796.332   88,293
Poplar, Michael G.
Fumble! The Browns, Modell and the
  move: an inseder's story

DATE DUE   24.00

FUMBLE!

The Browns, Modell and the Move

An Insider's Story

by Michael G. Poplar
with James A. Toman

ISBN—0-93676011-7

Library of Congress Number
LC 97-69596

Published by
Cleveland Landmarks Press, Inc.
13610 Shaker Boulevard, Suite 503
Cleveland, Ohio 44120-1592

Printed by
Bookcrafters
Chelsea, Michigan

Design, layout and desktop publishing by
Russell Schneider Jr.
Moonlight Publishing
Hinckley, Ohio

DEDICATED

To the 53 former Cleveland Browns and Cleveland Stadium Corp. employees and to their families who were left behind when the organization moved to Baltimore; to the countless thousands of Clevelanders who worked those many Browns' Sundays through all kinds of weather at Cleveland Stadium and whose earnings were severely impacted by the move; and last but certainly not least, to the hundreds of thousands of Cleveland Browns' football fans everywhere who lived and died with every Cleveland Browns' game.

Author Michael Poplar just days before the Stadium walls were demolished.

TABLE OF CONTENTS

ACKNOWLEDGEMENTS

The contents of this book spans some 35 years. Some of the earlier events in the 1960s and 1970s described here were conveyed to me by long-time Browns' followers and employees who shared their knowledge of the Browns' organization. These veteran observers include Hal Lebovitz, John Minco, Gib Shanley, and the late Edward Uhas. I am grateful for their willingness to contribute their recollections.

Significant contributions were also made by many former employees of Cleveland Stadium Corp. and the Cleveland Browns, including Dino Lucarelli, Bruce Gaines, George Hoffman, Mike Srsen, Larry Staverman, Marilyn McGrath, Ernie Accorsi, Kevin Byrne, David Frey, Jim Bailey, Vince Patterozzi, Bob Metzger, Helen Jelencic, and many others. It was their stories and many like them that helped form an integral part of this book. My thanks to all of them. A debt of gratitude is also owed to John Hubbell, director of the Kent State University Press, for his critical insights and encouragement.

Over the years the Browns' teams were covered very skillfully by local sports reporters. Their reporting significantly helped me as I tried to recall the many years and the many events which affected the operations of the team and of Cleveland Stadium Corp. Many times I also relied on these reporters to keep me abreast of what was happening with the team, especially when precarious times and delicate situations kept my colleagues in the Berea training facility unusually tight-lipped.   Many of the reporters' accounts and comments which I included here were taken directly from their newspaper columns. I sincerely hope that I have given proper credit to those talented men and women for their colorful and informative work which served as major contributions to my book.

In my opinion, the best in-depth reporting of Browns' football since 1981 was found in *Browns News Illustrated.* Much of the Browns' history which I repeat in this book was framed and reported by BNI editor-in-chief Ray Yannucci and columnist Pete Franklin, and others. Special thanks to Ray and Pete.

The writings of sports reporters from the Cleveland *Plain Dealer,* Akron *Beacon Journal,* Lake County *News Herald* and the *Sun Newspapers* also are well represented here. I would like to extend my deepest gratitude to Tony Grossi, Russ Schneider, Bill Livingston, Bud Shaw, Bob Dolgan, Mary Kay Cabot, Jeff Schudel, Paul Hoynes, Ed Meyer, Terry Pluto, Chuck Heaton, and Bob Kravitz. Likewise, the insights of PD editors Tom Vail and Brent Larkin were drawn upon often in telling this story, as were extracts from columns of PD talents Joe Dirck and Steve Luttner. I am grateful for their work.

The writings of four authors also worked their way into this narrative. Bill Levy (*Sam,Sipe and Company*), Sam Rutigliano (*Pressure*), Jack Torry (*Endless Summers*), and Linda Goodman (*Linda Goodman's Sun Signs*) all offered insights in their books which I found pertinent to my narrative. My deepest thanks to each of them for allowing me to share again their previously published thoughts with the readers of this book.

Writers at both the *Baltimore Magazine* and *Cleveland Magazine* are to be commended for their in-depth coverage of the events leading up to the painful Move. This story could not effectively have been told without their input. Thanks to all who were involved in the reporting and analyzing of that tragic (at least for Clevelanders) event.

I am deeply indebted to accounts from various other newspapers, including *Crain's Cleveland Business*, the Baltimore *Sun*, the Washington *Post*, the Elyria *Chronicle Telegram*, *USA Today*, the *Wall Street Journal*, *Point of View*, and publications such as *Sports Illustrated*, *Money Magazine*, *Barron's*, *Newsweek*, and *Financial World*. Commentary from these periodicals filled in various bits of Cleveland Browns' history and their move to Baltimore.

A special thanks to the local sports media writers/commentators/columnists who served as reviewers for me: Russ Schneider, Dan Coughlin, and John Urbancich, along with good friend Dino Lucarelli. Their reactions and helpful suggestions along with a lot of encouragement helped an accountant more accustomed to numbers than words write his first book. Their collective years of following the Cleveland sports scene are many, and their voluminous experiences and insights proved invaluable.

The efforts of Bill Becker (Cleveland State University Archives), AP phototgrapher Tony Dejak, Nancy Yodice (*Plain Dealer*), and designer Rusty Schneider are greatly appreciated. Without their help, this book would be less than complete.

And of course the biggest thanks must go to veteran Cleveland chronicler Jim Toman, who took a series of vignettes and a tangled web of diaries describing a myriad of events from my computer, and wove these segments into an interesting piece of history. As my editor, Jim helped me make my recollections and assessments clearer and more reader friendly.

And lastly, but most importantly of all, this entire effort became a reality because of my wife Sunnie and my children who encouraged me to continue whenever intermittent bouts of frustration set in. Sunnie provided the title *Fumble* even before I was sure there would be a book. Sons David and

Michael shared the memories of days at the Stadium that we shared together; daughters Carol, Jennifer, and Dana also worked at many odd jobs around the Stadium and were always there for me during the 15 months it took me to complete this story.

Hopefully I have covered everyone and given proper credit to whom it is due. My deepest apologies to any contribution I may have inadvertently overlooked.

To all who helped in any way, I am eternally indebted, for you assisted me in telling a more complete story of the ups and downs of the Cleveland Browns and of their infamous move to Baltimore, Maryland.

PREFACE

"But frankly, it came down to a simple proposition. I had no choice."
Art Modell, Baltimore, Maryland
November 6, 1995

The November 6, 1995, announcement that the Cleveland Browns were moving to Baltimore stunned the community. Coming as it did without apparent prior warning signals, it left Greater Clevelanders shocked, hurt, and angry. It also raised many questions. Was Art Modell's statement an adequate or even accurate explantion of why the Browns left their home of 50 years?

The pain stemming from that decision was foisted not only on the loyal long-time fans of the team, but also on the majority of Cleveland Browns' employees and on all Cleveland Stadium Corporation employees. Not only were these folks losing their team, they were also losing their jobs. Concessionaires, ushers, security guards, restaurant personnel, and program salespeople were some of those affected. I too was affected. I had served Art Modell for over 20 years as his executive vice president for the Cleveland Stadium Corporation, and his statement haunted me.

Few of us were prepared to face the end of what had been so significant a part of our lives. The end came like the proverbial thief in the night. Each of us struggled to find his or her own way of coping with the loss. By profession, I am a C.P.A. By nature, I am a guy who needs to lay out all the pieces of a puzzle before I look at the whole picture. And so I began to sort out the clues that would help me understand how it had all gone wrong.

Each night after that bleak November day, I would head home from my office in Tower B of Cleveland Stadium, thinking about some aspect or other of the tragic situation. Once home I would sit down at my word processor and jot down the memories, the ideas, the theories that kept running through my mind. After some days of doing this, I decided that I would try to put all the pieces together in the sequence of events that eventually led to the last game in 50 years of Cleveland Browns' history. I could not avoid thinking that the people who could have saved the "game" for us, fumbled when it mattered most.

When I started writing, I was only intending that it would be valuable personal therapy in dealing with the stress that the end of an era had brought. My wife, of course, took an interest in my nightly session with the word processor, and we would talk about the events I was attempting to describe on paper. Then she asked to read some of sections I had finished. After reading she frequently remarked that she didn't think many people knew about that particular event or this particular detail.

Eventually, my bitterness over what had happened began to ebb, and I gave up my nightly writing sessions. It seemed like a futile exercise. I told my wife that I didn't think it mattered if I ever completed the puzzle after all. "No one really cares," I told her.

She said I was wrong, that only a handful of people were aware of all the facts that led to Art Modell's decision to leave town with his football team and that what had happened was a significant part of Cleveland history. She said that I was one of only a few who could tell almost the whole story, and that maybe I had an obligation to share what I knew.

Her case was strengthened by conversations I had with my friends. Invariably their questions were much alike: "Mike, what really happened? How could Modell do such a thing?" I began then to see that people really were interested.

That's when my strategy changed. My energies were recharged. I decided to turn my personal journal and my yearly diaries and meeting summaries into a book.

At that point I began my research and writing in earnest. I went back into the corporate files as I relived nearly 21 years of my life with Art Modell, the Browns, and Cleveland Municipal Stadium. My being an accountant proved a real help to me. I had naturally retained reams of records, and so details I could not recall came back to me as I perused financial statements, minutes of meetings, or activity logs. I had also saved newspaper clippings.

Some of the things that I have included here will be familiar to some readers. Many of the events were covered by the media, but here the apparently unrelated events of twenty-some years are brought together and woven into what I perceive as the slowly developing pattern which ultimately resulted in the November 6 announcement. Other things that I relate come from inside the various Modell organizations. I was there. And when my own recollection proved foggy, I was able to turn to my colleagues; their memories sharpened my own.

Ultimately, I am not sure what factors mattered most. Some of the causes underlying the move can certainly be attributed to the Browns' and Art Modell's management decisions. Some can be traced to the public's rather general dislike and distrust of Art Modell and/or of his decisions. Some undoubtedly is due to a lack of effective and cohesive governmental leadership on the local, county, and state levels. Some is due to the fact that the Greater

Cleveland community had a great many important financial matters on its plate all at the same time. Each person may assign blame where she or he thinks it best fits.

What I hope, though, is that by recording these events and memories, that I may have provided a perspective that will help keep the record straight.

Some may say this is not an objective book, that it was prompted by sour grapes, since I was not invited to make the journey to Baltimore. I can only insist that it was not motivated, even in the smallest way, by the lack of such an invitation. This book simply offers a look from the inside by someone who witnessed, and was part of, some of the thinking that prevailed in the organizations.

Some of the references to events that occurred over the 22-year span are cited to highlight the realities of life in the Stadium and Berea offices. They are not presented as irrefutable evidence that anyone in particular was right or wrong in discharging his or her responsibilities. Rather, these points are made to illustrate the gap in attitudes between internal management levels, and at times those of the highest echelons of Browns' management, and the public.

What I know for sure is that what none of us ever thought could happen, and what should never have happened, did happen. The Cleveland Browns left town.

PROLOGUE

November 4, 1995, was a cold and snowy Saturday in Cleveland. My alarm clock radio sounded at 6 a.m., and I vaguely wondered why I hadn't turned it off before I went to bed Friday night. Normally I would have allowed myself to sleep until the sunlight woke me about 7:30 a.m. I reached to turn off the radio and go back to sleep when what I was hearing made me freeze.

The voice did not belong to WWWE's (now WTAM) normal Saturday morning host, but to sports reporter Mike Snyder, who was conducting a live telephone interview with Cleveland Browns' owner (and my boss) Art Modell. What made me pause was the tone of Art's voice—it just didn't sound right. Normally confident, even brash, in his speech, Art's delivery that morning seemed measured and careful. In fact, he sounded as though he had been awakened from a deep sleep to answer Snyder's questions.

Art was forthright when he told Snyder that he had participated in several discussions with Maryland officials about relocating the Browns to Baltimore. This was the first time that I or anyone I knew had heard Art talk about moving the team. Art said that everyone would know more on Monday, November 6, after a meeting with Maryland politicians.

What the hell was I hearing? Was Art dancing around the fact that he was moving the Browns? Or was he only threatening to move, given the fact that a vote was coming up on Tuesday, November 7, for the $175 million Cleveland Stadium renovation package? Although Art said the final decision would not come until Monday, something about his tone suggested that he had already finalized the deal.

Listening to Art Modell on the radio that morning, I feared the worst. As executive vice president and treasurer of Modell's Cleveland Stadium Corporation, I worked downtown in Cleveland Stadium's Tower B, while Art spent most of his time in the Browns' Berea complex. Still, there was considerable contact between the personnel in the two offices, although it had dropped off significantly in recent months. Rumors had been multiplying since early summer, when Art had declared a moratorium on discussions about renovations to the 64-year-old Stadium.

I was aware of many daunting challenges facing Modell and his dual operation of the Stadium and the football team. I was fully cognizant of mounting financial pressures. I knew of Art's frustration over the protracted discussions about how to finance the renovations acutely needed to restore Cleveland Stadium to a first class venue for football. I had also learned of an increasing number of recent closed-door meetings in Berea, although their subject had remained a closely guarded secret from most of us "insiders." On the nature of those discussions almost all of Art Modell's employees remained outsiders.

By mid-October 1995, the rumor mill was in high gear. I was pretty sure that something "big" was in the works, but I still wasn't ready to accept that it would mean the end of 50 years of Browns' football in the city. Perhaps Art was going to sell the team to other Cleveland interests. Perhaps the moratorium and all the last-minute media speculation was only a cleverly designed plan to promote the November 7 ballot issue for Stadium renovation financing.

Then on November 6, 1995, like hundreds of thousands of other Greater Clevelanders, I watched the fateful news conference in Baltimore. The months of mystery and speculation were finally over. Cleveland was going to lose its NFL franchise; the Browns were going to Baltimore. The ensuing furor that erupted in the city was unprecedented.

As for me, I was numb. I had been closely involved with the Browns organization since 1965, and in charge of Cleveland Stadium operations since 1975. What I had spent most of my adult life working for and towards was about to be lost. I couldn't help but think of how ominous the first week in November had been in recent times. In 1990, that was when Bud Carson met his fate. In 1993 that was the week when the Bernie Kosar episode erupted. And now this!

While I was numb, most Clevelanders felt enraged, and all of that rage was directed at Art Modell (with perhaps a bit left over for Bill Belichick). Radio, television, and the *Plain Dealer* covered the decision exhaustively, and fans had ample opportunity to vent their anger. Anti-Modell signs cropped up in office building windows, on front lawns, and on the tops of automobiles. Modell was burned in effigy, and sadly within hours of that fateful announcement, some individuals had even gone so far as to physically threaten him and his family. He and his family had to be given police protection. And while the vast majority of Cleveland fans would not and did not condone the level of violence such behaviors threatened, nonetheless their anger over a sense of betrayal burned red hot.

For most Clevelanders, the cause of their rage was obvious. Art Modell was deemed a traitor to Cleveland and its people. He had asked for money to renovate the Stadium, and the voters had said yes in an overwhelming way (albeit anticlimactically). For years the fans had supported the Browns with sellout crowds and intense loyalty, even though their beloved team had never rewarded that devotion with a trip to the Super Bowl. Modell had promised he would never move the Browns, but now he had done so. Clevelanders were seeing their historic and envied support of the Browns rewarded with treachery. Modell said he made the decision to move because he "had no choice." The fans did not believe him. To the fans Art Modell was a deceitful villain. Pure and simple.

But I knew it was not quite so simple. Multi-million-dollar decisions are not made lightly, nor are they the product of short-term thinking. I began to reflect on where things had all begun to go wrong.   In hindsight, I could see that the first pieces in Art's eventual decision to move the Browns out of Cleveland had really occurred several years earlier.   The love affair between Art Modell and his Cleveland Browns organization and the Cleveland political and business community had begun to sour in 1988. The rupture grew perceptibly larger, and it was a complex series of interrelated events and circumstances that contributed to it. The story of these intertwined factors behind the move deserves to be told. It is an interesting tale, but it is not simple.

Though the Browns were very important to Cleveland, their loss cannot be considered a tragedy in the classical sense. Nor is the unfolding of their loss an epic tale. So, the convention of beginning in the middle does not hold here. Let's take our story back to its logical starting point, to when Art Modell became the owner of the Cleveland Browns. Those early years, though not without difficulties and controversy, were filled with promise—and success.

CHAPTER 1

THE EARLY YEARS

I first met Art Modell in 1965.

At the time I was working in the Cleveland office of Arthur Andersen & Co., a national accounting firm, which had responsibility for conducting the annual audit of the Cleveland Browns football franchise. Because of my strong interest in professional sports, my superiors at Arthur Andersen gave me the Browns' assignment, and that was when I was first introduced to Art Modell.

Modell had then been owner of the team for four seasons. In 1961 Modell was a television advertising executive in New York City, but he felt a keen interest in becoming involved in the National Football League. He put together an investment group, which included R. J. Schaeffer of the Schaeffer Brewing Company, and on March 22, 1961, for some $4 million, his group bought controlling interest in the Browns from the existing ownership of Dave Jones, Ellis Ryan, and Homer Marshman. Bob Gries, Sr., and founding coach Paul Brown retained their existing shares of Browns' stock and became hold-over minority owners. With the purchase of controlling interest, Modell became the Browns' chairman of the board and chief spokesman for the team. One year later he also became club president.

Modell did not buy the team merely as an investment, as was typical of many owners. He was a hands-on kind of guy, and he intended to be an active and involved owner. He wanted the team to bear his imprint.

At the time, of course, the person with the Browns' highest profile was Paul Brown, coach of the team since its 1946 founding in the old All-American Football Conference (AAFC). His success with the team had made him a genuine coaching icon. Just as much as Modell wanted the team to reflect his ideas and leadership style, equally intent was Paul Brown on keeping intact the system which had brought the franchise so much success during its first 15 years. Like oil and water, Modell and Brown were destined not to blend.

From the very first day of their professional association, the tension began to build. An early anecdote illustrates the point. Art Modell's office in Tower B of Cleveland Stadium was just across a reception area from that of Paul Brown. On one of the first mornings at his new desk, Modell dialed Brown's secretary and asked if Paul was in. She informed him that he was, but that he was in conference; his office door was closed (Brown usually worked with the door closed). Modell told her that he would like Brown to stop over to his office when he was free. After lunch, Modell phoned again to find out when Brown would be free, explaining that he was eager to talk to the coach.

Brown's secretary, Mercedes O'Toole, informed the new owner that Brown would not be meeting with him that day, since he had already left the office. Despite the air conditioning, the temperature in the Browns' offices went up a degree or two.

Over the next two years the two men were never able to achieve a harmonious working relationship. Art Modell said the breach became irreparable after the Bobby Mitchell trade to the Washington Redskins for Ernie Davis was made in 1962. Modell said he was embarrassed when Washington owner George Preston Marshall called to congratulate him on the first deal between them, a trade which Paul Brown had made but about which he had not apprised Modell.

Only rarely were Art Modell (standing, center) and Paul Brown (seated) in a photograph together, this one taken just months after Modell acquired the Browns. Brown doesn't seem excited about having his office used for the photography session. *Cleveland Stadium Corp. collection*

On January 9, 1963, following a 7-6-1 Browns' season, Arthur Bertram Modell announced the firing of head coach Paul Eugene Brown. It was clearly a gutsy move, but it also illustrated Modell's determination to be the one man in the organization who called the signals. On that day it became crystal clear that the Browns were his team. That paired identity, Modell and the Browns, remained in place over the next 32 years. Modell named then-assistant coach Blanton Collier to replace Brown.

The first year under Collier the team improved to 10-4, and in 1964 the Browns won the NFL championship. The 27-0 victory over the Baltimore Colts in the championship game laid to rest, at least for the time being, any lingering doubts about Modell's capacity to build a winning organization. Cleveland had claimed its first football crown in nine years. The rest of the 60s was also a success. The Browns made it to the playoffs four times, and to the league championship game three times, each time, however, coming up short of the final prize.

Modell continued as a strong owner, willing to take risks. In 1966 he boldly challenged Jim Brown to choose between football and Hollywood, that he couldn't have both. Art was determined to be the man in charge, even if it meant losing the services of the premier runner in the game.

The Browns under Collier were a higher-scoring team than they had been in the past, and this brand of football appealed to the fans. Attendance, which had stood at 422,043 during Paul Brown's last year as coach, jumped to 578,360 at the end of the decade. The Browns had become a consistent success not only on the field, but at the box office as well. After financial losses during Modell's first three years as owner, the team became profitable in 1964, and for the next ten years averaged well over $1 million in annual pre-tax profits, a very handsome sum. Art Modell's moves had paid off, and while perhaps not everyone was then willing to call him a football wizard, he had relatively few detractors.

He was soon to make even more contributions.

Modell and Blanton Collier sign first-round draft pick Paul Warfield in 1964. Warfield (lower left) joined Jim Brown and Gary Collins (below) in generating a more prolific offense to lead the Browns to the title in 1964. *Cleveland Press collection, Cleveland State University Archives.*

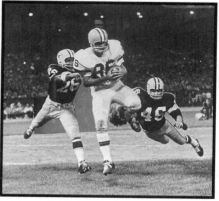

Modell detested the Brownie elf (below) which had been the Browns logo for years, and instructed the PR staff to gradually eliminate it from programs, pennants, letterheads, etc. By 1968 the elf was virtually a memory. *Cleveland Press collection, Cleveland State University Archives.*

CHAPTER 2
ART BECOMES
A LANDLORD

I became a full-time employee of Art Modell's new company on March 1, 1975. I still remember it vividly. Dino Lucarelli and I joined Modell's Cleveland Stadium Corporation the same day, bringing the number of people in the organization to nine. I was hired as the Stadium Corp.'s controller. Dino came on board as director of public relations and loge marketing. Art Modell was the president, and he was also treasurer for several years until passing that title on to me.

Despite the fact that Modell and I had known each other for the ten years previous when I was one of the outside auditors of the Browns' books, I still had to go through a formal executive search process before landing the job. Ernst and Ernst, as the Big Eight accounting firm was then known, conducted the process for Modell and recommended me for the job. I had to decide between my career at the well-established Arthur Andersen & Co. and Art Modell's newly created Stadium enterprise. I chose Modell and the Stadium Corporation. To my knowledge, it was then the only private management of a publicly owned stadium in the country. As an early example of privatization, the Stadium job offered an exciting challenge.

Working for Art Modell also held an attraction for me then. People who know Modell well consider him a risk-taker. Art never viewed a business "reach" as a gamble because his judgment was usually framed by supreme self-confidence. If there was any chance of turning an enterprise around, no matter how remote, Modell inevitably would view that challenge as an opportunity, and he would attack it with vigor.

Art considered himself a man of action. Occasionally he'd criticize some of the executives around town (though not by name) who would talk at length about community problems but who would never lift a finger to help solve them. Modell, on the other hand, always seemed ready to swing into action, although in my opinion sometimes a little too quickly. A good example of his action orientation came when Art signed a lease with the City of Cleveland and took over operation of the aging Cleveland Municipal Stadium. I'm doubtful anyone other than Art Modell would have entered into the type of lease that he did. But because his main business, professional football, operated out of that building, he felt he knew more about its possibilities and limitations than anyone else. For Art, the Stadium represented both a challenge and an opportunity. In those days Modell was everything that Clevelanders had come to know him as. He was brash, but charming. He was impulsive and visionary. He was dominating and demonstrative. I felt energized working for that kind of man.

It seems to me that given the opportunity to operate the Cleveland Stadium, most other businessmen would have placed much more weight on the negatives visible in the building, and these factors would ultimately have slanted their final decision against getting involved. But Art would always "pooh-pooh" such negatives, dismissing them as minor impediments that could be easily corrected. Modell was an unusually positive thinker.

Art Modell and Mayor Ralph Perk were all smiles at the 1973 announcement of the signing of the Cleveland Stadium Corporation lease.
Cleveland Stadium Corp. collection

The 25-year lease on Cleveland Stadium was finalized a year and a half before I signed on full-time. The contract between the Stadium Corporation and the City of Cleveland was signed in October 1973, and Cleveland Stadium Corporation began operating the building in 1974. It was not until late in 1974, however, that the first major construction project and first major bank borrowing took place. It was this increasing financial involvement that made my job necessary.

All Art had needed to reach his decision to become responsible for the Stadium was completion of a survey of loge marketability. Once the survey team delivered a favorable conclusion that sufficient demand from Cleveland-area businesses existed for over 100 loges, he was eager to complete his deal with the City of Cleveland. The major problem he had to deal with was the snail's pace with which City Council proceeded with the legislation and approvals. Art is not a patient man, and the 18 months that transpired before all documents were in order certainly tested him.

One of the hangups along the way centered on the city not feeling it was getting enough in return for use of one of its assets. At the urging of Dick Hollington, former City law director, Art upped the ante and offered the city not only a guaranteed rental (one sufficient to cover both the payoff of the existing bonded indebtedness on the Stadium and all real estate taxes), but also an incentive rental in which the city would share in the "upside," if there was any. Art thought that this represented a better situation than the city then had, since the city had often been unable to make bond payments from Stadium operating proceeds. Records showed the city also suffered a cash loss almost every year on Stadium operations. Council estimated these losses at between $300,000-$500,000 a year, with the major variable the Indians' attendance. During this era the Tribe was typically a fifth- or sixth-place finisher. Very simply, the worse the Indians played, the lower the attendance, and the larger the city's operating loss. According to Hal Lebovitz, local sports columnist and sports historian, even in 1948 when the Indians drew 2.6 million fans en route to winning the World Series over the Boston Braves, the city reported a loss of $30,000 from the operation of the Stadium. Under Modell's lease terms, the city would not have to lift a finger, and yet it would be guaranteed to be "in the black" every year.

His proposed incentive rental allowed the city to share in the gross rentals from all events. If the Stadium enjoyed some lucrative concerts, football playoff games, a college football game, or even (though in the 1970s it certainly seemed far-fetched) a pennant or World Series, the city would earn increased profits for the year. Art believed that all participants should share in the spoils. In addition to these cash rental terms, Modell also committed the Stadium Corporation to spend $10 million on improvements to the building.

As landlord, Modell also had to negotiate a new lease with the Cleveland Indians. By offering the Indians an increased share of concession and scoreboard revenues, he was able to sign a ten-year lease with the baseball club. He also assured the Indians that the new loges would bring corporate Cleveland back to the Stadium where they would be able to entertain business customers in a modicum of luxury for baseball games. Similar to the psychology behind the incentive rental feature of the city lease, Art offered the Indians an additional reduction in their stipulated 8% rental by allowing them to earn a rebate equal to 10% of all the rentals earned by Stadium Corp., including the rent paid by the Indians. This unique idea, as Art would repeat from time to time, was to create for the Indians and Browns a mutual interest in each other's success, and thus end the petty bickering that had long existed between the two tenants. The hope was that each team would cheer the other's success at the gate, as increased gate sales for all Stadium events would financially reward both tenants. (We found this rebate feature was overlooked and misunderstood by the Indians when troubles emerged over the renewal of the lease in the 1980s.)

When the arduous negotiations surrounding the two leases were finally completed, Modell turned his attention to loge construction. Successful operation of the loges was the only means that could make Stadium Corp. a profitable enterprise. To achieve this objective, two things were necessary. First, the loges had to be built within budget, and second, all had to be leased at reasonable rates. Art personally managed the loge construction program through Peter O'Donnell, a close friend who acted as his general contractor. Art's wife Pat worked with the designer to augment the loges' aesthetic qualities and comforts. Under O'Donnell's judicious scrutiny, the loge project was completed on time and within budget.

Throughout the construction period, Art personally marketed the 102 suites so they could all be sold before the start of the 1975 baseball season. Many of the leads, and eventual sales, were cultivated among the cocktail party set and among the board members of the many civic and charitable causes for which the Modells worked. With the help of long-time friend and Browns' program director, John Minco, the Modells leased all 102 marketable loges within eight months. The suites were fully occupied by the Indians' Opening Day 1975.

When Art got involved in a situation, he led the charge. His secretaries referred to him as a "whirling dervish." It was fun to work with Art on these projects. Not many of us were able to keep up with him, but it was fun trying.

The entire amount of money needed for loge construction was borrowed. Along with other projects, including replacement of major electrical components in the building, repainting the concourses, and installing new light fixtures, the Cleveland Stadium Corp. sported a $5 million bank loan as a very prominent liability on its first annual balance sheet.

Art was a big believer in leverage. He had no fear of incurring debt, because he was supremely confident of his own business acumen to generate sufficient profits to retire it. Interest rates were then fairly reasonable, ranging between 6% and 8%, and Art the entrepreneur felt that even if the borrowing rate reached 8%, the loges could generate enough profits to cover both interest and principal, given a long enough term in which to operate. All Art felt he needed was a friendly banker, progressive enough to see things in Art's optimistic way. Modell was launching a one-of-a-kind business--the private management of a publicly owned stadium. There was no track record. All Art could tell the banker was, "Believe in ME. I will take a building which has operated at a loss every year, and I will create a profitable business out of it. Just loan me the money."

Art was persuasive, and he secured the loan from a consortium of three banks in Cleveland, with Central National Bank as the lead bank (Central later merged into Society Corp., which has now become KeyCorp.) Securing the loans, however, did require Modell to give the bank his personal guarantee.

Cleveland Stadium thus became the first privatized stadium operation in the country which invested private funds in leasehold improvements and assumed the bottom-line risk of turning a profit. If red ink resulted, according to the lease Cleveland Stadium Corp. suffered the loss and had to fund it. By contrast, most private operating companies existed only as management firms. They earned a percentage of revenues (perhaps 4%) "off the top," recovered every dollar of expenses, and then shared on an incentive basis if a profit was earned (20% of the bottom-line is commonplace). In these arrangements, losses were not incurred by the management company but instead were passed on to the governmental body which owned the facility. This was the typical arrangement, especially when a long history of operating losses was in evidence. The City of Cleveland, however, needed someone to come along and guarantee its losses would be eliminated. That's what the Modell lease did.

Over the years, controversy continued over the purported benefits of the lease. Art Modell often said, "The most agreed upon aspect of the lease is that it is the most misunderstood lease in existence." To understand it fully, one would have to quantify each paragraph to see if it cost or saved the city money, compared to (a) when the city had operated the building itself, and (b) what other cities (such as New Orleans or Philadelphia) received in their leases with private management firms. Art Modell and I did this often, and we were satisfied the city got a good deal out of its lease. Modell gave up a lot to get control of this building. At times we thought it was too much.

When Dennis Kucinich became mayor in 1977, he was urged to delve into the Modell lease to assure the citizens of Cleveland that Modell was not "ripping off the city." This deprecatory view of the lease had become common in some sectors of the media. Kucinich, elected on an "anti-big business" platform, led a charge against anything smacking of corporate privilege. In this he was ably supported by his close advisor, Bob Weisman. One of Weisman's goals was to wrest the Stadium from Modell's control, to give back to the city what was the city's. So one of Kucinich's first pronouncements was that he was going to investigate the Modell Stadium lease. He sent Public Properties Director Peter Pucher to visit me at the Stadium offices.

Pucher had joined Kucinich's cabinet based on a close friendship formed when he was Kucinich's high school football coach. Kucinich described Pucher as his "father image." Pucher could stay focused on a goal until the job was done, and he was someone in whom Kucinich had complete confidence. When Pucher told me the investigation was starting, I told him, "I'm glad somebody from the city cares about what we're doing down here. Art Modell has plunged a lot of his money into their building."

I had batched into project categories every invoice paid since 1974. I went into my cabinets and pulled out at least 50 pounds of paperwork ($6 million of invoices and canceled checks) and offered the pile to Pucher so he could begin immediately. I told him it would do us both good to document for the public that Modell was in compliance with the lease. Pucher reviewed with me each and every project, and he scheduled an outside audit firm to finish the work professionally. This firm not only completed the audit of capital improvements but stayed on to audit the annual rental payments on the building and the ancillary parking lots.

The most beneficial thing to come out of this audit was Pucher's coming to realize that privatization of the Stadium, the concept derided by Bob Weisman, actually was a good thing for the city. His responsibilities as properties director also extended to the Convention Center, the Zoo, and the West Side Market. After the audit, Pucher learned that the Stadium, under Modell's management, was the best-run of this entire group and yielded the best return to the city. When he finally drew that conclusion and passed it along to Kucinich, Weisman told Kucinich that Pucher had been brainwashed during his Stadium visits. Roldo Bartimole, journalist and perennial critic of the lease, after hearing that nothing negative had come from the audit, called for the prosecutor's office to get involved. He charged that the city had done an inadequate job on the audit.

Pucher stood by his conviction. He believed that Modell's lease had been scrutinized eight ways to Sunday, that it was a very good deal for the city, and he so convinced Kucinich. To my consternation, I couldn't figure out what possibly could be up when several weeks later Pucher called me to set up another meeting. I wondered what else the city could want to review. To my total surprise, Pucher had called the meeting to inquire whether Art Modell and the Stadium Corp. would have any interest in managing the Cleveland Zoo for the city. Contrary to what the public might have expected, the Kucinich administration was actually looking to put more city properties into Modell's hands to operate.   Sadly, the results of the Kucinich investigation were not made public, and so the negative perception persisted.

(Fourteen years later, during an interlude in Kucinich's political career, the former mayor was hired by Art Modell's Stadium Corporation to serve as a consultant on how to secure state financial support for Stadium renovation.)

The initial pressures on the Cleveland Stadium Corp., however, were brought by Art himself.   In 1974, soon after getting Stadium Corp. up and running, Modell struck a deal with Jules Belkin of Belkin Productions, offering him an exclusive arrangement to promote major concerts in the Stadium. Belkin responded by booking four shows in 1975, featuring the Beach Boys, Rolling Stones, Rod Stewart and Faces, and Yes.   The shows attracted more than 200,000 concert fans to what was billed as the "World Series of Rock." The Rolling Stones concert played to a sellout crowd on June 14, and the front page of the Sunday *Plain Dealer* carried an overhead photograph of the sardine-packed crowd on the Stadium field.   After Art learned that the Rolling Stones took 90% of the net gate receipts for the two-hour concert, he quipped, "In my next life, I have to learn how to play a guitar!"   The venture with Jules Belkin produced good results in its very first year and for many years thereafter.

A 1976 World Series of Rock concert featuring festival seating, which was later abolished in favor of the more orderly rows of chairs installed on the field.
Cleveland Stadium Corp. collection

To Modell's surprise, several days after the Rolling Stones concert, Robert Gries and his attorney made an appointment to meet with Modell to inquire whether Gries could purchase stock in Cleveland Stadium Corp. Gries had substantial minority ownership in the Cleveland Browns, and by virtue of this ownership he asked to invest the same percentage in this related company. Modell reminded Gries that with Modell's stock ownership also came the responsibility of a personal guarantee of the Stadium Corp. debt. Modell said that he was willing to offer Gries the same share of stock that he held in the Cleveland Browns, as long as the Gries group would also share in the personal debt guarantee. At the meeting, Modell had his lawyers, and Gries had his lawyers. It appeared unlikely the deal would be resolved in one sitting.

Modell wondered out loud: Why hadn't the Gries group requested stock ownership when the conversation about starting up the Stadium Corp. was first announced several years earlier? Had Gries perhaps waited until the loges were all leased and the sold-out concerts began appearing in the papers?

While Modell was drawing the conclusion that Gries was forcing his way into Stadium Corp., Gries remembers it differently. He said that Modell had mentioned years earlier the possibility of taking over Stadium management, and at that time he assured the Browns' shareholders that he would keep them apprised of the progress. Gries claimed that Modell failed to communicate that progress to him or to other stockholders.

After some deliberation, Modell was advised by his attorneys to make the requested percentage of ownership available so as to avoid a charge against him of something I soon learned was called "corporate opportunity." The Gries party, however, balked at acquiring the same percentage of stock as it owned in the Browns, largely over the issue of having to carry that same percentage of liability in personal guarantees on the bank debt. After several meetings, the Gries group decided to acquire 10% of the stock, with no contingent liability relative to corporate debt whatsoever. (I believe everyone realized that while at that moment the company was on the line for $5 million of debt, that number would eventually rise to $10 million when the full commitment in leasehold improvements would ultimately be completed; therefore, any personal guarantee of debt would eventually be even larger). Whatever the reason, the Gries group seemed content to buy 10% of the stock of Cleveland Stadium Corp.

At the end of this ordeal, Art called me into his office to reflect on what he had been through. Without pointing a finger at anyone, Modell said, "Listen, kid, never, EVER, let a lawyer run your business for you. Some of my best friends are lawyers, mind you, and they are great guys, but they just don't have the instincts for dealing in business." I took Art's advice to heart. Whenever I had any choice in the matter, I resisted any lawyer having final say on the business aspects of a transaction. Sadly, little did Art heed his own advice some 15 to 20 years down the road.

There were times when Art Modell would also become frustrated with accountants and tax advisors who were convened to help pull a deal together. He'd say, especially after a potential deal hit a snag, "You know, I'm tired of accountants telling me, 'you can't do this and you can't do that.' They're forever telling me that. What I want to see is a guy come in here and say, 'I found a way to get it done.' That's what I want. Some creative thinking."

Those were Art Modell's basic instructions: Find a way to get done what he wanted done.

Knowing that I was a C.P.A. he was basically telling me the rules that we were going to work under. One of the challenges that I had in front of me was how to tell Art what he really had to hear when he couldn't, or shouldn't, do something that he wanted to do.

To survive for a long term with Art Modell, as I would come to find out, one had to be good at his trade, confident, but not too assertive in making points to the owner.

Modell was a very generous man. He paid his executives well, and he was extremely generous to charitable causes. He gave to virtually every worthy cause that solicited him. Never in all my auditing years with Arthur Andersen did I see a corporation make donations in the large amounts the Cleveland Browns did. I once had to caution him that his companies were no longer able to take tax deductions for some of the contributions because they were exceeding the maximum allowable under the Federal Tax Code. He just shrugged his shoulders, thanked me for the advice, and said that was not the reason that he gave.

In that first year of doing business, Art wanted to be one of the check signers on the Stadium Corp.'s main disbursement account. Most of the payments that first year were made to contractors working on Stadium improvement projects, and such invoices were quite sizable. One day I walked into his office with a large batch of checks. As was typical he would question me on each one as to how far along on the job so-and-so was, just to make sure that we weren't paying someone for work not yet completed. Then he would sign the checks in my presence. On-the-job training for both of us, I figured. I learned what he was particularly interested in knowing, and he learned how detailed I was in reviewing the disbursements at hand. One day he became distracted while signing checks. He quickly put down the brown felt tip pen he had been using, and picked up his blue one. I looked at him quizzically. "Oh, I forgot I'm signing Stadium checks. I only use the brown pen for Browns' checks. I should be using the blue pen for Stadium Corp., since the Stadium colors are blue and white." He chuckled, and kept signing the checks. Boy, I thought, Art had everything planned, right down to the color ink he used.

After Modell took over the lease of the building, sky blue became the predominant color throughout the Stadium. While there was dark blue, navy blue, and midnight blue added for accent, the main theme was always blue. (Later on, our maintenance staff pleaded with me to ask Art to change the sky blue colors since walls and railings always seemed to become dirty much more quickly. It took some time to get Art's approval to replace the sky blue with a much deeper national blue. That didn't happen until 1982).

A large part of Art's motives with the formation of the Stadium Corp. was to protect the value of the Browns' franchise by improving the house in which the team played. Realistically, he knew he couldn't make large amounts of money on the new company. In fact, most projections we had generated were geared to getting the company to break even, which required just enough operating profits to pay interest and retire debt. We were realistic enough to know we would need plenty of luck to break even, so we weren't going to be reckless and plan much beyond that. After all, since the perennial cellar-dwelling Indians played 85% of the Stadium dates, the only way we could see enormous upside in the profits was for the baseball team to become a contender. The Browns were already playing to 72,000 fans on average, so the upside from football was less than 10%.

Our most realistic expectation was to make this investment self-liquidating; that is, to pay off the entire bank debt of $10 million, and interest thereon, over the 25-year lease. We felt comfortable that this expectation was achievable (little did we know that player strikes and work stoppages were to become commonplace in the 1980s). To achieve the break-even point, Stadium Corp. had to operate on a tight budget, and those were Art's continuing instructions to me. The understanding was that the only way we could ever spend more than budget was if Modell himself approved the expenditure. We operated that way for all 22 years of our corporate life.

When Art offered me the Stadium Corp. job in 1975, I did not hesitate. I knew I was the right guy to manage the business, given that mandate. I knew this situation was the right opportunity for me. I thrive on the challenge of getting the most done for the fewest dollars. I realized that Modell's personal guarantee to the banks was on the line, so I knew that the preservation of his personal wealth was at stake. It was the kind of responsibility that appealed to me and that kept me motivated.

Those early days were fun. "King Arthur" would preside at lunch at the "roundtable" reserved for us in the northwest corner of the Stadium restaurant in Tower A. Lunch time was whenever Art wanted to go. It was at the lunch table that Art held his daily staff meetings where each person would be available to answer questions on the status of anything he wanted a report on. It also gave each of us the opportunity to hear how other departments were operating, and where their focus was pointed each day.

While a lot of Stadium and football business was conducted during the lunch period, it was also time for Art to fire off a few of his jokes. Art usually brought levity to the roundtable, and lunch provided him an opportunity to sharpen his delivery techniques. He always had a story to tell, and sometimes as he would run through his repertoire, he might pause and say, "Stop me if I've already told this one, but these three old guys were sitting on this park bench..." Of course, no one ever told Art that they had heard it before, even if they had heard it a dozen times. It was interesting to hear how Art could put a new spin on an old story.

One of the first jokes I heard him tell did not appear to be a joke at all because he delivered it with a straight face. "Do you know how to become a millionaire from owning a sports team?" he asked.

I thought I was going to hear a lesson in high finance. Everyone attending lunch shook his head, since none of us had any idea how to answer the question. "Start out as a billionaire," he guffawed (it is sad to note that 20 years later that joke has a much greater ring of verisimilitude to it).

Lunch was also a time for Modell to vent. One day soon after I started working for him, he came to the roundtable particularly angry. I realized then that not every lunch was reserved for jokes. It seems that Art had received a call from one of the team's cornerbacks who wanted his contract renegotiated. The player told Art, "I had a really good year last year, and I feel I should be paid more."

Art replied, "What do you think I paid you for, to have a bad year?"

He then said to us at the table, "I'm still waiting for the player to come into my office and say, 'Art Modell, I had a lousy year, so cut my pay 20%.'"

All types of business were discussed at the roundtable. If a promoter came looking to produce a different kind of event at the Stadium, he was usually invited to join the staff at lunch and was told to feel free to discuss his proposal openly, even in front of employees from other departments. Thus Art would get more feedback. In those days Art liked to get opinions from as many people as he possibly could; sometimes he was looking for a consensus, other times for a different slant on things.

On some occasions, Art might invite the head groundskeeper to join the confab. The rest of us would chuckle as Art explained how he wanted the grass-cutting pattern to look. "Give it a criss-cross cut," he'd say, "so it has the Boston Garden floor look." He would cross his hands emphatically to illustrate how he wanted it to look. Conversation then would likely extend to: how short the grass would be cut (depending on which team had the speedy running backs); when painting the yardlines would be scheduled (weather consideration); whom we were currently buying our paint from; how much sand was being added to the turf each year; when we were scheduling our last effort to overseed the field; and so on. Art wanted to know all the answers, reasons for the answers, and the opportunity to make the final decision.

Even in later years when things began going bad, Art could still muster a joke or two at lunch. "You have to keep a sense of humor about you," he'd say, "to get through times like these."

Those roundtable lunches not only helped build esprit de corps, but they also helped each of us understand what others were doing in the company, and how the departments dovetailed with each other. (Sadly, this facet of Art's modus operandi disappeared after the Browns moved their headquarters to Berea in 1991. Meetings there were handled on a more selective invitee basis, generally dictated by whom Jim Bailey, Browns' executive vice president, thought should attend. I have long felt that Art was deprived of some much-needed information after the roundtable lunches stopped).

1976 - While the playing field was being lowered to bring better viewing to the fans in the lower box seats, renowned groundskeeper Harold Bossard found time for a litle horseplay, as he sharpened his pitching delivery from the elevated "mound." *Cleveland Stadium Corp. collection*

The loges, suspended from the bottom of the upper deck, provided both indoor and outdoor seating.

Each bi-level loge provided a kitchen, lavatory, television and storage amenities. *Jack Muslovski photos*

CHAPTER 3
BUSY DAYS ON
THE LAKEFRONT

It was probably fortunate for Art Modell that he had all the Stadium Corporation activities to occupy him in 1975. The Browns had experienced a miserable 1974 season, going 4-10 under Nick Skorich. It had been Modell's first losing season as an owner, and he did not take losing easily. Skorich was dismissed, and Forrest Gregg was named the new coach.

I was hired at about this time and given Nick Skorich's old office as my work station. This led Chuck Heaton, veteran *Plain Dealer* sports reporter, to remark upon meeting me, "I wish you better luck than Skorich had."

I did have better luck than Forrest Gregg. Gregg's 1975 Browns' team ended with a dismal 3-11 record. But for the moment, people in town were now applauding Art's achievements in rehabilitating the "old" Stadium, and they were dismissing as temporary the plight of the Browns. Art told us one day after attending a civic luncheon downtown that his place had been reserved in the name of "Art Modell, President, Cleveland Stadium Corp." He wondered why it had replaced "Art Modell, President, Cleveland Browns."

Fortunately, in 1976, the Browns were blessed with one of their rare successful drafts, as all top five rounds yielded starters: Mike Pruitt; a trade for Gerald Irons; Dave Logan; Mike St. Clair; and Henry Sheppard. All five selections contributed to a delightful turnaround 9-5 season. Near the tail end of the season, Art got himself involved quite by accident in something that eventually led to his greatest honor, in my opinion, outside professional football.

Citing Art Modell's business acumen and referring to him as the one person able to take a losing stadium and turn it into a successful business venture, Judge John T. Patton, who had gotten to know Art well during Modell's recent stint as Cuyahoga County Grand Jury foreman, called upon Art to save a dying (or was it already dead?) Sheraton-Cleveland Hotel in downtown Cleveland (today's Renaissance Cleveland Hotel). The hotel had been placed in receivership in November 1976.

Art had a fond place in his heart for the hotel. When he first moved to Cleveland, he made his home in the hotel, and each morning he would take a cab to his office at the Stadium. After hearing the judge's invitation (or maybe more exactly, his request) Modell accepted the role of court-appointed receiver. Following two successful years of Stadium Corp. operations, Art was brimming with confidence and was flattered to have been selected as *the* one to help with the city's downtown renaissance. In fact, a typical Modell one-liner was quoted extensively in the ensuing weeks. Said Art, "The only thing I know about being a receiver I learned by watching Reggie Rucker (referring to the Browns' wide receiver). However I will do whatever I can to help keep the hotel alive."

Art enlisted me in the project. I needed to take the pulse of its operations and get a handle on its finances. We needed to evaluate if the hotel was doing as badly as reported. With the help of the Laventhol & Horwath accounting firm, a few of us CPA's rode herd on the business until March 1977. The operation was registering a paltry 12% occupancy rate, compared with the 60% required for most hotels to break even.

In the meantime, while we were safeguarding the few dollars of revenues that the hotel was generating, Modell called on many of the CEOs in town with whom he was familiar, asking them to join him in his efforts to save this prime asset for Cleveland. "It's our civic obligation," he implored the group. I can still recall Art's script as I accompanied him on each trip. His plea to the prospective corporate investors was simple and straightforward:

Gentlemen, we have in our midst on the most prime real estate in downtown Cleveland (on Public Square) a jewel of a hotel that has been allowed to deteriorate. If we corporations don't step forward to save this business, no one else will. If this hotel eventually becomes a parking lot, the city will decline further, and then where will our corporations be? This hotel has the largest banquet hall between New York City and Chicago, and when this hotel is rebuilt, the facility can generate more F & B (food and beverage) revenues through its banquet business than a normal hotel operation. Consequently, our projections show that with the generous contribution of profits to the bottom line from F & B, the hotel can break even with 45% occupancy, when the norm in the business is 60%. It looks like the hotel, when up and running after a total renovation, poses very little, if any, downside risk for an investor. All we need to do is closely control the construction budget, and I will take on that responsibility with my staff.

That was it, short and sweet.

Art made about 14 calls and ended up batting about .500. He found six corporations and F.J. (Steve) O'Neill, future owner of the Cleveland Indians, to invest $1 million each. The Cleveland Stadium Corp. then contributed $1 million, and Stouffer Corporation purchased a second unit. With this $9 million in hand, he personally called on his friendly banker, Central National Bank, to lend a like amount to the cause. Central put together a consortium of Cleveland banks and savings and loan institutions to share in the loan. We were told this cause represented the first time in Cleveland that banks and savings and loan institutions had joined in a loan for this type of civic effort.

With a commitment of $18 million and Cleveland-based Stouffer Corporation agreeing to manage the hotel, Art then led the investors through the renovation effort in conjunction with the Stouffer Hotel design group. Because he had such a high degree of confidence in Peter O'Donnell after his efforts in constructing the Stadium loges, Art selected O'Donnell as construction manager. Modell had read of the work done recently by world-renowned designer Carlton Varney at the Copley Plaza in Boston. Art suggested that Varney be hired to propose the theme and scope of renovation.

Under many layers of wallpaper and flocking added over the years, Varney found the lobby area's original marble. It was difficult for Varney to contain his excitement when promising the investors how beautiful the end result would be. He felt strongly that the hotel should be restored to its former grandeur.

Art had asked me to work along and pay heed to the construction budget, line by line, and to keep him apprised if we came close to exceeding any line item. He reminded me that designers don't like to be constrained by budgets. He also told me that he had given his word to the bankers and the other investors, and that his credibility was at stake. I knew what that meant. There was no room for error on this project.

There was no one to do our Stadium work when we were tending to the hotel renovation project. That Stadium work waited for us until we got back to it in the evenings. These were long and exhausting days, but rewarding at the same time.

Art made the hotel restoration project fun. The investors, besides Steve O'Neill, our Stadium Corp., and Stouffer Corp., included Eaton Corp., TRW, Diamond Shamrock Corporation, Chessie System, and the Higbee Company department store (later acquired by Dillard's). As the project unfolded, the entire exterior of the building was steam-cleaned, and new windows were installed, providing for greater energy efficiency and also adding a richer tone to the building's exterior. The dingy inner area between the guest towers, once debris-littered, was converted into an atrium with an overhead skylight and a swimming pool. All the suites were reconfigured and redesigned. The 2500-seat Grand Ballroom was extensively refurbished to include new carpeting and wall coverings. The hotel lobby, stripped back to its original rich marble texture, became the trademark of the project.

The hotel project was put on a fast track, and it was substantially completed within a year. In September 1978 Stouffer's Inn on the Square was reopened with a lavish black-tie celebration. Among the 2000-or-so guests in attendance that night were the investors and the lenders, all quite proud of their accomplishments. Of course, on that night Art Modell, who led the entire effort, was also proud of what had been achieved. After his achievements at

The hotel renovation featured a spectacular refurbished lobby.
Jim Toman collection

the Stadium and now with the hotel, Modell was being credited with having given the city of Cleveland a "physical and psychological high."

After the hotel re-opened, Art used to enjoy dropping in during the evening, reviewing operations with the manager, and having a drink in the renovated lobby area. He didn't have to specify his drink. He always had the same: a vodka martini on the rocks, in a glass jammed with as many as eight or ten olives.

Art Modell stayed on a roll. Editorial writers at the now defunct Cleveland *Press* lauded Modell's previous efforts to get involved with another project, the changing ownership in the Cleveland Indians. With Clevelanders facing a real threat of the team leaving town, Modell had sought to rescue the franchise by finding a new owner. The owner was his fellow hotel partner, F.J. "Steve" O'Neill, a substantial owner in Leaseway Transportation, and a former owner in the New York Yankees. The newspaper showed its appreciation for Modell's efforts when it claimed that "…..the reorganization of the Indians by Art Modell ...despite the burden of problems with the Browns, has factored a new front office structure that promises to make the Indians a respectable organization again."

At the time Modell was a media darling, but he would not remain so for long.

In 1978 the Cleveland Browns also began a new era. Sam Rutigliano was hired as head coach, charged with bringing the Browns back to respectability. Art had decided that after going almost three years with Forrest Gregg, a change in head coach was necessary. Gregg's regimented, drill-instructor-like practice sessions gave way to Sam's more philosophical approach. In 1978 Rutigliano's team evened out the won-lost record and in 1979 returned to winning ways with a 9-7 tally. Attendance, which had dipped below the 400,000 mark in 1975, rebounded to 593,821. With Sam at the controls and number 17, Brian Sipe, at quarterback, the Browns were once again playing exciting football.

In addition to the hotel and football, there was also more work under way at the Stadium as part of Cleveland Stadium Corp.'s ongoing $10 million capital improvement obligation. At the end of the 1977 football season, work began on a new electronic scoreboard to replace the archaic manually operated board that had been installed in the early 1960s.

It took several electricians to operate the old board. One would peer with binoculars through slits in the scoreboard and watch for the home plate umpire's ball and strike calls. He would then relay the call to another electrician below, who in turn activated the appropriate switch, illuminating the ball-strike count. Even by 1970s technology standards, this method of operation was embarrassingly obsolete, except in stadiums like Boston's Fenway Park, where it was considered part of the "old ball park" charm.

Addressing the design of the scoreboard, Art had walked through the Stadium grandstands with his staff, including Dino Lucarelli and me, and dictated exactly what he wanted in the new electronic scoreboard. He did not want the standard configuration which was shaped similar to the dimension of a television screen. Instead, he chose an exaggerated rectangular board (about 50 feet high by 136 feet wide). His rationale was twofold: First, the "irregular" shape of the board would more symmetrically fit the shape of the bleachers; and second, the new board would be visible to more fans. For fans sitting in the higher rows of the lower deck (rows Q through Z), the underside of the upper deck obscured their view of the traditional square-shaped board. Modell's unique board, however, would give these fans a full view of the message center.

We contacted several prominent companies to quote on the new board, only to discover that major contractors would not quote on anything but standard-sized boards, which were (and still are) prevalent in other stadiums. Since that would not work for us, Art demanded a custom design for what would be, at that time, the largest scoreboard in the country (20,160 lamps). Even though we were venturing into uncharted territory, Art's enthusiasm was contagious, and we all actually began to believe that somehow we would be able to find someone to build the board at an affordable price. The question was who.

Art turned again to Pete O'Donnell. We all agreed that Pete was the person to supervise the project. With surprisingly little prompting, Pete agreed, and we set out together to custom-make our new scoreboard.

The structure of the original scoreboard was retained, but everything else was gutted - - making room for the computerized scoreboard installation in 1978. *Peter O'Donnell collection*

Once the design was complete, Pete selected the subcontractors, with construction scheduled to start after the last football game of the 1977 season. Construction problems began on the very first day. As luck would have it, 1977-78 was the harshest winter in Cleveland history, bringing extremely cold temperatures along with a then-record 90.1 inches of snow.

The scoreboard was needed by the first baseball game in April, and we had missed several crucial construction days. O'Donnell also had problems with several subcontractors who did not deliver on time what they had promised. Somehow, though, we managed to have the board operating for the Indians' home opener in April 1978, but it was then a very fundamental operation, functioning at only 85% of its final capability.

As the spring weather warmed, we were able to complete some of the remaining pieces. While we made progress, we also began to encounter difficulties. We quickly learned how sensitive the components on circuit boards were to temperature extremes, so we installed heaters in the scoreboard cabinets for warmth during the cooler months and small fans to mitigate the summer heat. However, the little fans were not sufficient to control Cleveland's sweltering humidity, which caused condensation on the circuit card and resulted in "stick-ons" (bulbs that could not be turned off by the scoreboard's switching device).

Despite the nagging problems, the board was operating fairly smoothly, and we took stock of the costs of the project. By acting as our own general contractor, we completed the scoreboard at below-market cost. (The final cost was $1.6 million as opposed to quotes of $2.5 million from the professionals). With the scoreboard done, we figured that we were set in that category for the next 20-or-so years, possibly until the end of the lease in 1998. We were to learn otherwise.

We had fun with the operation of the board. We hired a young Clevelander, George Hoffman, as our programmer. A sports fanatic, George easily fit right in, and as he learned the system, he began to introduce new and better programming. From a public relations standpoint, Dino Lucarelli did a great job of marketing our board, the largest single-matrix message center in the country. As with most technology-based industries, scoreboard operators share information quite freely, and visitors from other cities were frequently meeting with George and Dino to glean ideas. Art Modell's privately managed Stadium Corporation was gaining some national attention.

Dino wanted to add visual appeal to the board and, together with George, found a young artist named Fred Schrier, whom they hired to incorporate his work into the daily operations. Fred created portraits of each player, and he also drew several creative caricatures. Some of the more colorful were:
* foul (chicken coming out of an egg)
* home run (Chief Wahoo, the Indians' lovable mascot, jumping up and down)
* OUT! (Chief Wahoo putting a cat outside a tepee)
* UGH! (Chief Wahoo covering his eyes in disgust)
* gigantic home run (batter hitting ball out of Stadium into Lake Erie, followed by a splash of water)
* double play (Chief Wahoo shooting an arrow through two base runners)
* stolen base (a masked man running away with a base)
* caught stealing (policeman catching the masked man with a base)
* thump 'em Tribe (Chief Wahoo beating a tom-tom, usually done in concert with John Adams, the drummer who sat in the bleachers for every game).

Some of the graphics used on the Stadium's new scoreboard.
Cleveland Stadium Corporation collection

Dino, George, and I were proud that Cleveland Stadium could boast the largest single-matrix scoreboard in the United States. Being the largest, and trying to be the best, fit the Modell agenda. However, we also learned about problems with electronics, and how climatic conditions--especially high humidity--can create havoc. After we experienced a blackout on an extremely humid July 3 "fireworks extravaganza" game (which, as luck would have it, was the Indians' only sellout of the year), Art called in a specialist to assess the sporadic malfunctioning. The recommendation was that the board needed further enhancements. Specifically, one recommendation was that Stadium Corp. provide a backup computer system so that if the original system failed, a toggle switch to the backup would keep the board operating with only a moment's interruption. So we invested in the backup system, only to later realize that we would never once use it. But such were the decisions we had to make in operating a building for public use.

The consultants also advised us to waterproof the scoreboard press box because we were beginning to experience leaks in the control room. The scoreboard room, located at the far end of the baseball press box, was directly beneath two major expansion joints, which served as conduits for draining rain and snow from the upper deck. Because of its location, this room had leaked since the day it was built. Needless to say, making the room watertight to preserve the costly computers became an expensive proposition.

The grand re-opening of the hotel was little more than a month old when Art Modell turned his attention back to football—but not professional football. Modell was eager to generate more special event income for his Stadium Corp. business, and so he followed up on his 1976 invitation to the Naval Academy, and raised his previous guarantee to $500,000 for the Academy to move its 1978 home game with the Fighting Irish of Notre Dame to Cleveland Stadium. We "lieutenants" felt Art stretched pretty far to guarantee the dollars to Navy, but his instincts had told him that Cleveland football fans would come out in big numbers to see "visiting" Notre Dame. Art felt that Cleveland boasted one of the largest Notre Dame "subway" alumni in the country, so on a hunch the Fighting Irish fans would substantially fill the Stadium, Modell offered Navy the increased guarantee. Modell would often say, "Trust my instincts on this one" when he was hell-bent to proceed despite concerns voiced to the contrary. No matter what anyone said, Art wanted that Notre Dame game played in Cleveland.

To cover the game staffing costs along with the guarantee to Navy and the cost of transporting and housing the Midshipmen, we calculated that Stadium Corp. had to sell 55,000 tickets just to break even. On Friday night before the game, only 53,000 tickets were sold, so despite the hoopla and hype over the game, Cleveland Stadium Corp. was still in the red when the box office opened on game day. "Modell weather" greeted Cleveland that Saturday morning, and 8,000 fans bought tickets at the gate, assuring the company a profit on the event. All said and done, 61,000 fans saw Navy, who came into the game with an unbeaten 7-0 record and ranked 11th in the country, lose to Notre Dame and Joe Montana by a score of 27-7. Navy seemed to play the Irish tough in Cleveland, and Notre Dame remembered all too well the 1976 contest where a tenacious and scrappy Navy team, going into the game as three-touchdown underdogs, only succumbed 27-21. In that earlier game it had been Notre Dame safety Dave Waymer just barely breaking up a last quarter, fourth-down pass in the end zone that saved the Irish from being upset.

Reflecting on the special events scenarios at the Stadium, I came to realize that a businessman had to spend money to make money. Not too many people would have taken the risk to lay out the big guarantee that Art did to bring this game to Cleveland. Certainly, the city charter had precluded the city from ever doing business like that when it operated the Stadium. But laying out a large sum still did not guarantee a profit. I also came to realize how important the timing of sunshine is to the temperament of the last-minute ticket buyer. The appearance of "Old Sol" at the right time has made a big difference in the success rate of many an outdoor event promoter. On this particular day, it made the entire difference between the Stadium Corp. making and losing money.

Modell was always concerned that his customer receive good value for money spent. He critiqued himself on the quality of the entertainment, as well as on the quality of the food served at the concession stands. With regards to the ND-Navy game, he wanted to provide more entertainment than the game itself. He insisted on paying to transport and house the Midshipmen, because having them at the game, waving their white hats and sounding their chants, formed a spectacle intrinsic to Navy home games. Art also made sure that the city permitted the Middies to parade down Euclid Avenue, through Public Square, and on to the Stadium field just prior to kickoff. Art wanted Clevelanders to enjoy the entire weekend and not just the game itself. Modell even urged Navy athletic director, Capt. "Bo" Coppedge, to tell the Middies to try the Flats for a taste of Saturday night entertainment after the game.

One of my clearest recollections of that 1978 Saturday afternoon occurred about ten minutes after the game. As the fans were leaving the Stadium, I was standing in the lower box seats watching Vagas Ferguson, ND running back, on the field for a post-game television interview after having gained some 200 yards that afternoon. Few people were left in the building, so a security guard easily found me to let me know I was being paged. I scurried to a phone; it was Art. He had left the game about 15 minutes earlier and was at nearby Burke Lakefront Airport, ready to board his private plane to Houston for the Browns-Oilers game the next day. Before he left, he wanted to get a feel for how profitable the Notre Dame game had turned out. He said, "Well, how did we do?"

I said, "Do you mean bottom-line profits?"

He said, "Sure, how much did Stadium Corp. make on the game?"

I said, "Art, I won't even have a preliminary count until Monday. Heck, the cleaners haven't even picked up their brooms yet. We don't know how much the cleaning costs will be. The guards and ushers haven't even punched out yet, so we don't have their hours totaled. The food and beverage revenues are still being counted and..."

He cut me off. "All right, all right, so you don't have an exact count yet. Just give me an estimate. Just give me your best guess. Within 1% will do..."

Recalling the profits from the 1976 game, I then told Art that a $100,000 profit should be a close enough guess. My answer was satisfactory enough to allow him to board his flight for Houston. I didn't have time to tell Art that out of $150,000 of event production costs, slippage of $1000-2000 in costs can happen in the seconds I was talking to him on the phone. The funny thing was that Art thought he was giving me plenty of latitude with the 1% allowance. Boy, what a kidder that Art was!

It was hard to win with Art on those "just give me your best guess" questions. If I would guess the profits low, he could assume I was giving myself an edge to cover up some oversight. If I guessed high, and the true answer came in low, I could be found guilty of "losing my fastball." And worse, if I were thought to have made a grievous error, I might never be confronted to provide an explanation. Someone else might be called in to talk over the predicament that involved my ability, or suspected lack thereof. In the last ten years, that someone turned out to be Jim Bailey, legal counsel for the Browns and Stadium Corp, who was fast becoming Art's confidante and close advisor on any and all issues.

Art had a real "promoter's feel" for entertainment. In his early years of Browns' ownership, he had become a private backer of professional golfer R.H. Sikes. He guaranteed Sikes an annual income of $50,000, as against one-half of Sikes' own golf earnings. Art's risk was that he would lose money if Sikes made less than $100,000; he would make money if Sikes made more than $100,000. Should Sikes earn exactly $100,000, Modell would break even. This deal was intended to take pressure off Sikes; hopefully, Modell thought, by keeping Sikes a little looser during his golf play, he might perform better. Over the years, Modell and Sikes just about broke even in this endeavor.

With his business instincts, I am absolutely convinced that Art Modell was the right man to be chosen to "privatize" the operation of the Stadium. Not only did he have good instincts, he knew how to promote. The man who invented the pre-season NFL doubleheader in Cleveland and who had urged the league to adopt Monday Night Football certainly had established his track record for creativity.

Art never stopped talking about having a prize fight in the Stadium. He didn't give much credence to the trend beginning around that time of presenting prize fights in small Las Vegas arenas like Caesar's Palace. The focus was also turning toward pay-per-view rather than the live audience. But Art dreamed of an 80,000 crowd for a big heavyweight fight at Cleveland Stadium, with the ring located on second base. At the roundtable he often sketched out how the rows of ringside seats could be laid out. He said it would be a natural, just like the very first event EVER held at the Stadium, the world heavyweight boxing championship between Max Schmeling and Young Stribling, on July 3, 1931.

Whenever Art got enthusiastic over an idea, he corralled four or five of us, looking for our reaction. At one meeting in 1976, he was trying to develop a calculation of the potential gate, and to develop a mythical ticket manifest with all the categories of ticket prices. He led us out into the Stadium. We tentatively priced the seats at ringside and in the upper and lower boxes at fairly high numbers ($100 and up), which probably were fair prices if someone like Muhammad Ali was fighting. But higher up in the reserved section, and much farther from the field, there was no consensus on the cheaper seats. Art was hoping to hear $50, but no one was agreeing.

So he turned to his oldest friend in Cleveland, John Minco. Looking for support, and also to finalize the discussion (we always knew when Art wanted to finalize the discussion from the tenor of his voice and the firmness of the upcoming question), he asked, "OK, John, you are sitting in the very last row in the lower deck, Row Z, for a heavyweight fight between Ali and the nearest contender. What would you pay for the seat?"

John hemmed and hawed, not offering an answer.

Art, becoming impatient, offered, "Well, you'd pay at least $40, wouldn't you? After all, it is a heavyweight fight."

John was being pushed hard for an answer, and he said, "Well, I would feel safe with $5 or $10."

Art became miffed. He apparently thought John was jesting with him, and he wanted him to be serious. John finally elaborated on his answer, but Art did not like his explanation.

John defended himself by saying, "The fight is only a rumor from this seat. They (the promoters) can tell you it's Ali, but it could be an imposter, and the guy in this seat is so far from the ring that he couldn't tell the difference."

Art became genuinely angry with John. "Why do you always have to throw ice water on my ideas?"

John said, "Well, you asked me what I thought. So, I told you."

In a huff, Art returned to his office.

When Art was in a mood for support, he expected support. But guys like John Minco, and all of Art's financial guys over the years, gave him their honest opinions. There were many times when that was not what Art wanted to hear, even though that's what it sounded like he asked for.

By the time 1980 rolled around, Cleveland Stadium Corp. was pretty active in a variety of ways. Profits were growing nicely, in that two very positive things were in place.

Loges had been sold out ever since they were brought to market, with not one vacancy in six years. For every loge cancellation, five or more corporations on a waiting list were ready to fill the opening. We had extensive discussions before we decided to adopt a policy urging customers to share their loges with those on the waiting list in order to offer more people the loge experience. This plan would also allow the customer to defray the annual cost. Obviously with the demand that had been created, price increases were more easily accepted when shared with a partner.

Special events were also profitable and became a regular item at the Stadium. A few of the smaller attractions lost money, but most of the large attractions did well. Outdoor concert tours were the "thing" in the 70s, and fans would drive hundreds of miles to see Belkin's World Series of Rock at Cleveland Stadium. It was commonplace to see the early cars arriving for concerts with license plates from Michigan, Indiana, Pennsylvania, and New York. Many Ohio plates came from cities like Cincinnati, which was a four-hour drive. The World Series of Rock drew the biggest names in rock. The Rolling Stones had been to Cleveland twice in the previous five years, joining the likes of Aerosmith, Fleetwood Mac, and the Electric Light Orchestra.

While Notre Dame-Navy had twice renewed their rivalry in Cleveland Stadium during the 70s, Art Modell remained unsuccessful getting Ohio State to play a non-conference game in the Stadium. Woody Hayes was adamantly opposed to playing off campus and insisted that he would never allow his Ohio State Buckeyes to play in off-campus sites like Cleveland Stadium.

As far as progress along the capital improvement commitment went, by 1980 $8 million of the required $10 million had been completed, and most of these projects came in within budget. Of course, since all of the funds to pay for the projects were borrowed, the liability side of our balance sheet showed that our bank debt had increased to over $7.0 million. We knew that the concessions department, in dire need of improvements, had not benefited much from any new capital spending since we had entered into this lease. So, of the last $2 million required under the commitment, we allocated virtually all for the food and beverage service areas.

That was the status on the Stadium operations front. Other than wanting to begin retiring some debt, everything appeared to be proceeding along expectations.

Unfortunately, that would not last.

CHAPTER 4

COURTROOM CONFLICT I: ART MODELL VS. BOB GRIES

As a businessman, Art Modell enjoyed the challenge of taking on a project and seeing it through to a profitable conclusion. Whether television, real estate, or football; certainly Modell's favorite venture, Art tackled the challenges with confidence and optimism. Modell, however, had not faced any significant litigation along the road. His personality was not well-suited to the protracted and emotionally draining realities of the court system. Yet during the 1980s, Modell would find that the courtroom occupied more of his time than the gridiron. The legal battles exacted a heavy price.

One set of legal battles was waged with Bob Gries, the Browns' minority owner. The second set was with Gabe Paul, president of the Cleveland Indians. Both were painful and drawn out, but the legal war with Bob Gries lasted four years, and ultimately it had greater long-range implications for the well-being of the Browns' franchise.

The controversy with Bob Gries, principal of Gries Sports Enterprises and minority owner of the Cleveland Browns with 43% of the franchise stock, stemmed from the 1982 sale of the Cleveland Stadium Corporation to the Cleveland Browns. But to understand the issues raised in the Gries' lawsuits, it is necessary to go back to 1980 and review the events that led to the sale.

Besides its management responsiblity for Cleveland Municipal Stadium, the Stadium Corp. had two other investments to deal with: the hotel on Public Square and 200 acres of land in suburban Strongsville.

Modell originally purchased the Strongsville land in 1973 when he was considering building a suburban stadium for the Browns, much like the New England Patriots had recently done in Foxboro, Massachusetts. At that time, Modell, like a string of Cleveland Indians' owners, had grown distinctly unhappy with Cleveland Stadium. The city had shown little interest or capacity in improving the decrepit condition of its aging facility. Therefore, Art decided the Browns needed some options, and one of them was to assemble the necessary suburban acreage near major highways on which to construct a football stadium with sufficient surrounding parking. The purchase also served to put pressure on City of Cleveland negotiators, who were dragging their feet during lease talks with Modell. When the lease for Cleveland Stadium was finally worked out, the Strongsville land became surplus.

Modell had held the land in his own name since 1973, but the cost of carrying it had proved considerable, especially since the investment failed to create any cash yield. Therefore, Art decided to sell the land to one of his companies. At first he was not sure which. One option was for the Browns to buy the land since the planned new stadium would have been owned by the Browns. But in the end Modell decided on Cleveland Stadium Corp. since he believed it was his acquisition of the land which had finally prompted the city to move forward with the lease and which in turn had required the company's formation.

So Cleveland Stadium Corp. approached the banks and added $4 million in borrowing: 1) to acquire the 200 acres of Strongsville land from Modell; and 2) to purchase a limited partnership in the Hotel Cleveland venture.

Stouffer Corporation had taken over the hotel's operation. By 1980 Modell felt the investors had done their job. They had saved the hotel for Cleveland, but some rumblings were then coming from the various contributors. Their investments were not intended as long term, and they began voicing the hope they might soon be able to cash them in. Over the previous three years, the investors had been receiving substantial tax benefits through depreciation writeoffs, but no cash dividends or profit distributions were forthcoming. The hotel was not yet sufficiently profitable.

At the urging of the other investors, Art began his campaign to sell the interests. Art explained his views to Jim Bailey and me. He said that he had hoped to increase the value of the hotel so that each investor could recoup three times his original investment. He told us that his goal was to show the investors that they could reach out to do civic good and still make a profit.

Bailey had joined the Modell companies during 1978 and split his time between the Browns and Stadium Corp. A young attorney, Jim had first worked with Art on the negotiations with the City of Cleveland back in 1972 and 1973. Almost all the wording in the lease documents and amendments was Bailey's work. With the unique contract terms then being designed by players' agents/ lawyers, Art felt it was time to bring a full-time legal staffer on board, if not to negotiate directly with the players, at least to advise the player personnel director on contract language. Bailey's legal expertise was also needed in Cleveland Stadium Corp. where a large variety of special event contracts had to be drafted, and where the Strongsville land business required someone knowledgeable in real estate law.

After meeting with Art, Jim and I had to wonder where Art had gotten the barometer of a 300% return on the hotel investment as something achievable. Art had casually dismissed the notion that doubling their investment was a convincing testament to success. A quick calculation showed that the hotel sale would have to net about $36 million (compared to the starting cost basis of $18 million) to yield that kind of result. In this scenario, after the bank loan of

$9.0 million would be paid off, $27 million would be left to split among the partners. (This is an oversimplified example, and it is merely an illustration of the appreciation necessary to achieve a threefold increase in equity; depreciation recapture and repayment of startup operating losses paid by the manager, among other things, would have to be factored in before the true return could be calculated). After determining how much the hotel sale would have to generate to achieve Art's goal, it became a matter of persuading someone to buy out the partners for $36 million.

Little did we realize that two other factors then coming into play would affect our ability to sell the hotel:

1)   a tax reform act was then being drafted by the IRS that would alter tax rates, making depreciation deductions on investment property less valuable to new investors; and

2)   interest rates were climbing precipitously, making investors less likely than in prior years to incur debt to buy investment property.

We also had to deal with the Strongsville property. Bishop Realty Co. of Berea was hired as Stadium Corp.'s land developer to begin designing the property into a residential subdivision, getting the proper zonings, building streets, and creating marketable lots for building homes. Subsequent land sales would raise cash to reduce the increased corporate debt.

At the end of each year, Art Modell and I would review the previous year and budget for the coming one. Art would establish the expected level of revenues, and I would factor in the expected expenses. We both evaluated the adequacy of what remained, the cash flow to be generated. This number had to be sufficient to cover bank interest and loan paydown.

In 1980 the revenues we were projecting included profits from another Notre Dame-Navy game, which we expected would return to Cleveland for a third straight time (the even years were the Naval Academy's home games; the odd years were played in South Bend). Just as we were about to finalize our projections, the Naval Academy called to tell us that it had opted to switch the site of its 1980 game to Meadowlands Stadium in New Jersey. It was explained that the Academy wanted exposure in the New York City area and that Notre Dame had acquiesced to the site change. We also felt sure that Navy expected to sell out the near 80,000 seats for the game, given the population in the area (as it turned out, 76,000 tickets were sold, generating over $1 million in gate receipts).

The loss of that event stunned Modell. He felt that he had delivered everything he had promised. But that's the way it had become; stadiums wanted new business and began bidding for college football events. We would later find out how the bowl games had come to be sold to corporate sponsors who paid millions to have their names associated with them. Later, after Woody Hayes had passed on, we also learned, much to our chagrin, that Ohio State Stadium had begun competing with us for major rock concerts—all to generate more money for the school's athletic budget.

Another factor also crimped our revenue projections. Late in 1979, Ohioans were shocked by a tragedy that occurred at a Who rock concert in Cincinnati. Thousands of teenagers were jammed near the doors of the arena. When the gates finally opened, many people were trampled in the rush for the seats closest to the stage. After order was restored, 11 youths were found dead, asphyxiated in the panicked mass of humanity. The result was a public outcry against concerts and the way seating was handled.

The State of Ohio reacted quickly and outlawed general admission seating at concerts. The legislators felt that the "festival seating" atmosphere so popular at concerts had led to the tragedy, not to mention other forms of unruly behavior. It forced fans to rush for the best seats the second the doors opened. Fans would arrive early and stand in long lines for hours—even over-night—for an edge in getting to the "best seats" first. The new law stipulated that all concert seats must have a given location stamped on each ticket. The rationale, of course, was to save patrons from being required to get to the venue early for a choice seat. Seat location was guaranteed. It seemed like a simple solution to an ugly problem.

We all thought so until promoter Jules Belkin called a meeting with us at the Stadium. It was more bad news. Rock stars were going to pass up Ohio venues on upcoming tours because they did not want to play concerts without their fans up against the stage. The performers had come to enjoy that ex-change, and since the legislature had taken that away from them, they would bypass Ohio. Belkin foresaw no likelihood the Stadium Corp. would be host-ing concerts in the near future, unless rock groups eventually accepted the new seating layout.

With this news in hand, we went back and revised the budget down-ward. We removed the Notre Dame-Navy game, then deleted concert rev-enues from the 1980 projection. After having earned substantial concert rev-enues in recent years, I found it strange writing a zero on that line. (It would be 1984 before the idea of placing rows of folding chairs on the field in a *reserved* format would be appealing enough for a major group to again bring its act to Cleveland Stadium).

Since the Stadium Corp.'s bank borrowings were geared to the prime rate, every time the Federal Reserve nudged rates upward, interest expense rose accordingly. Revenues were declining rather abruptly, and our bank bor-rowings and interest rates were rising. Interest expense had, in fact, become the Stadium Corp.'s largest annual expense. Between 1978 and 1981 interest rates had risen sharply, from 10% to 21%, and interest payments were consuming virtually all of our operating profits. At Stadium Corp., we found we had no cash left to reduce our loan principal for the next several years. Thankfully the banks understood, and they were willing to restructure our loan repayment schedule.

These challenges kept Art Modell's mind working full time. He knew something had to be done, or the positive start he had made with Cleveland Stadium Corp. would come to an abrupt halt. Looking for assets to sell, he focused on the Stadium concessions business, at the time an in-house operation. Most stadiums and arenas, however, sold the rights to the food and beverage business to outside companies. Modell felt the time was right to try the same approach. The proposal would be two-pronged: a percentage of concessions sales to be paid to Stadium Corp, as well as a fixed, low-interest-rate loan sufficient to replace the entire Stadium Corp. bank loan. Art Modell was tired of suffering the slings of double-digit interest rates.

After reviewing proposals from the interested parties, we decided that Servomation (name later changed to ServiceAmerica) had made the "best" offer. It offered a 9% fixed-rate loan, plus a reasonable percentage of future food and beverage revenues. The loan included $1.5 million more than the Stadium Corp.'s then-outstanding loan balance. Stadium Corp. would use this extra sum to make sorely needed improvements in the Stadium's concession facilities.

It was another stroke of genius on Modell's part. What he accomplished was to guarantee that the Stadium Corp. could survive under almost any conditions. If concession stand improvements could generate more gross sales, as everyone speculated, then our new percentage of participation might even get the company back to the revenues it had earned earlier.

One other consideration involved in this undertaking affected our very limited staff. Our concessions manager, Alvie Friedlander, a long-time veteran of this business, had been hinting at retirement, so this move was also timely from the standpoint of keeping professional management in place.

Our stadium management team was lean in numbers. Friedlander managed the entire $8 million concessions department; I managed the business as executive vice-president under Art Modell along with being his treasurer; Mike Srsen was added as controller to help manage Stadium, hotel, and land development business; we also had Larry Staverman as vice president of Stadium operations and the land development business; Dino Lucarelli remained in charge of public relations, loge sales, and loge relations; and Jackie Lax was director of loge services. To define Jackie's duties in simple terms: She managed a 108-unit motel (102 loges were leased; six were for Stadium Corp. use).

With the proceeds from the Servomation loan, our next project was to complete what we thought was our final construction project under the Stadium lease commitment. The concessions project would take the total commitment to over $10 million, thus satisfying our obligation to the city within the required 10-year time frame. The work was done under the direction of Servomation designers and began immediately. Projected completion date was April 1, 1982, better than a year ahead of the deadline. What made the undertaking so comfortable was that the financing was already in place and at an interest rate about seven points below the market.

While this project was under way, and with our future now relatively secure, Art set in motion the sale of the Cleveland Stadium Corporation to the Cleveland Browns. Unlike the positive outcome of the concessions sale, this one set off a real furor, and brought on the four-year legal battle with the Gries interests.

To prepare for the sale, Art enlisted the professional services of McDonald & Co. to perform a valuation study of the Stadium Corp. Based on that study, he would be able to recommend a documented buying price to the Cleveland Browns. The sale would then be submitted to the Browns' board of directors for approval. While this transaction was actually a sale of an Art Modell-80%-owned-company to an Art Modell-50%-plus-owned company, it was the other side of the coin, so to speak, that ultimately led to a lawsuit. Although Bob Gries and family owned parts of both companies, Gries was not prepared to agree to sell a company he owned 10% of to a company that he and his family had 43% of. He simply did not believe Stadium Corp. was worth what McDonald & Co. said it was worth, and as he later contended in court, he believed his family was getting the short end of the stick.

The valuation process took months to complete. The experts not only had to value the seven different revenue centers contained within Stadium Corp., but also to estimate the ultimate values of the hotel interests and the cash value of the Strongsville land as if it were fully developed into sublots and sold. The final worth of the company was to be based on a calculation of discounted cash flow, using a 12% discount rate. This rate was applied to a fixed profit/cash flow number as projected in 1982, and as expected to occur each and every year through 1998. The experts needed to figure how much profit and cash flow would be generated, and as importantly, WHEN the profits would be realized.

When McDonald & Co. put the finishing touches on its study, its took into consideration the new arrangement with Servomation Corp. and how it impacted future cash flow. The McDonald study gave no effect to inflation or its ability to impact future earnings. By refraining from doing so, the McDonald team felt it provided an element of conservatism to the valuation. I felt that the selling shareholders were being hurt by understating the company's real future value. Nevertheless, McDonald and Co.'s preliminary valuation of Stadium Corp. was set at between $7.2 and $8.0 million.

Art asked for our opinions. I told him I believed the real value of Cleveland Stadium Corp. was almost $9.0 million, if one built only modest inflation into future revenues and earnings. I thought $7.5 million was unrealistically low. Then Art asked, "What is the value under the worst possible conditions?"

I said, "Under worst conditions, between $6.5 and $7.0 million."

After further discussion, Art reached a decision. "I think I want to propose a price even lower than that, so that there isn't one element of suspicion of self-dealing here. I'll propose a selling price of $6.0 million."

I responded, "That price is way low, but so low it certainly should eliminate any suspicion of profiteering. However, I feel you're shortchanging yourself." I was both right and wrong. Modell was shortchanging himself by 30% (80% of the Stadium Corp., less 50% of the Browns), but the low price did not prevent the Gries faction from charging bad faith.

In March 1982, the Cleveland Browns' board of directors approved the purchase of Cleveland Stadium Corp. for a price of $6 million. At this time the Browns had only $2 million of long-term debt on the books, so the Browns had plenty of borrowing power. The Browns therefore borrowed the $6 million needed to acquire 100% of the stock of Cleveland Stadium Corp. All Cleveland Stadium Corp. shareholders, including Bob Gries and the Gries family, but excluding Art Modell, tendered their shares and received payment. Then the Gries family (as Gries Sports Enterprises) filed suit in Cuyahoga County Common Pleas Court to prevent Modell from selling his shares in Stadium Corp. to the Browns on the basis that the price was exorbitant, and in excess of Stadium Corp.'s true value.

In fall 1982, quite possibly as a result of the controversy surrounding the Gries charge that Modell was selling Cleveland Stadium Corp. stock to bail himself out of debt, Cleveland Mayor George Voinovich decided to conduct an audit of the Modell lease. Maybe the city had fears that Modell was close to bankruptcy, as Gries had been alleging, or maybe it was just an opportunity to review the last batch of improvements that were being installed in the concessions department, but whatever the intent, the Voinovich administration proceeded to audit the years 1978-1981, picking up where the Kucinich administration had left off. Voinovich hired Coopers & Lybrand (Laventhol & Horwath had conducted the prior audit for Kucinich) to audit all rental and capital improvement payments. By this time the concession stands had been renovated, bringing Modell into full and final compliance with his commitment to invest $10 million into Stadium improvements.

When the audit was completed, the exact amount of $10,017,725 was verified as an accurate representation of the capital improvements installed in Cleveland Stadium—and one full year ahead of schedule. In addition, during this review, the parties had agreed to make a determination on the value of the benefits the city was deriving from the private management of the Stadium. In short, the answer ranged between $1.5-$2 million a year. The savings came about in three different ways:

1)   The city no longer was incurring the losses it had previously been experiencing, which amounted to about $500,000 a year;

2)   The city had a private party investing private dollars into a public building; the annual cost of retiring a $10 million debt at an average 9% interest (although interest rates then were 14-16%) a year would be at least $1 million in debt service costs which the city did not have to pay;

3)   The city was beginning to receive a cash rental in excess of its debt service and real estate taxes, and as debt service declined and Stadium rents increased, this amount would grow every year from the $50,000 it was then getting (in 1993 the city received more than $400,000 in excess cash; after the Indians left for Gateway, this excess cash figure was still over $300,000).

Over the term of the lease, the city would derive more than $40 million in cash or cash benefits, without having to lift one finger to get it.

When the audit was completed, unfortunately for Art Modell, no public announcement was forthcoming. I know he would have liked Mayor Voinovich to issue a public statement to the effect that through Modell's efforts, Cleveland was earning millions of dollars from the lease. Art said that Voinovich had told him privately that the city appreciated all he had done for it, but Art felt that a more dramatic statement would have quelled the whispering around town about Modell being as a "rip-off" artist.

The "rip-off" terminology had appeared in the March 27, 1980, Cleveland *Press*, and it still rankled Modell. The Cleveland *Press* was then struggling for survival, and it assigned two of its best investigative reporters to delve into the Modell Stadium lease, to settle, once and for all, the continuing controversy that had dogged the arrangement since 1974.

The Cleveland Press

Thursday, March 27, 1980

Stadium lease —is it a ripoff?

By PETER PHIPPS and DOUG CLARKE | First of two articles

Critics thought they heard the staccato melodies of "The Sting"...

both Modell's critics and his supporters. The questions first raised at City Hall six...

How Stadium lease

Art Modell

Stadium Corp
- 8% of Browns and Indians t
- Scoreboard and other adver
- 80% concession proceeds
- Stadium Club, loge and parl

Stadium profitable for city, study shows

By David W. Jones
News-Herald Politics Editor

Cleveland benefits more from its lease agreement ... Stadium ... a study by an

In some cases, cities also are offering to make capital improvements to their stadium at their expense to ... professional

expense to lure or retain professional sports teams," the report said.

Under a 25-year lease signed in 1973, Modell agreed to spend $10 million on capital improvements during the first 10 years of the lease.

The accounting firm said if Cleveland paid for the improvements, it would have cost taxpayers $1.1 million a year. That's assuming the city borrowed money and paid 10 percent annual in-... for 25 years.

Stadium lease benefits taxpayer

Continued from Page One

Steelers have not been asked to repay.

• In New York, the city's Shea Stadium lost $300,000 in 1969 in spite of the fact the Mets drew 2.1 million fans on their way to a world championship.

• In New Orleans, the $175 million Superdome was expected to lose $2 million to $2.5 ...

In the years before the Modell lease, city officials estimate the Stadium cost the taxpayers $300,000 to $500,000 a year in operation subsidies.

Frank Duman, Stadium commissioner from 1968 to 1974, when the Modell lease was si... thought the ...

It is on this point that softball magnate and Indians investor Ted Stepien enters the picture as perhaps the most persistent thorn in Modell's side.

Indians' seven-member board of directors to seek a new ...

Metro ⋆⋆ **Races**

Cleveland Press

Friday, March 28, 1980

...dium lease — better than most

By PETER PHIPPS and DOUG CLARKE

...nd's Municipal Stadium ...ned less than $100,000 a ...he city since 1974, but tax-...re appear to be better off ...Art Modell's controversial lease than those in other Press study has found.

...because most city stadiums are subsidized from the ...nas which ...treasury — subsidies which ...d along to the profits or re-

ranks among the most profitable public stadiums in the country, according to The Press study and findings of The Brookings Institution and the National Collegiate Athletic Association.

In addition to direct rent subsidies, most stadiums do not pay property taxes and a number don't pay an admissions tax — two taxes collected for Cleveland taxpayers.

"Public subsidy of professional teams is the rule and not the exception," Benjamin Okner wrote in a ... study titled "Gov-...

... had failed after 10 years to pay ... ...struction

2-1-95

THE PLAIN DEALER / WI

Leasing of Stadium has benefited city

By STEPHEN PHILLIPS and STEPHEN KOFF
PLAIN DEALER REPORTERS

'If the city were still

Stadium Corp. also does share its parking fees. Is this a good deal for the city

---

A few newspaper headlines lauded Modell's stadium management efforts over the years. However, note the word "rip-off" coincidentally placed next to Modell's picture, which left a negative impression in many readers' minds.
Cleveland Stadium Corp. collection

The investigatory article began with: STADIUM LEASE---IS IT A RIPOFF? One had to read the entire story to learn that, in fact, the lease was a pretty good deal for the city. After extensive interviews with many people around town, including Modell, the *Press* headline on the second day was better than the one on the first day: STADIUM LEASE--BETTER THAN MOST. The text of the article made reference to findings of the Brookings Institution and to the NCAA through which the reporters established that Cleveland Stadium ranked among the most profitable public stadiums in the country. Brookings stated that public subsidy of professional teams was the rule and not the exception. In Cleveland, by Modell privately managing the building, there was no public subsidy to either the Indians or the Browns. When asked to comment on the report, Mayor Voinovich only said, "If the city had held onto the Stadium, it probably would be closed today."

Once again the Stadium Corp. lease had received good marks, but most of the public were left with the impression formed by the first headline's "ripoff" language. We felt that we were ill served. Three times the Stadium lease had been shown to be a real benefit to the City of Cleveland. All of us wondered if we were ever going to see our side of the story get the attention we felt it deserved.

Jim Bailey was extremely upset with the treatment by the city during this audit, especially since we thought we were dealing with friends in the Voinovich administration. He indicated the initial drafts of the report presented to us for review were harsh, even accusatory in some respects. Some issues were indirectly pointed at Bailey who had handled the negotiations almost ten years earlier. Because the city at that time failed to document its intentions, Jim's explanations why certain things were done (or not done) were challenged. In 1982, after his dealings with the auditors, and while he was trying to cool off, he rifled off a memo to Art and me, letting it all out when he said:

You know, we don't ask much from this city. We just pour our capital improvement money into this place and quietly run it. I have long since given up expecting any sort of acknowledgment that it has been a worthwhile civic endeavor. All we really ask is not to be condemned. But I guess, that is not meant to be. Art has never asked for one bit of relief from the obligations he undertook in 1973, despite soaring interest rates, despite the miserable performance of the Indians, and despite last year's baseball strike and now the football strike. It is one thing for the city to raise legitimate questions, but it is another thing to subject us, and Art Modell, to the indignity of the way this has been handled. I think there is a lesson to be learned here. In looking at a site for the new year-round Browns facility, I think we need to keep in mind the enthusiasm with which the City of Cleveland greeted the formation of Cleveland Stadium Corp. in 1974, and the way the relationship has since evolved. I for one do not want to spend the rest of my career with the Browns "defending" whatever deal is made, and I don't think Art deserves that either....

Bob Gries filed his initial lawsuit (which came to be known as Gries I) in March 1982, wherein he alleged the Browns' board of directors had acted improperly in approving the purchase of Cleveland Stadium Corp. for a price far in excess of the true value of the company. Gries followed with two more lawsuits. The second lawsuit, Gries II, was filed in June 1982 and charged that the Gries interests were under-represented on the Browns' board of directors. Most court observers viewed this suit as subsidiary to the first, and essentially filed for its add-on or corroborative value.

The lawsuit, though, that really frosted Art was Gries III, filed during the sixth week of the 1982 NFL strike. In the latter part of October, while Modell and other owners were trying to negotiate a settlement of the labor issue, Gries challenged Modell's conduct as president of the Cleveland Browns. The lawsuit charged that Modell failed to properly account for his personal expenses and caused the company to pay for his and his family's expenses, to the detriment of the minority shareholders. Part of the complaint was based on Modell's having entered into a new employment agreement with the Browns, which Gries alleged provided for an "excessive and unreasonable" amount of compensation. In the 20 years Modell had been in Cleveland, he had received a salary of $60,000, plus a bonus based on profits, as defined by contract. After all those years, the board had seen fit in 1982 to adjust Modell's base salary to $200,000. Art drew no salary from Stadium Corporation, as per his agreement with the lenders. His other investments at the time were yielding sparse, if any, income.

The *Plain Dealer* noted Modell's reaction to the lawsuits. It reported, "If Modell seemed upset at Gries I (first lawsuit), and exasperated at Gries II, he was downright furious this time." Modell immediately called a press conference in his attorney's office, appearing red-faced and angry. He described Gries' latest charges as:

outrageous, irresponsible, and scandalous.....especially during what is the NFL's darkest hour. My salary has not changed in 21 years, and at $60,000, places me with the bottom 30% of all NFL players. I do not need Gries to approve my business expenses. Arthur Andersen & Co. has verified our books each year without so much as a question as to my business conduct. My record is clear. Gries has no moral or legal right to question that record. I do not understand Gries' motivation, but I can tell you that he will be held accountable for damaging the Browns organization and the Modell name.

Preparations for the Gries lawsuits took a long time and consumed time we needed for our other work. Plaintiffs are permitted to review and copy any documents not deemed privileged information. Altogether Gries was given more than 20,000 pages of Browns' and Stadium Corp. documents with which to prepare for trial. It was months before some of the files were returned. On more than one occasion I had to discontinue work on a project because I didn't have the files I needed; they were in "discovery."

The main Gries lawsuit, Gries I, a contract equity case, kicked off in Judge John Angelotta's courtroom on June 18, 1984. Under Ohio law, such a dispute is tried directly by a judge. The Browns were accused by minority shareholder, Robert Gries, of paying too much for the stock of Cleveland Stadium Corp., which brought personal benefit to Art Modell. Gries testified, "I thought, and still think, that this transaction is damaging to the Browns."

Gries contended that Modell was deeply in debt, and that the transaction was geared so Modell could pay down his bank debts. Modell argued that how he used the proceeds was a personal matter, that the only issue to be discussed was the valuation of Cleveland Stadium Corp. Was it fair?

Art Modell did have bank debts, but that was, and probably always will be, Modell's style. Art borrowed to accumulate assets. He was not born into money. He would not have been able to buy the Browns, or any of his other businesses, including Cleveland Stadium Corp., for that matter, if he wasn't able to borrow money to do so.

When Modell received his share from the sale of Cleveland Stadium Corp. stock, more than one person remarked how Art would be sitting pretty, since all he had to do was put those proceeds into a 10% CD or Treasury Note (interest rates on bond investments were quite a bit higher then) and start drawing interest. Since his 80% share of the $6.0 million selling price fetched him nearly $5 million, folks concluded that he could earn much more than his salary just in interest income. But that was not how it was. A capital gains tax on the stock sale and a temporary cash infusion into the Browns so the team would be able to sign several players accounted for most of the proceeds.

But, no matter the amount of money Art received, it was not his style to put it into a passive investment to earn interest. That offered no challenge whatsoever. Saving money in a CD was for the timid, not for Art Modell. If Modell came into a sum of money, it would be consistent with past practice for him to go out and borrow as much new money as he could get, and coupled with his own funds, buy a new business and try to make it grow in value. Just as he had done with the Cleveland Browns! Art always figured that his return on the growth of a successful business would outpace interest income on a short-term CD. He didn't believe in accumulating cash in a savings account. I once heard him break into laughter when asked where he had his savings accounts.

Unfortunately, two of his business ventures in Cleveland, a vacuum cleaner company and a metal box fabricating plant, ended up closing their doors several years later. The money he invested to try to resuscitate the businesses was lost. I sensed that both companies were too far gone when Modell decided to make the acquisitions.

Judge Angelotta lamented the fact the Gries-Modell skirmish had come to trial. He said he wished the dispute between two upstanding Cleveland citizens, both of whom happened to be his friends, could have been mediated outside the courtroom. He also recognized the case involved complex financial and real estate analyses; he asked both sides to talk in lay terms during the trial so that he and observers would be able to grasp the issues more readily.

One of Gries' experts testified the Stadium Corp. was worth a minus $69,000. We presumed this meant that if this expert had his way, Modell should have sold the Stadium Corp. to the Browns and delivered along with his stock a personal check for $69,000. One of Modell's experts, on the other hand, testified the company was worth around $8-9 million, far more than the $6 million the Browns had paid for it. It was no wonder that the judge appeared to be in a dilemma. If the so-called experts couldn't come close to a consensus on value, how was he going to do so?

Actually, Modell had tried one last-ditch attempt to avoid a court battle. Just prior to finalizing preparations for the board meeting back in 1982 to vote on the transaction, Modell had offered Bob Gries and his family a "guarantee." Modell pledged that if the transaction did not yield the financial results projected by McDonald & Co., Gries' and his family's interests would be compensated fully. Modell made the guarantee because he was absolutely confident the Browns were buying the Stadium Corp. for less than market value. Modell said at the time, "Gries can only make money on this deal. He cannot lose. He's in a no-lose situation."

Gries, however, seemed unimpressed by this assurance, and said the transaction gave Modell an "unwarranted windfall" and unloaded much debt. Jim Bailey and I had developed and presented the guarantee in detail to Gries Sports Enterprises. At the time we felt that Gries was not very interested in learning how the guarantee was intended to work. What Modell guaranteed was that there would be no loss to the Browns' shareholders from the investment in Stadium Corp. What Gries expected, however, was that Modell guarantee a profit on the investment. There seemed to be no way to reconcile these drastically-differing viewpoints. We agreed with what Modell had said to a *Plain Dealer* reporter. From all indications "Gries was hell-bent on litigation."

Many of us thought that Gries pursued the process of litigation in order to focus public attention on Modell's debts. Trial testimony recapped

Modell's personal financial transactions during his Cleveland years. Gries' lawyers pointed out that Modell lived with bank debt during his entire life with the Cleveland Browns, even beginning with a loan to provide the down payment for the bank loan used to buy the Browns in 1961. They pointed out that he borrowed to begin the Stadium improvements, borrowed to invest in oil wells, borrowed to purchase a radio station, and so on. They pointed out that Modell's personal interest expense was averaging over $1 million a year during 1980-82, while his salary and bonus was averaging only $180,000. They were hoping to paint a picture of a man facing financial ruin. Yet, as Modell told an Akron *Beacon-Journal* reporter shortly after the sale of his stock to the Browns in 1982, he made an interest-free loan to the Browns to provide signing bonus money for Tom Cousineau and others.

A big part of the valuation discrepancy centered on the Strongsville acreage. Depending on the underlying predicates, there can be a vast difference in the valuation of a land parcel. For instance, if valued as RAW land, the results would be far less than if valued after development. Since the Stadium Corp. operated a land development subsidiary known as Whitney Land Development Co., which had experience in land development and was continuing with development work (when we were not giving depositions or spending time in a courtroom), we felt it appropriate to value the land on a developed-parcel basis. The Gries group had difficulty believing the Stadium Corp. executive team could pass muster as land developers.

It gave me added satisfaction, then, when we were eventually able to prove otherwise. Over time we completed converting the land into a successful housing development. Although this was not our given vocation, we ultimately developed 192 acres into 520 single-family parcels. The project was finally completed in 1993, after 15 years of installing streets and sewers, and then selling the finished 1/4-acre parcels to six different builders. All the money invested in the land was fully recovered, with a little bit of profit left over.

One of Modell's experts, a Wall Street financial analyst, ignored the more controversial assets in setting a valuation on the company. John Adams Morgan, a descendant of J.P.Morgan and John Quincy Adams, testified Stadium operations ALONE were worth between $8-$9 million, even before adding in the land and the hotel units. Furthermore, he increased the value of the acquisition by another $1 million as a premium for "control," adding this amount only under the condition that the Browns bought the stock. He said any sports team that controlled the venue in which it played also controlled its own destiny and would ultimately increase its franchise value. Then ascribing only minimal value to the non-stadium assets, Morgan's valuation approached nearly $12 million, almost double the $6 million transaction price.

Jim Berick, one of the Browns' directors who took the witness stand, defended his vote in favor of the purchase of Stadium Corp. He said that, unlike Gries, he was not concerned the Browns would go $6 million further into debt to make the purchase. He said that in his view the Stadium Corp. assets and future earnings brought much more than $6 million to the Browns.

Pittsburgh Steelers' president Dan Rooney also testified. He claimed that from a team standpoint, it was essential to control one's stadium. The purchase of Cleveland Stadium Corp. by the Browns would accomplish that objective.

Sam Rutigliano was the last of the nearly 20 witnesses to testify. Sam likened a football team to a family. He said discord at the top spread "negativism" throughout. Rutigliano continued, "It makes the job of winning much more difficult. Professional football players are very fragile people, and when 43% shareholders make negative statements, it's not in the best interests of the Cleveland Browns. The owner is the single-most important person in the organization." Rutigliano said Gries had "made many irresponsible statements" that had hurt the team. Sam was particularly disturbed by Gries having been quoted that the team's record the last 10 years had been an embarrassment. (Rutigliano had been head coach for six of those 10 years).

Bob Gries did not escape the cross-examination of Modell's lawyers. Pat McCartan, Modell's lead lawyer, pointed out in court that Gries, as a 10% shareholder in Cleveland Stadium Corp., had first accepted the $32 per share buyout offered by Stadium Corp. and only then sued the Browns for paying the same ($32 per share) for Modell's shares. Gries' answer? "If they want to give me $32 a share for the Gries shares, it would be silly of me not to take it."

Setting a value on a company can be tricky. With the uncertainty of the volatile prime interest rate, there were varying calculations on the value of the Stadium Corp. stock. Value is based on expected future earnings, and those earnings are impacted by interest expense. Depending on the interest rate one uses when projecting the future, value will be impacted accordingly.

As we were projecting our estimates internally, we knew that such a valuation process could be challenged. If we were wrong, one of our companies would be hurt while the other would benefit by a like amount. We knew that we could not allow this to happen. With the sale of its concession rights and the procurement of the fixed-rate 9% loan from Servomation Corp. to replace all the Stadium's outstanding debt, we knew that future earnings could be better defined.

The trial lasted six weeks, the proceedings duly covered by all the area newspapers. Often during recess, Gries and Modell were solicited for quotes. On one rare occasion late in the trial, conversation turned away from the issues in the courtroom and onto football, and both owners found it possible to agree on one thing: It should be an interesting season for the Browns. Gries said, "Since there is no dominant team, the division is up for grabs." Modell said, "If my football team is as good as my legal team, we'll make the playoffs. This could be the best Browns team in 20 years." Neither owner knew it at the time, but they were in for a big surprise.

At his summation, the judge said that the trial had been very difficult. Weeks had gone by as expert after expert had authoritatively rendered contradictory arguments. He acknowledged the difficulty of his arriving at a fair conclusion as to value, when the experts who were schooled and experienced in valuation methods and techniques had reached such diverse and contrary conclusions.

Modell was visiting relatives in New York City on August 2, 1984, when he received word that the judge had announced his verdict. When told that Gries had prevailed in the case, Modell made it clear that he planned to appeal the decision immediately.

I was dejected by the ruling. From the very beginning of the lawsuit, I felt that it was my judgment being attacked since all the values developed were the product of my thinking. McDonald & Co. took my calculations and further trimmed the profits to stay on the conservative side.

No matter what the court ruled, I believed Stadium Corp. was worth $8 million. That belief was based on the confidence I felt in the company's future, a company whose results I was responsible for. But then it dawned on me. How could I ever prove it? I could explain my rationale, but I couldn't *prove* it was valid.

The value we were discussing was the result of a conglomeration of future events, the expected profits from as yet unknown eventualities. That was something I couldn't prove in a court of law. Nor, I hasten to add, could the opposite be proved either.

While in most courts of law the burden of proof falls upon the plaintiff, the one making the charges, in this case, the burden fell on the defendants (the Browns) to prove that the transaction had been fairly valued. In retrospect, given that scenario, it was futile to have thought we could win the case.

When the settlement was reviewed in its full written form, we learned that not only was Modell to pay back the $6 million, but also interest on that amount since March 1982 (another $1.2 million), plus Gries' legal bills, which some estimated would be close to another $1 million. The judge, when asked to elaborate on his decision, said that in his final analysis, "the defendants failed to prove that $6 million was a fair price. The four directors who voted in favor of the transaction abused their discretion."

On September 7, 1984, Modell's lawyers filed for appeal. In the court papers, Modell indicated that if the Browns did not buy Cleveland Stadium Corp., he would sell it to a third party. There was wild speculation that party was Marvin Davis, an oilman and a close friend of Art. Few were aware that the man whose interest Art was piquing was Al Lerner. That was how Art Modell operated. He was always working on a backup plan, and he would be ready with one if he had to move quickly.

Despite the fact that he had appealed the Angelotta decision, Modell had to plan for the worst case scenario. If he were ultimately to lose the appeal, he would be forced to buy back 100% of the Stadium Corp. from the Cleveland Browns. He therefore needed to be ready to put the company up for sale again, in whole or in part, and in preparation, asked McDonald & Co. to "freshen up" its valuation report. Three years had passed since its 1981 report had been completed.

There were many positive factors to take into consideration in this re-valuation. The Stadium Corp. had been financially stabilized by the 9% fixed-rate loan from Servomation, by the reduction in the prime interest rate and consequently the discount rate used in the valuation study (which would make future earnings more valuable today), and by buyers showing increased interest in the hotel notes held as assets in the Stadium Corp. There were also increased construction activity in the Strongsville subdivision and renewed interest in holding special events and concerts at the Stadium. All these things made Art Modell confident that the company in 1984 would be valued even higher than it had been in 1981, even with three fewer years remaining on the lease. His instincts proved to be absolutely correct.

On November 3, 1984, McDonald & Co., using the same present-value method of valuing future expected cash flow it had used three years earlier, assigned a value of $9,935,000 to the Cleveland Stadium Corp. This valuation represented an increase of almost $2 million over its earlier calculation and almost $4 million more than the Browns had paid for the stock. While the conclusions in the revised report were gratifying, I can honestly say that those of us active in the operation of the business were not surprised, as we always felt its value was nearer $10 million than $6 million.

Bolstered by the updated McDonald & Co. report, Art initiated a plan to sell the company to Lake Erie Radio Company. Having disposed of its stations, the company was then a shell corporation which he owned in equal partnership with Al Lerner. Art asked Jim Bailey and me to meet with Lerner and apprise him of the details behind the Stadium's business operations and the outside investments (the hotel and land development business) and then to give him a copy of the revised McDonald valuation report.

This was my first meeting with Al Lerner. I knew of him only by reputation as a successful businessman, a private person, and a Modell business associate. Lerner listened patiently as we spoke of the slow but steady progress of the Strongsville housing development, the new "cluster" housing being introduced to go along with the traditional single-family housing, and the different economics that each style offered. We talked about progress towards selling the hotel notes, and of course, we talked about the basics of the seven operating departments within the Stadium (loge rentals; rentals from baseball and football games; concessions, both food and novelties; scoreboard advertising sales; parking lot operations; special event activity; and the restaurant in Tower A). Lerner thanked us for our time and promised to get back to Art after completing his review.

Several weeks later we reconvened with Al Lerner in Art's office. I recall that he had only two questions, none about Stadium operations. He explained, "I go to all the football games, and I see the loges filled to capacity, the long lines at the food and beverage stands, and the parking lots filled to capacity. That is what it is. The only big risk is if the Indians leave town, and we'll deal with that issue when the time comes."

His first question was geared to the hotel notes, and the likely timing of when they would be turned into cash. His second question was about how much money was invested in Strongsville land at that moment and how much additional money might have to be invested in the future. He seemed to want to be sure that this wasn't going to be a future cash drain by pouring money into streets and sewers that might remain an idle investment.

We assured him that we always exercised prudence in undertaking future phases, that we did not proceed with a new street until we recovered substantially all the money invested in the last street developed. By doing so, we never had more than 40 lots or so in inventory, while much of our competition had as many as 100 lots available. While at times there may have been less variety for customers to choose from, we were able to limit exposure should the housing market go into a nosedive. The good news was that no additional money was needed; the funds for all future development would come from selling the developed lots already in inventory. Lerner seemed to accept that answer as a positive.

It seemed to me Lerner's approach was to examine the investment from a "worst-case" scenario. How much could he lose if external conditions turned bad? Was there more upside than downside? It was only a matter of minutes before he said, "OK, we got a deal. Let's get the lawyers to draw it up." Lerner and his partner Arthur B. Modell agreed to have Lake Erie Radio Co. make the acquisition.

Was that it, so nice and simple? Jim Bailey and I thought so, but we really should have known better. In April 1985 the Ohio Court of Appeals ruled in Modell's favor and reversed the Angelotta decision, holding that it was not the role of a court to decide on whether a corporate board's decision had been sound or not. So far, each litigant had won one round. This time Gries immediately appealed to the Ohio Supreme Court.

When Gries learned of the pending sale of Stadium Corp. to Lake Erie Radio, he filed a motion with the Ohio Supreme Court to block the sale. The Supreme Court granted Gries' motion, blocking the sale, until it could decide on the Court of Appeals ruling. Gries' lawyer said after filing the motion, "The web of self-dealing in the proposed 're-sale' is even more insidious than in the 1982 transaction which resulted in this litigation."

Bailey and I laughed, probably out of exasperation. We wondered what Art had ever done to these folks to warrant the tag of "insidious."

Modell, now completely flabbergasted, issued a statement saying that Gries had spent four years trying to nullify the Stadium Corp. deal. "We now have an opportunity to sell the company for a higher price than the Browns paid," Modell said, "and what does Mr. Gries do? He sues again, this time to stop the transaction, which represents a price of $7.169 million more than his own expert witness testified under oath in court that the company is worth." The reference was to Gries' witness who had testified that Stadium Corp. was worth a minus $69,000.

"His latest lawsuit might be the best indication of the problems we have in trying to deal with this man," Modell continued. "According to Mr. Gries, the Browns can't buy, nor can they sell, this company. The lack of logic and business sense and the motives of this man boggle the mind."

On August 20, 1986, almost two years after the Gries-Modell lawsuit had been decided in Common Pleas Court, the Ohio Supreme Court rendered the final decision. In a 4-3 split decision, the highest court in the state ruled in favor of Gries, stating, "The Browns' directors who voted for the transaction acted out of conflicting loyalties and for personal financial gain. Those motives led to a deal that was intrinsically unfair to the Browns and their minority shareholders, and therefore, is null and void."

Sometimes in my more cynical moods, I also reflect that of the eleven judges who were involved in reaching the verdicts, all of those who decided against Modell were Democrats, and all of those who had judged in his favor were Republican (as Art was). Was this just coincidence, or is it possible that judicial judgment might have been tempered by political preference?

After Arthur Andersen & Co. put away the calculators, the final sales price agreed upon was $7,213,522. (including interest). The Lake Erie Radio

Co. purchased Stadium Corp. from Modell literally hours after Modell was instructed by the courts to buy back the investment from the Cleveland Browns for $6 million plus accrued interest. By virtue of the Supreme Court decision, it would be Lake Erie Radio that enjoyed the fruits of Stadium operations in later years, rather than the Cleveland Browns.

Several weeks after the court-ordered sale took place, Cleveland Stadium Corp., a wholly-owned subsidiary of the Lake Erie Radio Co., began liquidating its peripheral assets. The company sold the two hotel units for $2,445,000, with all the proceeds going to retire bank debt.

Gries had won the first lawsuit, and he had also come away with another victory in the subsidiary Gries II. With those lawsuits out of the way, and Bob Gries commenting that he and the other minority shareholders had emerged victorious, Gries, Modell, and their lawyers conferred extensively over Gries III. This suit, of course, was the one in which Gries had charged Modell with using corporate funds for personal benefit. After four years of pre-trial discovery, this matter still had not come to trial. Several judges urged both combatants to "lock themselves in a room and settle this between themselves," and eventually a settlement was reached and the suit dismissed.

The agreement was treated as "extremely" confidential. Apart from the attorneys and Jim Bailey, no one else in the office knew the details. Someone close to the scene, however, dropped a note to a newspaper reporter that one facet of the agreement was that any future disputes between the two owners would be settled by an arbitrator.

The Gries III lawsuit was the most damaging to Art Modell, both personally and to his public image. Art was not a "crook," and he deeply resented any inference that his corporate dealings were in any way tainted. Those of us who worked in the corporate finance area knew Modell's dealings within the corporation were always beyond reproach. Like any of us, Art took umbrage when someone impugned his integrity.

What made all of this worse was that the average person typically assumed that when someone made charges in the form of a lawsuit, that some degree of wrongdoing lay at the bottom of it. That is especially true when the person bringing suit is someone of stature. Even in our dealings with those in business, that assumption held true. Gries III had left most people with the feeling that Art Modell was to some extent guilty of something underhanded. That was the real damage. Even though Modell denied all the charges in Gries III, and although four years of document review by the plaintiff revealed nothing improper, the only thing reported in the newspapers was the simple fact that the lawsuit had been dismissed. Unfortunately the taint and the hurt were not so easily dismissed.

Our accounting department tallied up the legal bills for all this court action. One thing became crystal clear: it was expensive to defend oneself. For the defense of the three Gries lawsuits, including the payment of Gries' legal fees in addition to the Browns' legal fees , the total payout to lawyers for Art Modell-owned companies was more than $3 million. This was equivalent to almost two good years of profits for the Browns..

Bob Gries was the only winner in these venal and petty proceedings. Art Modell was certainly a loser; his reputation had been smeared, and as a result, his ongoing ability to influence governmental policy to protect the best interests of the Browns had been weakened.

Art Modell shares a laugh with Mayor George Voinovich, Vice President George Bush and Governor James Rhodes during a Republican fundraising dinner in Cleveland. Some say Modell's activism in Republican politics may have hurt his efforts with Democratic Cuyahoga County politicos in the 1990s. *Cleveland Stadium Corp. collection*

CHAPTER 5
COURTROOM CONFLICT II: ART MODELL VS. GABE PAUL

If Bob Gries had been the only source of legal maneuvers against Art Modell's leadership of the Browns and Stadium Corporation, perhaps the wear and tear on Art's inner resources could have been manageable. Unfortunately, though, while Modell fought for his ability to lead the Browns' organization as he saw best, he was also assailed by two lawsuits from his baseball counterpart, Cleveland Indians' president Gabe Paul. These lawsuits did not happen in a vacuum. In 1981, our relationship with the Indians was becoming increasingly strained at various levels. Some background will help set the scene.

After three straight sixth-place finishes, the Indians started out the 1981 season in exciting fashion. During May, the Tribe surprisingly found itself in first place, and the home fans had the rare experience of witnessing a perfect game by Len Barker that month. At our roundtable in the Stadium restaurant those days, we found ourselves getting increasingly optimistic about the Indians' prospects. One day at lunch Art remarked, "It's been an awful long time to wait with this baseball team, but it looks like this team is finally going to create some excitement. With the loss of our college football series and the concert tours, it's a relief to finally get some help at the turnstiles from baseball." Collectively we shared the feeling, and we thanked God for Lenny Barker.

Several weeks later the boom was lowered on baseball fans everywhere, but the biggest boom was felt in Cleveland. As the Tribe was sitting in first place, Major League Baseball went on strike. For 59 playing dates, most of June and all of July, no major league baseball games were played.

I felt we were snakebitten. Having lived in Cleveland all my life, I had grown accustomed to baseball frustration. Being in first place during the summer just didn't happen. But in 1981 the first-place Indians were going to rescue our budget when everything else was failing. With the strike that little flicker of hope was dashed.

Gabe Paul had succeeded in getting the 1981 All-Star game scheduled in Cleveland to mark the 50th anniversary of Cleveland Stadium. With our large stadium and the excitement that started the season, we had high hopes for a king-size crowd. So when the strike was settled, it was agreed that the first game to be played would be the rescheduled All-Star game. Major League Baseball was aiming for Saturday, August 8, but the Browns were scheduled to play the Steelers in a sold-out preseason game at the Stadium that day.

Gabe Paul had considered asking Art to reschedule the Browns' game to another day, but thought better of it, and the All-Star game was played the next day, Sunday August 9. The game was a huge success. The crowd of 72,086 set the all-time All-Star game attendance record, and the National League won in a nail-biter.

After the regular games resumed, to everyone's disappointment the Indians resorted to their old style of play and steadily slid backwards in the standings. The team had virtually no offensive firepower. Bo Diaz led the team in home runs that year with seven. The shortened season brought only 661,395 fans to the Stadium, and the Indians again finished in sixth place.

The Indians' Stadium lease was due to expire at the end of the 1983 season. Our typical profit projection with the Indians always started with a 1,000,000 - fan base, but we knew pretty early in the 1983 season that this was to be a "down" year. With the loss of revenues that both Stadium Corp. and the Indians suffered from the 1981 strike, and with the 1982 football strike further impacting Stadium Corp. revenues, neither party was in a financial position to make concessions. Nonetheless discussion got under way. Steve O'Neill and Gabe Paul selected Bernard "Bunny" Goldfarb, O'Neill's favorite attorney, to represent the Indians.

Several things made the negotiating atmosphere tense. Modell still remembered Gabe Paul's anger over rescheduling the 1981 All-Star game. Paul had complained how difficult baseball had it in Cleveland, co-existing in a stadium controlled by the football tenant. Gabe later made reference to this being an example why sharing a stadium with pro football just didn't work out. A game as sacred to baseball as the All-Star game shouldn't have to take second place to a "meaningless" pre-season NFL game.

Indians' President Gabe Paul.
Jim Toman collection

Signs of football activity seemed to irritate Gabe Paul. He once saw the ground crew throwing footballs in the outfield on a day in September when they were supposed to be watering the baseball infield. Paul had operations director Dan Zerby go out to the field and threaten them with their jobs. Zerby told us later that had they been throwing baseballs around, nothing would have been said. Every September, the remnants of the chalk lines representing the yard markers were still visible, maybe only faintly, when the Indians played their remaining home games. This would gnaw at Gabe, and during games he would grumble about it to whoever was sharing his private box.

Another petty thing also soured the atmosphere between the Indians on the one hand and both Stadium Corp. and the Browns on the other. It occurred in the inner lobby leading to the home team locker room. On the wall near the entrance, Art had insisted that the logos of both the Indians and Browns be prominently displayed. He felt proud that two professional franchises shared the facility. Large framed plaques, one with the orange helmet and the other with Chief Wahoo, hung on the wall several feet from the door. Once baseball season started, for the most part, Stadium Corp. management folks didn't go near the locker room, since the Indians wanted it kept off limits to all but their own staff. But one day, Stadium maintenance folks were summoned to repair a hot water heater. They reported that the plaques had been tampered with. We learned that early in the baseball season, an Indians' employee had turned the Browns' plaque face to the wall. When Art received word, he turned three shades of red and demanded the Browns' helmet plaque be re-attached in a permanent fashion so that it could never be removed again.

Word also got back to Modell that Steve O'Neill had been questioning Gabe Paul about the Indians' continuing sub-par performance on the field. Paul reportedly told O'Neill that "the Indians will never be able to win...because of the poor lease with the Stadium." Yet it was common knowledge that the Indians' draft record was sub-par. In fact, not one Indians' first-round draft pick 1974-1983 ever reached the big leagues. But management didn't want to be held accountable for that failure; it was easier to blame the lease.

This background helps make clear why tensions were high as lease negotiations began. Jim Bailey and I represented Stadium Corp., and Bunny Goldfarb spoke for O'Neill. Goldfarb had simplified his approach down to one request: The Indians were looking for $2 million in additional revenues from the lease. He said the Indians considered their lease one of the worst in baseball. Bailey and I politely disagreed. We told Goldfarb that while we knew it was not the best, it was no worse than average. We also told him that most leases better than ours were the result of city subsidies. I asked Goldfarb to allow us to sit down with the Indians' representative who had compiled their statistics since our two conclusions were miles apart. I suggested that unless we agreed on the starting point, any conversation towards improving the lease was somewhat meaningless. Goldfarb refused my request.

The Indians' major contention was that the team received only 20% of concessions revenues. That was correct. The Indians did receive one of the lowest percentages in the league, but what the Indians wouldn't recognize was that in other venues when a team got a much higher percentage, with it went responsibility for cleaning the stadium. In Cleveland that cost was incurred by Stadium Corp., and it equated to eight percentage points on the concessions revenues. So, comparing apples-to-apples, in effect the Indians were receiving 28% of the concessions gross.   The average concession split of about 30-33% with some of the better leases was not that far off from what the Indians were receiving.

Modell felt that sparing the Indians an expense normally regarded as a tenant responsibility was the same as getting more revenues from another category. But, then again, Gabe Paul and Steve O'Neill were not present when the lease was first negotiated, so they did not have had first-hand knowledge of why some things were handled the way they were.

We tried to explain to Goldfarb that if one focused only on the gross amount of revenues paid to the Indians from Stadium operations, then one would incorrectly conclude this lease was the second worse of the 17 studied by the Stadium Corp. However, we pointed out, in order to evaluate the full economic picture, one had to go beyond the revenues received by the team and explore the responsibility for paying event expenses. A wide range of how expenses were treated between tenant and landlord existed throughout the league. After evaluating the expenses among other teams and juxtaposing these on the Indians' situation, the Indians' lease improved dramatically. We noted, for example, that where some teams got larger concession shares from their cities, the city admission taxes were much higher than Cleveland's. Of the 17 leases studied, we concluded the Indians' lease was the eighth best, putting the Indians just above the middle of the pack. Furthermore, less than $400,000 in economic value separated the Indians from the best lease in the league, when using a million-fan base for comparability. Our arguments continued to fall on deaf ears.

The Indians continued to claim that the lease was unfair. Modell kept repeating that the Browns enjoyed the identical lease terms as the Indians, and the Browns did not find the lease terms onerous. He suggested the Indians compare their present lease to the terms they had "enjoyed" with the City of Cleveland prior to 1974, commenting that it was he who had brought about the improvements in those terms. Modell maintained that if the ballclub would put a competitive team on the field, it would get more "asses in the seats," a common reference Modell used in these types of discussions. Modell's point was simply that with fans in the seats cheering on an interesting team, everything else would take care of itself. Besides the gate receipts picking up, concessions sales would also increase, and the team's share would increase accordingly.

Instead, the Indians complained about how little revenues they received from loge sales. (The Indians and Browns got per-ticket revenues in the loges equal to the highest-priced ticket sold to the public, i.e., the box seat ticket value). We reminded the Indians that Stadium Corp. policy to have every loge customer buy baseball tickets was designed to protect the Indians and in so doing had actually begun to alienate many loge owners due to the Indians' poor play. Modell reported that if the Stadium Corp. were to give loge customers a choice of tickets to purchase, many would not buy tickets for most Indians' games.

Paul also complained about concession revenues earned by the Indians in the previous year. Modell responded to him by letter saying, "It shouldn't surprise you that with the Indians' attendance ranking 22nd out of 26 teams that your gross concession revenues would rank at the low end of the chart." The Indians kept referring to the gross revenues earned by the Stadium Corp. from loge sales, and complaining that so little was shared with them. They were reminded that the net revenues, after ticket value paid to the teams, went to service the debt on Stadium improvements. At the Stadium Corp. we remained firm that there could be no financial improvement whatsoever in the Indians' lease if the team could not generate at least one million fans a year, since it was our experience that the Stadium Corp. could not break even at anything below that attendance level. In our negotiations we introduced improvements in increasing increments only as attendance rose above the million-fan level. We considered that the "floor."

The existing dilemma over the Indians' lease was disconcerting to us. The September 6, 1983, *Plain Dealer* quoted Indians' executives as saying that the better leases in baseball generated about $500,000 a year in revenues more than the Indians received. Another report furnished several years prior by Ernst & Whinney at the request of Gabe Paul showed that, at most, the Indians were approximately $200,000 shy in revenues as measured against the median of other ballclubs. We felt our comparison was valid since many of the other leases were better simply because of subsidies from city governments which owned the stadiums. In Cleveland, these subsidies were not possible because the city was not negotiating directly with the teams. It was puzzling for the Indians to be seeking $2 million more a year from the Stadium Corp., when they also were stating that only $500,000 would make them equal to the BEST lease in baseball. That lack of logic made the negotiations frustrating. When there were disagreements in interpreting benefits in other teams' leases, we opened the details of our study to explain how we arrived at certain conclusions. The Indians, however, refused to produce the details of their studies, making it virtually impossible to reconcile differences in perception. Bailey and I could only conclude the Indians were not being totally above board with us.

While Art was aware that improvements to the Indians' lease in some areas were overdue, he knew that Stadium Corp. did not have an additional $2 million to give the Indians in annual cash improvements. Modell said if the Indians held firm to their demands to get $2 million, then like other teams, they should get that kind of subsidy from the city.

Modell said he did not want to be cited as the reason the Indians wanted to leave the city. So he set forth a plan where the city could re-acquire the rights to its own building for the cost of the improvements he had completed. Art estimated that amount to be $16 million (which included an approximation of $6 million for interest).

In April 1983 Modell outlined his plan to the City of Cleveland. It included the concept of the city leasing the loges back to the Stadium Corp. for $1.25 million. Likewise the plan included the city receiving all other revenues and becoming responsible for all expenses. With the city gaining control over these revenues, Modell hoped it could give the Indians the benefits they were seeking. Art asked Bailey and me to prepare the proposal to have the city re-acquire the stadium lease for the cost of the capital improvements plus interest.

Modell had long-standing friendships and good rapport with many of the Indians' board members. Sensing that it was impossible to deal with Paul and his attorney, Modell began dialogue with these members, apprising them of his plans to get out of the landlord business, and turn the "damn building back over to the city."

As soon as the proposal hit the newspapers, Gabe Paul prepared a press release lambasting Modell's plan as a "sham." The release stated that "the efforts of the Browns [actually, Gabe meant to say the Stadium Corp.] to wheedle more than $10,000,000 from the city to surrender the lease while retaining the concession contract and control of the loges is a sham. If successful, they will have staged one of the greatest coups in the history of Cleveland, at the city's expense."

It took only a few weeks before Mayor Voinovich issued a negative response to Modell's proposal. He backed away saying, "When Cleveland Stadium Corp. agreed to take over the Stadium, the Stadium was losing money and was a definite drain on the general fund. By the Stadium Corp.'s performance under this agreement, the cash drain had been stemmed....each year since then has resulted in a positive effect on the general fund." Besides, he said, "the city has other priorities for (spending) the $10,000,000." Brent Larkin, *Plain Dealer* columnist, wrote that "the mayor and those around him are convinced that there's more than meets the eye surrounding the offer by Browns' owner Art Modell to serve them the 52-year old building on what seems to be a silver platter. 'It's falling apart,' said one city official last week. We'd end up on the short end.'" Larkin also reported George Forbes' viewpoint on the matter. The Council president thought it was a fair offer, but impossible because the city would be incapable of managing it properly.

The city had a good deal, and it was not about to give any of its benefits back to anybody. At the same time, the mayor kept urging Art Modell and Gabe Paul to get together to work out a favorable lease renewal.

Paul's press release was the second that year in which he took a swipe at Modell's reign as Stadium operator. Several days before the opener, Paul had prepared a release lambasting the "high" concession prices which were established under the control of the Stadium Corp. He said he was trying to protect his fans from overpricing. He cited the cost of beer. "... $2 is too much to pay for a beer, I know that." Gabe never mentioned the size of the beer. The fact was, Servomation had gone to a new 20-ounce cup that year, thereby creating a new price category. Up until 1983, beer was served only in 12-ounce and 16-ounce cups. Dino Lucarelli, Stadium director of public relations, said the Indians' protest was a flagrant attempt to embarrass the Stadium Corp. and the concessionnaire. "I am amazed that the Indians would send out a news release on this matter," Lucarelli added.

Headlines such as these portended troubling times for Art Modell off the football field in the 1980s. *Cleveland Stadium Corp. collection*

Gabe Paul didn't stop there. He seemed loaded for bear. Several days later, the Indians filed a lawsuit charging that Cleveland Stadium Corp. had shortchanged the Indians in concession revenues over the previous ten years, to the tune of $1.25 million. The lawsuit was filed during the first day of the annual NFL college player draft in April, while Modell and the front office were at team headquarters in Berea. Asked to comment, Modell said, "This is a disgrace. If the Indians had a complaint over the concessions sharing methods, why hadn't they raised the issue in the last 9 1/2 years? Also, their announcement was timed to almost precisely the exact moment we selected our first draft choice."

Sports columnist Hal Lebovitz, a good friend of both Modell and Paul, was thoroughly confused by Paul's behavior. He pointed out in an article that he couldn't understand why Paul objected to Modell wanting to let the city back into the picture as Stadium operator, since that might be the only way the Indians could receive the lease improvements they were seeking. Other writers chided both men for acting childish and engaging in name-calling via the newspapers. Some writers thought Gabe was just being opportunistic in jumping on Modell when he was most vulnerable, since at the time Modell was also dealing with Gries' three lawsuits. But they didn't know how determined Art could become when under fire. Those of us who worked near Art knew how tough he really was. He never viewed the odds as unfair. He knew he was in a fight, and he wasn't going to run.

Some Indians' investors, most notably Ted Bonda and C. C. Tippitt, were upset over Paul's lawsuit and asked to act as intermediaries. They respected Modell and felt that they could reach a reasonable compromise on behalf of the Indians with the Stadium Corp., if permitted by Steve O'Neill to do so.

Writers continued to take sides. One writer blasted Paul for being a hypocrite in citing concession price increases, while at the same time raising ticket prices. Jeff Schudel of the Lake County *News-Herald* (LCNH) said that Paul:

> pounds the table indignantly because the fans have to pay another dime for a hot dog this year, while box and reserved seats were hiked one dollar for the 1983 season. On Opening Day, normal general admission seats are expanded on the manifest, and relabeled as box seats, so the Indians can get $8 instead of $3.50 for the seat. Does that sound like a man concerned about the fan paying an extra dime for his wiener?

Schudel finished off, "Fans aren't fooled. They are staying away from the stadium not because the lease is bad or because hot dogs now cost $1.20, but because the team they're paying to see isn't as exciting as mowing the yard."

Bob Dolgan, *Plain Dealer* columnist, presented a contrary view:
Art Modell has this image, however inaccurate it may be, of an opportunist who got lucky and is nifty with a dollar. Most fans prefer to feel he just fell into it and that nobody should be that fortunate. They just feel that they cannot completely trust him, no matter how much his superb public relations team makes it look as though he only makes money for the fans' benefit. Now they are happy to see people of substance--Gabe Paul and Bob Gries--take shots at him. It lends substance to their suspicions.

In discussing his reasons for going forward with the lawsuit against Stadium Corp., Paul asserted that he believed Modell had accepted a payment of $4 million from the concessionaire "under the table." Paul didn't necessarily charge any wrongdoing with that statement; he only wanted the Indians to share in that payment.

Modell had arranged for former Secretary of State Henry Kissinger to speak to the 50 Club in downtown Cleveland's Union Club in early June. Art and his secretary Marilyn McGrath had temporarily set aside the legal problems to plan this meeting right down to the last detail. After the successful evening ended, Modell was driving home late into the night when he experienced a scary tightening in his chest. "Indigestion, I guess," Art said to himself. "Maybe I'll try to slow down a bit this week and start taking it a little easy."

When Art reached his house, he was struck with another chest pain. His wife Pat looked out and saw Art leaning over in the front seat before coming into the house. He explained to Pat that he was only reaching over to gather up some files.

Art did not return to the office until late Friday afternoon prior to going out for a social event. Jim Bailey and I had been ruminating over ways to revise our lease proposal to the Indians. We had been working on four different options, including one where the Indians would acquire 50% interest in the Stadium Corp., and we were discussing these with Art when the phone rang.

It was Art's good friend and one-time broadcaster for the Browns, Gib Shanley, calling to see if Art wanted to comment on Gabe Paul's latest lawsuit, filed that day. Art had no idea what this was all about until Gib told him that the Indians had filed a suit against Cleveland Stadium Corp. for $25 million for failure to negotiate a new lease. Art was aghast! The lease still had seven months to run before expiration, and almost everyone in Cleveland knew that efforts to find common ground were continuing. Art left the office that night, quite dejected, and went on to his social event.

When my phone rang at home the next morning, it was Jim Bailey telling me that Art Modell had been rushed to the hospital in the early hours of the morning with a massive heart attack. Bypass surgery was being planned as soon as Art regained enough strength to endure the procedure. Afterward I sat in my room reflecting on what I had just heard, and the events of the recent months. As strong as I thought the 57-year-old Modell was, I wasn't surprised by what had happened. The previous three years had been hell.

Preparatory work on the trials continued. Depositions of some of the Indians' investors revealed that Gabe Paul had several times referred to Modell as "a crook and a liar" during meetings of the baseball team's hierarchy. In one deposition, an investor testified he heard Paul say he believed Modell had received an improper payment in return for the concession contract. Modell responded by calling that a "blatant untruth," and he wanted to search out the source of the rumor. Paul then claimed that he never accused Modell of taking money "under the table," but rather "upfront money" in return for the contract, which Paul acknowledged was not uncommon in the industry.

While this was going on, Art Modell remained at home, recuperating from quadruple bypass surgery. Following the surgery, complications had set in, and he had to be rushed back to the hospital for more surgery. When he was strong enough to return home, he remained on many medications. Art spent the entire summer of 1983 recuperating, and his wife Pat watched his recovery closely. He did not travel with the Browns to the pre-season games. While he was physically getting back on his feet, he was mentally gearing up to fight the lawsuits against him. It was a fight to defend his integrity. He vowed to win all of them. Most office conversation dealt with the progress on the litigation, not a pleasant topic with Art. He wanted to do more constructive things, but he was not going to run from these accusations. Since Art's daily direct contact was with Bailey on mostly litigation matters, Art began to direct all his dealings through Bailey. For all intents and purposes, Bailey became the man in charge.

Art's lawyers recommended that he retaliate with a lawsuit against the Indians. As repulsive as that option was to Art, he went along, if for no other reason than to show that the string of "nonsensical" lawsuits against his company had to stop. Nobody had yet ventured a guess, but the legal costs were going to be substantial, and the efforts of our management team (few of us that we were) were not going into running the business but defending the company against our erstwhile friends(?).

In federal court Modell's lawyers struck back at the Indians with a $10 million counterclaim for damaging Modell's corporate name. The *Plain Dealer* followed the series of events closely, reporting that even the lawyers on both sides were becoming emotionally involved in the issues.

The Indians were not only demanding an opportunity to audit Stadium Corp.'s revenues from Servomation Corp., they also insisted on the right to audit the concessionnaire's books. While the lease provisions gave the Indians the right to audit Stadium Corp.'s records, it did not permit auditing another tenant's records. Accordingly, we refused the Indians' demand to audit Servomation, because the Stadium Corp. had no right to grant such permission.

While the debate over the audit continued, the ensuing hostilities led to a cessation of lease negotiations. As Stadium Corp. president, Modell stated that talks would not resume until the Indians dropped the lawsuit and issued a public apology. Depositions in court brought forth the information under oath that Gabe Paul had been heard in the Indians' media lounge before a ballgame to call Art Modell "a crook." Paul was reported to have been invited to watch a taped television interview with Art Modell, to which Paul responded loudly that he "wouldn't watch the interview because...Modell was a crook and a liar." Paul was asked by reporters whether he actually called Modell a crook, to which he responded, "I don't want to comment at all."

Both Jim Bailey and I had to appear for depositions during the heat of the summer. I still remember those long days at the law offices. Art was home recuperating, and no one was back at the ranch "watching the store," a phrase Art used when he wanted a report from the in-charge, on-site manager. For many weeks, the only "store-watching" was happening after 6 p.m.

It was during one of the depositions of the Indians' in-house legal counsel, Michael Fetchko, that the boredom of the long, drawn-out process was broken. Bob Weber, a Jones, Day lawyer representing Stadium Corp., was questioning Fetchko about various things surrounding his responsibilities with the Indians. Weber became increasingly frustrated with Fetchko's answers (or lack thereof). Almost every question was being answered by either "I don't know" or "I don't remember." Weber began mixing in very simple questions which would hardly merit anything but a straight answer. But still the response was "I don't recall." Weber turned his back and paced through the room, appearing deep in thought. It seemed clear that Fetchko felt he might have succeeded in stonewalling the interrogation. Then, abruptly, Weber turned and almost leaped at Fetchko, screaming, "Fetchko, I am sure that you realize that if you knew the answer to any one of those questions I just asked you, to which you answered 'I don't know,' or 'I don't recall,' that you just committed perjury. Let's take a break!" After a 15-minute recess, the question-and-answer session started again. It was amazing to note the improvement in Fetchko's memory.

Steve O'Neill was one of the last parties scheduled for deposition. The other depositions had been completed, and O'Neill was scheduled on August 30, 1983, to answer questions pertaining to the Indians' two lawsuits against

Modell. O'Neill never made it to the deposition; he died the day before. Hal Lebovitz wrote in his next column, "One has to wonder if Art Modell's recent heart attack and O'Neill's sudden death might not have been tied to the stress and aggravation resulting from the legal hassles." Lebovitz added, "The lawsuit against his old friend Modell was so uncharacteristic of Steve that close friends wondered who was calling the shots, and why."

Art Modell felt the same way. He often said he would never forgive Gabe Paul for turning his good friend against him. Art remembered how O'Neill had willingly joined him in contributing $1 million in the effort to save the hotel. In 1978 O'Neill had trusted Art with his money and told him he was confident Art would do his best. Modell felt that in the intervening five years somebody had worked to change O'Neill's mind about him.

After cautiously watching the negotiations brouhaha from a distance, the Mayor's office finally decided to become involved. Advised that the chemistry between Gabe Paul and Art Modell was so bad that the Indians might not get their desired lease improvements, and thus be forced to pack up and leave town, Mayor Voinovich scheduled a meeting with Gabe Paul to discuss the team's impasse with the Stadium Corp. He offered to mediate in any way the Indians might suggest. Very quickly, the mayor learned his services would not be required. Voinovich said, "I don't think they really paid a lot of attention to my offer to mediate. Their attitude was they're going to get an audit, and this thing will be resolved in court."

Following the death of Steve O'Neill, trustees for his estate began the process of finding a buyer for the team. One interested person was 37-year-old Donald Trump, owner of the USFL New Jersey Generals. Trump had earlier indicated his interest in buying the Indians, and he was not bashful about stating his intent to move the club to the Meadowlands Stadium in New Jersey. Another interested party was New York attorney David Eaton LeFevre, grandson of the late industrialist Cyrus Eaton, who supposedly was heading a group of Cleveland investors. LeFevre made it known that he was going to push hard for a new stadium. Paul Hoynes of the *News Herald* reported that while LeFevre was a proponent of a domed stadium, he actually favored a smaller, open-air baseball facility with a 40,000-45,000 fan capacity. Art Modell began to realize that any new owner would sound that same theme: a new, baseball-only ballpark would be needed to keep the Indians in town.

While the O'Neill estate was evaluating purchase offers, Servomation Corp. was bristling over the comments issued by the Indians' front office. It hadn't been particularly helpful to the concessionaire's professional standing to hear the charges being hurled about, and quietly the company had urged Gabe Paul to issue a public apology for his unsupported allegations. When no response was forthcoming, Servomation took action of its own and in turn sued the Cleveland Indians and president Gabe Paul for $6 million, charging Paul with slander. The suit stated that "Paul claimed recklessly and maliciously that Art Modell personally benefited from a $4.1 million payment." The suit further claimed that Paul's comments were false, defamatory, and slanderous, and left the impression that Servomation engaged in "nothing less than criminal activities and unethical business practices. These charges have caused Servomation clients to look upon the firm with distrust, contempt and ridicule." Servomation's legal counsel said that the company had waited for a retraction, and only reluctantly took this legal action. A Servomation vice-president said, "We want our good name cleared. If you want to call that an apology, well, you can then call it that. What we are looking for is a clarification. Where did these remarks come from, and why?"

After pursuing dialogue directly with Servomation Corp. and asking their auditors to go as far as they legally could with the company, the Indians asked the concessionnaire for affidavits spelling out the full extent of the deal with Cleveland Stadium Corp. The concessionnaire said it every which way it could: There was no "upfront" payment to Cleveland Stadium Corp. or to Art Modell. Several months later, Paul finally issued his letter of "clarification."

Paul said it was not an apology, since he claimed that he never did say that Art Modell and Cleveland Stadium Corp. received any "under the table" money. He further said that anyone who attributed those comments to him was wholly incorrect. A full-page ad was run in Cleveland-area newspapers and carried a reprint and copy of Gabe Paul's letter to Servomation Corp. apologizing for any embarrassment caused from the statements falsely attributed to him. Apparently satisfied the air had been cleared, Servomation Corp. terminated its lawsuit against the Cleveland Indians.

David LeFevre and Patrick O'Neill, trustee for the O'Neill estate, were designing the purchase agreement of the Indians ballclub in 1984 when concerns arose over Modell's control over Cleveland Stadium. As reported by the local papers, this issue appeared to be the stumbling block to completing the deal. When a reporter asked Modell, for what seemed the umpteenth time, for a comment on the lease, exasperatedly he said, "I concede that this is not the best lease in baseball, but it is far, far from being the worst. We rank it eighth or ninth of the 17 leases that we have been able to review." We were able to tell the public, the Indians, the *Plain Dealer*, and whoever else wanted to know that the Indians fared better in their lease than did Seattle, Pittsburgh, Montreal, Atlanta, Oakland, Philadelphia, and Toronto, primarily because these teams all paid expenses that the Indians were spared.

In another conversation with an Indians' director, we were told that this particular director was having difficulty convincing Gabe Paul to be reasonable in his expectations of what the Stadium Corp. was capable of giving in cash improvements. This director asked Gabe to take the historical audited income statements of Stadium Corp. and to make demands based on what the Stadium was able to reap from the baseball operations. Gabe replied by saying that Bob Gries, minority owner of the Cleveland Browns, had said the statements contained "lavish and unnecessary costs to run the business," and therefore Gabe felt they should not be used to limit the demands for lease improvements. At the time, it began to appear to us that a connection of sorts existed among the five lawsuits by the two plaintiffs, Gries and Paul. Subsequently, however, Gries has stated that he never had any such conversation with Gabe Paul.

Months passed without any final word on the Indians' purchase. Lefevre seemed to be hitting roadblocks that prevented the deal from closing. All the while he continued to say he needed a "fair" lease from Modell before he could sign his purchase agreement.

In the meantime newspaper reports began to pick up on the differences between the very good leases and the Indians' current one. The range of difference bandied about was $200,000-$500,000, which sports reporter Paul Hoynes remarked was "the price of a utility infielder's salary." How could this trifle be enough to hold up a multi-million dollar business acquisition? Then came a satisfying revelation in Lebovitz's column in the *News Herald* in November 1984 that LeFevre had the accounting firm of Price, Waterhouse make yet another analysis of the Indians' lease at the Stadium. The firm's report found the Indians' lease with the Cleveland Stadium Corp. an excellent one. Lebovitz remarked as to how this must have wounded Gabe Paul.

As the O'Neill family continued its pursuit of buyers for the club, they also began a search for a new president. Gabe Paul announced he would retire on January 1, 1985. The O'Neill family retained well-known baseball consultant Tal Smith to conduct the search. The new president was expected to get the team's house in order in preparation for a sale. Tal Smith eventually tapped Peter Bavasi, son of long-time baseball executive "Buzzy," for the Indians' new president.

Bavasi, in sharp contrast to Gabe Paul, hit it off with Art Modell. He stayed with the negotiating process, and one month later, in January 1985, an agreeable arrangement was concluded. The proposal provided the same basic benefits that were offered to Gabe Paul two years earlier. It increased the revenue sharing percentages gradually as fan levels exceeded 1,000,000. If the Indians would ever reach 2,000,000 fans, the proposal was structured to make the lease the fourth best in baseball. All the Indians had to do was put a

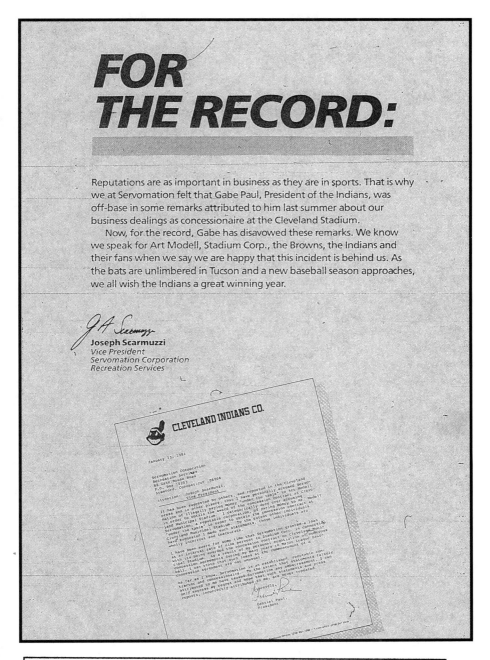

FOR THE RECORD:

Reputations are as important in business as they are in sports. That is why we at Servomation felt that Gabe Paul, President of the Indians, was off-base in some remarks attributed to him last summer about our business dealings as concessionaire at the Cleveland Stadium.

Now, for the record, Gabe has disavowed these remarks. We know we speak for Art Modell, Stadium Corp., the Browns, the Indians and their fans when we say we are happy that this incident is behind us. As the bats are unlimbered in Tucson and a new baseball season approaches, we all wish the Indians a great winning year.

Joseph Scarmuzzi
Vice President
Servomation Corporation
Recreation Services

After some persuasion, Indians' president Gabe Paul decided to issue this "clarification" letter which was placed as a full page *Plain Dealer* ad by Servomation Corp. *Cleveland Stadium Corp. collection* competitive team on the field. Included in this proposal was an escape clause for the benefit of the Indians, but only to permit a move to a new building in Cleveland. Bavasi understood why the Stadium Corp. could provide no meaningful increase in lease terms while the Indians attendance stayed below 1,000,000.

It was not difficult to prove to Bavasi how little revenue was being generated from baseball operations, for in the previous two years the Indians had drawn a mere 768,000 and 730,000 fans. With no increase in season ticket sales, the 1985 season did not look to be any better.

While reviewing the proposal with all the involved parties, and after extensive thought, Bavasi, in the spirit of promoting harmony between the companies, recommended the O'Neill family end all pending litigation. On February 20, 1985, the Cleveland Indians Co. agreed to drop the two lawsuits against Cleveland Stadium Corp. In return, the Cleveland Stadium Corp. and the Cleveland Browns dismissed their counter-claim on the anti-trust lawsuit.

So, after one year and almost nine months, Art Modell and the rest of us at Stadium Corp. finally felt vindicated. Bavasi had proved to the O'Neills and their attorneys that there was nothing to gain from further legal action. Today I still am not sure who was the provocateur of all this litigation, and what his motives might have been. Art Modell told us, however, that he was pretty sure he knew who it was.

Whatever the case, the lawsuit cost the Stadium Corp. over $500,000 in legal fees, and the loss of almost one year in management effort spent in depositions and processing files for two sets of lawyers.

Despite settling the lease, in 1985 the Indians were heading for an even more dismal record in fan attendance. We never thought the Indians would draw fewer than the 700,000-plus fans they had in 1983 and 1984, but 1985 attendance dropped to 650,000. At that rate, no one could make a profit. The Indians certainly were not, the Stadium Corp. lost money every night we opened the doors but drew fewer than 10,000 fans, and the concessionaire and parking lot operators were not making money either. All entities servicing the Indians had to cut back to save payroll and fixed costs, and the economy moves affected service. No one was talking any longer about improving the lease. Peter Bavasi did try to make the ballpark fan-friendly for the few fans still coming to the Stadium while the "FOR SALE" sign was still hanging from the wigwam.

When the 1986 baseball season started up again, my 12th season with Cleveland Stadium Corp, things felt different. It was not the typical Indians' spring in the old ball yard. During May, the Indians found themselves in a very unusual place--first place--after a successful West Coast trip, during which they had won ten games in a row. For the first home game back, the Tribe was greeted by 48,000 fans on a Friday night, and two weeks later, 61,000 fans appeared for what Mayor George Voinovich had been energetically promoting as Citizens' Night. With this surge in attendance and renewed interest, Bob August, veteran *News Herald* sports editor, was prompted to write that certain Indians' owners and execs had long been convinced that a baseball team could never make it at Municipal Stadium, their only hope a new stadium. "But," August said, "the stadium is not the Indians' major problem. It probably isn't even a minor problem."

Then, after three years of trying, possibly advanced by the Indians' success at the gate and on the field, the team was finally sold. In December 1986 the estate of F. J. O'Neill sold the franchise to Richard and David Jacobs.

CHAPTER 6
DOMED STADIUMS
IN THE AIR

In the early 80s, it was certainly not clear to us at the Stadium Corp. just what all the lawsuits were about. Even today, with the benefit of hindsight, the real purpose(s) of the litigation can be little more than speculation. Yet the suits, in and of themselves, did not seem to represent the actual issues at stake.

If one considers the Gries-Modell courtroom situation, for example, one can see in Gries I that the merits of the case resulted in a split decision. Gries won round one, Modell won round two, and the third and deciding round went to Gries on a split decision of the judges 4-3. Gries III was settled out of court. If the merits had been so clear, would not the verdict also have been easily reached?

The Modell-Paul skirmish ended in the parties withdrawing their lawsuits. After considerable expense, nothing was resolved.

Perhaps, just perhaps, the litigation was meant to be instrumental in focusing the attention of the community on the issue of just how important a stadium can be to an overall sense of civic well-being, or to just how valuable a new stadium might be. The timing of the issues may offer some insight.

While the suits were being battled in court, forces were at work to convince Greater Clevelanders that a new stadium was necessary and that community support for it was vital. The Domed Stadium issue became another headache for us to handle and led to increasing insensitivity on the part of the political community to the conditions necessary to keeping old Municipal Stadium a first class facility.

While the estate of Steve O'Neill kept searching for a new owner for the Cleveland Indians, the condition, limitations, and age of the Stadium, and the economics of the lease became key issues. Newspaper reporters were speculating that anyone interested in buying the team might only be doing so with ulterior motives in mind. After all, how could a newcomer to the scene obtain improvements in the lease with Modell when preceding owners had been unable to? The commentators concluded that a new owner would be interested in procuring the team only in order to move it to another city. There were cities interested, too, such as Tampa, New Orleans, and Denver, to name those most prominently mentioned.

Because of fear Cleveland might lose the Indians, the State of Ohio entered the arena of concern in the person of Governor Richard Celeste who himself launched the idea of a Domed Stadium in downtown Cleveland as a means of showing the next owner of the Indians that the team would be able to attract fans with modern-day amenities in a brand-new weather-proof baseball stadium.

Clevelanders, in general, seemed ambivalent about the issue. Some, however, were strongly opposed. The county commissioners eventually decided to fund the Domed Stadium through an increase in real estate taxes, a burden that would fall heavily on the working homeowner. At that point, many Clevelanders became quite vocal; they didn't see themselves footing the bill for a building they claimed they would never use. Even Celeste turned against the issue, feeling the property tax was not the way to go. On the other hand, on May 6, 1984, just days before the vote, a *Plain Dealer* editorial urged readers to "Help the City, Approve the Dome."

Such was the ambivalence toward the issue, however, that in the days following, *Plain Dealer* columnists James Neff and Jim Parker urged the same readers to "Forget the Dome." Whose thinking were the readers going to follow? As it turned out, it was not that of the *Plain Dealer* editorial board. On May 8, 1984, the issue was soundly thumped by a 2-1 margin. Columnists and some men on the street added that "if Modell wants to put his team in a dome, he should build it himself."

What? All of us at Cleveland Stadium Corp. were stunned by comments like these. Art Modell NEVER wanted the dome. As Hal Lebovitz stated in his column, "There are those opponents of the Dome who strain to make Modell the villain, seeing him as the beneficiary." At the Stadium Corp. we all knew that Modell had only reluctantly agreed to support the campaign, and then only because he felt a new facility would be good for the economic health of downtown Cleveland.

The issue of the Dome grew out of a perceived need to save the Indians, not the Browns. But the times had changed. Whereas in the 1970s Modell was commonly seen as a committed leader in the fight to revitalize the city, it had become the fashion, both by the media and by the guy in the street, to blame Modell for any difficulty arising from stadium issues.

All we could do in Tower B was scratch our heads in wonderment. Modell himself issued one more comment, and then dismissed the whole thing. "The Browns don't need a new stadium. We're happy where we are."

Art Modell was then being scrutinized rather harshly by the public. Some media members charged that he was arrogant. Some fans felt he was a know-it-all, a man who had all the answers and didn't need to listen to anyone.

Sometimes I felt that he may have been too outspoken when hyping his product in the marketplace, such as claiming the Browns' draft picks, or receivers, or the coach, or the defense the "best ever since I've been with the Browns." I thought a smidgen of restraint would have done wonders for Art's image. The people in Cleveland didn't want blowhards leaving them with unfulfilled promises over and over again. "Leave that up to me. PR is one area I think I know a little bit about," he would say. Humility was not something that came easy to Art, because to him, I believe, he felt a display of humility was a sign of weakness.

Amid all the controversy over the Dome, *Plain Dealer* publisher and editor Thomas Vail wrote an opinion piece on Cleveland sports and the issues raised by the teams' houses of combat. He referred to "confusion" on the Cleveland sports scene. He cited several unsettling areas: discussion about a new convocation center at Cleveland State University (CSU); whether the Cavaliers would be playing at downtown Public Hall or the future CSU arena or staying put at the Richfield Coliseum; the lawsuits flying back and forth at Cleveland Stadium between the Indians and the Browns; the mayor and his staff refusing Modell's proposal to again take over control of Stadium operations; and the uncertainty about the Governor's position on all this aforementioned confusion. Vail added:

> The whole Cleveland sports scene sounds like a disaster waiting to happen....A Cleveland failure on a new stadium for our community could mean eventual loss of the Browns and the Indians....If Cleveland had a new exciting modern downtown Stadium, then the old stadium....could be torn down to make way for a whole new development on Cleveland's lakefront ....including an aquarium, marine museum, park and lake facilities, followed by restaurants, apartments, hotels, just like the Harbor development in Baltimore....There are lots of important arrangements to be worked out: Art Modell's Stadium Corp. should be compensated for its Stadium investment...."

Joseph Rice, PD columnist, added some reflections of his own. He wrote that Governor Celeste had to be the one to step forward and provide state support for a new stadium. Rice explained that "if Celeste produces a smaller domed stadium that lures away the Indians, Modell's prime tenant at Municipal Stadium, then Modell is left with two options: either cancel his Stadium Corp. lease with the city, or move the Cleveland Browns." Rice suggested that Phoenix had been wooing the Browns.

It brought us some comfort to know that the media understood that a new ball park for the Indians was not an issue without significant impact on Art Modell and the Browns. Unfortunately, this understanding did not seem to be equally shared by other segments of the city's leadership.

In 1984 Stadium Corp. was finding its revenues severely crimped. There had not been a major rock concert at the Stadium since Bob Seger performed in 1980. Since then there had been two major sports strikes, baseball in 1981and the NFL in 1982, and legal bills from all the years of courtroom battles were pouring in. Art Modell wasn't very happy, then, when the Michael Jackson Victory Tour initially decided to bypass Cleveland. The tour started in June as one of the hottest ever, but then a series of bungled situations turned it into a nightmare. Outrageously high ticket prices, bickering among the many managers introduced at various times during the tour, and a complicated advance ticket mail order system were contributing to a fan backlash. These negatives manifested themselves in disappointing crowds in venue after venue. The Sullivan family, owners of the New England Patriots, had bought in as the tour promoters. When the tour didn't show the financial promise the Sullivans had expected, they decided to schedule more concert dates in order to cover their guarantees, and so negotiations for additional locations began in earnest. Art Modell decided to take action himself, and he called fellow NFL owner Billy Sullivan to arrange a show for Cleveland. As a result, Cleveland Stadium received a contract for back-to-back shows on October 19 and 20, 1984. Ticket prices were set at $30, at a time when the highest priced concert ticket at the Stadium generally ranged in the area of $18. Despite the high prices, crowds of 34,000 and 47,000 braved chilly weekend weather to see the legendary Michael Jackson in his sequined glove dazzle the crowd in a 90-plus-minute spectacular. The fans went wild when amid the glitter and glamour Michael came on with the opening lines of "Beat It." It was typical of Art to jump in and make special events like this one happen.

In 1985, when Bruce Springsteen and his E-Street Band planned to go on tour and showed interest in coming to Cleveland, we accepted immediately. Having done reasonably well with the two-night Michael Jackson event the year before, we realized that a recovery in the rock concert business would brighten our lagging profit picture. Apparently rock fans were starved for entertainment, for the Springsteen show sold out in a little over three hours, an almost unheard-of record pace of ticket sales. Tickets were priced at $18.00, and 64,000 tickets were sold by a little after noon that day. A few days later obstructed seats in the bleachers, directly behind the stage, went on sale. The Springsteen tour was in such demand that fans wanted to hear "the Boss," even if they couldn't see him.

Springsteen's show was really a-l-i-v-e. He performed for three-and-one-half hours, pumping out 26 songs, from "Born in the U.S.A." to "Born to Run." It was fun to watch the 71,000 excited fans come through the turnstiles. Concerts attracted a wide spectrum of folks, and that night was no exception. We talked to drill press operators and attorneys, mothers and their pre-teen children, college kids, and even a few clergymen. Maybe deep down they appreciated that Springsteen had become a spokesman for the underprivileged. During the concert he pleaded with his crowd to do something about the hungry in their hometown. He asked them to call the hunger hotline the next day and make a contribution. After the show we learned that Springsteen contributed $25,000 from the proceeds to the Cleveland food bank.

In 1985 there was yet more talk about a Domed Stadium. A Domed Stadium Committee was formed, and one of its first announcements was that the complex would be built for both baseball and football. The design was not yet decided, but the committee seemed interested in a new concept called the Hexatron, a hexagon-shaped stadium with a retractable roof. Governor Celeste pledged his support, as he followed up on the promise he had made prior to the May 1984 vote. The governor's suggested funding plan was not based on real estate tax increases, but rather on some type of entertainment and user tax. Jeff Jacobs, son of future Indians' owner Dick Jacobs and a state representative, proposed funding the $100 million Hexatron with taxes on cigarettes and alcohol, a method which was soon dubbed a "sin tax." "Admission taxes might also have to be increased, if necessary, to cover the rest of the cost," Jacobs said. The Hexatron proved an exciting concept because it emphasized providing more 50-yard line seats than any other stadium design. The Dome Committee and the Hexatron group continued dialogue over a period of time, but little progress resulted.

Talk about a domed stadium attracted little attention from the man on the street. Mary Boyle, county commissioner, when questioned about Clevelanders' tepid support, pointed out, "Previous failures taught Clevelanders not to be too enthusiastic about any project. People in Cleveland are very distrustful. They don't believe they're not going to be ripped off."

Dome planning nonetheless did inch forward. In February 1986, the Dome Committee announced its next priority, formal negotiations with the Browns and the Indians for long-term leases. The *Plain Dealer* expected that negotiations with the Indians would move along more smoothly than with the Browns. Negotiations with the Browns would involve both the Browns' tenancy and the resolution of Cleveland Stadium Corp. lease matters, since Modell's lease still had outstanding loans for Stadium improvements. The *Plain Dealer* went on to say that the City was willing to forgive the remaining years of the Stadium Corp. lease, but Council President George Forbes was adamant that the city wasn't going to make the Stadium Corp. "whole" on its improvements.

The Dome Committee chairman explained that income from loges was to be a critical component of the financing, and that there "seems to be excess demand for loges, with expectations that at least 200 loges will be constructed in the new building."

This optimism stemmed from a recent newspaper report that Cleveland Stadium Corp. continued to sell out its loges, and although price increases were enacted annually, there had been no resultant loss in occupancy. The Dome Committee asked Modell to turn over his loge customer list for its own use. That was too much for Art. Modell told Jim Bailey and me, "Wait a minute. That list is proprietary information to our company. We developed that listing through our sales efforts over the years. Most of these customers prefer to remain anonymous and certainly wouldn't appreciate being made part of a mailing list being passed all over the city. Besides, why would I hasten the process of the city putting me out of business?" Art added, "They don't understand the situation; we need to iron out a lot of things." Members of the Dome Committee couldn't seem to understand why Modell wasn't more cooperative.

If public interest was the barometer, the Dome seemed to be losing ground, and County Commissioner Timothy Hagan couldn't see much support for it either. Hagan said that Mayor Voinovich told him the Dome Committee folks were outraged by the county commissioners' reluctance to make the dome tax a higher priority. Hagan defended his position by saying, "I haven't received one letter from a constituent asking me to put the issue on the ballot." He also indicated that the sin tax plan was a loser. Then, several days later, the official word came. Commissioners Hagan and Virgil Brown announced that any dome tax vote would be delayed until 1988. The county would instead address more pressing issues, such as road and sewer repairs and human services. Hagan said three factors which neutralized the dome backers' points of contention and which led to the County's decision:

1)   The Jacobs brothers' purchase of the team seemed to ensure the team would stay in Cleveland;

2)   Not one Indians' game had been postponed since April, so the weather issue wasn't as pressing as Dome backers had indicated; and

3)   Indians' attendance was on track to hit 1.5 million fans in 1986, indicating that fans did not have a problem attending games at the Stadium.

Before the year wound down, the *Plain Dealer* ran one more column about the domed stadium. Russell Schneider said the future of the dome lay clearly with the Jacobs brothers, new owners of the Tribe, in concert with baseball's hierarchy. The only comment forthcoming from that sector was that the Jacobses preferred an open-air, small and intimate, baseball-only stadium. Schneider sought out Modell for his views, and once again Modell said, "All I know is that Bobby Brown (American League president) told me that baseball favors a baseball-only stadium that seats about 35,000 fans, and I can't say that I blame them."

Modell continued:

If that's the case, and if the Dome is put on the back burner and the Indians go ahead with a stadium of their own, I would be perfectly happy staying where I'm at. But I'd want some economic relief for the improvements I've made in the Stadium and the loss of my principal tenant. At this time, I wouldn't take the Indians or anybody for granted, and that includes the Browns.

A strange turn of events then hit the papers with regards to Cleveland Stadium. The *Plain Dealer* reported on September 19 that the National Park System advisory board recommended Cleveland Stadium as one of four Major League Baseball parks to be designated as National Historic Landmarks. The Stadium would join the downtown Arcade as the only other Cleveland building nominated for that distinction.

This proposed designation led to an outcry from City Hall. Voinovich strongly opposed this designation, noting that "the venerable ballpark occupies a site proposed for future lakefront development." Voinovich then wrote letters to five northeastern Ohio congressmen asking them to oppose such a designation. Hunter Morrison, director of the City Planning Commission, took an active part in fighting the designation. He argued: "We don't in fact meet the criteria, in terms of significance of architecture, or its role in the development of sports, or its role in the history of Cleveland, and recommend it not be nominated." The result of the disagreement was a compromise. In November 1987 the National Register listed Cleveland Stadium on the National Register of Historic Places, a less protected category than landmark status would have conferred.

Modell was certainly receiving a message that City Hall did not want him in the lakefront Stadium much longer. But, he wondered, where would the Browns play their home games? No one was offering an answer to that.

At about the same time, the State gave Cleveland $8 million, to go along with $36 million in federal funds, to complete the first phase of a waterfront project then known as Inner Harbor. The development was located at the east end of the Stadium parking lot, at the foot of East Ninth Street. With city finances tight, this improvement was undertaken under the auspices of the state. While everyone heralded the Inner Harbor plan as a great step forward for northeastern Ohio, to us at Cleveland Stadium Corp. it sure seemed to be coming at the expense of Stadium patrons.

The problem we faced was that the Inner Harbor would significantly shrink the size of the main Stadium parking area. While there appeared to be some passing sympathy for the loss of our fans' parking accommodations and lip service to finding some makeup spots in the general vicinity of the Stadium, no one was sure where these would be. Follow-up meetings were held, and some spots were designated, but the costs of clearing, paving, and developing new parking areas were to be at the expense of Art Modell and Cleveland Stadium Corp. "if they wanted them." Jim Bailey and I tallied up the total costs required to recover about one-half of the lost spots by expanding the West Third Street lot. The cost came to a tad over $110,000.

In addition, we were flabbergasted to learn that the real estate taxes imposed on what was left of our East Ninth Street lot had doubled. Since the remaining land was one half of the original parking lot, the taxes should have been sliced in half; instead the rate was quadrupled. The county explained that since the parking lot bordered the Inner Harbor, the land was now classified as "waterfront property" and was valued significantly higher, on a par with the commercial properties in the Flats. I guess we were to forget that parking a car next to the water fetches no more revenue than a car parked anywhere else! In the interest of downtown development, the Stadium Corp. gave up half of its main parking lot, suffered a permanent loss of established parking revenues, incurred higher property taxes, and received the privilege of paying for improvements to provide new parking spaces to replace those lost to the Inner Harbor, all so the City of Cleveland could enjoy a lakefront renaissance. When we asked whether there would be any recovery forthcoming from the city for these additional costs, Bob Jacquay of the city's law department told us, "We're sorry, but the city has no money."

At the same time, Stadium Corp. continued to need repairs and improvements to the aging Stadium. One problem we had to face was random lamp failures in the scoreboard as toothpick-thin wires began to fray due to corrosion. Cleveland is in the heart of the rust belt, its steel mills spewing heavy doses of pollutants from towering stacks located just a few miles south of the Stadium. Whenever the wind blew north, oxides in the air matriculated into the Stadium and through the scoreboard's vents, landing on the board's delicate electronic components. Electricians were hired to reconnect the wires to the scoreboard lamps in order to keep the board operating.

As talk about a new stadium for the Indians gained momentum, and ground began to be removed from the Stadium's main parking lot for the Inner Harbor project, Art Modell began to sense a one-way street developing. Everything was for "the good of Cleveland," but much of the progress was coming at Modell's expense, and yet no one on the committees seemed to notice or care. Art has plenty of money, and the city is broke, seemed to be the cry. Modell was expected to cooperate, even when it meant giving up the Browns' fans' parking lot, because "after all, the Browns only need it ten times a year."

During the 1985 football season, *Sports Illustrated* (SI) ran a survey of serious injuries suffered by players from artificial turf surfaces. The article claimed many careers were shortened by turf injuries. The players' union stated it was committed to pressure ownership to convert artificial surfaces back to natural grass. Browns' players often asked Modell to promise never to change the Stadium's natural grass surface. Building a dome in Cleveland would necessitate installing an artificial surface, so sympathy with his players' feelings further cooled Modell's attitude toward a domed stadium in Cleveland.

Art was in a frump because of the cool treatment he was receiving from the city. In the early 1980s, the Indians were barely averaging 800,000 fans a year, and the Tribe regularly ended up as sixth-or seventh-place finishers. Yet the City was falling over itself to build a new stadium for the Indians, ostensibly to assure that the baseball team would not move. On the other hand, the Browns, a franchise which was self-sustaining and which asked for no municipal subsidy, received nothing but the "opportunity" to take over the city's responsibility of maintaining its aging building.

Before long it would become apparent that the city was not even willing to support that "opportunity." Art Modell's plans for further improvements to Cleveland Stadium would gather dust in City Hall.

Along with the lease of the stadium, Stadium Corp. had rights to the 2500-car parking lot to the east. By 1995, however, that lot was replaced by the Inner Harbor and its museums, prompting Art Modell to observe, "They left me with enough space to park a few motorcycles." *Jim Toman collection*

CHAPTER 7

THE KARDIAC KIDS
AND MARTYBALL

So much time and attention had to be devoted to "outside" concerns during the 1980s that football became a saving distraction from the financial and legal controversies that dogged the organization. It brought us some real thrills, but ultimately left us feeling disappointed too. The Browns would come tantalizingly close to the brass ring, but then would let it slip away.

One bright spot during this era was the 1980 coming of age of Sam, Brian & Co. Sam, of course, was Rutigliano, head coach from 1978 to 1984, and Brian was Brian Sipe, a 13th round draft pick from San Diego State. Together they forged a high-scoring offensive machine and helped the Browns gain their first trip to the playoffs since 1972. The outcomes of 13 games in that 1980 season were determined by a touchdown or less in garnering a record of 11-5. The close contests and a succession of come-from-behind Brown-and-Orange victories resulted in the team gaining the nickname "Kardiac Kids."

The magic, unfortunately, ran out by playoff time, as Clevelanders suffered a pain that they would feel again years later against Denver. Cleveland Stadium hosted the playoff game against Oakland on January 7, 1981. Once again, the outcome was decided in the final minute.

The game was a nail-biter throughout, and most fans were so caught up in the drama that they didn't notice the minus 37° chill factor that enveloped the lakefront that afternoon. It was so cold during the game that several water pipes on the concourses froze and burst.

Oakland held a 14-12 lead over the Browns in the fourth quarter when Cleveland took over the ball on its own 15-yard line. Brian Sipe then engineered another one of his heart-stopping drives, bringing the Browns to the Raiders' 13-yard line with a minute showing on the clock. Then Sipe launched one more pass. Clevelanders' hopes were soaring, but then Mike Davis of the Raiders stepped in front of Ozzie Newsome in the end zone to pick it off. The Browns' media guide would later refer to the throw as "an ill-fated" pass. The game was a crushing loss for both the team and the front office. It was Art Modell's greatest playoff disappointment in 20 years as Browns' owner.

Disappointing as the loss was, it still inspired hope for the coming season. Those hopes, however, were frustrated when the team began to crumble as the 1981 season approached its end. Five straight losses closed the campaign at 5-11.

Brian Sipe did not have the same productive year that he had in 1980. His 25 interceptions were too many, and his 17 touchdown tosses were too few. At year end, Sipe had a quarterback rating of 68, and he was starting to hear boos from the fans. His throwing six interceptions in a game against arch rival Pittsburgh probably had more than a little to do with his falling from favor.

The season took a bad turn in the tenth game, a 23-20 overtime loss in Denver. On that day a win was needed to turn the year around and get back to a 5-5 record. I usually did not accompany the team on the road, but I did attend that game, since I wanted to see first hand how the Broncos' Prescription Athletic Turf (PAT) system worked (the field was constructed in a large bed of sand on top of an irrigation system; grass was watered from below through a computer-controlled system.

I took the early bus to the stadium that morning with the players so I could get a pre-game tour from the groundskeeper before the gates opened. Sitting near Joe DeLamielleure and several other players, I was eavesdropping on their conversation, wondering what they talked about on their way to the field. The conversation was mostly about the city of Denver and some of the sights along the way to Mile High Stadium. Then, just as the players were ready to exit, Joe D. said to his teammates, "Hey, now, come on, we can beat these guys today. They're just not that good." Joe D. was a veteran, and I figured he knew what he was talking about. I hoped the rest of the guys were as confident.

I was one of about twelve persons in the owner's box that day. I could feel a tension-filled afternoon building. Joe D.'s optimism aside, this wasn't going to be an easy win.

An amusing thing had occurred at halftime. The Browns trailed 10-7, and Art just had to do something to change our luck. It is one of his major characteristics: Art can never stand around doing nothing. If something is awry, he has to jump in with a plan. If he doesn't have a plan ready, he creates one. Well, at halftime, he said the loge seating arrangement needed a shakeup. He moved all of us around "for good luck." Art moved 6'8" Larry Staverman away from the seat in front of the TV set, because whenever Art had turned around to check an instant replay, his view was blocked by Staverman's bulk. The other seat changes were incidental, but in true Modell fashion, the reassignment was done with flair. He pronounced it our strategy to bring victory back to Cleveland.

In regulation the game ended in a 20-20 tie. Cleveland had played well, especially the defense behind Lyle Alzado, who was playing against his former team. Then the foot-stomping began. In Denver, there are thousands and thousands of aluminum bleachers, and as the fans stomp, they create a deafening crescendo of noise. Even in the glassed-in loges it was difficult to hear a normal conversation. When Cleveland took over the ball in overtime, luck seemed with us. Sipe began engineering a drive. Then came a sweep to our side of the field. The ball was pitched back to Calvin Hill, but as he was nearing the sidelines, it became apparent he was going to get bumped out of bounds. Just as he was getting knocked over the chalk line, the ball came loose. Hill went out of bounds, several tacklers went out of bounds, the referee got swept out of bounds, but the ball landed in bounds, and bounced high, *straight up in the air*, one of those rare times a football bounces true. That fumble on the Browns' first possession in overtime told the story of the season very succinctly. The Browns argued that the ball had to have gone out of bounds; it just could not have stayed in with all the rest of the momentum going to the sidelines. The referees ruled otherwise, and Denver recovered the fumble. Minutes later Denver put us out of our misery. The Broncos sent their fans home with a 23-20 triumph, and they sent us home with a 4-6 record and the feeling that the season had ended.

About half the seats in our loge box emptied before the referee raised his arms to signify the Denver field goal kick was good. It seemed that our people were needed in the locker room, the pressbox, the ticket office, and on the field. I didn't make many road trips, so I didn't know everyone's duties, but at that particular moment, about seven people scurried out of the box. They didn't want to be near the owner at that moment. Art turned around and looked at the few of us left. He shrugged his shoulders, and all he could think of to say was, "Just wasn't meant to be, I guess." He looked on the verge of tears. I felt for the man. He wanted so badly to bring home a winner.

Not being a regular on these trips, I trudged back in the dark looking for the team bus. There were so many busses around the stadium, I was not sure where to look for ours. When I finally found it, I squirreled away into a seat and watched everyone exiting the stadium. It took a long time for our bus to fill. It was almost 10 p.m. Cleveland time, and Art was still not aboard. Then I spotted him just ahead near the players' bus. He was hugging Calvin Hill, and for a long time neither man moved. Calvin Hill had tears streaming down his face and never moved to wipe them away. It was a vintage Art Modell scene.

The flight home was sad. Most of the players on the plane were quiet. As I sat there, I recalled an earlier flight with the team. That was not a happy trip either.

In 1980 the Minnesota Vikings were playing their last season in their old outdoor stadium before moving into the Hubert H. Humphrey Metrodome. Their stadium director thought that Cleveland Stadium might have use for some equipment that would become available when they moved indoors, and so he invited me to the game. I spent all day Saturday and before the game on Sunday rummaging.

That game was an important one. It could have clinched the Browns' first division title since 1972, but Minnesota's Tommy Kramer and Ahmad Rashad changed all that. Cleveland fans remember that game as featuring the "Hail Mary" pass that beat the Browns on a deflected tip on the last play of the game.

Waiting on the bus, I was thinking, maybe it's me. Those were two really weird losses. Was I the common denominator underlying the bad luck that dogged us when I traveled with the team?

I thought again about the strange trip back from Minnesota. Waiting for the plane to take off, Art was especially angry over how the game had been lost. I was seated across the aisle from him and his wife Pat. In our section there was total silence. As the plane was final-loading the football gear and everyone was buckling in, Pat broke the silence. Art needed to erupt: scream, shout, throw a glass, anything to let off steam. Because she knew Art was raging inside, Pat tried to console him. "You know, Art, we should have won that game."

That was all he needed. "Woulda, coulda, shoulda, dammit, we DIDN'T win the game," he screamed, loud enough to be heard in the cockpit. His outburst was not directed at Pat, because Art would never do anything to hurt his wife. Art was fuming about the frivolity of some of the players. Several rookies in the back rows of the players' section were harmonizing some Beatles' hits in honor of John Lennon, who had recently been murdered in New York City. Modell had made his remark to no one in particular, but he was glaring at the row of rookies. The plane still was not moving, and Art had that look like he was about to get up. Oh-boy, I thought, those guys should realize the owner just experienced a very tough loss. Well, our diminutive kick-returner Dino Hall had no clue, and he took the lead, singing "We all live in a yellow submarine...." As he was waiting for other players to chime in, I heard a "click," and that was it. Art had unbuckled his seat belt, and he looked tense as he fidgeted out of his seat. Several players up front had begun harmonizing until someone spotted Art coming up the aisle. Voices dropped off quickly. Big offensive lineman Cody Risien, who was facing the front, didn't know what to think when Art grabbed him behind the neck and said point-blank, "We didn't have a very good day today, did we? Well, let's act like it." Things got really quiet, really quick.

It was after the 1980 football season when Art returned from one of the many NFL owners meetings that he began talking of going into the newspaper business. He had learned the Dallas Cowboys were publishing their own newspaper. Many Cowboy faithful lived outside the Dallas-Fort Worth area, and residents in the open stretches of western Texas had little newspaper coverage of the Cowboys. The Cowboys announced that subscriptions reached 50,000 in the first year.

With the Browns coming off their Kardiac Kids playoff year, Art Modell felt it time for the Browns to try the same thing. Art assigned Nate Wallack, veteran public relations man with the team, to lead the effort, while I was asked to oversee the budgets and prepare profit projections. This was the first time that Art asked me to be directly involved in the financial picture of the Cleveland Browns. John Minco was invited to come into the project as an advertising sales executive, but John did not jump at the opportunity, and Minco's hesitation had Art miffed. Minco put it bluntly, "Does anyone realize that it took *Sports Illustrated* 12 years to finally break into the black? How many years will Art really wait for this project to become profitable?" I told Art that my projections showed the Browns would lose money for a while, and I did not know for how long. A lot depended on the quality of the publication and probably also on the team's won-loss record. Art was irritated at both of us because again he wanted unstinting and uncritical support.

Despite our objections, the Browns went into the newspaper business.

Art called a meeting and laid out the qualities he wanted in the newspaper product:

1) The paper would have 36 pages. He didn't care that Dallas had from 24 to 32 pages;

2) He wanted a thick, bright-white look to the newspaper stock, not the chintzy ecru-looking off-white stock standard in most tabloids—he wanted the paper to be a collectible;

3) He wanted a lot of color photos of players and a lot of features about the players' home-side, with the wives and kids.

So, besides running Stadium Corp. operations, trying to re-start the housing business, and trying to sell the hotel investments, I was participating in the Browns' publishing business. Still, it was fun, as with any of Art's ventures, to launch a new business. The businesses were all different and involved different managers who were brought in to oversee them. My responsibility was straightforward: to make sure our investment interests were protected and, to the extent possible, to maximize our profit potential. The directives in any of these projects were simple: 1) keep Art apprised of the progress, 2) make him aware of any problems that surfaced, and 3) be accountable for deviations from budget. *Browns New Illustrated* was launched in training camp 1981, with a full-page color cover photo of Brian Sipe.

The strike of 1982 was a devastating setback for the Browns. The players had been talking about their commitment to get a "percentage of the gross." They were seeking 55% of the owners' gross revenues to be paid out in players' payroll costs. The 57-day strike resulted in the loss of four home games and a total of seven regular season games. Outsiders might have viewed this as only a seven-week strike, but in football parlance this was 7/16ths of a season. Therefore almost a half year of revenues was lost. In a normal manufacturing environment, the 1982 NFL strike was approximately equivalent to a six-month work stoppage at a company like General Motors, for instance.

I do not believe the Browns ever recovered from the financial damage of that strike. When Art had asked me to calculate the strike's impact on the Browns, I informed him that although the cash loss for the strike-marred 1982 season showed $4 million on the year's income statement, its true cost wouldn't be fully calculated for four years. An estimate, however, showed the strike would eventually cost $10.5 million. I summarized the costs as follows:

1) $5.0 million severance pay, to be accrued over four years; this was negotiated in the bargaining agreement and was something the players did not have before;

2) $2.2 million "money now," a payment to players to return to work; this approximated the amount of wages the players would have earned during the seven-week strike;

3) $2.3 million in team revenues lost during the strike;

4) $1.0 million legal fees paid by the team for strike-related work.

Since the Browns had been earning on average about $1.3 million a year prior to the strike, I concluded the organization would need more than eight years of normal earnings to recover totally. Because funds to pay for the strike did not exist, bank borrowings were required. A large portion of this borrowing became part of a Browns' loan base that never got repaid.

Although the Browns returned to profitable ways in 1983, records show they had operating losses for each of the 1984-1986 seasons. By 1984 the fledgling USFL football league was competing ferociously for NFL front-line players, and this served to drive up player payrolls. Between 1981 and 1984, Browns' players' salaries rose more than 100%, from $6.2 million to $13.4 million. Then, of course, came the strike of 1987, the one that forced the owners to use "replacement" players. The 1987 strike just plunged the Browns (and other NFL teams) deeper into debt.

Art Modell was heavily involved with the NFL brain trust trying to deal with labor unrest, and he was one of the owners working with Pete Rozelle in rebuffing the players' request for a "percentage of the gross," a notion totally unacceptable to the owners.

Once the strike was settled, Modell and Bailey returned to the huddle, discussing among other things, the future of the Browns. Sensing the players would eventually get a bigger piece of the pie, quite possibly in the form of a "percentage of the gross," it was important, they felt, that the Browns begin generating non-football revenues in order to survive. Many NFL team owners already had other businesses and investment interests, and that might be what the Browns' ownership would also have to pursue. Modell and Bailey felt that those revenues would be excluded from others subject to sharing with players, should they succeed in winning "a percentage of the gross."

One opportunity Modell investigated was ownership of a travel agency. Because of the charter travel incurred by the team and its fans, and even more through the commercial travel done by scouts, Modell figured it might make sense for the team to earn some profit back from its sizable travel expenses. As it turned out, the Browns actually bought two agencies--one small agency in downtown Cleveland and half-interest in a larger agency in Berea which handled the scouts' travel. Because travel agencies usually operate on a budget comprised mostly of fixed expenses (as opposed to variable costs), Modell hoped that a combination of these two businesses would provide economies of scale. If the revenues of both agencies could be combined and the expenses of the smaller one eliminated, further profits could be realized.

Bailey, Modell, and I caucused over the acquisition. I was beginning to see our management team being stretched too thin. We had many business demands at present, and I didn't see any sense in adding another business unless it offered a substantial return, which this one didn't. I reminded both Art and Jim that the land business hadn't taken off as we had hoped, due to high interest rates, but that as soon as rates began dropping, we would be developing streets and selling lots to builders to satisfy pent-up demand. I cautioned that we needed to have time available to nurture this part of the business when the upturn arrived. The hotel investment was still in a prolonged state of negotiations, then for over three years. We were about to begin lease negotiations with the Indians. We were also active in the management of the BNI newspaper, which was in its second year and losing money as subscribers were canceling in droves due to the football strike. We were then also facing the demands of preparing for the Gries' trials.

As we reviewed profit projections for our new business-to-be, it became apparent that profits would be limited to 50% of whatever this new combined entity could generate. After a one-hour meeting, I knew this was not the business for us. The reason these agencies were becoming available was because the airlines' price wars were squeezing their profit margins.

Art and Jim viewed this business acquisition as a "strategic" decision, not an economic one. Many companies, including ours, called decisions "strategic" when the economic conclusions based on net present value came out negative. This was an opportunity Art felt he had to seize, or it would be lost. I continued to have mixed feelings. I didn't want to put a damper on Art's enthusiasm, but an opposite view can certainly be healthy during the decision-making process.

I had to be careful how I stated this to Modell. When I had given him my views on the newspaper, he viewed me as a turncoat "fighting" the team. If I didn't jump on the bandwagon and say "let's go," I would again run the risk of being viewed as a traitor. Art expected total support. I kept telling myself that while Art expected that, it wasn't what he should have. He needed his people to stand up and honestly tell him their views for his own good. I realized I could view it differently: If the losses started mounting, those would be Art's losses, not mine. Why should I even care? It wasn't money out of my wallet.

But I couldn't adopt that attitude. I felt strongly that for such a paltry return, it made no sense for the Browns to go into the travel business. I was scheduled to leave on a four-day break between Christmas and New Year's with my family, but before I left, I told Art and Jim straight out that as I saw it, the ultimate profitability of this venture would depend on interest rates in the coming years. If rates dropped, the business could be profitable, but still not profitable enough to warrant, in my opinion, the risk of interest rate uncertainty. Modell and Bailey then sent me off and wished me a good time.

When I returned on January 2, 1983, I learned from the Browns' controller, Gordy Helms, that Art had approved the purchase of the travel agency. Helms had been given the responsibility of forming the subsidiary and bringing it in under his wing.

After a quick start in 1981, losses on the *Browns News Illustrated* began to mount. The football strike of 1982 unofficially marked the end of the Kardiac Kids era. The excitement generated by come-from-behind football turned into indifference. The early eager subscribers who couldn't wait for the next issue to arrive began to cancel their subscriptions. Our records showed that the newspaper registered cash losses each of the four years before the front office began to tire of the business. It wasn't hard to figure that the subscriber list was not going to grow when other events beside the 1982 strike were factored in.

The other events? Brian Sipe defecting to the USFL, Sam Rutigliano starting out the 1984 season at 1 and 7 before getting fired, and Paul McDonald indicating that he too might jump to the USFL, just to name a few. Art Modell's directive was: SELL the newspaper business and try to get back at least the money that had been lost on the venture. The Browns took a payout on a long note to eke out a small gain on the whole venture. We said among ourselves, "Let's get back to our main businesses of football and Stadium operations."

Football. That's why we were in business in the first place. Because he felt that Jim Bailey was being stretched too thin by our other ventures, Art decided to hire an executive to deal with player procurement and signings. There had been no one in this position since the resignation of Peter Hadhazy in 1981. With complicated contractual arrangements becoming more common following the 1982 strike, and because of the competition from the USFL, Art felt someone was needed to deal solely with player matters. That someone was Ernie Accorsi, who had just resigned from the Baltimore Colts as they were leaving that city for Indianapolis.

Still, it was Jim Bailey who had become the one man that Art was increasingly turning to for all his business and legal advice. Knowing Bailey was there to "watch the store" allowed Art to feel comfortable at home while his post-operative recuperation process continued.

Among the problems Art Modell and his Browns' management team were dealing with, the severe drug problem that pervaded the team in the 1980s might have been the one issue that caused Art the most grief. The dramatic decline after the Kardiac Kids' exciting 1980 season was the first tipoff to the problem. Few of us in the office knew much about this dilemma, because the team took pains to maintain a veil of secrecy. All that the rest of us knew was that this effort was consuming a lot of Sam Rutigliano's time and keeping Art Modell tense most of the time. It was many years later, after reading Sam Rutigliano's book *Pressure*, that we learned how the Inner Circle came into existence. Under Coach Sam's leadership this fraternity was formed to provide aftercare for recovering addicts. As the Browns learned more about the demons of drug use, the Inner Circle was expanded to deal with the prevention, intervention, cure, and aftercare of the player/victim.

Serving as their brothers' keepers, Art and Sam had a sizable undertaking on their hands, and the program was expensive. With the significant number of players enrolled, more security had to be hired, more doctors were needed, and at least three full-time executives were on staff to deal primarily with this issue, all of which added up to one large expense. Over a period of years, the entire Inner Circle program cost the Browns well over $1 million. But Art and Sam valued their players as human beings and never questioned how much money to spend in this regard.

In 1984, pre-season expectations for a great Browns' year were running high. *Playboy* picked Cleveland to win the conference championship and then lose to San Francisco in the Super Bowl. But not everyone, at least locally, was in agreement, although the sound of Super Bowl and Cleveland in the same breath was refreshing. Radio commentator Pete Franklin laughed at the pick, saying the football knowledge of the magazine's football critic could "fit on the nose of a gnat." Franklin asked, "Could a new quarterback step right in and exceed what Brian Sipe has done?" Reference, of course, was to Cleveland's southpaw backup, Paul McDonald, who had played sparingly in 1983 and finished with a lowly 42.7 quarterback rating and one touchdown pass. On defense Franklin paid tribute to the Browns' linebackers, but wondered where the pass rush would be found. All Super Bowl-bound teams find part of their success in the prowess of the defensive line. In 1984 the Browns were also going to introduce three new faces into the defensive secondary, joining lone repeat starter, Hanford Dixon. Added were newly drafted Don Rogers and Chris Rockins, along with Frank Minnifield, a recent USFL defector. The coaches were hoping this foursome would jell as a respectable pass defense unit. Too much to hope for too soon, Franklin felt. (As time would tell, when January 1985 rolled around, *Playboy* magazine proved to be half right in the prognostications; the 49ers rolled to an easy Super Bowl triumph, but over the Miami Dolphins, not the Browns.)

In 1984 Sam Rutigliano was starting his seventh year as Browns' head coach. Asked for his reaction to *Playboy*'s prediction, he said that he too was optimistic, but added that the key to the Browns getting to the championship came down to three things:

1)   Paul McDonald getting the job done at quarterback;
2)   finding new speed at wide receiver; and
3)   improvement in rushing the passer.

Over the years, those of us who worked in the Modell organization came to realize how knowledgeable Browns' fans were. They didn't swallow the party line without assessing the data on their own. Sports talk shows proliferated in Cleveland, and more than 50% of the subject matter centered on pro football and the Browns. Callers debated everything to do with the team. While they wanted to hope that the Browns were good enough to warrant the *Playboy* prediction, they also listened to and read Pete Franklin; they would not lightly dismiss his concerns.

Ray Yannucci of BNI, in his pre-season column, said that the Browns would be better in 1984—period. Fans responding to his column were skeptical, saying they were not convinced about Paul McDonald since McDonald had been unable to beat Sipe out in either 1982 or 1983.

Most fans agreed with Coach Sam's three-point checklist, adding that these were three big "if's." They elaborated on the wide receiver dilemma, namely finding speed at wideout. Finding the speed, though, was only part of the answer. Once found, speed had to be synchronized with the new quarterback. Duriel Harris, recent acquisition from Miami, Dwight Walker, and speedster draftee Bruce Davis were the three likeliest candidates to join Ricky Feacher and Willis Adams at the position. The fans knew that none of them, with the possible exception of Harris, had ever been a big-time player. Another concern that received relatively little attention was the change in offensive coordinator. Larrye Weaver had departed, and Coach Sam named Joe Scanella to replace him.

A new offensive coordinator, an inexperienced starting quarterback, two new receivers with speed—all had to come through with high grades for the Browns to reach January's promised land. How often in the NFL had that happened before?

At the start of the season, Art Modell extended Rutigliano's contract three years to 1988, saying, "Sam Rutigliano is going to be here a long time, whether it's as a coach or not a coach." Art was given to making this kind of sweeping statement. It would not be the only time he would have to eat his words.

Pete Franklin's talk show, broadcast on Cleveland's most powerful radio station weekday evenings, was very popular. He liked to reiterate: "This show is heard in 38 states and over half of Canada." The preferred whipping boy for a lot of his callers was Art Modell. Many called him "cheap." Franklin might agree with some charges against Modell, and many times he did, but he would really take callers to task when they labeled the Browns' owner as penurious. Franklin would fire back, "How can a guy be called cheap when he pays the kind of salaries that Art Modell pays? How can you call the

Art and coach Sam Rutigliano evaluating the talent on the Baldwin Wallace practice fields. *Browns News Illustrated*

Browns cheap when they were the first team to sign all their draft choices?" Franklin was right. Modell paid his people well.

Art was extremely sensitive to charges of "cheapness" and "stinginess." He rarely talked about it, but observing him when he overheard any such comment made it apparent. He would flush with anger.

In fact, signing Tom Cousineau in 1982 to what at that time was one of the biggest contracts ever paid to an NFL linebacker found Art publicly defending why he spent so much. Before he completed his answer, he said, "Maybe now they won't be calling me cheap anymore."

Perhaps more than anything, Modell wanted to be loved by the people of Cleveland. Getting booed when he was introduced in the streets of downtown Cleveland years later when President Ronald Reagan was in town certainly hurt his feelings. But it wasn't hard for some of us to figure this hostility out. Art was known to be worth millions of dollars, and ordinary people generally like to take aim at the wealthy. The average guy reacts adversely to the display of wealth. Clevelanders would make snide reference to Art's "camel hair coat," his common winter garb.

It was not unusual for a team owner to become a public target. One story relates the advice Frank Lane, legendary baseball executive and former Indians' general manager, gave to Chuck Comiskey during a power struggle in the Chicago White Sox front office. Lane urged Comiskey to refrain from being too visible in baseball matters, since the average fan could not relate to an owner. "Remember, Chuck," Lane said, "no millionaire is ever going to be popular with the masses. The fans trust me because I'm just a working stiff." Although Lane was talking about White Sox fans, he could just as well have been talking about fans in New York, Detroit, or Cleveland, or about any sport.

In Cleveland, many fans told Pete Franklin they did not want to hear Art Modell speak out on football matters. They preferred hearing from either the head coach or the personnel director.

The 1984 regular season began with a trip to Seattle. Just before the team was about to launch its drive for the Super Bowl, the Browns received the terrible news that Cody Risien was lost for the season with knee surgery. The editor of the *Browns News Illustrated* thought this would make the Super Bowl a distinct long shot. His ominous outlook was based on several things. In addition to the Risien injury, he felt the coaches were expecting too much from rookie safeties Rockins and Rogers, and he worried over the lack of a pass rush. But Rutigliano kept saying that the Browns do "not hope to, but expect to, make the playoffs." Other Central Division sportswriters were seeing things the same way as BNI. Either Cincinnati or Pittsburgh was being chosen as the eventual Central Division winner by almost all the scribes.

Off to the Seattle Kingdome the team went, a location where they had not fared well. Sadly, the trend continued in 1984. The Browns may have had their worst overall team performance up to that time, getting annihilated by the Seahawks, 33-0. Super-Bowl bound teams just didn't start off a season this way.

For a number of reasons, including two straight West Coast trips and Paul McDonald ranking last in the conference with a 46.2 quarterback rating, the Browns opened the season 0-3. We kept in mind Coach Sam's words: "If Paul McDonald has a great year, we'll win."

In week six the fans witnessed one of the most controversial and bizarre sequences that ever occurred in Cleveland Stadium. The Browns' record stood at 1-4, following a tough 10-6 loss to Kansas City, a game that Rutigliano said should not have been lost. Their opponent was a good New England Patriots team. The Browns entered the contest with the top-ranked defense in the AFC, but with the lowest-rated quarterback in the league. With nine minutes left in the third quarter, Cleveland was surprising its fans with a nice 16-3 lead. Then came a flea-flicker pass by the Patriots and a fumble by the Browns, giving the lead back to the Pats 17-16. The Browns had one chance to recover the lead, but Matt Bahr narrowly missed a field goal that most fans thought was good.

Very late in the game, they had yet another opportunity when the top-ranked defense forced a punt. Trailing by only one point, the offense behind McDonald drove deep into Patriots' territory with 23 seconds left in the game. A timeout was called with third down and the ball on the 21-yard line. Instead of lining up for a field goal, Rutigliano called for an out-pattern pass to Duriel Harris. Harris cut at the five-yard line, slipped, and the pass dropped right into the arms of the cornerback breaking to cover him. An 85-yard interception by Raymond Clayborn resulted, and the game was over.

The slim crowd of 53,000 was stunned. This was a game the Browns deserved, and needed, to win; instead, memories of the infamous pass against the Raiders in the 1980 playoffs resurfaced. Sam Rutigliano admitted that he took a gamble he should not have, much as he had done in that playoff game. Once again, he disdained the field goal for a pass play that was poorly executed. Maybe Sam lacked confidence in his kicker, who minutes earlier had missed from about the same distance. Maybe he was playing psychologist and hoping to give his quarterback a much-needed boost in confidence. Maybe Sam and his coordinator Joe Scanella liked what they saw Duriel Harris do that day against Raymond Clayborn, by amassing seven catches for 120 yards and a touchdown. All that notwithstanding, some players commented about confusion on the play. The personnel sent onto the field (two tight ends) did not fit the play that was called (three-wide-receiver set). McDonald ran the play anyway. Later he said he should just have thrown the ball away.

Not only were the fans and the media stunned by the call, but so was Art Modell. He called the decision "inexcusable," adding that the final seconds "defied comprehension." Leaving the stadium that day, fans were heard booing and chanting, "Goodbye Sam." The media in the pressbox were also aghast.

Art Modell must have been wondering what had gone wrong with his high hopes for the season. But when reporters questioned him about the coach, Modell was supportive and said, "I intend to make no coaching changes this season. I don't believe in coaching changes in mid-term. It has never worked in the NFL, and it's an owner's cop out to make changes when things go bad."

Then it was Sam's turn to comment. First of all, he said, "After the New England game, Art fired me, but I had enough time to talk him out of it. I do have a little bit of a gift. I was able to talk him out of it for one more week. So this week, the Jets game is critical." He went on to rebut his mounting chorus of critics:

Let me tell you something. I am good for the City of Cleveland, both as a coach and as a person, and I think you are all lucky that I'm here. And when we win, it will even be better because I stand for all the things that are right in the National Football League and the things that are important. I frankly believe in this country. I never thought I was as good as everybody thought I was when I was named coach of the Year in 1979 and 1980, and I'm not as bad as everyone thinks I am today.

The Browns went on to lose the next two games by a total of seven points----24-20 to the New York Jets, and then 12-9 to, of all teams, the 1-6 Cincinnati Bengals.

That evening after the loss to the Bengals, Sam sat in his family room expecting a phone call. It was quite unusual that Art Modell did not fly back with the team from Cincinnati that day, an ominous sign in Sam's estimation. We all knew that's how the end usually started with Art. The separation process began when he stopped communicating directly and started keeping his distance. Messages would arrive through an emissary. Sam said that for the last week he felt as though he had leprosy. After the loss to New England, he sat in Art's office, and Art's chief lieutenants, Ernie Accorsi and Jim Bailey, wouldn't even look at him.

About two hours after the loss to the Bengals, Modell decided to make a coaching change. He called Sam's residence, just a few minutes away in Waite Hill, and asked him to come over. Both Jim Bailey and Ernie Accorsi were already in Art's family room, ostensibly to give Modell support when he told Sam that he would no longer be the head coach of the Cleveland Browns.

At a noon press conference the next day at Cleveland Stadium, Art explained that a change "was in the best interests of the organization." He went on, "I asked my friend and associate to step aside." Modell then introduced Marty Schottenheimer, the team's defensive coordinator, as the new head coach. Marty was not named interim head coach but given a contract through the 1986 season. Rutigliano left the Browns with a 47-50 record. In seven years as coach, he had twice taken the team to the playoffs.

A reporter reminded Modell of his comment just two weeks earlier that he would not be making any coaching changes during mid-season. Modell responded, "Two weeks ago I didn't feel the organization needed a change, but I do feel that way now." Modell denied that losing to Cincinnati was a final determinant in the decision.

Rutigliano said all the right things in announcing that he was "stepping aside," and his final advice to his successor-coach was, "Make sure you kick field goals." A week later, Art Modell added one more incisive comment, saying:

Sam and I have been very close. Adversity brings people closer together, and we have probably been closer than ever the past few weeks. I won't get as close to any coach in the future. I look forward to a good relationship with Marty Schottenheimer, but now I realize that an owner has to stand back some.

A source in the front office, who insisted on remaining anonymous, tried to explain further to the media Modell's rationale:

Behind this whole thing, Art saw the pressure getting to Sam. Sam was suffering inwardly. Art saw the pressure being reflected in the way he ran the team and affecting its play. He did it for Sam's personal welfare as well as the team's.

The 1984 season was clearly not the one people had expected. Even the scalpers who worked West Third Street near the Stadium's Gate A were complaining. Two $16.50 tickets to the Houston game went for $30. The scalpers still made money since they were able to buy "extra, unused" tickets for $5 or $10, but they were not making their accustomed margins. If they made $100 on a Sunday afternoon in 1984, they had to be satisfied. As the Browns headed into November, they were averaging 58,000 fans per home game, compared to 70,500 in 1983. A 1-8 record usually does that to gate receipts.

The team finished the season with a disheartening 5-11 record. Fans were asking how the coach, the owner, and others close to the scene could have misjudged the talent on the team so badly. Joe Fan hadn't been fooled. After all, he had called into those talk shows expressing skepticism. Maybe he saw the team for what it really was--mediocre at best.

BNI editor Ray Yannucci wrote that the 41-7 humiliation at the hands of the San Francisco 49ers near the end of the season showed how far away the Browns really were from being a substantial team. He summed up the season thus:

This offense appears light years away from being good enough to compete against the upper-echelon teams in the NFL. Being last in touchdowns scored isn't a misleading statistic, folks. It's a sobering fact of just how ineffective the Browns' offense is.

So much for Super Bowl expectations.

There was talk in the Browns' brain trust of using the top pick in the 1985 draft for a quarterback. Like the rest of the country, Modell had seen on national TV the game-ending heroics of the holiday college game with Doug Flutie battling Bernie Kosar. Art was particularly interested in how our team's scouts were evaluating Flutie. I was having lunch at the roundtable in the Stadium Restaurant with Art Modell and several scouts, when Art asked the most veteran scout, "Can Doug Flutie, given his size, play in the NFL?" (Flutie was less than six feet tall.) The scout answered, "Well, Art, there are some scouts in the league who think he can play, and there are some scouts who don't think he will make it."

Art was miffed at the evasive response, and asked with a little more emphasis, "Well, what do **you** think? Can Doug Flutie play in the NFL?"

The scout didn't even hesitate, and repeated, "Like I said before, some scouts think he will be a good player, and an equal number think he won't be."

Art was exasperated and dropped the subject. People who worked for Art learned to tell from his tone when he wanted them to state their position— with support attached. If they waffled or had an opinion without logical support, especially when it ran against the current, they could be in for trouble. There were always one or two in the group, and we all knew who they were, who would try to figure which way Art was leaning and then throw their full support that way. They knew they didn't need to support their conclusion if they were siding with the owner. I once challenged one of these loyal "supporters" as to why he told Art only what he wanted to hear, rather than giving him an honest answer. His response? "Art expects support from me. I am there to support him and concur with his thoughts. That's my role."

I said, "Well, what would you do if Art swung 180 degrees right after you agreed with him?"

Without a skip, he answered, "I would swing 180 degrees, announce that I had changed my mind too, and agree with him."

Answers like the one Art received from the scout would prompt him to don his businessman's hat. He grew skeptical of the value the Browns were deriving from the scouting department. He knew scouting department costs (primarily salaries and travel expenses--which were substantial) ran about $800,000 a year. Art grumbled during one draft that it was costing the team almost $100,000 for each pick. When he wanted to get really depressed, he used to divide the $800,000 by the number of picks who actually made the roster. In the leaner drafts, costs might be calculated at almost $200,000 a player.

Pete Franklin had strong opinions about the two quarterbacks in the upcoming draft. When he learned the Browns were interested in acquiring the Number 1 draft choice from Buffalo, possibly to select Doug Flutie, Franklin shouted, "Phooey on Flutie. He is not the answer. He will be an average NFL quarterback at best." Now there was a guy not afraid to state his opinion! That's how Art Modell wanted his scouts to speak. Franklin continued, "There is only one quarterback worth moving up for, and that is Bernie Kosar." And that's the way it turned out.

MAKING THE GRADE	
Production	9.0
Leadership	9.0
Poise	9.0
Judgment	9.0
Locate secondary receiver	9.0
Arm Strength	7.5
Quick release	6.0
Accuracy	8.5
Ball handling	8.0
Set-up quickness	6.5
Scramble ability	5.0
Average rating	**7.9**

The Fort Lauderdale *News* interviewed NFL personnel directors grading Miami Hurricane quarterback Bernie Kosar in 11 categories. The rating was on a scale of 1.0 to 9.0. *Browns News Illustrated collection*

The 1985 season was the first full season under new head coach Marty Schottenheimer, who brought in a new offensive coordinator, Joe Pendry, and a new quarterback coach, Greg Landry. Landry greeted five quarterbacks at training camp that year: top draft pick Bernie Kosar, newly-acquired Gary Danielson, 1984 starter Paul McDonald, Terry Nugent, and Tom Flick. As is commonplace when a new coach takes over, many veterans were released to make room for younger players. Veterans Mike Pruitt, Joe DeLamielleure, and Ricky Feacher were waived, along with recent draftees Dwight Walker and Bruce Davis, two wide receiver hopefuls who did not pan out. Room was made for two acquisitions from the defunct USFL, Kevin Mack and Dan Fike, and for newly drafted Reggie Langhorne and Fred Banks.

Schottenheimer watched the quarterback derby unfold during pre-season, and although fans were clamoring for local favorite Kosar to start, Marty leaned in the direction of experience and named Gary Danielson his opening day starter. Modell supported his coach, saying, "It's like the fine wine commercial. I will not play Bernie Kosar before his time."

It was amazing to us at the Stadium Corp. that Art was so often accused of meddling with the football team. Perhaps it was the way he phrased things. Whenever he did come out and say that he would not play so-and-so, it did not imply that it was his decision rather than the coach's. It may have been wiser, though, to use the pronoun "we" or "the organization" or better yet, "the Browns."

Even with the experienced Danielson starting the season, few observers were confident about the offense since the team wasn't blessed with Pro Bowl talent nor with speed at the wideout position. The depth chart on opening day showed Willis Adams and Fred Banks as the starters (by the end of the season this tandem between them had 14 catches for 184 yards). Brian Brennan was out with injuries, but the team had Ozzie Newsome at tight end. Every fan in the stands (and certainly every defensive coordinator in the league) was able to guess that Ozzie would be the primary target that year.

The Browns got off to a slow start, which Schottenheimer attributed to inconsistency on the offensive line. While the coaches were working toward the desired consistency, Ernie Accorsi and his personnel staff were scurrying around for free agent wide receivers to bring in for immediate impact. To the organization's credit, both John Jefferson, former San Diego great, and Clarence Weathers, released by the Patriots, were on the roster by the fourth week.

In the fifth week of the season Bernie Kosar got his chance to play, as Gary Danielson went down with a separated right shoulder. Danielson had guided the Browns into first place, alone, in the AFC Central division, the first time since 1980 that had happened. Brian Brennan was back from his injuries and starting. Rookie Kevin Mack, running out of a two-back set along with second-year back Earnest Byner, and Ricky Bolden, Dan Fike, and Don Rogers were all making significant contributions. Along with the linebacking corps, the team's strength, the Browns had developed an air of confidence.

In Kosar's first start, which took place in the Astrodome, never an easy place in which to win, Bernie was 8 of 19 for 208 yards, outdueling the Houston Oilers and Warren Moon, who accumulated only 108 yards through the air. After Kosar's first start, which the Browns won, 21-6, Art Modell was quoted as saying, "The only thing I'll say about Kosar is he's not a prototype quarterback as we know it. He's not very pretty, but he's resourceful. He can improvise on a broken play."

Kosar and Danielson alternated the rest of the season, with Gary playing whenever he was healthy. This quarterback tandem led the Browns through the season, and on to the post-season playoffs by winning the AFC Central division title with an 8-8 record. This was the first time in the NFL record books that a division had been won with no better than a .500 record.

When post-season analysts looked at the Browns' roster for who had made major contributions to the team's success, once past the obvious first-round picks (Kosar, Matthews, Chip Banks, Rogers, Cousineau, Dixon, and Newsome), the next group of contributors were free agent acquisitions. This prompted Pete Franklin to headline his next feature article in BNI: BROWNS HAVE BETTER LUCK WITH FREE AGENTS THAN HIGH DRAFT PICKS. Citing Felix Wright and Harry Holt from the Canadian Football League, the USFL's Kevin Mack, Frank Minnifield, and Dan Fike, and the many free agents starting (Bob Golic, Robert Jackson, Al Gross, Jeff Gossett, Clarence Weathers), Franklin wondered why there were so few starters from recent drafts. After complimenting the Browns' personnel department for discovering and landing the castoffs, he also lamented the failure rate in the key draft rounds from which many long-time starters should be secured.

The Browns actually backed into the playoffs as Cincinnati, Pittsburgh, and Cleveland all lost on the last Sunday of the season. The Browns were heading south to face Dan Marino and the explosive Miami Dolphins without Tom Cousineau, out of action with a broken wrist. The day before the game, Modell, hoping for the club's first playoff victory since 1969, was heard to say, "I just hope we don't get embarrassed on national TV."

Schottenheimer eventually found the consistency he sought in the offensive line. By adding the blocking of tight end Harry Holt to the attack, the Browns achieved something rarely found in the NFL: two 1,000-yard rushers on the same team, in the persons of Mack and Byner. The running attack continued in that playoff game, as Byner rushed for 161 yards, establishing a new Browns' playoff game record. Hanford Dixon and Frank Minnifield also rose to the occasion, holding the two highly heralded Marks--Clayton and Duper--to one catch between them as the Browns cruised to a 21-3 third quarter lead. Then Marino went into action, finding Tony Nathan, Bruce Hardy, and Nat Moore with a patient short passing game. Marino's effective passing, plus two questionable officials' calls, led to three straight Dolphins' touchdowns enroute to a 24-21 Miami victory.

After the game, the Browns' play-calling was discussed at length, leading even rookie QB Bernie Kosar to speak out about its conservative nature. Kosar said, "We're going to have to improve our passing philosophy. It's not up to a professional level. We just don't take advantage of certain defensive situations. That's what we've been doing all year. Whenever we get ahead, we become as predictable as you can get." One of Kosar's criticisms was the failure to call deep pass patterns. Bernie, and some of the receivers too, expressed hope that the Browns' offense would "open it up a little next year."

Whether Kosar's post-game comments had anything to do with it or not, a new offensive coordinator was employed by the Cleveland Browns for 1986. Lindy Infante would help bring an exciting season of football to the lakefront and another trip to the playoffs.

In 1986 the Browns sported a very good 12-4 record, but the season itself had not been without down times. Five wins came by a field goal, games which were close enough to have gone either way. Among the low lights of the season were the Browns getting trounced by the Bengals, 30-13 on national TV, over which Art confessed to being embarrassed by the team's performance, and a loss to a down-and-out 0-6 Packers team at home, 17-14.

Modell commented to Tony Grossi of the *Plain Dealer*, "You should have seen the scene in my office after the Green Bay game....that's the low point of the season. I must confess, twice this year, Pat Modell said she's never seen me so depressed in the 17 years she's been with me in football....I don't want to be disappointed again. I've had too many of those, so I'm trying to keep myself on an even keel."

At the end of the 1986 season, the Browns travelled to Vero Beach, Florida, where Marty Schottenheimer had convinced Modell to take the team to escape the winter weather while they prepared for the playoffs. When Art joined the team in Florida, the skies were dark gray and dreary, mirroring what the year had been like for the owner (it was just two months after the final verdict had been rendered in the protracted Gries' lawsuits). He had also been spending considerable time in New York with Commissioner Pete Rozelle, negotiating on behalf of the league with the television networks. Modell said that while the Browns had enjoyed a banner season, that personally "it's been a very nerve-wracking year, and it's still nerve-wracking. I will say it's taken a toll on the whole family. I've had better days." Relative to the television contract, he remarked these were the toughest negotiations he and Rozelle had in 25 years. The networks were losing money, and they felt it was the NFL's job to help them alleviate some of the problems. Modell continued, "I am tired. This has worn me out."

Art had also been disappointed with a seeming lack of support and interest from Cleveland fans during the season. "I am not ashamed to say that I was down on this town," Modell said. "I thought we were playing good, entertaining football. We just didn't get the respect. I felt like Rodney Dangerfield most of the season." But he did add that before he left Cleveland to be with the team in Florida, he was invigorated by the resurgence of interest in Cleveland. "My greatest thrill is seeing the community respond. I walk down the street, and cab drivers and truck drivers want to talk about the game. That I like. That makes it very rewarding for me."

Grossi concluded his article by saying that Modell had done all he could to bring the Browns to the forefront of the American Conference. He had made the necessary changes after the Browns blew the playoff game in Miami a year earlier. Now all he could do was sit back and watch his team finish the job.

Art hoped the Browns would do just that in the playoff game in Cleveland on January 3, 1987.

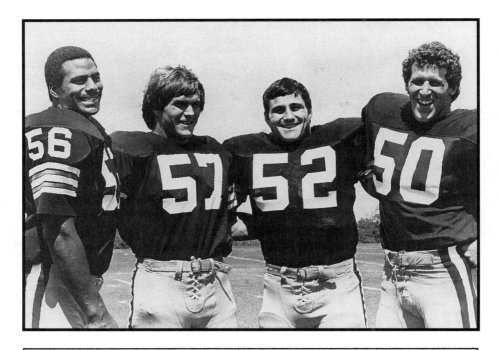

In 1983, the pride and joy of the Browns' defense were its linebackers- (L to R) Chip Banks, Clay Matthews, Dick Ambrose, Tom Cousineau. *Browns News Illustrated*

CHAPTER 8
SOME UPS - MORE DOWNS

January 1987 started off as the culmination of the 1986 football season, with the Browns playing two home playoff games. The first game, a double-overtime win over the New York Jets on January 3rd, exemplified a true "Kardiac Kids" win, as Bernie Kosar played spectacularly to bring the Browns back from a 10-point deficit with 4:14 left in regulation play. Bernie's 489 yards passing and the nine sacks recorded by the defense were record-setting performances. After a scoreless first overtime period, Mark Mosely kicked a 27-yard field goal in second overtime to win by a score of 23-20. Thousands of fans had left the Stadium early, despairing of the Browns having any chance to win the game. Many returned to the Stadium, though, when they heard the comeback story unraveling on their car radios.

The whole city was sky-high the entire following week. Pro football in Cleveland was fun again, and we could hardly wait for Sunday's matchup against Denver and John Elway.

On January 11, we watched what could arguably be called the most emotionally draining game ever viewed in Cleveland Stadium. The 79,915 fans in attendance will probably never forget the memorable 98-yard drive engineered by Elway which culminated in a 5-yard touchdown toss to wide receiver Mark Jackson, tying the game at 20-20 and sending it into overtime. Then Rich Karlis narrowly kicked his third field goal of the game to give Denver the game 23-20. Both playoff games had ended in overtime, with the same score, on the same field. How we wanted to add, "with the same winner."

The fans, however, were truly appreciative of this team's post-season (and regular season) efforts. They gave the players a standing ovation as they left the field. The grounds crew then went onto the field to take down the goal posts until the next season.

January 1987 started everyone at Stadium Corp. off on a emotional roller coaster, especially Art Modell. A big upper on January 3rd was followed by the big downer on January 11th, courtesy of John Elway. The roller coaster ride that began then would continue in the years ahead, but, sad to say, there would be more downs than ups.

Coaching changes were in order in anticipation of the 1987 season. Tom Olivadotti resigned as defensive backs coach to become defensive coordinator with the Miami Dolphins. Bill Cowher, who had done an exemplary job as Browns' special teams coach, replaced Olivadotti, and Kurt

Schottenheimer was hired by head coach and brother Marty to take over special teams. We knew Kurt would be on the spot, as he had Cowher's big shoes to fill. Kurt came from Notre Dame, after having spent a couple of years at LSU. Kurt had earlier recommended that the Browns pick up the undrafted Herman Fontenot as a free agent, and Fontenot repaid that confidence by becoming the Browns' second leading receiver in 1986 with 47 catches.

Attention soon turned to the NFL spring draft. Since it was generally felt that the Denver playoff loss was due to the Browns' inability to generate a pass rush on John Elway, and because defensive linemen Reggie Camp, Carl Hairston, and Bob Golic were not getting any younger, emphasis was on selecting defensive talent. Possibly the biggest surprise on draft day came before the Browns' first pick was made. That was the trade of Chip Banks to San Diego for an opportunity to move up in the first round. For several reasons, the final straw probably being his ineffectiveness in helping stop "The Drive," Banks was dealt for someone the coaches hoped would be there to play every play. The Banks' trade brought the Browns a move up to the number 5 pick in the first round, and the Browns decided to go for a linebacker. Both Mike Junkin and Shane Conlan were on the board, and both were rated by scouting services as top picks right behind Cornelius Bennett, who went second. The Browns selected Mike Junkin. In Marty Schottenheimer's mind it was a close decision. He was quoted in *Browns News Illustrated* afterward that he saw similarities between Junkin and Jack Lambert, and that "in my years of evaluating college players, he (Junkin) is one of the two best linebackers I have ever seen. The best of course is playing for the New York Giants" (referring to Lawrence Taylor).

The really big downer this draft day, though, was that this trade represented a surrender by the Browns. They were admitting they hadn't generated the yield they had hoped for from Charles "Chip" Banks, their top draft pick in 1982. Insiders knew Art viewed this as a major investment loss.

It didn't take long to get depressed over our inflated baseball expectations. We had reason to expect great things because 1986 was the first year the Tribe finished over .500 since the strike-shortened year of 1981. Under Pat Corrales, 1986 found the Indians only 11.5 games out of first, a respectable finish. Perhaps April's weather should have been an omen of more ugly things to come. To ready the field for the home opener, head groundskeeper David Frey and his crew had to shovel and plow out over 100 truckloads of wet snow. What a sight that was! A convoy of trucks lined up at home plate, extending past the dugout and out to the bullpen, all awaiting their snowy cargo. The trucks then proceeded two-tenths of a mile to the East Ninth St. pier and dumped the snow into Lake Erie.

We were amazed at the complaints some players made to Frey. Most guys never uttered a word, because they knew both teams played under the same conditions. Yet others, coming north after eight weeks in Arizona, seemed unable to appreciate that Cleveland had just experienced a heavy snowstorm, the kind we get here as our last snow about every five or six years. I suppose some expected Frey to go out there personally with an extension cord and a hair dryer to dry their positions.

By April 18, the Indians were 1-10, and by July 4, historically the annual benchmark of baseball success or failure in Cleveland, the Tribe was playing .341 ball and perched 23 games out of first. It was mightily clear that this season could already be labeled a downer.

One part of my role as Stadium Corp. treasurer was to periodically freshen up financial projections. Since many of our revenue projections depended on the success of other promoters, we had to constantly stay abreast of the success of those ventures, interpolating the most recent expectations of their success, or lack thereof, into the mix.

In the 12 years under this lease, we had gained an enormous amount of knowledge about the 55-year old building and found that most expenses could be anticipated and were somewhat controllable. That contrasted nicely with the early years when we found some sort of surprise in almost everything we tackled. Most maintenance then became, thankfully, preventive in nature.

Underground water line breaks were still a major nuisance. Before they were discovered, a lot of lost water and large water bills resulted. Winter cold spells caused pipes to freeze; the colder the weather, the more expensive the repairs. People would be amazed at how much damage ice can do. I'll never forget the ice break in a 4" water main after the 1981 playoff game against the Raiders. I do not believe any force exerted by man or tool could have caused that kind of rupture in so thick a fitting. But the ice that Sunday afternoon sure did.

In 1987 Stadium Corporation faced some financial setbacks. Cleveland suffered two major windstorms that year. Because most of the Stadium roof covering was over 50 years old and brittle, it did not hold up well to the gusting winds off Lake Erie, and good-sized chunks came off during the storms. Since the deductible on our liability insurance policy was $50,000, those two acts of God were the major reason our roof repair expense ran $110,000 in 1987, the largest amount ever spent in that category.

As I was trying to find money to pay the roof bills and losing hope of hosting a rock concert, Jules Belkin, Cleveland's foremost entertainment promoter, pleasantly surprised me by asking if the Stadium would be interested in hosting one, and maybe two, "big-name" fall concerts. He assured me these "biggies" would be playing in many NFL stadiums, and scheduling would be difficult because dates had to fit around the NFL schedule. Further complicating matters would be timing the shows in those NFL stadiums which also hosted major league baseball, such as ours and Pittsburgh's. Sometimes Cincinnati would also be considered, but if only one location was factored in for Ohio, the show generally came to Cleveland because of the Stadium's larger capacity. Jules assured me that our date would be given priority since few dates were available in September and early October, given both baseball and football schedules.

Why, I asked myself, does this have to happen in September? Fitting in a show on a tight time frame could be done, but it allowed no margin for error, and virtually no time for field repair in case of a torrential downpour. We had all June and July, but no shows were to be had. It was Browns' policy that to schedule shows after August 15, a special meeting was held with Browns' management, including Art, who wore his so-called "football hat" for the session. Whichever way Art ruled, for either the Browns or the Stadium Corp., was clearly his right. He voted for and against himself at the same time. In many cases Art made his decision on the best public relations stance, and these instincts allowed him to override the economics of the situation.

From my Stadium Corp. perspective, I was thinking how two concerts would help out the profit projections. We had reason to worry about income that year since the baseball team was in the cellar. The calls from Belkin were a godsend to the bottom line. At least that was how it seemed during August.

At the meeting, I advised Art that the first show was so big that it could lead to a two-night stand, a rare phenomenon in stadium concerts, and a rare opportunity for us to improve our bottom line. Art knew the downside. A two-night event added a multiplier to the risk of field damage. Risk would more than double if we encountered a hot or a wet spell. A wet spell meant the grass would begin mildewing, regardless of the type of cover. For any large concert production, the field was covered for a minimum 48 hours. Under the stage and sound towers, field cover could be down for as much as six to eight days. That's why the stage was always shoved as far against the bleachers as possible, since it was unrealistic to expect to escape damage there. During baseball season, this area was behind the outfield fence and generally not visible to most fans. But during football season, the entire field was visible. With a two-night show, there was no way there would not be at least minimal damage. The question really was: Could the grounds crew get it repaired before the next football game?

Art made it clear that he wanted the shows, but at the same time he did not want visible field damage, a contradiction in terms if you will, and he wanted the whole staff's maximum effort to that end. While we all pledged total support to the cause, we also knew that we could only do so much and that conditions, such as the weather, were beyond our control.

I told Belkin we would take the show, and in a matter of days, we entered into contract negotiations with Pink Floyd. Pink Floyd had excited the rock world when it had announced its first major tour in over ten years, and the tour was expected to sell out quickly. Because of this, the Ticketron ticket agencies introduced a new concept of the wrist band, designed to replace overnight camping, vandalism, and long lines that occurred at shopping malls from fans waiting to buy tickets. These colorful bracelets were numbered to guarantee a place in the ticket lines. The concept was very simple: no wristband, no place in the line. The bracelet was not removable, at least not until the ticket was purchased.

Cleveland was the only Ohio tour stop. When the concert was announced, the first day sellout occurred quickly, and so a second show was immediately announced. The concerts were booked on Sept. 16 and 17, and Floyd played two spectacular shows in an all-out rain. The performances during the "Momentary Lapse of Reason" tour were replete with smoke, videos, lasers, and inflatable pigs. Pink Floyd proved it still had magic.

While the reward from the concerts was evident, good fortune on the football field was slow to develop. The Browns opened up practice without first-round draft pick Mike Junkin, who was a holdout. The Browns opened the new season with high expectations, but it was infuriating not to have the services of the first round pick on defense. One can imagine Art Modell's disappointment when the Browns dropped the opener to New Orleans 28-21 (a downer). The Saints piled up big yardage on the ground as they ran at the Browns' left side almost all game, going at Anthony Griggs, who had started in place of Banks/Junkin. Art wanted to know how soon it would be before Junkin got in and started making an impact.

The growing player payroll was on Art's mind, and it became a typical topic at our Stadium Restaurant roundtable lunches. Usual attendees besides me were Ernie Accorsi, Jim Bailey, Mike Srsen, Larry Staverman, and Kevin Byrne. Art talked about impending doom if the wage spiral wasn't broken.

One day he began citing examples and asked, "Now let's start with the defense. Take the nose tackle for example. How much is Bob Golic making?"

Accorsi said nothing, defering to Bailey. Bailey, who negotiated the contract, said a few general words which were essentially a non-answer. Mike Srsen, who had all the figures at his fingertips, sensed that Art was still looking for a specific answer, and chimed in, "$500,000."

"What," Modell gasped, "for a nose tackle? How did his contract ever get that high?"

Bailey was trying to pretend he was not a part of this conversation, but at the same time he sent Srsen some darting looks. Accorsi, who negotiated most of the player contracts, must have felt that Modell was blaming him for the exorbitant salary, and he kept quiet. Bailey, whose prior negotiations with Golic had resulted in the half-million-dollar contract, also remained silent. Art Modell should have demanded and received a detailed answer to the Golic matter right then and there. But he didn't.

Later when Staverman and I were leaving the table, Larry remarked, "Well, Jim came this close (holding his thumb and forefinger an inch apart) to being exposed."

Roundtable lunches with Art were held less frequently after that. Most of us felt that Bailey orchestrated scenarios which would keep Modell away from those of us who had the financial information. We posed a risk—not to Art, but to Bailey.

The Browns were scheduled to face the Steelers in the home opener three days after the second PINK FLOYD show. After two nights of constant rain, the field was finally uncovered late Friday. It had been covered by a protective material known as Geotextile, but we found the material was rendered totally useless after it absorbed the first inch of rainwater. By the second evening, the continuous downpour made the material a sopping mess, and the lush grass beneath began fermenting. The grounds crew viewed the result with horror. The heavy equipment needed on the field to tear down the sound towers and the stage only made matters worse. In hurrying to clear the field so the grounds crew could get to work, a bulldozer flipped over and imbedded itself into the 20-yard line near the bleachers. Needless to say, when the Steelers came to town on Saturday to work out on the field, they were denied access since so much work remained to be done. Chuck Noll was not happy, especially after the Browns soundly thumped Pittsburgh behind six interceptions, including two by Clay Matthews and two by Chris Rockins. Art Modell was so upset by the field conditions that he never even asked the financial outcome of the shows. For him, the embarrassment of the field overshadowed everything else, including the victory (a downer).

Perhaps what really distressed Modell was the knowledge that a players' strike was looming. It took place later that week and caused an already sold-out Monday night game at home against Denver to be canceled. That game was to be Cleveland's opportunity to retaliate against Elway and his Broncos. Instead the week was spent getting replacement players into the fold. Modell became morose over the work stoppage. John Madden had quoted him after the 1982 players' strike as saying that he would seriously consider selling the Browns if another work stoppage occurred. The 1982 strike had taken that much out of him. The 1987 strike began as a one-week work stoppage, while the owners were individually trying to decide whether or not to put their product on the field with less than their front-line players. This time Art made no remarks about selling his team, but he did say that he got sick to his stomach when the players walked out. He believed the labor disputes eroded the popularity of the NFL that he had worked so hard to build.

Soon after Pink Floyd had sold out, Belkin called with an opportunity to follow up with a new group called U-2, which was going out on a stadium tour in October and early November. When Art gave his okay, I pleaded with Belkin to get Cleveland on the schedule as early as possible, given the likelihood of cool-to-cold October nights on the lakefront. The show was booked for Tuesday night, October 6, and U-2 played in a driving rainstorm before 50,000-plus deliriously happy, but soaking wet fans.

I recall the group's business manager being very upset since they were assessed a $10,000 field repair charge because of the heavy equipment damage done to the soggy turf after the show. While most groups realize that field repair costs are charged to the show, neither side wants to pay for what is commonly viewed as an act of God. Most regular touring acts do, however reluctantly, pay for field cover and field damage from their enormous gate receipts. U-2 threatened never to play Cleveland Stadium again after the charge back of $10,000. I'm sure the band did not realize that pittance would come nowhere near the real cost to repair the field.

When football began again in October, the replacement Browns won their first game in New England behind running back Larry Mason's two one-yard touchdown runs. The next game was at home against the replacement Houston Oilers, and the field was not in very good shape. Only 38,000 less-than-enthusiastic fans watched the Oilers down the Browns, who were quarterbacked that day by replacement player Jeff Christensen.

Watching home football games in October in front of a small crowd was surely a downer, watching the home team represented by replacement players was a downer, not knowing when the cock-a-mamy strike was going to end was a downer, watching a rutted and soggy field of play was a downer, and having the baseball team end the year with 101 losses, 37 games out of first, was a super-downer. The Tribe's stellar pitching staff of the prior year ended 1987 with the following records: Ken Schrom (6-13), Tom Candiotti (7-18), Greg Swindell (3-8), and Rich Yett (3-9).

By Sunday October 18 the NFL players' walkout was resolved, and the regulars returned. Cleveland went on to win six of the remaining nine games to advance once again to the AFC playoffs (an upper, but only a partial one, since we had expected a repeat trip). Facing the Colts in Cleveland Stadium on Saturday, January 9, before 79,372 fans, the Browns demonstrated a nicely balanced attack, featuring three Bernie Kosar touchdown passes, and Earnest Byner's 122 yards, to come away with a 38-21 win. Kosar and the other players credited Lindy Infante's genius in calling the offensive schemes. The explosive offense had averaged 346 yards a game in 1987, slightly better than the 337-yard average attained in 1986 during Infante's first season. It had been a long time since Cleveland fans had seen that kind of firepower. Unfortunately, soon after the season ended, Infante resigned to become head coach with Green Bay. The Browns' offensive production slipped to 313 yards in 1988 and to 315 in 1989, and it dropped below 300 yards per game in most years thereafter.

But in January 1988 the Browns and their fans were getting ready to face Denver once again, this time in Mile High Stadium. The fans hoped for a reversal of fortune, this time beating them on their home turf. The Browns went into battle on Sunday, January 17. Kosar outdueled Elway, as he set an AFC Championship record with 26 of 41 passes for 356 yards, 3 TD's, and one interception. Elway completed 14 of 26 for 281 yards, 3 TD's, and one interception. Again the Browns showed Kardiac Kids spunk as they fought back from a 21-3 halftime deficit and scored 30 points in the second half, but fell short at the whistle by a count of 38-33.

When the year ended, Kosar emerged as the top passer in the AFC, winning the title with a 95.4 QB rating. The Browns roared through two play-off games with enormous offensive stats, scoring 71 points and averaging 434 yards a game. There were a lot of reasons to feel good about the Browns, but because we had failed in two straight years to beat Denver and get to the Super Bowl, a certain fixation began to develop in the Browns' front office about beating Elway and Denver. Among those on the inside, concern was growing that the Browns might have a head coach who, despite his defensive prowess, might be unable to get the Browns to the Super Bowl (let's call this a downer).

Art reflected on the back-to-back playoff losses to Denver. He lamented, "It's gnawing away at me. It hurts to read about the Super Bowl and see over and over again the last two minutes of those two games."

After Lindy Infante resigned, Marty Schottenheimer announced that he would not be hiring an offensive coordinator. He explained his decision by saying that if he were to bring in an experienced coordinator, that person would undoubtedly expect to incorporate his own philosophy. Considering the potency of the Browns' offense, he felt it best to leave the system intact and elevate someone already on the staff. On February 7, he announced that he himself would serve as offensive coordinator during 1988.

While critics wondered whether a defensive-minded head coach should direct an offense, Art Modell was not one of them. According to the *Browns News Illustrated*, Art said, "Marty is a very bright student of the game. I don't have the slightest qualms about him taking over the offense."

Gary Danielson had served an important role in Bernie Kosar's development. He was a sounding board, a quarterback coach, and an advisor. With Danielson thinking of retirement, Marty felt the Browns needed to bring in a QB coach. The Browns decided on Marc Trestman, a 32-year-old former quarterback coach at the University of Miami, who had tutored Kosar during those great Hurricanes years of 1983 and 1984. Trestman and Joe Pendry were both going to provide input into the offensive schemes to assist Schottenheimer.

In January each year we held pricing discussions for the coming season. The loges at Cleveland Stadium were renewed every January, and the decision about price changes sometimes was based on what happened right up to the last game of the previous season. A decision about Browns' ticket prices was usually done concurrently with the loge decision but announced later. Top price for an upper box for the coming season was hiked to $27, a nifty increase of somewhere in the neighborhood of 16%.

Art always hated the time when price increases were announced. In most years he would just happen to be out of town when the announcement was scheduled. About five days after the announcement went out, he would begin calling in daily. "Are the loge renewals coming in? How many came in today? How many have renewed as of today? How does that compare to the number of renewals over the same number of days last year? How does it compare to the number of renewals over the same number of days the last year we had a price increase?" They were the right questions, but I required a constantly updated set of data at my fingertips. After a while I was able to anticipate his questions, and I could tell him the data before he asked. Lacking patience, if Art had to wait too long for an answer, his employee might get charged with "losing your fast ball." That term could indicate that Art thought one's better days were past.

The general acceptance of the 1988 price increases made it apparent that Cleveland fans were fairly satisfied with their sports teams, even the Indians. The baseball team had some exciting players, with Cory Snyder and Joe Carter hitting the long ball, and Greg Swindell showing big-time promise. In the past, most of the complaints we had received from our loge customers were over the horrible performance put on by the baseball team. Many loge tenants even suggested to Art that he eliminate the mandatory purchase of baseball tickets and thus be able to lower the prices for the loge suites. After all, they would say, we buy the loge for football. The loges provided corporate Cleveland the comfort of staying warm during brutally cold football games. The tenants therefore had plenty of customer demand for loge use during football season, but they often couldn't give away the baseball tickets. During baseball season we would note about 40% of the boxes unused during most games. The season opener and fireworks nights were just about the only dates when the boxes were used near capacity.

Soon attention turned to the 1988 draft. It was a pretty simple guess that the offense would not be a priority. After all, with the offensive production the club was generating behind Bernie Kosar, why change anything? Since Marty had cut his football teeth on the defensive side of the ball, it was a safe bet that he would tend to look there first. As it turned out, the Browns' first four picks in the draft were defensive players. Not until the eighth round was an offensive player selected, that being wide receiver J.J.Birden.

More interesting than the picks themselves, however, was the growing power struggle over who would have the final voice in selections. Was it to be the head coach who was gaining in stature within the organization, or would it be the acting general manager of football operations (Ernie Accorsi), or would it be the owner, who would "jump in if he felt he had to"? Marty had selected the prior year's number one pick, Mike Junkin, who had nowhere near the impact on the team's performance that most people felt that pick should have provided. In 1988 it was assumed that Marty would want to have that same right to make the selection.

Many football managers feel coaches should not have the final say on personnel procurement. After all, during the football season when the players are on the college gridirons, pro coaches are deeply involved preparing for their own games. The scouts in the organization accumulate the best feel for a college player's total performance. Pro coaches normally get to see the players only in post-season all-star games.

I passed Ernie Accorsi's office one day on the way to get a cup of coffee when I noticed him watching a tape of the game between LSU and Florida. He kept rerunning a play over and over again. I remember that LSU had the ball and had just converted a running play on third and six for a first down. Ernie was grumbling about someone's ineptness. He said something about three LSU linemen not good enough or big enough to get drafted by the NFL, and about a little 175-pound junior third-string running back filling in for an injured starter who dominated Florida's highly-regarded defense on that play. He told me to watch number such-and-such, whom he identified as Clifford Charlton. He said Charlton was playing terribly, and as an example he showed me how this little back juked Charlton out and got outside for a first down. I didn't exactly understand Accorsi's point, but he seemed to be downgrading Charlton from draft consideration.

I wasn't really sure how the mechanics of his operation worked. I had figured if a team had no interest in a player, it would simply leave him off its "wanted list," but Ernie seemed to be doing something beyond that. Before I left the room, he whispered that the coaches were beginning a campaign to draft Charlton in the first round, and he thought that would be a disastrous move by the Browns.

It was going to be interesting, I thought, to see how this played out. Charlton was rated a first-rounder by almost all scouting services, but Accorsi was not convinced. In the end Charlton was the Browns' first draft pick in 1988, the guy penciled in eventually to replace ageless Clay Matthews, then going into his eleventh year.

Art Modell had to make the decision whose judgment he was going to rely on when there were conflicting opinions. In most instances, Art deferred to the head coach. Why? Because it was easy for the head coach to not play a first-round pick if it was not his choice. That had happened in the past, and sometimes it was the coach's way of getting even. So, once again in 1988, Schottenheimer prevailed.

In the second round, Modell expressed an interest in taking Michael Dean Perry, a defensive tackle still on the board when the 50th pick overall came up. Art was impressed with his play when he had seen him in post-season games on television. Schottenheimer was overheard saying that Perry was too small to play for him, that 6'1" was too short for a defensive tackle in the NFL. "Well," Modell supposedly said, "but at 6'1", he's not too small to play for me." Perry became a Cleveland Brown in the second round.

Round three came up, and Van Waiters, a guy deemed to have first round potential, was still available when the Browns' turn came. Rumors were going around about personal problems with Waiters, and Marty said he didn't want to deal with outside problems. Schottenheimer had been assistant under Rutigliano, when Sam had gotten personally involved with players' problems. While Sam may have felt his program was a success, Schottenheimer probably saw this as a distraction. He would rather avoid a problem, if in fact there was one, at the outset. Besides, he now had two young outside linebackers, Junkin (draft of '87) and now Charlton, and he may have thought another outside linebacker wasn't a high priority. The scouting report on Waiters described him as having great speed, great jumping and pass-rushing ability, and long arms. He had recorded 18 blocked passes and 8 blocked kicks at Indiana. Art Modell supposedly said that if the Browns could use the ability that Waiters' possessed, then the team should take a chance on him, getting him whatever help or treatment that he might need, if he in fact needed any. Waiters was the Browns' third-round pick.

It appeared confusing to many of us not on the "very" inside. Schottenheimer had just led the Browns to three consecutive post-season play-off years, but he seemed to be losing stature that draft day. Then again, he had prevailed in not hiring an offensive coordinator and in selecting the first-round picks in both years. All that notwithstanding, something seemed to diminish his subsequent influence. Marty won round one over Accorsi, but Art Modell called the shots in rounds two and three.

BROWNS

CHARLTON, CLIFF \
LB   FLA U
6.023 232   4.72 ▬

PERRY, MICHAEL 2
NT   CLEMSON
6.004 271   ▬

WAITERS, VAN
OB   IND U
6.034 229   4.81 ▬ 3

BLAYLOCK, ANTHONY 4
DC   WINSTON SALEM
5.107 188   4.56 ▬

The board in the Browns' draft room listed defensive players taken in each of the first four rounds in 1988.
Browns News Illustrated

Art and Marty forged closer ties as the team grew into Super Bowl contenders.
Browns News Illustrated

CHAPTER 9

'SUPER' HOPES IN 1988

The feature story in the July 24, 1988, training camp issue of *Browns News Illustrated* was headlined:

IS THIS THE YEAR ??

'Super' Hopes Begin at Lakeland

Lakeland, of course, referred to the Mentor, Ohio, community college where the Browns' training site was located, about 25 miles east of Cleveland. That is where the team would once again begin its pursuit of the elusive golden ring, an appearance in the Super Bowl. After close losses to Denver in post-season play the previous two years, many so-called experts felt this was the year the Browns would win it all. The team was posted as a 4-1 favorite in Las Vegas to win the Super Bowl, ahead of Denver (6-1), NY Giants (6-1), and Seattle (8-1).

Playboy Magazine was the first to pick the Browns to win the coveted bowl. Folks believed that the team had matured enough and made the necessary progress via the draft to bolster its defense. Paired with the team's prolific offense, the hoped-for defense made the Browns appear a solid football team. If the team could get the pass rush it had recently lacked, Cleveland would be the team to beat. Talent sleuth Joel Buchsbaum said that while he rated New England, Seattle, and Houston as having better overall team talent, the difference in his mind was what Bernie Kosar brought to the table. He felt Bernie's leadership could take a team with slightly less talent and still win it all.

On the Cleveland Stadium Corp. side of Art Modell's business, there were no outside summer events held in 1988. No major concert tours were scheduled that year, and given the grief generated over what the 1987 shows had done to the field, no one in either front office (Browns or Stadium Corp.) was complaining.

The Indians had shown signs of recovery from 1987's pathetic performance, and though they improved only one place (to sixth), attendance had returned to the 1986 level, about 1.4 million. That attendance helped to create a fairly healthy bottom line for the Stadium Corp. Actually anytime the Indians could generate one million fans a year, we felt that Stadium Corp. should be able to pay all its bills and meet its loan payment schedule. But given the losses still accruing to the Stadium Corp. due to the two football strikes, we knew that we could use an additional contribution to profits. We had some catching up to do.

Sports Illustrated came out with its pro football issue, and Bernie Kosar was featured on the cover. Local media asked Art about his feelings going into the season and specifically how he felt about the so-called *Sports Illustrated* cover jinx. Art still had the Denver playoff losses on his mind as he responded, "I sure as hell would rather be on the cover than on the obituary page. I don't think that it'll add any more pressure than we've imposed on ourselves. We had it in our hands two years in a row and we blew it. That's enough pressure."

The Browns were not quite ready with their roster. Just before the season started, Mike Baab was traded to New England, and the team slated Gregg Rakoczy, going into his third season, to start at center. On defense, neither Mike Junkin, Clifford Charlton, nor Van Waiters, all highly-touted draft picks, was ready to start at outside linebacker. The Browns agreed on David Grayson, a 1987 replacement player, for the starting slot. Junkin started the season at left inside linebacker, as the coaches thought it was his more natural position.

The Browns traveled to Kansas City for the opener. In a game of field goals, the Browns emerged victorious by a 6-3 count, despite six key injuries, the most notable being one to Kosar which sidelined him for the next six weeks. Kosar was nailed cleanly on a safety blitz by Lloyd Burruss, when just as he was following through on a pass, his elbow caught Burruss' helmet. Gary Danielson came in to finish the game, and everyone knew that he would have to lead the team until Kosar could return.

It took just one game to be jinxed by that damned *Sports Illustrated* cover.

The 1988 season, projected to be a Super Bowl season for the Browns, turned out to be as much of a disappointment as 1984. Like 1984, it would also mark the year of a coaching change.

With four different quarterbacks playing that year due to an unusual rash of injuries, the team could not stay on track. Special teams play was horrific, with fumbled punts and blocked field goal and punt tries in almost every game. On one particular punt late in the season, the Browns found themselves with only nine men on the field. The announcers were quick to point out the special teams' failures, as most of them were beginning to anticipate some type of player or coaching miscue in any special team alignment. Modell and Accorsi felt embarrassed by these situations. We learned the head coach was spending more time helping brother Kurt address these shortcomings, and the front office felt this effort detracted from Marty's dual role of head coach/offensive coordinator.

The Browns were not getting much help from their recent draft picks either. Neither Clifford Charlton nor Van Waiters made much of a contribution, and Mike Junkin was lost for the year. Michael Dean Perry was listed as a backup on the depth chart behind Carl Hairston in the three-man defensive front.

More than halfway through the season, with Kosar back from his injury and their record at 6-3, the Browns traveled to Houston where they were beaten in a very physical game. The Oiler running attack ground out 148 yards, compared to the Browns' 44. The Oilers unleashed a potent pass rush which had Kosar's attention during the whole game. Bernie said later, "I can't remember ever getting hit this hard." Although Bernie was sacked just once, on virtually every play he was hit as he threw.

From the booth upstairs where the front office sat to view the game, the real hard questions came at the end of the first half. With the Browns close enough to assure them of at least three points just before the half, Marty called a pass play to try for a touchdown. Marty had cut it too close, and time ran out as the pass dropped incomplete. The decision led to Schottenheimer being perceived as having a problem with "clock management." The front office also began to second-guess itself as to whether it should have allowed the head coach to bear the additional burden of offensive coordinator.

After the disheartening loss in Houston, the team had a short practice week before leaving for the high altitudes of Denver. The Broncos were tied for first in the AFC West at 5-5, and this game was as crucial for them as it was for Cleveland. During the year Denver had shown some signs of weakness against the run, and Elway was having a sub-par year, as his interceptions and touchdown passes were running about equal. If the Browns could generate a pass rush and contain Elway, the game appeared winnable.

There is no point in trying to state it equivocally: the Denver game was simply horrifying, as the Browns were humiliated by a score of 30-7. The game was actually over at halftime as the Browns went in for intermission down 30-0, after four first-half turnovers. Kosar was sacked six times as Denver rolled to its tenth straight win over Cleveland. The game started ugly as running back Tim Manoa fumbled on the first play. That was followed by fumbles after the catch by receivers Reggie Langhorne and Clarence Weathers and a late second quarter interception.

At halftime, the Browns' execs with Art in the owner's booth felt embarrassment, indignation, rage, and a host of other unpleasant feelings. Why bother playing the second half? Why can't we beat Denver? Why do we keep beating ourselves? How can five other teams manage to beat Denver and Elway this year, while Cleveland, picked by many to represent the AFC in the Super Bowl, gets annihilated in just two quarters? The rage was directed, fairly or unfairly, at the head coach, as usually happens in professional sports. The focus turned to Schottenheimer's ability as offensive coordinator.

The Browns managed only seven points against Denver, a team that had just surrendered 55, 39 and 42 points to the Colts, Steelers, and Saints, respectively. We had to wonder what had happened to the prolific offense the Browns had possessed only a year earlier under Lindy Infante. After all, the core of skill players was intact, and except for the center position, this was the same offense as in 1987.

After the game the mood around the team busses was, as one might expect, not very good. Modell was waiting for the coach, as he expected answers for the miserable team performance. People standing nearby saw Ernie Accorsi go over to Marty and ask him to see Art before the busses left for the airport. Marty indicated that he would as soon as he took care of some business, but no one ever saw Marty and Art meet. From then on, whispers began among those close to Art referring to "the snub" by Marty.

Modell publicly expressed his unhappiness with the poor pass protection being afforded Bernie Kosar. He said he didn't want to see him injured a second time, especially since he still had hopes the team could pull it together down the home stretch. About the same time, Marty went public in a Q & A forum with *Browns New Illustrated* editors. On the subject of his role as offensive coordinator, he said he enjoyed the challenge, and he stated he would remain the offensive coordinator as long as he was with the Browns. Naturally this statement was relayed to Art. It was not a thing for Marty to have stated so strongly when it appeared to anyone viewing recent games that the offense was clearly not in sync.

Another tantalizing script was also being written. As the season was winding down, some media representatives claimed that they heard a Browns' executive say that Marty would not be back with the team in 1989 unless he got them to the Super Bowl.

The front office of Modell, Accorsi, and Bailey seemed to be on edge for the rest of the season. The team was not playing well but did manage to get into the playoffs to face the Houston Oilers at home. Because of continuing injuries, Don Strock was slated to be the starting quarterback for that game.

While the team was supposedly pulling together in preparation for the game against a dangerous Oiler squad, unpleasant rumors were circulating. Published reports from unidentified offensive linemen indicated some displeasure with quarterback Bernie Kosar. The extremely high number of sacks made the offensive line (and its coach Howard Mudd) look incompetent. The linemen, however, felt that Kosar was holding the ball longer than he had in prior years because he was looking to go deep more often. Other players were openly complaining that their talents were not being recognized and/or utilized by the coaches. Art Modell was saying that an overhaul might be forthcoming, and several coaches were feeling vulnerable. The fans generally put all that aside and were looking forward to the playoffs even though they knew the team would start without Kosar, Kevin Mack, and Hanford Dixon, all out with injuries.

Losing by a 24-23 count that day marked the earliest exit from the playoffs in Schottenheimer's four years as head coach, and it came the year the Browns were picked to go all the way. Marty, though, did not blame the injuries, although he had lost five starting quarterbacks to injuries throughout that strange season, and both Frank Minnifield and Hanford Dixon in the post-season game. He also refused to blame the officials for some strange calls that certainly could have adversely impacted the outcome of the game. Nor did he mention that Byner's two back-to-back 15-yard penalties in the second half, due to what some felt was Byner's overzealousness, may have taken the Browns out of field goal range. No. Marty could have, but he did not mention any of those as excuses.

In fact, according to some players, Marty was not his usual self that day. He showed less reaction than usual to the questionable calls. Also missing was his typical sidelines feistiness. The players were wondering whether something major was brewing.

The strange 1988 season came to a close on December 24. Modell was uncharacteristically quiet during the season, but his displeasure was evident as the season progressed. He had commented to Jeff Schudel of the *News-Herald* just prior to year's end:

To say that the entire coaching staff will remain intact going into 1989 would be misleading....the organization will not preserve the status quo for 1989. I try not to disturb matters during the season because you can't do it during the season. Now it's my ballgame. I'm going to run my ballgame. I'm the owner, coach, president, general manager and trainer.

That was strong language from Art, and at that time of the year, it was obvious he was sending a message. For those of us who recognized some of his select phrases, and maybe more importantly the inflection that went along with them, we knew that Art had had it!

It was a matter of who would be included in the housecleaning. The usual sign was that the victim-to-be was closed out of close personal dialogue with Art. Art was still talking to Ernie Accorsi, and both still appeared to be on friendly terms. In my mind, Ernie was safe, and if the issue of poor draft selections was one of the cards on the table, Ernie was not going to take the heat for that. After all, Ernie had concurred with Art in the selection of Michael Dean Perry, the one, maybe the only one, of the early draft picks in the last two years, who showed signs of emerging as a notable player.

Some doubted Art would make any significant changes. They believed those comments were just Art's way of issuing a warning. After all, the Browns were the only AFC team to advance to the playoffs in four straight years. Marty Schottenheimer was the coach for those same years, so how could the owner even think of firing someone with that kind of record?

Still, the message was coming through in what Art said about it being his team, that he was this and he was that. What this meant was that Marty had gained too much control. So we felt a showdown of sorts was in the making, pitting owner vs. winning head coach. We did not believe that Marty could think he could win this matchup, if in fact that is what it turned out to be.

The four straight post-season playoff games could be overlooked because that success could be attributed to the presence of Bernie Kosar, Modell's chosen leader to get the team to the Super Bowl eventually. Since Browns' management would never accept injuries as an alibi, it wouldn't be mentioned that Kosar, Slaughter, and Mack had only been on the field together for the very first quarter of the first game of the year. Injuries had plagued one, two, or all three of these players during every game in 1988.

Something more trivial—at least it would seem trivial in comparison to the significant things that happened on the field that year—had begun to fracture Marty's relationship with Art. It splintered around the time Marty received his contract renewal offer from Art some time earlier. Modell called Marty in and presented him with what he perceived as a very generous contract extension, a reward for his demonstrated success with the team after replacing Sam Rutigliano. Marty's "mistake" may have occurred when, instead of accepting the contract on the spot with an expression of gratitude, he told Art that he would take it home and "mull it over." I learned that the phrase "mull it over" had stuck in Art's craw. "What's to mull over?" Art asked his aides. There wouldn't be any negotiation, since this was an offer to extend his contract at an increased salary, a gift from the owner. Even though Marty eventually accepted the contract extension, insiders felt Art's view of Schottenheimer was never the same after that. After the details of this meeting seeped out among the front office staff, it became commonplace to use the term "mull it over" in lieu of "reflect" or "think about." More than once we overheard Modell tell Jim Bailey that something was being "mulled over." Those words were delivered with a special inflection, and sometimes a slight sneer.

It was December 27, the first work day after the loss to Houston, when Marty came down for a meeting with Art, Accorsi, and Bailey. Art initiated the meeting by giving a list of changes he wanted for the 1989 season. The program was lengthier than Marty probably had expected, and Marty asked to be excused after the meeting. He promised to call back two hours later. He obviously had to "mull over" the list of requests which Art had made, which included the following:

1)   several assistant coach reassignments,
2)   the hiring of an offensive coordinator, and
3)   the firing of several assistant coaches.

When Marty called back, he stated that he could not accept these conditions. At that point both men understood the situation had become irreconcilable, and later they both described Marty's termination /resignation in that way.

It was rumored that Art had asked Marty to re-assign brother Kurt to the scouting department and hire a new special teams coach. Art supposedly told Marty that Kurt would not have to take a cut in pay, even though scouts normally are compensated at a lower rate than coaches. Art as usual was generous in matters of compensation when handling personnel matters. The other issue the two men couldn't agree on, and what led to the "irreconcilable differences" was: Who should have the final say on the selection of assistant coaches: the head coach who had to work with the assistants, or the owner, who pays the individual and who as owner should have the final say on almost anything he wants to.

Judging by Art's comments after the meeting, it sounded like the major point of disagreement centered on Art's wanting Marty to give up the role of offensive coordinator. Art explained to Marty that even though he was originally in favor of Marty taking on both roles, the team needed Marty's attention on all phases of the game, and hiring a coordinator would allow Marty the opportunity to reassume that kind of leadership. Marty contended that bringing in a new offensive coordinator would be a step backward.

Soon after the press conference announcing that Marty would not be back as head coach in 1989, Art announced that Ernie Accorsi would be in total charge of the draft, that he would supervise all scouts, and would come up with the recommendations of the players to be drafted. Art went on to point out that several things that had occurred with Marty in 1987 and 1988 would no longer be permitted. In other words, there was to be no interference from the head coach at the draft. Art also questioned the timing of the trade of Mike Baab which occurred the week of the season opener. Art hinted that Rakoczy probably did not have enough time to develop the chemistry with the more veteran offensive linemen, and this could have impacted the teamwork on the line for the whole season. Another coaching era in Cleveland Browns' history thus came to an end.

The Browns' most successful head coach since Blanton Collier (and the only Browns' coach with a winning record since Nick Skorich) was rumored to be leaning toward taking a job with either the Kansas City Chiefs or the San Diego Chargers. As for Art, he seemed tired, extremely disappointed with the season, but apparently relieved that a situation which he had found untenable, was finally resolved. Art could not accept having his authority as owner and president questioned. While Art would accept suggestions, timing was important in determining how far to push them. Whenever one crossed Modell's line, even though he might never know he had done it, there was no turning back. With Marty, some say that "mulling over" the contract offer was where the line had been reached. Whether Marty crossed over that day only Modell knows for sure. Others say the line was crossed in the Denver parking lot, at the meeting near the team busses that never took place.

MARTY DEPARTS
Irreconcilable differences were stated as the reason.
Browns News Illustrated

CHAPTER 10

STADIUM PLANS STYMIED

Art Modell shifted his attention back and forth between his companies quite readily. He liked the hustle and bustle of switching subjects, and as long as progress was being made toward his final goal, he stayed on an even keel. He'd like to start off on an entirely new subject by saying, "OK, now where are we on this?"

The pattern that Art followed between football seasons was pretty predictable. After the football season ended, he was off to the Super Bowl, unless he had just terminated a head coach. He did not make an appearance those years, choosing to lay low. Instead he would send his associates, and more than likely his son David.

Upon returning from the Super Bowl, Art usually crammed any lingering business matters into the first two weeks of February, and then he was off to a lengthy winter getaway, either to Beverly Hills or to West Palm Beach. He would then leave from his vacation spot to go to the NFL meetings in mid-March for the week, where he would catch up on business with Jim Bailey, Ernie Accorsi, and Kevin Byrne. He would return to Cleveland for the opening day of baseball and view the game from his loge box 8A, which sat on the 50-yard line for football, but for baseball, was positioned directly above the right field foul pole. If a fly ball landed in his loge, it could be either a foul ball or a home run, depending on where it landed. The baseball foul line, if extended into the seating area, would literally go right through the middle of his compartment.

Art also used this visit to give the Stadium's condition a once-over, checking for things that he felt had been overlooked. If he found something not to his liking, he would threaten, "Heads are going to roll..." Away since the middle of February and in tropical weather, he sometimes lost sight of the fact that we continued to have winter conditions in Cleveland. I remember one year when he challenged Larry Staverman as to why the right field wall hadn't been repainted in our traditional Stadium blue for Opening Day. Art always wanted to open a new baseball season with fresh paint everywhere. The operations director had to tell him that we couldn't apply paint over the coat of ice remaining on the frozen wall.

If the Indians were looking like potential contenders, Art made it a point to attend several games in opening week, but his primary focus was on the upcoming football draft in the last week of April. Then rookie camp or "meet the rookies" week followed in early May. There may or may not have been a mini-camp in early June, depending on the coach, but for the most part June was the vacation month for coaches, and they did not return until about July 10th. So, football went on vacation, and Art turned his attention to Cleveland Stadium Corp. for the better part of May and all of June. During this six-week period we could always count on being asked for an updated profit projection, for how many houses we had sold, or what new streets we had added to our Strongsville development.

Cash flow was picking up, due in large part to stronger attendance, and with the loan retirement program back on schedule, the prospect of a record year of profits loomed on the horizon. As we had learned before, however, good times are usually tempered by troubles.

In 1987 the scoreboard albatross returned. We once again began to experience frequent scoreboard failures, and we discovered that our scoreboard had become technologically obsolete. Replacement parts were no longer readily available. We were beginning to think we would have to install a new scoreboard and invest more into the Stadium than originally planned.

Ever the optimist, Art was hoping that the Indians' ownership (not to mention the City of Cleveland) would be encouraged by Stadium Corp's willingness to continue making capital improvements, even though we had long ago fulfilled our initial $10 million commitment. During the late 1980's, we still were hoping to sign the Indians to a long-term lease in order to be in a financial position to continue upgrading the Stadium.

Over the course of several weeks of discussions, we began to formulate plans for a new scoreboard. With all the difficulty we experienced constructing the first board internally, prudence dictated that we do what every other stadium did and hire professionals, which also meant a higher price tag. Regardless of the cost, a second scoreboard was certainly not something for which we had budgeted in our initial capital improvement plan.

Art's opinion was that if we were going to replace the board, we might as well add a video screen similar to those that had been added in other stadiums. Art had formed the habit of listening to some of the sports radio call-in shows that proliferated in the Cleveland market, and he often remarked about how many callers griped about not having a video board in Cleveland, why other stadiums could have one while our fans were being deprived, blah, blah, blah.

We therefore began to research those types of boards. Advertising dollars had to be adequate to liquidate the board's cost, plus the interest thereon, or most scoreboards were not afforable. As we set out to benchmark other operations, that issue remained foremost in our minds.

Wading bravely into our sea of unanswered questions, we began traveling the country, visiting Atlanta's Fulton County Stadium and Miami's brand-new Joe Robbie Stadium, sites of the most recent installations. We also spent a lot of time in the New Jersey Meadowlands, learning the characteristics of the board in the stadium the New York Giants and Jets shared. Over time, we began to eliminate some types of companies from consideration. Eventually we settled on the Whiteway Corporation in Chicago.

Art started talking about making the new video scoreboard the centerpiece of a much larger improvement program, expanded to include locker room renovations and the installation of concourse television screens for fans waiting in line at the concession stands or rest rooms (our concessionaire, ServiceAmerica, had implored us to consider doing this, as fans often became ornery when they missed significant portions of the game while waiting in the food and beverage lines).

As he was devising his renovation plans, Art took time to walk the entire Stadium. Sitting in the top row of the lower deck seats, he realized that the fans' view would be obstructed by the proposed auxiliary scoreboards that would hang from the facade of the loges. He immediately ordered Whiteway to develop a quotation for installing 35-inch televisions, one every three sections, throughout the entire lower deck. The televisions would give fans the opportunity to watch instant replays from the network broadcasts.

Watching Art get caught up in his improvement plans, I understood how tired he was of negative comments about Cleveland Stadium. He wanted fans in the lower-priced seats and those stuck in lines on the concourse to have the same access to the game as those in the loges. Perhaps most of all, he was tired of the media's negative comments about the locker rooms. In what had become an annual ritual, Jerry Glanville, head coach of division rival Houston Oilers, would spout off about the poor conditions in the visiting team dressing quarters at Cleveland Stadium, saying, "The locker room walls don't even have a nail to hang your coat on."

Not everyone agreed with Art on the locker room issue, though. Ernie Accorsi was among those who felt that small visiting team rooms were part of Cleveland's home field advantage. Ernie felt that the more uncomfortable the visiting team was, the better. When the Browns came from way behind in the 1988 season finale to defeat the Oilers at the Stadium and force a home wild card rematch, a member of our maintenance staff sneaked into the visitor's locker room between games and pounded a nail into the wall. In black magic marker, he wrote, "Hang it here, Jerry."

When Whiteway finally delivered its quote on the entire project, aforementioned extras included, the tab totaled $4.6 million, minus the video screen. I had the responsibility of developing a cash projection to ensure Art that we could pay off the investment by the end of the ten-year lease, given our revenue estimates of scoreboard advertising. My calculations confirmed that if we could realize the same advertising revenues that cigarette, beer, and soft drink companies were paying in other NFL stadiums, then we could pay off the board, minus the video screen, within the allotted period. At that time, we could not afford to siphon any other revenue sources for this new project, since every dollar in place was necessary to pay off the original improvement loan. Encouraged by my response, Art issued two directives.

The first was to try for the top-of-the-line scoreboard. Why not, he asked, go for the video replay board right away? He wanted to know how much more it would cost and how much more in advertising dollars we could expect to generate because ads would be surrounding a huge television screen, along with game-in-process data and constantly changing statistics. He turned this project over to Jim Bailey, John Minco, and me.

The second directive was in response to an earlier caveat from Jim Bailey. "Remember," Bailey had warned, "that any changes to the exterior of the building or new installations on Stadium grounds must receive city approval." Bailey was assigned this task, which we all perceived to be merely a perfunctory step in the whole process. We would later realize that dealings with the City of Cleveland were never as simple as we might have hoped.

While Bailey was awaiting a response from the city, he, Minco, and I went to work to quantify our projected advertising revenue increases. After several days, Whiteway submitted a revised quote to include the video board, and we quickly learned that video boards were pretty damn expensive--$3 million! That boosted Whiteway's tab for the entire project to a total of $7.5 million.

Armed with the new particulars, I began some calculations. Simple economics painted a fairly bleak picture: given only ten years to pay off the entire scoreboard, we would need $300,000 more in annual revenue simply to pay the additional loan principal, plus up to $250,000 more for interest (assuming a rate of 10%) in the early years, plus maintenance costs in later years when the inevitable repairs would be required. Altogether our total annual cost to liquidate the borrowing for the video screen alone came to approximately $550,000.

Meanwhile, Minco had contacted several advertisers about upping their current contract value a notch or two. He found that a typical advertiser who previously might have paid $150,000 for an ad might stretch to $175,000 with the new board, but most said they would have a hard time justifying any increase. All told, Minco figured that we might be able to generate a maximum increase of $100,000 in advertising revenues, and even that, he said, was a stretch. It was a far cry from the $550,000 we needed.

Art Modell had sure financial instincts; he was quick to capture the essence of any deal. So even though he had sent me back to calculate the specifics, I think he knew before I left his office that the answer could hardly come back positive. Art was never difficult to read. Typically an optimist who exuded a contagious enthusiasm to rally more pragmatic types like me, his hesitations were also easy to discern.

When I reported to him with the news, I was essentially telling him what he had already guessed. Bailey and I assured him that we definitely needed to do something, since maintenance on the present board was starting to increase. I told him that we probably would be lucky to survive the 1988 season without an embarrassing mid-game scoreboard failure. Disappointed, but by no means resigned to failure, we sat on the deal for a few days. We had already established we couldn't fund the new scoreboard with a video board included. Without some creative thinking, our new scoreboard would never become a reality. As Bailey and I relayed the disappointing information to Art, I could sense he had already started to formulate plan B.

And so he had. Modell told us that he intended to present the scoreboard renovation as part of a $10 million capital improvement program which would include a $1 million locker room renovation (apparently to appease Jerry Glanville and the rest of the NFL) and public restroom expansion and renovation ($1.5 million), along with the $7.5 million scoreboard.

The restroom renovation, not unlike the locker room project, was more in response to a problem of perception than function. Granted, the bathrooms were old (the toilets and urinals were mostly of original vintage, with parts replaced as needed), but they were always 100% functional at the beginning of every game; our maintenance staff made damn sure of that. Problems would start when some idiot would try to flush a (take your choice) diaper, apple, sanitary napkin, roll of toilet paper, or stack of paper towels down the toilet. Many times our maintenance staff would respond to a distress call during a game, enter a men's restroom, and find fans standing in an one-inch-deep mix of water and urine, only to find that the cause of the problem was a paper cup that a fan had strategically placed over the drain in a urinal trough.

Although we could never comprehend the thought process behind such actions (we usually attributed it to stupidity), the public perception of restroom problems demanded our attention. We hoped that Mayor Voinovich would see it through our eyes. Most of us, especially Ernie Accorsi, were less enthusiastic about the visiting team locker room renovation, but if that's what Art wanted, we would forge ahead with his plan.

And so onward we went. Art, Jim, and I carefully reviewed the economics of the proposal which Art wanted to fund privately, asking nothing from the city except a ten-year extension to the lease. If the prime rate would stay in the moderate range (around 6 to 9 percent) and if the Indians would stay put through 1998, we would be able to retire our original borrowings.

We did not, however, see how we could generate enough additional revenues to retire an additional $10 million loan--unless, that is, the city would give us ten years beyond the existing lease to continue operating the Stadium. The reason was very simple: of the three phases included in the renovation program, two were non-revenue producers. Fans using renovated bathrooms were not going to generate any new money, nor was the visiting teams' use of a new locker room. After the three of us had discussed the plan, Art asked Jim and me, "Isn't what we are proposing a win-win for both sides?"

We certainly thought so. City officials recently had acknowledged that the current lease was one of the best in professional sports, so granting a ten-year extension to 2008 would seem to have been mutually beneficial. The key points of the proposal were:

1)   Stadium Corp. would fund the program ($10 million); the city pays nothing;

2)   Like all of the previous improvements that we had made, the city would get title to all the improvements at the expiration of the lease; and

3)   All the city had to do was grant a ten-year extension to the present lease, assuring the continuation of this income to the year 2008.

Art felt certain the city would approve our proposal immediately. All of the economic risk fell entirely on his shoulders, but as an eternal optimist, he felt no apprehension about this whatsoever.

Whiteway in the meantime was designing the basic scoreboard so that a video section could be added at a later date. Four of the nine sections of the message center could be removed to make room for the video This flexible plan enabled Whiteway to begin work on the board even before we would hear from the city.

Confident despite the lack of certainty regarding our payback abilities, Art decided to move with what we had. On September 1, 1987, we made arrangements to deliver our proposal to George Forbes, city council president. Art had asked Forbes to evaluate the likelihood of the city's accepting our proposal, that it was also a matter of some urgency since our scoreboard was failing fast. Whiteway would hold its quote for only so long, and architects were already designing improvements to the restrooms. Forbes told Art he would handle the matter directly with Ed Richard, who presumably would advise Mayor Voinovich.

Richard completed his review fairly quickly and advised Art that negotiations could start immediately. While Art was somewhat miffed that we did not receive immediate approval, he directed Jim Bailey to drop everything else and attend to this matter. Art wanted quick approval from city council. Then he wanted to draft the papers, sign off on the obligatory lease amendments, and immediately begin construction.

Discussions, however, did not move quickly. Over the next seven months, Bailey and Richard met many times to hammer out the lease specifics. The city was asking for concessions. Among other things, it was asking for higher rentals during the ten-year extension period and, interestingly enough, a $10 million penalty payable by the Browns should they ever leave the city. The city also asked to receive the use of a Stadium loge. There was one last but very important item from the city's standpoint. The city asked Art for his promise to work toward a new stadium. (Art privately indicated that the way things moved in Cleveland that it could be ten years before any new stadium was built, and the present stadium sure needed work in the meantime.)

Art also knew that the key issue was keeping the Indians in town. The baseball club wanted its own intimate ballpark, fashioned after Boston's Fenway Park, not one shared with pro football. Baseball purists consider baseball fields sacred; neither football cleats nor concert stages should ever set foot thereon. Indians' officials were making this need ever clearer. At the time, a note in Chuck Heaton's OFF THE CUFF column quoted Hank Peters, "This is just my personal opinion but long range, we (the Indians) should have a park for baseball only. The size (of the present stadium), general atmosphere and playing conditions are somewhat of a detriment to us."

Bailey duly transmitted all of the city's requests to Modell, and he acceded to them. All that seemed to be left to finalize this deal was council approval. On May 21, 1988, the *Plain Dealer* reported that Voinovich, Richard, and Modell were all in agreement on extending the Stadium Corp. lease.

On September 6, 1988, almost a year after the initial proposal had been aired, the *Plain Dealer* reported that council was reviewing two major proposals: the stadium lease extension request and a tax abatement request presented by the Jacobs brothers for a second downtown hotel and office complex. That being an election year, and politics being politics, the *Plain Dealer* speculated that nothing much would happen on either of these proposals until after the November 8 election. The newspaper added that Modell's lease extension to 2008, and possibly even to 2018, didn't sit well with some leaders of North Coast Development Corp., planners for the North Coast Harbor, which had aspirations to use Stadium land for housing.

When Art read this, he shouted to Bailey and me, "Well, the city will just have to decide whether it wants the Cleveland Browns or more housing, I guess. With all the land available for housing in the city, why do they have to build on our 17 acres?"

The *Plain Dealer* ran a lead editorial soon thereafter, entitled, THE BROWNS' DEFENSIVE LINE, challenging Modell's position on the lease extension request and his tactics, referring to his original 25-year lease in the editorial as a "sweetheart deal" and questioning his right to recoup money lost from the eventual move of the Indians. Art couldn't understand why the PD had reversed its position from four years earlier. Art bristled over the reference to his "sweetheart deal." Back in July 1973, both newspapers in town (at that time the Cleveland *Press* was still operating) had run editorials applauding the proposed lease as "good news" and "a fair deal" for the Stadium. Fifteen years later, Art was no longer getting support from the city's only newspaper. It now saw his lease differently, and Art knew that could be devastating down the road.

On Sept. 13, 1988, the smaller Lake County *News-Herald*, the paper which serviced Modell's Waite Hill and surrounding eastern communities, reported that George Forbes feared Modell might move the Browns if he did not get his lease extension request. Modell told the reporter, "I have to look out for my own interests and realize the value an NFL franchise has to some communities who don't have one." He said any agreement to move the Indians from the Stadium should have a mechanism to compensate Stadium Corp. for the loss of its tenant. He also lamented the delay. He thought a deal had been reached with the mayor a year earlier and was surprised the lease request had become "mired down" in council.

As to a dual-purpose stadium, Modell again explained that dual tenancy didn't seem to work anywhere, and probably wouldn't work in this case either, since this was the point constantly made by the Indians for wanting their own ballpark. "You just can't design a stadium to fit the needs of both teams' fans, i.e., sight lines are different, schedules overlap, etc.etc.," Modell said.

It looked like no one but Modell and Stadium Corp. management felt the lease extension made sense. Apparently, Mayor Voinovich didn't feel strongly enough to fight council and bring the matter to resolution. Apparently council didn't see the benefits to the extension, nor did the leaders of the North Coast Development Corp. The *Plain Dealer* thought that of all the options available, renovating an aging stadium made the least sense of all.

Despite the fact that we had conceded practically everything the city wanted, council still had not acted. Art and the rest of us were both shocked and disappointed. How could council not act? It made no sense to us.

Deep down inside, though, I could tell that Modell's mind was not on the scoreboard. He knew something was terribly wrong. Despite the fans' love affair with the team, the politicians seemed to have taken an entirely different view of both the Browns and the Stadium Corporation's efforts. We thought it strange. Any other city would love to have a major sports tenant invest its own money in a public sports complex, but Cleveland apparently wanted no part of it. What had happened, we wondered? Jim Bailey concluded that plans were being developed for the lakefront that would extend farther west of the Inner Harbor and which did not include the Stadium on that land beyond 1998.

Approximately two weeks after the termination of Marty Schottenheimer, on February 6, 1989, Art Modell, through Jim Bailey, quietly withdrew his bid for the 10-year lease extension. The city had begun its review of the proposal in September 1987, but 17 months later there still had been no word. Modell quite frankly got tired of waiting.

Art told the *Plain Dealer* on January 14 that he had learned of behind-the-scenes maneuverings by some politicians and certain business lobbies to kill the lease extension. Apparently they feared it would foil plans for the proposed new downtown stadium. Modell felt that if the mayor truly thought the extension was good for the city, as he had expressed publicly, then he would have exerted the necessary leadership with the council to get it passed. We came to believe that at best the mayor was lukewarm to the proposal.

Art was not going to beg city council for the "privilege" of borrowing $10 million to create an additional debt burden. If the city politicos couldn't see this was a "win-win-win" situation (besides Stadium Corp. and the city, Art viewed the fans as winners because they would benefit from the video board and renovated bathrooms), Art said that maybe this city wasn't smart enough to get out of its own way.

Daily I heard comments about the lease extension from typical Cleveland sports fans who were obsessed with what Art Modell was getting out of it. Such was the anti-Modell mindset that existed among many Clevelanders. They wouldn't believe the lease extension could be a win-win situation. If Modell would come out as one of the winners, then the plan was no good.

Local writer Roldo Bartimole possessed the same thinking and constantly ripped Modell for no reason other than having become wealthy through his ownership of the Browns and his operation of Cleveland Stadium. While Roldo ripped most politicians, major corporations, and business leaders, Art Modell was a favorite target. Roldo took Modell on for his lease extension request. He called it one big ripoff. That came as no surprise because Roldo still thought the original lease was wrong. While Roldo criticized Modell for the revenues he earned through Cleveland Stadium Corp., never once to our knowledge did he credit Modell for the benefits the city received under the lease. I knew those benefits were substantial.

In many ways, the entire Cleveland Stadium Corp. venture had been a headache for Modell, going back to the difficult negotiations in 1972-1973. In hindsight, what probably had made the original process so difficult was the pressure the city fathers felt over the potential perception that the city was giving away a public asset to a private business interest. Some of that worry was probably still in place 16 years later.

Modell had lived under the strain of the personal guarantee required as part of his original $10 million loan. In 1987, when the personal guarantee was finally removed, Art felt like a man released from bondage. For the first time in 12 years he was free from having his personal assets tied up indefinitely. When the city failed to respond to his lease extension offer, it meant he did not have to borrow and become liable for another $10 million. As bank loans on the Browns were then starting to escalate, maybe it was the wiser course to save his borrowing power for other things.

In an interview Modell explained:

The forces working against us, in their own perception, were well-intentioned. Some people thought that if I got that extension or option to extend I would have no interest whatsoever in discussing the new stadium at Central Market, even though I committed in writing to the mayor and everyone involved that it would not discourage me at all from discussing any viable plan.

Mayor Voinovich declined further comment on the matter, saying only that he thought Modell's plan was fair to the city.

Modell added, "Some of the corporations in town got involved...the Cleveland Tomorrow group...and we found ourselves negotiating with the law departments of major corporations, instead of City Hall, on the lease extension." Modell said some political and business leaders, whom he refused to name, were "busily at work to kill the legislation. That's why this was delayed and delayed and delayed." The *Plain Dealer* reported that there was never even a single council committee hearing on the ordinance. Finally, Modell made clear his views about the Browns' facility needs:

The only facility that we will be interested in talking about at the Central Market would be a TWIN (emphasis added) facility....a smaller facility for baseball and a larger one for football. We have a dual purpose one now. Why should we move? I am happy with the Browns' occupancy of the stadium. Obviously, Dick Jacobs (Indians' co-owner) is not. And I am urging that the city and county direct their efforts toward accommodating his needs for a smaller baseball-only grass facility. If the developers cannot do a twin complex, then they should concentrate on baseball, and maybe an arena....Should the community end up building a baseball-only stadium for the Indians, I expect the city fathers and powers that be to give Cleveland Stadium Corp. some help to keep this place going absent a baseball tenant."

The reporter asked him how much that would be?

Modell said, "In the neighborhood of $1 million a year, which would be a pittance compared to what a football facility would cost to build."

Modell was then asked if he would move the team elsewhere if he did not receive what he wanted.

Modell answered, "I've never threatened to do that as long as I've been in Cleveland. I'm not looking at that option right now. I dread the prospect of being made to look at that option. I just don't think the city fathers would treat us in that fashion. I hope not."

That was the first time I heard Art express any doubt that he would be compensated for the loss of the Indians. Over the years Art had thoroughly discussed the matter with George Forbes. Art reported that Forbes had always told him that he needn't worry. The city would do what was right for him. Bailey and I often told Art that he could count on whatever Forbes had told him, at least as long as Forbes remained in a position of power.

In 1988, the loss of the Indians would have meant $1 million in lost revenues annually, the amount that Modell specified at that time. Seven years later that compensation might have bought the Browns one starting offensive lineman. Then again, it might not. That was just how chaotic the economics of the professional sports scene had become.

While the rejection by the city and the so-called "powers-to-be" (whoever they were) was upsetting to Art, he nevertheless proceeded with the completion of the scoreboard project. With the Browns coming off two consecutive outstanding seasons and Super Bowl fever running rampant throughout Cleveland, Art did not want to dwell on the negatives of lease failures. We tried to put it behind us, and so we quickly turned our attention to formulating an alternate plan with Whiteway for the scoreboard minus the video display.

It had also become time to "freshen up" the loges with a $500,000 undertaking, as new carpeting, decoration, and reupholstery was badly needed. Before the new look could be added, all the steel plates under the old carpeting had to be sandblasted and primered, as substantial rust had begun gathering during the 13 years that the old carpeting had been down. Sometimes we would forget that ours was an outdoor stadium, situated on the lakefront. Even though the loges were enclosed, the loge balconies and the undersides of the living compartments were made of steel and exposed to the elements.

Art didn't care about rust, or the lakefront, or the Indians, for that matter, just then. All he told me one particular day was that after he spent this $5 million in 1989, he wanted a moratorium on all capital improvements until he could figure what direction things were headed. At that moment, Art did not want to hear about the other needed repairs which we already had on the drawing board.

Whiteway installed the new board, complete with a redesigned sound system, on time. It functioned almost perfectly, demanding very little repair or maintenance. The new board was operational by the Indians' Opening Day, 1989.

Looking back on it, I realize now that City Council's inaction on our lease extension proposal would prove to be the beginning of the end of the Cleveland Browns as we knew them.

While performing a test run of the new scoreboard on April 1, 1989, the computer operators found time to pray. *Tony Dejak, AP Photo*

Laventhol & Horwath
Certified Public Accountants

National City Center
1900 East 9th Street
Cleveland, Ohio 44114
(216) 696-4770

The Honorable George Forbes
President of Council
Cleveland City Council
219 City Hall
Cleveland, Ohio 44114

Dear Mr. Forbes:

Pursuant to your request and based on available pertinent data, we have prepared this report summarizing our findings and conclusions regarding the lease between the City of Cleveland and the Cleveland Stadium Corporation.

The scope of our work is explained in the various sections of this report. Information for our study was made available by the City of Cleveland (Finance Department and Convention Center - Fiscal Department) as well as the Cleveland Stadium Corporation.

Based on our analysis, it should be noted that the City of Cleveland generates a sub<u>stan</u>tial cash benefit from the stadium lease arrangements.

We sincerely appreciate the continued confidence that City Council has shown in our firm and the courtesy and cooperation extended to us by employees of the City of Cleveland and the Cleveland Stadium Corporation.

Laventhol & Horwath

December 5, 1988

A member of Horwath & Horwath International with affiliated offices worldwide.

By 1988, 13 years after the Stadium Corp. was formed, a fourth analysis of the stadium lease had been prepared - - each one showed increasingly more cash benefits accruing to the city. In spite of the lucrative arrangement, city council saw no merit to extending Modell's lease by another 10 years. *Cleveland Stadium Corp.*

CHAPTER 11
THE SHORT REIGN
OF BUD CARSON

I could not help but feel the stress as the calendar page turned and 1989 opened. Terminating Marty Schottenheimer had been stressful for Art Modell. He tended to see his organizations as extended families, and for Art the termination of an executive was as gut-wrenching as divorce proceedings could be. A dismissal became easier if he could find clear evidence of some kind of outright wrongdoing, but there was nothing like that in the Schottenheimer decision.

Actually the tensions that were taking their toll on the chief and which permeated the Stadium Tower B offices had begun early in the season. The ups and downs of the 1988 campaign only compounded the stress load. Since the Browns had been pegged to go to the Super Bowl, the impact of these swings of fortune was further exacerbated by those early expectations.

Some of the stress Modell was feeling went back two years. The back-to-back Denver playoff losses still gnawed at him. Then, of course, on top of the Denver disappointments were the back-to-back first-round draft failures and the rift between his head coach and head of football operations over who had authority to make the final choice in the draft room.

The lack of peace on the NFL labor front was also constantly on Modell's mind. He worried that if the free agency advocates prevailed, the NFL would face ultimate ruination. Nor had all the problems behind the strike of 1987 been resolved. Since he felt he had always been more than fair to his players, he needed to constantly reassure himself that his Browns had walked out only because a show of league unity had been required. He believed strongly that most players had not wanted to strike and that if they could have voted by secret ballot, the majority would have been against the work stoppage. Art was convinced that the union required an open vote so that each player would be pressured to support the its position.

Modell was also troubled by the damage to the playing field caused by the Pink Floyd and U2 concerts. When we watched the 1987 Browns' highlight film in spring of 1988, it delivered a sharp reminder of how horrible the field had looked. Since much of the film focused on whipping the Steelers (always good footage) in the Browns' opener, we also got repetitive views of the torn-up tundra, reminding us of the price required to keep the Stadium operation viable. Art knew we needed the concert revenues, but he was unwilling to risk further damage to the playing field for football, and more importantly, for baseball. That was why he had turned down an opportunity to host a Van Halen concert in 1988.

Art was then still hopeful that the Indians would sign a long-term lease, and he didn't want to create any animosity over field damage with Indians' ownership. As it was, the Indians were already sharing in all Stadium Corp. rock concert rentals by virtue of their lease with the Stadium Corp. which was then being renewed on an annual basis. But deriving revenues from the Stadium Corp.'s shows didn't seem to appease the team when field damage was concerned.

Art was hoping to show Dick and Dave Jacobs his readiness to invest additional money in the Stadium to provide Cleveland sports fans with an array of betterments and improvements. Modell believed that in Cleveland the only way things got done was for the private sector to spend its own money. That was why he was willing to risk further debt with his lease-extension offer to the city.

Art and the Browns' front office knew they had to get busy on the football front. The Browns were without a head coach, and a decision in this matter had to be made soon. It was disconcerting to Browns' followers, and I presume to Art also, that the Browns were going to be led by their third head coach in six years, a situation most organizations would view as a sign of dangerous instability. Art often said that he preferred continuity over change, but if he felt change was absolutely necessary, then change it was. Stability in top positions enhances a team's chances of winning championships because philosophies, systems, and directions don't change significantly. Changing a head coach often affects the types of players used, drafted, and released, and as a result of too many coaching changes a team can find itself in a constant state of flux.

As far as changes in the team's general manager were concerned, there were none since that title was always held by Arthur B. Modell. "I act as my own general manager," he would often tell reporters. The late Armond Arnson, who represented Modell in several business deals, said, "Art operated almost with blinders on. He was focused on building his image. To Art Modell, image was everything, perception was everything. He wanted to be known as a very keen operator of the football team."

I had come to believe the real reason Art never hired a football G.M. was because he didn't want to compete with too strong an executive over the direction of the Browns. I can still recall a discussion in 1972 when Art was forced to relieve Bob Brodhead of his duties (Brodhead came the closest to acting as general manager with the Browns). In explaining the reason for asking Brodhead, once a fair-haired boy in the organization, to resign, Modell said simply, "I want someone who wants to work for Art Modell, not be Art Modell."

While Art had a good knowledge of all aspects of football, he needed to rely on other experienced voices within the organization. If he couldn't rely on his head coach as his primary confidant in football matters, he turned to his director of football operations. If he had no one in that slot, then he looked to the player personnel director. Unfortunately, the man in that slot also changed often. Bill Davis, Paul Warfield, Ricky Feacher, Chip Falivene, Ernie Accorsi, and Mike Lombardi all had a major voice in drafting and evaluating talent between 1984 and 1989. Having had three head coaches during this six-year span also contributed to divergent views as to the direction the Browns should be heading.

In 1989 the search for head coach actually moved quickly. Bud Carson was the front-runner as the Browns remembered him vividly from his years as defensive coordinator with the Steelers whom they had to face twice a year. During the last season his New York Jets' defense obliterated the Browns in the opening home game with a never-ending series of blitz calls.

Most of the interviews took place at Art Modell's Waite Hill home. The screening team included David Modell, Ernie Accorsi, and Jim Bailey, in whom Art had developed a tremendous confidence and who was included in virtually every meeting and team decision. Occasionally, Kevin Byrne, director of public relations, would join the huddle.

The Browns were leaning toward Carson, and they had asked him to come in for his third interview. Troubling some members of the screening team was that Bud Carson, at age 58, with years of successful coaching behind him and his defensive achievements a matter of public record, had never been selected as a head NFL coach before. Art, tired by recent events and frustrated at how the process was being dragged out, eventually instructed Accorsi to make the final decision.

It must have been the accumulation of all the tribulations of the prior months that finally caught up with the usually indefatigable Art Modell. The disappointing end to the 1988 season, the firing of another head coach, and what he regarded as a slap in the face from the politicians and corporate elite left him too depleted to continue the selection process. What had always been Arthur B. Modell's most important decision, selecting his head coach, he left to others.

Accorsi announced Bud Carson as his choice. Accorsi had known Carson from their days together with the Baltimore Colts. Accorsi was impressed with the way Carson handled his players. Accorsi said, "Bud made an impression on me that I won't forget. His knowledge of the game vastly exceeded the talent that we put on the field. His defensive schemes were always a few years ahead of time."

Actually, it is not really known how many coaching candidates were still available once the final round of interviews started. The front office had stipulated several conditions which the successful candidate would have to accept. Some of us close to, but not on, the inside felt the brain trust wanted to rectify all the problems they thought arose under the Schottenheimer regime. The front office had decided to hire an offensive coordinator first. A condition of employment for the head coach-to-be was to accept the coordinator. Another stipulation was that the head coach would not "interfere" with the college draft process.

Bud Carson with "sackmeister" John Teerlinck. *Browns News Illustrated*

The subject of the offensive coordinator became an important issue with the Browns' front office simply because all the final candidates were defensive-minded coaches, just as Schottenheimer had been. No one in the Browns' hierarchy wanted to risk having a defense-oriented head coach call offensive plays again. So Marc Trestman, though unproven as such, was promoted to the position of offensive coordinator; whoever was to become the next Browns' head coach had to accept that decision. The desire was to keep the offense intact, and the front office felt the Trestman/Kosar combination was the best bet to achieve that goal. Art and Ernie saw a rising star in Marc Trestman. Several people close to Art felt that because Bernie Kosar had a strong opinion of Trestman, Art's own positive opinion on the young coach had been fortified. Soon after, Modell went on record that Trestman would be head coaching material within three or four years.

Carson had ample time to interview Trestman and talk over football philosophies. In the end, Carson indicated he was comfortable that he and Trestman could work well together.

So on January 27, 1989, five days after San Francisco had edged Cincinnati in a 20-16 comeback victory in Super Bowl XXIII, Art Modell announced Leon (Bud) Carson as the next head coach of the Cleveland Browns. Modell said, "We are absolutely confident that Bud Carson is the right man to help us make the next step...I have never been involved in a more exhaustive search for a coach. We wanted to make sure that we studied the whole field, and when we did, Bud Carson became the clear-cut choice."

During the press conference, Modell went on to state that Ernie Accorsi would have complete control over the draft. When asked what Carson's role might be in the draft, Modell said:

He'll have a voice, and he'll be able to express himself as to what the team's priorities are. But we are convinced in the front office that we can only be successful at the draft table by having the scouts pick the players. Our scouts work nine months a year from spring practice through the post-season games looking at players, and they know more about these players than the coaches can gain in one or two looks.

Modell acknowledged that the Browns' fans expected the Browns to win, and to win big. He was then asked if there was pressure on Carson to get to the playoffs. He responded:

Yes, but it is pressure that is self-imposed. It's pressure brought upon us by our friends in the media, by the public, by the people who buy tickets, by the players. It's a pressure business. We've come awfully close in the past four years, especially the two losses to Denver. It took a lot of heart out of the organization.

Yet again a reference was made to the Denver playoff losses. Paranoia over the formidable Broncos' reign continued.

Privately Modell compared Bud Carson to Blanton Collier, Art's first choice as Browns' head coach and a man for whom he had a great fondness. He said there were so many similarities that it was "almost eerie." Besides both men having the same initials, both succeeded coaches who were head-strong men (Paul Brown and Marty Schottenheimer). They both were the same age when they got hired (58), and both were failures as college coaches. Both were grandfatherly-types, according to Modell, and excellent teachers and communicators. Modell said he hoped that another comparison would come to pass, that Carson would duplicate what Collier had done and win a championship. While Modell was expressing his hopes for success with Carson, Jim Bailey was saying to his colleagues, "we finally got a coach we can control."

In the *Plain Dealer* Tony Grossi reported that Modell had stated, "This is my last coaching change. If this doesn't work out, I'm through." Art did not expand on what "through" meant.

Once the final selection of the head coach had been made, the Browns found themselves facing the upcoming draft. With so much emphasis on defense in recent drafts, the offense had been overlooked for some time. No young, top-quality, speedy running backs had been added to the stable in several years, so in the 1989 draft, emphasis was placed on looking at blue-chip

backs. Barry Sanders seemed the consensus choice as the top running back.
Ernie Accorsi seemed to focus not only on a speedy back, but on one who
might also provide big-play ability. The Browns had seen both the Bengals
and the Oilers blow by them in 1988 with their "high-octane" offensive weap-
ons. The Browns felt they had some catching up to do. Accorsi wanted to add
the running back with the speed to get outside and around the corner quickly.

Ernie always spoke highly of Curtis Dickey, the Colts' running back
of the 80s. He felt Dickey had been a tremendous weapon, especially near the
end zone, where he could get from his running back position to the pylon at the
corner of the end zone quicker than any other back in the league. That kind of
outside speed would give the offensive scheme much more firepower.   Besides Sanders, who everyone was certain would be gone in the first round, a
couple other good backs were available.

Mack and Byner had been the featured backs under Schottenheimer,
but while they were effective runners, they lacked outside speed. Adding that
ingredient to the Browns' 1989 attack became a priority. With Sanders, Tim
Worley, and Eric Metcalf all available, Accorsi started planning how to achieve
the goal.

Come draft day, the Browns were able to trade up in order to achieve
two things: 1) draft Eric Metcalf, a back with the ability that the team had
lacked since Greg Pruitt's heyday; and 2) acquire a big wide receiver with
sprinter's speed by the name of Lawyer Tillman. It was felt that the 6'5" Tillman
would give the Browns a height advantage over the little bump-and-run
cornerbacks then dominating the league. The acquisition of Metcalf also gave
the Browns an ideal special teams' player and possibly a guy with the ability to
be a receiver out of the backfield.

Callers phoning in to the sports-talk shows applauded the choices. Most
felt confident that the acquisition of these two exciting players had rounded out
the Browns' offensive arsenal. Fans couldn't help but feel that a healthy Bernie
Kosar now had the tools to get the Browns to the Super Bowl.

In one of Carson's first press conferences, he let the cat out of the bag
regarding his plans for the defense. With Bob Golic departing the Browns to
play for the Raiders, Carson was going to convert the Browns from the 3-4
defense, used since the early 80s, to the 4-3 where the emphasis would be on
the pass rush. To help accomplish this, Carson brought in John Teerlinck, an
enthusiastic coach who had earned Little All-America honors for his defensive
play at Western Illinois and who later had played defensive line for the San
Diego Chargers under Tommy Prothro. His obsession with producing quarterback sacks had become legendary during his USFL coaching career.

The brain trust achieved what they had set out to do. They had to mortgage a little of the future, but to get two offensive stars seemed worth the risk. Art Modell was heard to say, "The future is now," and in accord with that philosophy Accorsi made the trades.

Accorsi and his staff then began planning for the upcoming minicamp and negotiating with the players' agents. He suspected the signings were not going to be easy. After all, agents read the newspapers, and when they heard Browns' executives throwing around superlatives (ostensibly to help market next season's tickets) about the rich talent procured by the personnel folks, they wanted to get paid accordingly. Jim Bailey often cringed when he heard the plaudits Modell used because he knew they would eventually come back to haunt the team in the form of higher signing bonuses.

Back home Bud Carson got a surprise. He found out that his first game as Browns' head coach would not even be played in the United States. The Browns were to play the Philadelphia Eagles in Wembley Stadium, London, England, on August 6, in a game that would feature Bernie Kosar and Randall Cunningham, two fine American quarterbacks. Bud didn't relish traveling 3,500 miles and enduring the logistical headaches that went along with the honor. He figured there were plenty other challenges down the road to which he might better devote his energies.

What a difference a year made, I thought. Just one year earlier, Marty Schottenheimer had been the talk of the town, the Browns were the favorite to go to the Super Bowl, and Bob Golic and Earnest Byner were the veterans who were going to lead the Browns there. One year later the Browns were going into the season with an untested head coach, an untested offensive coordinator, Kevin Mack facing incarceration following a drug-related arrest during the summer, questions about whether there was enough talent on the defensive line to provide the Browns' new attack "Carson-style," an aging offensive line that had to learn how to protect the "most important person in the franchise"— Bernie Kosar—and both top draft picks, Eric Metcalf and Lawyer Tillman, still unsigned.

Carson must have thought how much easier remaining a defensive coordinator would have been. Who needed all these problems? Signing players to contracts is an organizational thing. The front office must get the players into camp for him to coach them. The offensive coordinator was not his choice, and despite accepting Trestman, he most probably would have preferred someone more experienced. Kevin Mack's problem was not unusual in pro sports, but Mack was the team's number one running back, and his being a major contributor that season didn't look promising. Tim Manoa, next on the depth chart, had accumulated 500 total career yards in two years, hardly encouraging numbers for the top running back in a year of high hopes. Tillman's agent was demanding first round money for his client since that is what the Browns gave up for him—forget that Tillman was taken in the second round. Management and player were not even in the same neighborhood as negotiations continued.

The Browns got through the pre-season with a 1-4 record and with very little offense to show for it. During five pre-season games, the offense tallied two touchdowns, a far cry from the offensive machine of just two years before. Even Bernie Kosar went out of character to chide his offensive unit by saying, "The meanness and intensity just aren't out there for everybody. The concentration isn't there. It's not evident on game day, and it's not there on the practice field or even in the meetings." All the new faces may have been part of the problem. Of the five running backs on the roster, only Tim Manoa had been with the 1988 team. On the offensive line, chemistry was slow to develop, due to injuries to Cody Risien and Ricky Bolden. But despite the setbacks, the Browns surprised their fans. They went into Three Rivers Stadium on opening day and walked away with a 51-0 victory. What a coaching debut for Bud Carson! Despite the problems that had developed since he had come to Cleveland, his team shut out the Steelers in the most lopsided shutout victory in Browns' history.

What a miracle worker this Carson must be, we all thought. The statistics were overwhelming as the Browns defense held the Steelers to just 53 total net yards, while recording seven sacks and creating eight turnovers. The next week, the Browns treated the fans to another win, trouncing the Jets, 38-24, in Carson's home debut. The defense picked off four passes. After two games, the defense had either accounted for or created plays that resulted in six touchdowns. So far, Carson had made the front office look like geniuses.

Then a major blow to his stature occurred with a 21-14 loss the following week in Cincinnati on Monday night. As coaches before Carson had found out, nobody can lose to Cincinnati and still keep Art Modell happy. The Browns' offense was lackluster in the second half. They went three-and-out in every possession during the third quarter, and twice within the ten-yard line in the fourth quarter, failed to come up with the tying touchdown. The letdown was short lived, and Carson regained his foothold in the organization, for on the next Sunday the Browns ended the Broncos ten-game winning streak over the Browns, 16-13, on a game-ending field goal by Matt Bahr. In Bahr's own words, "It was good by a coat of paint." The Browns finally found a way to whip Elway. The defense forced three turnovers, to bring their league-leading total to 16 after four games. They also sacked Elway four times. The offensive game was also good, as Kosar spread his passes around to eight different receivers. Everything seemed to be hitting on eight cylinders that day, and the Browns were sporting a nifty 3-1 record. Wasn't it great to have Bud Carson's defensive wizardry here? We finally found the answer to stopping Elway, we all thought!

The next two weeks spelled trouble, however, as the Browns lost to the Dolphins in Miami in overtime, 13-10, after two missed Matt Bahr field goals cost the team an opportunity for a win. Then the team performed miserably one week later, losing to Pittsburgh at home, 17-7. In those two weeks, Kosar had no TD's and six interceptions. Against the Steelers, the Browns converted only 2 of 10 third-down conversion attempts, and went 0 for 3 in fourth-down attempts. The one bright spot was that Carson's defense continued to play well, allowing Pittsburgh to convert only 1 of 14 third-down attempts.

Noticeable in-house grumbling had begun about the offense and its schemes. Complaints focused on the offensive line as the major reason for the lack of a running game. The offensive linemen, though, redirected the criticism to the offensive coordinator's play selection, chiefly about the small number of running plays he called. Whatever the cause, opposing defenses were expecting the pass play calls and gearing toward Kosar. More passes were being batted down at the line of scrimmage. After starting the season with a hot hand, Kosar slumped badly in the following weeks, leading Ray Yannucci of *BNI* to speculate that there might be something wrong with Kosar's throwing arm. Yannucci expounded on where he felt the offensive problems lay. He felt that Bud would prefer to play power running football, but he had neither the type of line nor the power running back (especially without Mack) to try it. The Browns were lacking the big-time blocking tight end, and until the roster could accommodate the need, the Browns would limp through the season with a less than formidable running attack. Soon after, the Browns went out and acquired tight end Ron Middleton.

Maybe because the Browns played so badly against the Steelers with their seven turnovers, or maybe the grumbling among the offensive players led to a clearing of the air, but whatever it was, the Browns regrouped and went on to win four games in a row. Metcalf was more comfortable with the system. It had taken him a little longer to catch up since he had missed so much training camp time due to his holdout. Newly acquired Ron Middleton was adding blocking strength.

In that spell of winning four games, the offense looked totally revamped, scoring 114 points, as surprise plays were pulled out of the bag and made to work. We saw an infrequent flea-flicker from Metcalf to Kosar to Slaughter for 80 yards, another TD pass to Slaughter for 77 yards, and a Metcalf halfback option pass to Langhorne for a 32-yard TD. In this series, Kosar hit Slaughter for a 97-yard touchdown on Monday night TV, setting a Browns' record for the longest TD pass in club history. Metcalf gained 233 all-purpose yards against Tampa Bay, setting an NFL record for the season, while the defense picked off four Vinnie Testaverde passes that day. Even Lawyer Tillman began to make his mark as he scored touchdowns on "alley-oop" passes in back-to-back games. This was a truly exciting time for Browns' fans who were beginning to see some immediate results from first-year draft picks for the first time since Bernie Kosar had joined the team in 1985.

With a record of 7-3, the Browns awaited the arrival in Cleveland of Marty Schottenheimer and his Kansas City Chiefs. In a closely played game, defenses dominated play. Cleveland held KC to no offensive touchdowns, while piling up three interceptions and five sacks. However it took the help of Nick Lowery's three missed field goals to allow Cleveland to come away with a 10-10 tie. That tie would prove important, because at the end of the season the Browns would win the AFC Central Division by one-half game.

But before the end of the season, the bottom fell out. For different reasons, the Browns lost three games in a row. The first came against Detroit on Thanksgiving Day. Despite Barry Sanders rushing for 145 yards; the Browns racking up 90 yards in penalties, many in untimely situations, and a couple on questionable calls; and despite a strip of Webster Slaughter on a long crossing pattern late in the third quarter, Cleveland still could have tied the Lions with a Bahr field goal later in the game. Instead, the attempt missed, and Cleveland suffered a 13-10 loss. Fans were wondering, and we were sure that Bud Carson was too, whether Matt Bahr's career in Cleveland was coming to an end.

Next, the Browns were embarrassed 21-0 by, of all teams, the Cincinnati Bengals. Not only were the Browns never in the game, this marked the first time a Kosar-led Browns team had been shut out, and this by a team with the 17th-ranked defense in the NFL. Carson laid part of the blame on the offensive line when he stated, "We're not moving anybody off the line of scrimmage." Some people questioned whether Gregg Rackozy had peaked in his development at center, although his problems against Detroit's Jerry Ball in the previous game were not unusual, as Ball dominated many centers in the league. Rushing stats at this point showed that Tim Manoa, Kevin Mack's replacement, had registered only 261 yards in 11 games. So much for Carson's hoped-for power rushing game. Metcalf was leading all rushers on the team with 520 yards. Carson was growing impatient for Kevin Mack to return. Mack had been sentenced to serve time in prison during the season and was not expected to rejoin the team until late in the season. Carson must have been thinking that an injection of a fresh runner of Mack's caliber might be the spark needed to make the playoffs. Maybe a back like Mack could even make the offensive line look better.

Kosar's play regressed at the tail end of the season. He was en route to playing 20 straight quarters without throwing a TD pass. During the three-game losing streak, he tallied four interceptions, the last one leading to a Colts' TD in a 23-17 overtime loss to Indianapolis. Although the offense showed some life that day, accumulating 470 yards, a Bahr field goal attempt from 35 yards out hit the left upright near the end of the game and cost the Browns a victory. Carson said that we lost because "we did all the things that losers do. We self-destructed with interceptions, fumbles, penalties, and missed field goals." People who had watched the games with Art Modell during these three weeks said that Art registered disgust with the offensive failures to score touchdowns and that he was directing much of the blame at Marc Trestman, his own pick for offensive coordinator.

The joke in the media was: "Don't blame the Browns' problems on the offense, because they don't have one!" Where was Lindy Infante when we really needed him? Others close to the team said Carson considered going to Mike Pagel, but Art would have none of that with the franchise quarterback still healthy. Surprisingly, Bobby Beathard, reporting on the "Insiders" segment of an NFL TV show, blasted Trestman's ineptness, saying Kosar was getting absolutely no help from him. Beathard predicted Trestman would be gone at the end of the year. Many of us knew that Modell had tremendous respect for Beathard; he had often raved of Beathard's achievements, especially his successes with free agent acquisitions.

The really BIG surprise in 1989, though, was the defensive play of the team, which was a tribute to Carson and Teerlinck. Big plays were registered regularly by Michael Dean Perry, on his way to earning 1989 AFC defensive player of the year honors. He was spurred on throughout the season by two veteran players, the ageless Carl "Big Daddy" Hairston, who was having a banner year, and "Bubba" Baker, the defensive end who was always filled with enthusiasm. Bubba was the Browns' sack leader in 1989 with 7.5, and the entire defensive unit, urged on relentlessly by Teerlinck, set the all-time Browns sack record with 45. From the opening of training camp, Teerlinck had set this as the defensive unit's goal, and he had them chant "45, 45, 45" every day, so as never to lose sight of it. The defensive unit played with abandon, and even when they didn't register sacks, they created enough pressure to hurry the opposing quarterback. Many defensive coaches welcomed "hurries" almost more than sacks, because a hurried pass can often be intercepted.

The Browns were 7-6-1, and awaiting Minnesota's arrival to Cleveland Stadium. It was desperation time, a victory an absolute necessity. The game was another nail-biter, but this time Matt Bahr made a 32-yard field goal with less than one minute left in regulation to tie the game and send it into overtime.

It then took a trick play from Marc Trestman's bag to provide a big win for the Browns, as Mike Pagel leaped up from his position as holder on a field goal attempt, rolled to his right, and hit Van Waiters with a touchdown pass to give the Browns a 23-17 win. All Cleveland then had to do was win the last game in Houston, and the AFC Central title was theirs.

Art Modell was not telling many people about the tightness he was experiencing in his chest. He just wrote it off to the anxieties and stress of the season.

The only thing usual about the 1989 season was that the games every week proved to be unusual. The Houston game was a "typical" unusual game. While the Browns got out to a 17-0 lead, they eventually had to come from behind on a memorable Kevin Mack run in his first game back with the team. With tacklers draped over him, he forged a four-yard TD run with less than a minute left to give the Browns a 24-20 win. This win set several Browns' records: the defense registered five sacks to set the single-season record of 45, and by winning, the Browns went to the playoffs for the fifth straight season. There was unbridled joy in the locker room after the game. Despite all the setbacks during the year, and even during this game, the players had fought and scraped and clawed back. Kevin Mack, only recently able to rejoin the team, stood in the locker room with tears streaming down his face as Art Modell hugged and kissed him. Modell told him how proud he was for his comeback from that summer's drug-and-jail-term nadir.

At the conclusion of the wild and crazy season, it was time to get ready to meet the Buffalo Bills in Bud Carson's first playoff game as head coach. What a great feeling there was in Cleveland for Browns' fans. Everyone was a Browns' fan in January, everyone was a Kosar fan, and a lot of people were even Art Modell fans. Art enjoyed being in public these days, receiving plaudits from well-wishers around town. All week the Browns' orange and brown were prominently displayed everywhere.

The Buffalo game was not one for those with weak hearts. It came down to the wire once again. Jim Kelly was attacking the Browns' end zone with time running out until William Clay Matthews, Jr., number 57, intercepted a Kelly pass to end the Bills' drive. The Browns held on for a 34-30 win, a game in which the teams combined for 656 yards and seven touchdown passes (three by Kosar and four by Kelly). A sparkling 90-yard kickoff return by Eric Metcalf for a touchdown may have been the most exciting play of the game. It was the first kickoff return TD in Browns' playoff history. This big win gave the Browns the right to visit Denver the following week, once again to face the Broncos and John Elway.

As that game approached, it was learned that Bernie Kosar had a broken hand but would play with a gadget strapped to his hand that would allow him to throw, albeit a bit awkwardly. To see the "franchise player" struggling that day in pre-game to make his passes work tugged at the heart, and most fans appreciated his gutsiness and wished him well. But against Elway, the pass rush would have to be awesome, and the rest of the defense would have to close everything else down. Denver came into the game with the fewest points given up in the entire NFL (226), so everyone knew our offense would have to be sharp. The players knew it would take the whole team to carry the Browns to their first Super Bowl appearance.

The defense, however, did not play one of its better games, giving up 497 yards to Elway and the Broncos. A total of over 900 yards given up by the defense in the two playoff games was hardly a Carson trademark. As most people had feared, Kosar, with the custom-made contraption on his throwing hand, suffered through the afternoon, completing only 19 of 44 passes, and throwing three interceptions to go along with his two touchdown passes to Brian Brennan, who made more than one spectacular grab that day.

Disappointment once again, this time by a 37-21 score! How much longer would this frustration continue? Did Cleveland fans have to wait until Elway retired before the Browns could beat the Broncos in the playoffs? How could we beat Denver during the season, and then come up short in the play-offs? These thoughts ran though Modell's mind. Modell reflected on Kosar's performance. Kosar had one of his poorer years; his quarterback rating had slipped to 80.3. Despite having the lowest all-time NFL interception percent-age (2.4%), he threw a career high 14 interceptions in 1989, and he went 20 quarters without a TD pass, all un-Kosar-like numbers. People remembered that only two years earlier under Infante this same quarterback looked and played completely differently. It looked like Marc Trestman was in for his share of the blame.

It wasn't long after the season that the expected change was made. Marc Trestman, touted not too long before as promising head coach material, was out as offensive coordinator, and Jim Shofner was hired, becoming the Browns' (and Bernie Kosar's) fifth offensive coordinator in six years. Shofner was no stranger to the Browns, nor to Art Modell. Some of the happiest days experienced with the Browns' offense in recent times involved Shofner, Brian Sipe, and that memorable "Kardiac Kids" year of 1980, when Brian Sipe passed for 30 TD's and over 4,000 yards. Sipe had earned the accolade of NFL Most Valuable Player, and many insiders believed Jim Shofner had contributed sig-nificantly to that achievement.

On the player front, Carson decided that several veterans were at the end of the road. Hanford Dixon was going to retire, and to replace him at right corner the Browns proceeded to shop the free agent market, landing Raymond

Clayborn, a former number one pick of the Patriots and three-time Pro Bowler. Carson also felt a more veteran center was needed, and former Brown Mike Baab was signed, also as a free agent, from the Patriots. The coach planned to move Gregg Rakoczy back to guard, thereby opening up the center position. On the defensive line, Hairston called it quits after 14 seasons.

Art Modell still regularly ate lunch with his staff at the roundtable in the restaurant at Tower A of the Stadium, often ordering lemon sole, "dry, no butter, please" and his vegetables. He seemed to eat heart-healthy foods, avoiding butter, red meats, creamy sauces, and the like. After his first heart attack and quadruple bypass surgery in 1983, Art became attentive to a healthy diet. So it was a total surprise to all of us at the roundtable when in early April Art tapped his chest and announced that his heart doctors were a "little" concerned at his last checkup. He had been experiencing pains and twinges. He told us that cardiologists usually placed a useful life of ten years "if you're lucky" on bypass surgery before the surgery would have to be redone. We all wondered why Art's first surgery in 1983 had only lasted seven years and if the stress of the last few years actually had reduced the optimum useful life of the surgery. In April 1990 Art had his second quadruple bypass surgery at Cleveland Clinic.

The 1990 season started off with a new set of problems: holdouts. With the signing of cornerback Raymond Clayborn for big free-agent money, long-time Browns' cornerback Frank Minnifield announced that he would not play for the Cleveland Browns without more money. Minnifield's situation was not resolved until the fourth game of the regular season, and he played on and off the rest of the year with a nagging heel injury. His performance certainly was not up to the level of past years. Over the years, we noticed a basic problem with holdouts, one that stretched into the season. It seemed that the player seldom could get into the proper physical and mental shape when he returned to action, especially when the player missed all, or almost all, of camp. Coaches rushed starters in as quickly as they became available, but the player was often so far behind the rest of the unit that the squad was out of "sync" for several more weeks while waiting to get him "up to speed."

With members of the defense either out or slow to return, and a total of 20 new players gracing the roster, the Browns started off in a real slump. There was a feeling of diminishing confidence by the front office. Accorsi and Lombardi noted that training camp practices had seemed less organized. New players were starting in key positions, but many were not those coming in as high draft choices. Chris Pike was penciled in as starting defensive tackle to replace the productive Carl Hairston. On offense it was Ben Jefferson and Kevin Robbins, two 300-plus-pound free agents with no pro playing experience, being asked to start at guard. These two were playing alongside Mike Baab, who though a veteran, was also new to the system of the new offensive coordinator. (In 1996 Carson said on a talk show that he had told the front office that he could not win with the offensive line as constituted, but the response was that he had some great young athletes that only needed to be developed, that they would be fine.)

The team was 1-3 after a sound whipping in Kansas City by Marty Schottenheimer and the Chiefs, 34-0. Of course, everyone knew that besides Cincinnati, it was now Kansas City that no Browns' coach could lose to without incurring Art's wrath. Poor Bud! To add to the embarrassment, the Browns had two punts blocked for KC touchdowns, these orchestrated by the Chiefs' special teams, then being coached by Kurt Schottenheimer. During the game, to shake things up a bit, Carson even pulled Kosar out and replaced him with Pagel, who registered 14 of 27 passes for 159 yards and one interception.

Circumstances did not bode well. The Browns were headed to Denver for a Monday night game, and everyone expected the worst. Rumors began circulating at Browns' practices that Bud was feeling the pressure. When Bud had conversations with Accorsi as to his status, he kept hearing that "nothing will solve this situation as quickly as winning." The Cleveland sports media fully expected Bud Carson to get fired immediately after the game if the Browns lost, and most writers expected the Browns to get beat that night. To almost everyone's surprise, the Browns emerged victorious when Jerry Kauric, the newly added kicker from Canada, split the uprights to give the Browns an upset 30-29 victory.

The win over Denver, Cleveland's first in Mile High stadium in almost 20 years, was only a blip. The Browns then lost the next three games. Included in these beatings was a thrashing by the Bengals, 34-13. This came against a Bengal team with the worst-ranked defense in the NFL. Kosar had a weak 17-for-33 performance for 190 yards, two interceptions, and no TDs, and he was sacked four times. Carson seemed to be demonstrating to the front office that he could not beat the Bengals (then winless against them in three attempts). Carson's trademark defense had given up 233 yards on the ground to the 18th-ranked Cincinnati offense. Worse yet, the way Cleveland was losing was embarrassing. After eight games, the Browns were 2-6, and in those games, Kosar had been sacked 23 times and had more interceptions (8) than touchdowns (5). The Browns led the league with the ignominious record of having had four punts blocked. And the Browns' injury list included Tillman and Oliphant out for the year, and Langhorne out with broken ribs. Ralph Tamm and Rakoczy were inserted to replace the Robbins and Jefferson tandem in an attempt to shake up the offensive line.

Modell was visibly upset. The media was pressuring Art whether he would give Carson a vote of confidence, to which he avoided giving an answer. What he did say, though, was that Carson had been given a fine group of young athletes (a statement that Carson would later say was debatable), and Art wanted to see them developed. Modell went on to say that the Browns had the best record in the AFC over the last five years, and he wanted that streak continued.

Art was also upset with Carson for having pulled Kosar out of two games in favor of Pagel, although in both cases the Browns offense had stagnated, and Pagel had been able to re-start the offense, although not to much avail. Art made it clear to *Plain Dealer* reporter Mary Kay Cabot that although the season looked bleak, he was not giving up. He acknowledged, though, that his patience was wearing thin after falling one victory short of the Super Bowl in three of the previous four years. Had we heard this before?

In the ninth week, Buffalo came to town and handed the Browns their worst defeat ever, another shutout to the tune of 42-0. Almost everyone in the Stadium sensed that they were watching Bud Carson's last game as head coach. Carson's calling card was defense, and yet the Browns were humiliated twice that year by lopsided shutout scores of 34 and 42 to zip. As Modell said the next day, November 5, when he terminated Carson, who ended his head coaching career with a 12-14-1 record, he was humiliated as he watched almost 32,000 fans leave the Stadium before the fourth quarter had even begun.

Browns' News Illustrated's Ray Yannucci had a good pulse on what the media were thinking during this period. He labeled the last month as the "Bud Watch." Speculation had run rampant as to when the execution would actually take place. After his termination, Carson told Ed Meyer of the Akron *Beacon-Journal* that his relationship with the front office had worsened following the 1989 playoff game in Denver. Carson said he was told by Modell and his staff at that time that none of Carson's coaches were worth a (bleep), and the front office wasn't sure how Carson himself would be evaluated. Carson said he told them to fire him then (after his first year) if they weren't satisfied. Carson said the tone of that meeting was to beat him down so he didn't get to thinking he was some kind of great football coach. He said he thought they were fearful of him because he had a good relationship with the media. Bud pointed to Mike Lombardi as the one specifically cautioning him not to talk to this guy or that guy because they were his enemies. Carson later stated that he made these comments "off the record," but Modell and the front office were miffed at seeing the articles in print, so the Browns sent Carson a certified letter reminding him that if he wanted to continue getting paid on his contract through 1991, he needed to heed the "no criticism" clause in his contract. Bud was careful about what he said from then on.

The week after the termination, Yannucci pointed out in his article that he thought the problems went deeper than head coaching. He held Carson responsible for many things, including the lack of discipline among the players, which is usually traceable to the head coach. But in his article Yannucci also pointed out that since Modell had tried hard for years to get to the big Bowl, he also must be doing something wrong. The writer suggested one fault was Art's over-inflated appraisal of the talent on the 1990 football squad. He also suggested that the Browns hire a football director, much like Bill Polian of the Bills and George Young of the Giants. He even suggested Bill Walsh come out of retirement.

Browns' players began dropping hints about the power that Mike Lombardi was starting to exhibit. Lombardi quickly denied the charge, saying, "The Browns' organization is run by three people, and they are Art Modell, Ernie Accorsi, and Jim Bailey. I certainly have no voice in running the show around here."

Accorsi brought himself in for a share of the blame. He knew that some of Carson's stipulations were true. He knew the personnel department failed to provide Carson the quality of offensive linemen necessary, and he added, "He (Bud) didn't fail alone. We failed as an organization. I've gotten a lot of blame and I deserve it. Evidently I didn't do a good enough job. Carson was my choice from day one."

To finish out the season, Art Modell replaced Carson with Jim Shofner. Carson thus earned the dubious distinction of having served the shortest tenure of all seven full-time Cleveland coaches. During the press conference, Modell cited Carson's demonstrated inability to stop opposing quarterbacks as the major reason for the former head coach's demise. Art also responded to a question about player holdouts, but refused to admit that the five veteran holdouts, of which three were All-Pros on defense, had anything to do with the defense's lapse. He said, "I can't lay the blame on the holdouts. These guys are old pros, and they don't need many weeks to recover their abilities. I think if I had to single out one major disappointment, it's been the defense this season."

In one press conference Art made it apparent that Carson's replacing Kosar with Pagel had not sat well. Saying that Kosar was "the franchise" and then having the coach put him on the bench sent contradictory signals. It was against the Bills on November 4 when Pagel started the game that Art was deeply hurt. Modell said he wasn't aware that Pagel was starting until ten minutes before the game. Modell told his friends that he was offended that Carson had failed to inform him of the quarterback change. "I don't think that was exactly conducive to a harmonious relationship. I think it would've been a courteous thing for him to call me and say that he was starting Pagel. I would've told him that that was his call." Art also admitted that his impatience to get to the Super Bowl factored into the decision. "I'll stay with it until it happens, and it will happen," Art finished.

The Browns went on to win one more game that year, with the team playing unimaginative and unenthusiastic football. The defense went on to give up 35, 30, 38, and 58 points in the next four games. Another humiliating shutout loss occurred in Pittsburgh late in the year, 35-0, as the Browns lost eight fumbles in that game, including one on each of their first three possessions from scrimmage. Bernie Kosar ended the season with a fractured hand, and Mike Pagel led the Browns in the last games. Kosar had his worst year ever as a Brown, registering 10 touchdowns, 15 interceptions, and a dismal QB rating of 65.7.

Bernie was asked for his views on playing under Carson. While he was careful with his choice of words, Bernie felt that he was not a "Carson-type" quarterback from day one, since he felt Bud was defensive-oriented and wanted to win games with defense and special teams. Kosar was not being critical of the philosophy itself, because a lot of people had won with it, but Bernie questioned whether the makeup of the Browns' offensive personnel possessed the kind of people needed to play Carson's brand of football. Kosar added that to play Carson offense, one needed to be set up to play ball-control, safe, possession football. What he was describing was a team of big power run-blocking linemen with big power backs who didn't fumble and a quarterback who only threw high-percentage passes. This was not the type of football Cleveland fans had become accustomed to in the 1980s.

Bernie was asked how his relationship was different with Marty Schottenheimer, in that Marty was also a defensive-minded coach who must have shared some of Bud's basic philosophies. Bernie indicated that Marty wanted to learn to be an offensive-minded coach, and the two spent many hours together, allowing Marty to learn about offensive schemes. Because of this start, Bernie and Marty had a good relationship which allowed for a lot of open dialogue.

But the big question that many people had a hard time answering was: How could the Browns go from being one win shy of the Super Bowl in 1989 to a 3-13 record in 1990?

Yannucci of *BNI* asked that question of Bill Walsh, and Walsh told him that whether they recognized it or not, the Browns were in transition in the 1990 season, since they went into the season with a new offensive line, and with players like Ozzie Newsome and Clay Matthews at the tail end of their careers. Members of the media tossed around other ideas, but the consensus kept coming back to the following:

1)   in spite of Modell's assertion to the contrary, the veteran holdouts really did hurt the team; some of the defensive players who came back never played up to their past abilities;

2)   the offensive line was not only new, but played poorly;
3)   the team lacked leadership;
4)   coaching was unsatisfactory, and
5)   last but not least, poor draft performances.

Yannucci summarized the last five drafts, and found that only five play-ers were starting. The only starting first-rounder was Eric Metcalf. Good NFL teams expect their first-round picks to be starters, hopefully in the first year, but at least by the second, and Pro-Bowlers down the line. Second and third round players are expected to be starters and key players for a number of years. A look at the Browns' results over the last drafts would show that nothing close to these expectations ever materialized.

Art Modell set February 1, 1991, as his deadline to name the next head coach. The one hint that Art threw out was when he said this was a job for a young guy with a lot of energy and enthusiasm. He said the selection process would be done by a group made up of himself, Accorsi, Lombardi, Shofner, Bailey, and David Modell.

When the Browns' record books were updated at the end of the 1990 season, 24 new records had been set, all of a dubious nature. Most of these were established by the defense, but the offense allowed themselves to be em-barrassed also. Fewest points scored since 1975 (which was a 14-game sea-son), most fumbles lost in a game, most games shut out in a season: these were on the offense's shoulders. Giving up the most points, touchdowns, passes, and so on, however, made up the bulk of the record-setting performances. Ugh! The new coach would have his work cut out for him.

After talking to George Young and Bill Parcells of the New York Gi-ants, and Indiana basketball coach Bobby Knight, Art Modell was confident that he had hired a good man. The new coach was a youthful 38, and Art Modell compared him to Don Shula, in that Shula was only 33 years old when he became the head coach of the Baltimore Colts. Art Modell often made the comparison to Shula when he introduced the next head coach of the Cleveland Browns. Time would eventually make it clear that Bill Belichick was not go-ing to be a Don Shula.

CHAPTER 12
GATEWAY

In 1989, as Art Modell was getting used to Bud Carson as his new coach, he was also busy planning his next step in regards to Cleveland Municipal Stadium. He, along with the rest of us, vividly recalled the sound thrashing the proposed $150-million domed stadium took at the ballot in 1984. So much voter animosity built up over the attempt to get the issue passed that it cost Cuyahoga County Commissioner Vincent Campanella his job. Based on that voter reaction, we were convinced that area taxpayers would not soon sanction any additional taxes for a new stadium. At the same time, everybody knew something had to be done with the Stadium, or Cleveland could very well lose both its baseball and football franchises.

Art decided to take a larger overview of the situation. He felt Cleveland sports fans could still get something "almost new" for a reasonable sum with a large-scale renovation of Cleveland Stadium. Rather than limit his thinking to the $10 million renovation, he decided to propose a complete makeover, a totally rebuilt and renovated stadium designed by nationally-known architects. Art's plan covered both baseball and football needs. He hoped the renovation would cost less than $100 million, an amount far less than for a new stadium.

During spring 1989 Art ran this idea past Mayor George Voinovich, suggesting it as a more practical approach to solving the stadium dilemma. He said Stadium Corp. would fund a $50,000 feasibility study. Work on the study by Ron Labinski and HOK would begin immediately, and the results could be available by summer 1989. Modell told Voinovich that he had discussed his plans with Dick Jacobs, and that he thought Jacobs was supportive. The mayor encouraged Art to proceed with the study. Although Art was of the opinion that Jacobs was excited about the study, neither Bailey nor I could understand how Jacobs could have changed his preference for a baseball-only facility, unless, of course, Jacobs also believed there would not be enough tax money for everyone's needs.

Everything came back into focus in June, when *Crain's Cleveland Business* reported that Jacobs was talking with what remained of the directorship of the Greater Cleveland Domed Stadium Corp. about a 44,000-seat, $120-million outdoor stadium. Greater Cleveland Domed Stadium Corp. was still in existence five years after the domed stadium issue had been beaten down at the ballot box. It still owned the 28 acres of land which had been assembled for the project, along with $22 million in a corresponding liability for related bank loans, which were in arrears. *Crain's*, citing three unidentified sources who spoke on condition of anonymity, cautioned that the talks were far from the point of a "done deal," but that Frank Mosier, president of Dome Corp., was privately expressing optimism about a new baseball park. *Crain's* also reported that Labinski and HOK were well underway with their study of the "old" Stadium, and although not all work was yet completed, Labinski was of the opinion that the cost of renovation would be at least $80 million. These same sources thought Voinovich, who had made known his intentions of running for governor in 1990, would be faced with weighing the corporate community's often-stated desire for a new stadium against Art Modell's concerns over his investment and the eventual loss of a baseball tenant at the Stadium. Council President George Forbes had said that he was certain a new stadium would be built and privately added he would support the new stadium if he won his mayoral bid.

Art wondered what Jacobs' support for this new project meant. Although Jacobs had not said a single word to reporters, Art wondered if there was some truth to the story. Art wanted to complete the renovation study and present it to the media and the public. Then he would let them decide between a new baseball-only park and a renovated Cleveland Stadium. Art was genuinely excited by the concepts being generated by the designers, and he thought he could convert the power brokers to his thinking once they were able to see the finished product.

Then, on August 3, 1989, the Jacobs Group publicly announced a proposed $150 million, 44,000-seat brand new stadium, which would be expandable for football by another 28,000 seats. It was hoped that the cost could be funded by a one-half cent increase in the county sales tax.

On the day of the Jacobs' announcement, Modell was in London watching his team prepare for Carson's first game as head coach. Mosier called Art in London the day before the announcement to advise him of what was about to happen. Art thought the timing relevant. His own conference on the renovation plan was just ahead, and he felt Jacobs' announcement was timed to steal some of his thunder.

In his column the *Plain Dealer's* Bob Kravitz said that building a new stadium was the right way to go. He agreed with those who objected to being taxed for the project, but he said that if Greater Clevelanders voted down the tax, they would be giving the Jacobs brothers the option of "loading the moving vans and blowing town." He said that Clevelanders owed it to themselves to continue downtown's rebirth and follow up on the contribution that the Flats and Playhouse Square were making to the city's renaissance.

Art held a brief news conference upon returning from London. He cautioned that folks should forget about the Browns moving into an expandable stadium. He reminded those assembled of baseball's strong preference for a baseball-only stadium, a position reinforced earlier by Hank Peters and American League President Bobby Brown. He urged the city to take care of the Indians, if that was the consensus. He did, however, remind his listeners that he expected fair and equitable treatment for the loss of the Indians as his tenant. Modell believed it would be unfair to him were the public to finance a new stadium for the Jacobs' interests and leave him bearing the losses from the departure of his main tenant. "Somebody has to treat us fairly, because it's my $28 million invested in this building," he said.

Two weeks later Art Modell stood on second base on the Stadium infield for a press conference in which he unveiled the mockup of the renovated stadium. The design showed the facility without its roof and upper deck columns, giving fans with the high-priced tickets an unobstructed view of the playing field. Many other features found in newly built stadiums were also incorporated in the design. While the conference was well-attended, conspicuous by their absence were Mayor George Voinovich and his aide Ed Richard. In the years to come, Modell often referred to the snub he received by City Hall that day.

The Stadium Corp. was enjoying a busy year in 1989. Requests for concerts had been coming in during the spring. The previous year had been a "down" cycle, and no one really knew when another series of rock concerts would turn up. Much depended on the willingness of rock groups to endure the arduous time-consuming journeys demanded of the successful tour which were usually coordinated with the release of new recorded material. Cleveland Stadium agreed to host a Who concert in July and the Rolling Stones' Steel Wheels tour in September. Since no new acts or groups were touring, 1989 became known as the year of the "reunion" tour on the outdoor stadium circuit.

The WHO celebrated its 25th anniversary in rock-n-roll with a sell-out at the Stadium on July 19. Pete Townshend, Roger Daltrey, and John Entwhistle delighted their fans with over 40 songs spread over three-plus hours. The band proved it could still recapture the aura it had developed over nearly one generation.

The Steel Wheels tour was being marketed by the Rolling Stones as its first major tour in eight years, thereby putting to rest rumors that internal strife was threatening to break up the band. At the press conference when Mick Jagger and Keith Richards were observed hugging and mugging for the cameras, Jagger told *USA Today* that the Stones would not be introducing too many new songs. Jagger said, "Nobody wants to hear new songs. You say to the audience 'and here's our new single!' and you can see them frowning. Very conservative, (our) rock fans." Jagger explained this was not a farewell tour, nor a retrospective tour, but just plain and simple, the Rolling Stones in 1989.

The Stones kept their promise to the fans that night, mostly playing their best-known hits. For the sold-out audience, the night started off with "Start Me Up" and finished with "Satisfaction" and "Jumpin' Jack Flash." Next morning the *Plain Dealer* headlined "Stones provide satisfaction at Stadium." That pretty much summed up the reaction of the fans who had attended.

While the Stadium was rocking, Art Modell carefully monitored the movement by the city powers toward appeasing Dick Jacobs and the Indians. Art's instincts told him he would soon have to go it alone at the Stadium, so he would need plenty of special events to make up for the loss of the Indians. He figured he might as well start early. I don't think he really cared as much about the concerts or their impact on field conditions as he had in the past, given the turn of recent events.

While the Browns began preparing for the draft leading into the 1990 season, and while Art Modell was preparing himself for his second quadruple bypass surgery, activity for a new ballpark accelerated. The political and business leaders were preparing the public for a county-wide sin-tax vote in May 1990 to finance the Gateway Project, as it had come to be known. The sin-tax had been chosen because a person who neither drank nor smoked could wholeheartedly support such a tax since it would not cost him or her one cent. This sin tax—and no other tax, the voters were told--was all that taxpayers would have to endure to bring Cleveland the finest 45,000-seat baseball stadium in the entire USA, along with returning the Cavaliers to downtown to play in a new arena. The Fenway-park-like baseball stadium would reportedly cost about $128,000,000, and the 20,000-seat basketball arena was expected to run about $75,000,000.

Ballpark backers had persuaded the Gunds, who owned the basketball team and the Coliseum, to move downtown. The Cavs' presence was seen as a critical component in securing voter support for the project. Certainly part of the merit of a major civic project like this was its ability to generate new revenues for the city over the long term. Since the Indians were already playing downtown, the ancillary spending that went along with the baseball team was already present. The possibility, of course, of increased Indians' patronage and a larger fan base could mean added city revenues (admission, parking, and other taxes). But with the Cavs, it was a different story. Every dollar spent on the Cavs would represent new spending in Cleveland. Gateway planners intended to capture that spending to create more jobs for Cleveland residents.

Another major accomplishment would be to capture for the city's coffers the income taxes on those multi-million dollar player salaries.

At the time, however, Richfield Coliseum was still an attractive and functional basketball arena. Nick Mileti had built it in the early 70s to take Clevelanders from the old Arena, a 10,000-seat dungeon on Euclid Avenue at East 36th Street, to a state-of-the-art building. Many people really enjoyed the 16-year-old Coliseum and questioned the need to replicate downtown what was already in place in Richfield. Politicians were aware this pocket of people posed a threat to the downtown political-business group pushing for the vote.

On the other hand, many Clevelanders hated the long trek to the Coliseum, especially in wintry weather. With a new basketball arena right next to the baseball park, people working downtown would be able to walk from their offices to watch Cavs' basketball. That would sure beat the one-hour trip that sometimes faced fans going to Richfield from the western suburbs. The timing of the vote was also auspicious, since the team was heading for the playoffs, and Cavs' fever would be running rampant at the scheduled May 8 vote time. Mark Price, Larry Nance, and Brad Daugherty were fan favorites, very easy to like, follow, and root for, and hopefully their popularity could translate into more "yes" votes.

The idea of a new baseball park was not an automatic selling point. Should Cleveland build a new ballpark to keep a last-place baseball team from leaving town? A lot of former baseball fans had been turned off by 30 years of baseball ineptitude. These folks just might vote "no," even if they weren't smokers or drinkers. Recent team performance had remained dismal. The Indians were coming off a seventh-, and two sixth-place finishes.

Therefore some backers of the project expected it would be difficult to get the fans to vote "yes" to house a terrible ballclub. Their tactics changed accordingly to include trashing the condition of the almost-60-year-old Cleveland Stadium. This angle was geared to the younger citizens, those not old enough to cherish memories from the old Stadium. It wouldn't take a genius to figure out that another element of opposition could well be the folks who had sat in that building and watched Ted Williams, Mickey Mantle, and Larry Doby clobber home runs, and Bob Feller mow down batters with his blazing fastball.

Despite the public ambivalence, one thing was crystal-clear: Under federal tax law, the county had until December 31, 1990, to issue $175 million in bonds that would qualify as tax-exempt. After that date, the bonds would be taxable and would carry a higher interest rate. Since the project appeared tenuous even at the lower tax rate, using one of Art Modell's favorite expressions, "you didn't have to be an MIT graduate to figure out" the project could never become a reality at a higher rate. So, Gateway backers knew they were battling the clock, and if the issue couldn't get on the ballot in May, the project would be dead. The business community behind the project had a major supporter in the person of new Mayor Michael White, and White began very actively adding his own input into the project.

But opposition continued to surface. The leaders of the United Auto Workers were opposed to the plan, and some segments of the community were bitter over the millions of dollars in tax abatements being awarded the Jacobs brothers, who were then acting as developers in other downtown real estate projects. Writer Roldo Bartimole took issue over these points with Tom Chema, an appointee of Governor Richard Celeste hired to steer the project towards reality.

Despite the opposition, in March 1990 the county commissioners finally committed themselves to place the sin tax on the ballot, even though many unanswered questions about the project remained. For instance, how did the project, as it was then being presented, get to become a $350 million project when the cost of the two buildings had initially been estimated at just a little over $200 million? Even if the sin tax passed, where would the rest of the funding come from? The commissioners announced that the rest would come from the corporate community and the teams. Mayor White said that the public would not have to compensate the Cavaliers in any way for the Coliseum, which would be abandoned.

Tower City, Cleveland's newest downtown shopping mall, had just opened to popular acclaim, and backers of the Stadium issue urged voters to continue the downtown renaissance momentum by casting their vote in favor of the sin tax. Plenty of positive TV commercial time was launched. Baseball commissioner Fay Vincent arrived in town about a week before the election, hinting that the Indians might move if the issue failed.

Art Modell had little to say during this period. He was battling to recover his health after his second open heart surgery performed that spring. What he did say was short and sweet. Reporters located him one day at the team's mini-camp headquarters in Berea. Responding to inquiries about the convertibility of the stadium for football, he said:

I support the project; in fact I made a $10,000 campaign contribution in support of it. However, the Browns will not occupy the new stadium, even though I am hearing that it is being designed to later accommodate extra seating for football. I think the Indians are an important asset to the city of Cleveland and should have their own stadium. But I want to quickly add that even though I support it wholeheartedly, the Browns will never play up there in an expanded baseball stadium, as had been proposed. We will continue to play where we are.

Art privately explained he would not knock the project, but he could not ask his fans to begin sitting on rollout aluminum bleacher seats. He said 26,000 ticket-buyers would have to be accommodated in this fashion, people accustomed at the Stadium to having single seats with arms and backs. In addition, he said, "What do I tell my 80,000 fans when 12,000 of them will not be able to attend future Browns' games in person?" (Reference of course to the capacity of 68,000 football fans proposed at Gateway). And, of course, and maybe most importantly of all, who at Gateway Economic Corp. was going to make up the shortfall in gate receipts from the loss of revenues from 12,000 tickets, which might amount to some $300,000 a game? Modell couldn't fathom the business leaders' total disregard for the revenues he would lose. "I wonder," he said, "how many of them would sit idly by and let revenues be wantonly removed from their businesses under the guise of civic progress."

Two years earlier, in a letter to Jim Biggar, President of the Greater Cleveland Growth Association, Art Modell had tried to get downtown business interests to understand his plight relative to moving into a new combination baseball-football stadium, whether domed or open-air. He wrote:

A new dual-purpose facility will duplicate the inevitable conflicts between football teams and baseball teams in design, capacity, usage, convertibility, operations and economics, and is not in the best interests of the Browns, or the Indians, and the city of Cleveland. Whether or not I agree with the ancillary civic benefits, I will not commit the Cleveland Browns to a bad business deal. Whether or not civic leaders agree with that business judgment, it is my judgment to make.

Apparently, Modell had failed to get business leaders to understand that a new stadium with 12,000 fewer seats would create a permanent negative impact on his team's future revenues.

Long-time Cleveland industrialist Cyrus Eaton had once remarked, "Anybody who goes through with a commitment...when he is going to lose money, is a sucker." Art Modell was not inclined to that role.

May 8, 1990, finally came, and the television stations carried the progress of the vote results throughout the evening. Votes from Cleveland's inner city wards were tallied first, and these were primarily negative; within the city boundaries alone, the issue was soundly rejected. However the suburban vote, which was counted later, was heavy and substantially positive. The suburban tally was enough to swing the total count into positive territory. The final tally showed county voters accepting the passage of the 15-year sin tax by a 51.7 to 48.3 percent victory.

Despite all the hoopla given the new stadium and the related sin-tax vote, the 1990 baseball season refused to start on time because of another in the long line of professional sports' management-labor disputes. This strike occurred during spring training and cut short the teams' normal training schedules. Peace among the parties was restored, but not until some ten days was lopped off the beginning of the schedule. Opening day in Cleveland had to be re-scheduled, only to find that a snow storm interfered with the new date, causing the "second" scheduled opener of 1990 to be postponed. Then on April 19, Thursday evening at 6:05 pm, the Indians finally played the opener against the New York Yankees in front of 6,000 fans, the smallest opening day crowd ever in Cleveland Stadium.

When Modell's request for the lease extension fell on deaf ears during 1988 and early 1989, he was disinclined to spend additional money of his own on further Stadium improvements. Nonetheless more expenses were soon on their way, and most of them were found on the roof, 115 feet above the playing field.

The Environmental Protection Agency (EPA) was making known its concern over the environment and the ozone layer. Any and all dangers to the environment were studied and addressed. Commodities used in industrial production were evaluated carefully, and consideration was given to forcing entities to use alternatives to protect the public from health hazards. The EPA folks made their impact in Cleveland in part by addressing old public buildings, and their review at Cleveland Stadium focused on the use of PCB.

PCB is short for polychlorinated biphenyl, a substance found in electrical equipment, and at the Stadium PCB was found in the large electrical transformers in use throughout the building and on the roof. When the Stadium was built in 1931, this liquid was considered a fine electrical conductor, the product of choice in transformers. PCB had recently been found to be potentially hazardous, but only if it should catch fire. The smoke would contain toxic gases which could be lethal to anyone nearby. Every Stadium transformer contained PCB. It was unlikely the transformers would ever catch fire, although it was possible that due to old age the transformers on the roof could leak PCB and the liquid then somehow ignite. In the liquid state, however, PCB was totally harmless.

The government issued a decree that PCB use be eliminated and that old transformers be replaced with new ones and the old properly disposed of. Compliance with this edict was required by April 1990, or jail sentences could be imposed. Some of us had just begun to figure what the EPA was all about, and now we were being faced with jail sentences if things didn't happen quickly enough.

When we conveyed the substance of this situation to Jim Bailey, he assigned the task to an outside law firm. Bailey had plenty of projects on his plate, so he couldn't find the time to address this problem, and after all, environmental law was a specialized field. We learned that the government threats were serious and that jail penalties were directed to the owner, not the user or operator of the building. At first, we thought this provision made the PCB problem the city's responsibility since it owned the building. The Stadium Corp. was merely the lessee. We found, however, that our lease contained clear-cut language that Cleveland Stadium Corp. was responsible for all necessary capital improvements, repairs, and maintenance. Was the replacement of all the transformers due to an EPA ruling our responsiblity? The lease did not really address such a situation, and I am sure Modell never intended to be responsible for expensive component replacements due to new federal policy. At the same time, we realized the public perception was that anything that needed to be done in the Stadium (and then some) had better be done by Mr. Modell or else. Bailey concluded that unless we wanted to be responsible for having Art jailed, we had better budget for replacement of all the transformers in the building.

Larry Staverman then began to seek bids on the work. There were 19 transformers on the roof and three other large transformers in the main power vaults. The total cost of the project was close to $365,000, with less than half representing the cost for the new components. The larger portion of the tab was for the removal, transportation, and proper disposition of the old transformers which contained the hazardous PCB material.

Staverman was able to shut down the Stadium completely for a full week in February 1990, so as to complete the project two months before the government deadline. Staverman and I achieved our goal: we kept Art Modell out of jail.

Many parts of the Stadium were showing their age, but none more than the roof lights. This was a problem not taken lightly by Major League Baseball. As a matter of policy the league sent consultants to each ballpark every year to check lighting intensity levels, which they posted in a continuing log file. When intensity levels declined to a specific level, the team (or the stadium, depending who, according to the lease, had that responsibility) was notified to take corrective action. In Cleveland Stadium, Stadium Corp. took on that responsibility. Nevertheless the Indians had a very real interest in making sure proper lighting levels were maintained, so when the annual review took place in Cleveland in April every year, the Indians always had a representative or two present for the test.

The logs on file with the American League showed the Stadium's lighting system deteriorating at the rate of 10% of candlepower a year. The situation became a little more severe each year because of the archaic condition of the ballasts and fixture gaskets. The Stadium's roof lights were mounted inside fixtures weighing about 50 pounds with a flip-glass door over the front, much like a car headlight within a glass casing. This prevented rain or snow from landing on the front of an extremely hot fixture and cracking the glass. The gaskets had become brittle and cracked, preventing the lid from closing snugly. The improper fit allowed dirt to be sucked into the fixtures and onto the front of the bulb whenever the lights were turned off and began cooling down. The buildup of dirt gradually reduced the intensity of the lights.

When league officials were in Cleveland in 1989, the readings were low, and we expected the Stadium would be put on notice. The existing lighting system had been installed in 1967, with one major overhaul since, this under Modell's stewardship in 1981. We were then going into our eighth year, with only periodic cleaning and spot replacement in the interim. So, it was no surprise that the American League reported that "the light readings in Cleveland Stadium were now the lowest in the American League." Art's edict about a moratorium on capital improvements would have to be revisited, we feared.

The cost of a total re-lighting was estimated at $375,000. If the new Gateway stadium was going to get built, it wouldn't be prudent to spend all that money for eight-to-ten more years of good lighting for baseball when baseball would be gone, especially since professional football does not require anywhere near the sharp intensity that baseball demands. In a meeting with league experts, we learned that their foremost concern was the lighting around home plate, to assure a batter's safety. If the officials were assured that home plate lighting would be replaced in time for the 1990 season and that additional roof lights would be replaced throughout the rest of the Stadium over the next two years, the American League would then sanction the program. (Modell was also getting complaints from the *Plain Dealer* photographer who worked the home plate area; his photos were coming out dark and lacking in clarity because of the the poor lighting).

So the Stadium Corp. scheduled another project, to be completed over three years, at a maximum investment of $125,000 each year.

The results attained from the first year's investment were astoundingly great! We learned that the "modern-day" roof light achieved much more intensity with a fewer number of lamps. If one counted the number of lamps on the home plate roof towers, he or she would see fewer than on the other towers. This favorable result also created a safer environment since there was less weight on the roof.

Several of the Indians' batters who were unaware of the lighting change even remarked to a reporter that they noticed that they were seeing the ball better at night games in the Stadium. It was always gratifying to hear that kind of favorable response to an expensive project at the "old" Stadium. Many times money was spent on projects invisible to the public, and they remained totally unaware of the improvement. Like the PCB transformer project, for example; aside from Stadium Corp. personnel, the suppliers, and the EPA, no one was aware of the expenditure or the need for it.

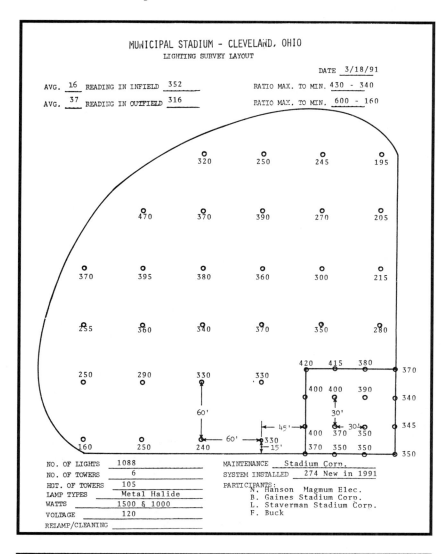

Sample of the American League field lighting survey monitoring the intensity levels at Cleveland Stadium. Requirements for the infield are substantially greater than the outfield. *Cleveland Stadium Corp. collection*

As agreed, Stadium Corp. followed through with the second phase of the roof light installation in 1991. Another $125,000 was invested, and when Modell wondered why we were spending the money now that Gateway was in the works, we reminded him that the second year's installation was necessary to get the average readings up into the upper third in the American League. After the survey was conducted that year, the American League applauded the program, saying that Cleveland Stadium would have one of the most uniform lighting systems in the entire American League when the program was finalized. I forwarded a copy of the report to Art, but I was not surprised that he had no interest in reading it or in hearing the plaudits.

Talk about the perils of budgeting and planning. We had gone into 1990 and 1991 planning to spend almost nothing on capital improvements or major repairs (which we budgeted differently from day-to-day repairs). As Art had told city council after his request for the lease extension was ignored, we were cutting back on all improvements. However, I guess he was referring to planned improvements. It was the unplanned ones that trapped us. Between the requirements imposed by the EPA and the American League, we found ourselves spending $700,000 for costly new items. What made it doubly irritating was that half the cost solely benefited the baseball team, which was planning to jump ship. With the new expenditures, the tally of capital expenditures by Stadium Corp. climbed over the $17 million mark, $7,000,000 more than required under the lease.

Late June 1990 was quiet as the Browns' coaches were on vacation or getting ready for the July football camp. The Indians were enroute to a relatively decent fourth-place finish (8 games below .500 by year-end), and the Stadium Corp. was getting ready to host a sold-out Paul McCartney World Tour concert in July. A quite prophetic column had been written by Dan Coughlin, a local broadcaster-reporter-feature writer, a man close to the Cleveland sports scene, and a good friend of the Browns. Coughlin was worried about the town's attitude toward Art Modell, and this prompted him to provide the following insights in his column in the *Elyria Chronicle* on July 1, 1990:

> I was wondering why no one had written that amidst all the hysteria over the passing of the sin tax for the new ballpark, one of the costs that wasn't being mentioned was what the city of Cleveland was to owe Modell for depriving him of his major tenant. The City already has a deal with Modell, (25-year lease to manage the stadium) and that deal was based on two teams being prime tenants. There's something unethical about the City stealing one of Modell's tenants. Even Nick Divito, the City law director who negotiated the Stadium lease with Modell back in 1973, acknowledged to me that the City owed Modell some relief. (Divito was in private practice at the time of this article. He is deceased today.)

Coughlin went on:

Don't the Browns deserve the same deal the Indians got? Of course they do. And the idea of expanding the new stadium for football seems to defeat the entire purpose of building a baseball-only stadium. I would expect that in 1998 the gloves will come off and Modell will do some real hard negotiating with the city. Having made a commitment to keep the Indians, Cleveland will have to make a similar commitment to the Browns or this city could lose its football team.

Gateway was in the newspapers regularly during summer 1990. With the sin-tax approved, designs of the buildings were being prepared, and lease discussions with the teams were underway. Plans were in process to secure the balance of the financing needed for the package, to include, among other things, proceeds from the sale of loges and negotiated sums of money from the teams under terms of the leases.

Gateway lease discussions with the Indians continued during summer 1990 and were on a fairly smooth course. Then, on August 23, the *Plain Dealer* reported a major behind-the-scenes disagreement over whose liability it would be to pay real estate taxes. Jacobs' representatives stated flat out that the Indians could not afford them after meeting all the other operating expenses. Representing the Indians in this matter was former City Council President George Forbes. Forbes was expected to resolve the Gateway property tax dilemma before the bond deadline of December 31, 1990.

Following normal real estate valuation practices, Gateway consultants estimated that the ballpark would generate $1.1 million in tax payments the first year, and escalate to $1.24 million by the fourth year of operation. The new arena next door (Gund Arena) would generate $750,000 in the first year and increase to $844,000 in the fourth year.

The *Plain Dealer* reporter learned from the Cuyahoga County auditor's office that a building with a valuation of $150 million should generate an annual tax (again, following normal taxation procedures) equal to approximately 2% of the building's value, or in this case, $3 million. That wasn't, however, what Gateway advisers were saying. Everyone wondered what the final real answer would be: $3 million or $1.1 million. In an attempt to get further information on other sports facilities, the *Plain Dealer* reporter called me at the Stadium to inquire what Stadium Corp. paid on our nearly 60-year-old building. I explained that based on an approximate tax value of $15,000,000 (the Stadium was estimated at salvage value), we had been billed $310,000 in the prior year. This, of course, was in addition to taxes of $46,000 for the land value on the eastern parking lot. Given the formula just stated, and compared to the Stadium payment, it seemed Gateway should be billed an amount ten times higher, or about $3 million, since its value was tenfold that of the Stadium.

Tom Chema, executive director of the Gateway Economic Development Corp., said he had no discussions with Forbes over this issue. Chema added that, "Gateway's assumption is that since taxes are an operating expense, they would be paid by the operating entities." The newspaper suggested that a fair comparison would be to Modell's Stadium Corp., which was responsible for the real estate taxes on the building that it operated.

During the campaign to pass the sin tax, literature had been distributed saying that $4.7 million in new property taxes would be generated. Cuyahoga County Auditor Tim McCormack specifically broke them down as $2.9 million for the ballpark and approximately $1.7 million for the arena. Despite the $4.7 million touted in the literature as one more reason to vote for Gateway, the accountants and consultants budgeting Gateway's operating expenses were using $500,000 as the cost slotted for first year operations. McCormack made the contrast even sharper when he pointed out that by comparison, the Stadium Corp. paid the county $417,000 (a number which also included personal property taxes) on a fully-depreciated building, thereby implying that the use of only $500,000 for tax budgeting purposes on a brand new building was ridiculous. The public was learning there was plenty confusion both over who was to pay the taxes and over how much eventually would be paid.

Some politicians and city leaders were still advocating that Gateway become a dual-purpose stadium. It would certainly provide economies and help with loge sales if all the major sports teams were housed in the same facility. There were pressures on the Browns to reconsider a move to Gateway, and despite Modell's continuing firm refusal, designers were told to budget for expandability to a larger capacity for football by making room for rollout bench seating to accommodate 72,000 football fans. It was said that Modell would not always be the owner of the Browns, and quite possibly the next owner (whoever that may be) might want to play in a new building. Therefore some city leaders felt it proper to ignore the present owner's position and plan for what they felt was the city's best long-term interests.

This growing sentiment in favor of a dual-purpose building caught the attention of Major League Baseball. When American League President Bobby Brown came to Cleveland to address reporters at Stouffer's Tower City Plaza Hotel, he pointed out that the League had taken a hands-off approach to the Indians' lease negotiations, but it remained the League's strong preference that the new stadium be developed as a baseball-only park (which flew in the face of the public mandate to develop a stadium enlargeable for professional football). He explained, "I am not going to say you veto it (a dual-purpose facility). But you certainly do everything you can to discourage such a thing, because it just won't give you what you need." He then urged political leaders to study other venues where baseball and football teams shared a common facility, so they could understand the problems stemming from those conditions. He also applauded the efforts in negotiating lease terms with the Indians, that so far those terms were favorable and offered the franchise "a chance to become viable and to operate in a climate that gives them a chance to be very competitive." He said the lease would guarantee the city a team for 20 years, even if fortunes on the field didn't improve.

It was interesting to hear Bobby Brown say just about the same thing that Art Modell had been saying. (In reality, Art had only been repeating what the American League has been saying for years). Still, it seemed that Modell's position was always interpreted by the politicians and business leaders as Art acting only in his own selfish interests. Ever since the 1970s Modell had known the Cleveland Indians wanted to control their own destiny. He heard it over and over again, first hand, from his tenant in Gate A. But when Modell spoke, people chose not to listen. Many of the entrenched community leaders were determined that Art Modell was not going to "dictate" to the city what should be done. Not until September 1992, did the *Plain Dealer* come out editorially in agreement with Art Modell, Bobby Brown, and others. "The stadium at Gateway is for the Indians. It is a baseball field and should remain that, nothing more," the editors wrote.

Even after Brown's visit to Cleveland, Mayor White and County Commissioner Hagan were still saying that the expandability feature for football must be included in the design of Gateway's ballpark. But not many voters remembered hearing anything about the Browns during the campaign. They only remembered a vote to keep the Indians in Cleveland. Jacobs was reported as telling friends that he wanted a baseball-only stadium—nothing else. A close friend of Jacobs said, "I think it's a deal-breaker. It'll be a question of who blinks first, and Jacobs doesn't blink."

Bob DiBiasio, Indians' publicity director, added, "We certainly want our own facility. One of the reasons we want to get out of the Stadium is because it's dual-purpose. To do it all over again at Gateway for another 50 years doesn't make sense."

Brent Larkin of the *Plain Dealer* wrote that "some city officials, especially Mayor White, want to ease Modell out of the Stadium in 1998 because they covet the lakefront land. Modell has indicated his unhappiness that the city is trying to force him out of the Stadium." Larkin went on:

If history is a guide, Jacobs will get what he wants out of Gateway in the form of a baseball-only stadium and he won't be bashful about backing out of the deal. What's needed here is basic fairness. If Jacobs gets his way at Gateway, Modell should get his way at the Stadium in the form of an extension of his lease. If not, expect Modell to start looking for land in the suburbs for a new stadium, maybe even outside the county. Keeping the Indians in Cleveland has long been a problem. Keeping the Browns in Cleveland could be the next problem.

All Art Modell was heard to say was: "Give me the same deal the city gave Dick Jacobs, and I'll be a happy camper."

By December 1990 a final lease had not been completed with the Indians. The issue of who would be liable for the real estate taxes was still unsettled. The Indians continued to maintain that there wasn't enough money projected in the operation to pay the tax. Something had to happen because the clock was running out before the end-of-the-year deadline to issue the tax-exempt bonds. Final leases had to be in place before the bonds could be marketed. Publicly, Tom Chema was starting to downplay the tax liability. The *Plain Dealer* on December 12 quoted Chema:

What all these projections come down to is what is fair value. The present Central Market property (site of the Gateway complex) is now taxed at $400,000 a year. If you tax Gateway on what is cost basis, we'd have to pay something like $4 million, and I don't think that's fair, and I don't think that's what will happen here.

Chema added that government needed to figure out an appropriate basis for evaluating sports facilities, but he said he didn't know why property taxes had to become an issue in 1990 when they wouldn't become a responsibility until 1994, when the buildings were completed. In the final draft of the leases with both the Indians and the Cavs, Gateway agreed to pay the real estate taxes.

At a press conference that day, Mayor White answered the barrage of questions posed by reporters with a written statement, but declined to field further questions on the subject. White said that Gateway would have to pay the tax, but the project must be given "fair and equitable treatment." There was no explanation for the disparity from the amount of the taxes promised voters in the Gateway campaign (co-chaired by Mayor White and Cuyahoga County Commissioner Tim Hagan). The $4.7 million promise had become a $500,000 pledge.

Back in Tower B at Cleveland Stadium, Art Modell and a few of us were wondering out loud whether any "fair and equitable treatment" would be forthcoming for our "salvage-value" stadium which obligated Stadium Corp. to pay $400,000 a year in real and personal property taxes. I couldn't help but wonder how much longer Modell was going to turn the other cheek.

Meanwhile, the Cavaliers lease was beginning to take shape, and some interesting insights were forthcoming. Roldo Bartimole reviewed the lease in his November 1990 issue of *Point of View* in which he indicated that the Cavaliers would keep **all** of their gate revenues. This suggested that the Gunds would get the arena rent-free. Bartimole explained that all concessions, scoreboard advertising, and loge and club seating revenues would be turned over to the Cavs. Bartimole appeared flabbergasted that Gateway was paying for, of all things, the Cavs' telephone system, since the system, according to the lease, had to be technically advanced, which apparently qualified it as a building expense.

At Tower B, we discussed with Art the concessions made to the Gunds. We wondered how long it would be before City Hall would call to tell Art that in the spirit of fair and equitable treatment, the city would no longer require rent to be paid by the Browns/Stadium Corp. The Browns could have used a new telephone system too, but needless to say, no City Hall call was forthcoming.

Modell summoned Bailey and me to review the benefits granted to the other sports franchises in town as a result of the sin tax vote, comparing them to what the Browns and Stadium Corp. then had. Modell was clear about his aim:

> I will keep a low profile while Gateway is being built. Heaven knows that I don't want to be construed as an obstructionist to progress being made in the City of Cleveland with its new sports facilities. But once the Indians get underway [scheduled to be in 1994] we will begin our campaign to get "equal treatment," and that includes being made whole for the loss of the Indians.

Bailey added one very significant point. While both teams retained the rights to almost all revenues, Gateway Corp. took on the responsibility to fund all necessary future capital improvements throughout the lease. As Jim was very deliberately making this statement, I saw Art's neck slowly turn red, before he let go with, "Yeah, and schmuck me, I'm sitting here putting my own money in this 60-year-old dump. I oughta have my head examined."

Gateway proceeded at a fast clip. Cost estimates were becoming more refined, and change orders were coming in just as fast. Many people justifiably were concerned whether the cost estimates were holding. Dick Jacobs took a reading of the situation and concluded in March 1991 that the project might be facing a problem of as much as $100 million in a combination of either costs over budget or revenues coming up short. The ballpark appeared to be running in the neighborhood of $179 million (compared to the original $128 million), and the arena budget was up to $105 million (compared to an original $75 million). In order to stem the rising costs of the baseball park, a decision was made to cut the capacity from 45,000 to about 42,000. There was no public discussion of exactly how much this 3,000-seat cutback would save. In addition, the Indians were going to contribute $20 million from up-front loge sales, an increase from the previously-agreed-to $12 million. Others were warning that the estimated revenues from naming rights were overly ambitious. If these critics turned out to be right, the problem with the budget would only be deferred until the tail end of the project.

While discussions over the new baseball park were going on, the Browns had to address a problem of their own, providing themselves with a new training facility. The Browns learned that their 20-year lease with Baldwin-Wallace College would not be renewed as the college's own sports programs were experiencing rapid growth, particularly for women's sports, and the school needed more space. The Browns would be practicing elsewhere in 1991.

Jim Bailey took leadership on this project, and one of his first steps was to try to locate land in the city of Cleveland for the facility. The Browns were hopeful that Cleveland would do for them what other cities were doing for their NFL teams, but the hopes faded when Cleveland officials were unable to find a suitable site. It began to look as though the Cleveland Browns' corporate headquarters, after being housed in Tower B of Cleveland Stadium for 40-some years, would no longer be located in Cleveland, Ohio.

The economic reality, of course, that follows such corporate moves is the consequential loss of city income tax collections on the salaries of the employees. The City of Cleveland stood to lose some amount of income taxes in this shakeout. While the move would not dramatically impact any change in tax collections from the players' salaries, since these salaries were already allocated among Cleveland, Mentor (stemming from training camp in August), and Berea, the same did not hold true for the front office. City income taxes on front office salaries were paid to the City of Cleveland; after the move most of them would be paid to another city.

After it became clear that Cleveland officials were either unable or unwilling to help the Browns find a training site in Cleveland, the City of Berea made an offer so competitive that it was clear to Modell how much Berea mayor Stan Trupo wanted the Browns to locate there. Very soon thereafter, the Browns entered into a long-term agreement to construct a $12 million state-of-the-art training facility in Berea. The City of Berea selected a site on the north end of the city which was zoned as an urban renewal area.

Much of the Browns' decision-making at this time was falling on Jim Bailey's shoulders, and Jim was finding it difficult to delegate much of his work. Jim's office became a bottleneck. It was the place all major decisions needed to pass through for approval, but these were becoming backlogged. Jim stated more than once that he didn't feel he had enough qualified help in the front office to assist him in business and administrative matters. So, to get through the pinch, he hired his wife Ann to help with the construction project.

Construction began in summer 1990, and in August 1991, the Browns, their new head coach, and revamped coaching staff moved into the new Berea corporate headquarters. They would return to Cleveland only to play their games on Sunday afternoons. When the total job was completed, with furnishings, cost of financing, and all change orders tabulated, the total outlay was over $14 million.

The Browns held an open house for the community in fall 1991. Many former players and employees came out to see the spectacular building. When Ed Uhas, assistant to president Art Modell during the 1970s, visited the building and complimented Art on the long-awaited accomplishment, Uhas was surprised that Art didn't seem very happy. Modell snapped back, "I sure as hell would like someone to tell me how I am going to pay for it."

What Art undoubtedly had been thinking when he made that remark was that around the NFL those days, other team owners were able to get cities to build the training centers for their teams. But in Cleveland Modell had just obligated his team to a new multi-million dollar loan. He must have thought he was still being a "schmuck" for not being able to secure the kind of deal his fellow owners were getting.

The training center represented one of the first matters on which the Cleveland Browns had to deal with the Cleveland administration of Michael White. It was the beginning of a relationship that would become increasingly acrimonious. Art Modell and Jim Bailey had come to see firsthand that it was virtually impossible for the Browns to work out a satisfactory business arrangement with the "new" City of Cleveland.

The 1989 Rolling Stones' Steel Wheels Tour. A view of the stage from a field seat.
Cleveland Stadium Corp. collection

CHAPTER 13

THE BEGINNING OF THE BELICHICK ERA

The tenth head coach in the history of the Browns displayed a rare bit of humor upon being introduced by owner Art Modell. In response to the introduction, Bill Belichick said, "I'm flattered to be compared to Don Shula, but to be compared to him is a joke. I mean, the guy is a Hall of Fame coach and I have yet to coach one game in this league. I hope he's not insulted."

As I remember, despite hiring a new coach and thereby offering hope to the Browns' fans hungering for a return to greatness, Art Modell did not have a happy look about him. Maybe he was worrying about his hip which would soon require replacement surgery. Who knew the cause? Art seldom discussed his health with the staff.

In the years that I worked for him, Modell often said that people lived on hope, hope for a better tomorrow, hope for an improved life, and hope for escape from the doldrums. But people had to have something to feed that hope. A new coach was what Art furnished his fans (and himself) to supply that hope.

I used to wish that as Modell was entering the twilight years of his career, he could be more at peace with himself and enjoy life a bit more. But as I would reflect on what he and his organizations had been through, I could understand why he was always uptight. "Wound tighter than a drum," we would say, "probably just waiting for the other shoe to drop." A recap of the last decade made it clear that starting in 1980 every year had brought some reverses. For example, how much worse could this menu be:

1980
- The playoffs ended with the Brian Sipe interception and loss to the Raiders. Super Bowl trip denied!

1981
- The two-month baseball strike damaged the financial hopes of the Stadium Corp. for the year.
- Browns collapse to 5-11 after nearly missing Super Bowl in 1980.

1982
- Gries files three lawsuits against Modell.
- NFL players' strike cripples the Browns economically.

1983

- Indians and Gabe Paul bring two lawsuits against Modell, reportedly making reference to him in public as being a "crook."
- Modell has a severe heart attack and requires bypass surgery.
- It is revealed that Charles White and other prominent Browns' players are being treated for drug abuse, forcing the creation of the Inner Circle, a drug/alcohol rehab program for team members.

1984

- Modell loses Gries lawsuit in Common Pleas court.
- Modell fires his dear friend Sam Rutigliano, after team falls to 1-7, in a season beginning with Super Bowl hopes.

1986

- Star player Don Rogers dies of cocaine overdose before the season starts.
- Modell loses Gries lawsuit by decree of Ohio Supreme Court.
- Browns lose home playoff game to Denver after Elway's 98-yard drive, foiling another shot at the Super Bowl.

1987

- Important first-round draft pick fizzles: Junkin never lives up to expectations.
- Another NFL players' strike devastates the Browns and Modell, leading to the introduction of "replacement" players.
- Enormous field damage from concerts proves embarrassing.
- Browns lose again to Denver in the playoffs, 38-33, thereby missing shot at Super Bowl for second straight year.

1988

- Another first-round draft pick fizzles: Charlton fails to develop.
- Friction arises between Schottenheimer and front office, leading to the second head coach termination in four years.
- City Council refuses to grant Cleveland Stadium Corp. a 10-year lease extension, despite Modell pledging $10 million in new capital improvements.

1989

- Modell's health takes a setback: arthritic hip keeps him in constant discomfort (surgery finally had to be done in 1993), and concerns over his cardiac condition return.
- After many months of preparation, Stadium renovation study proposed to city leaders; Mayor Voinovich fails to attend Modell's presentation.

- Kevin Mack sentenced to jail during the season for recurring drug abuse.
- Another playoff loss to Denver, 37-21, the third time the Broncos come between Cleveland and the Super Bowl.

1990

- Modell enters Cleveland Clinic for second open-heart surgery.
- Gateway project vote passes, greasing the skids for the Indians to leave the Stadium.
- No mention of financial relief is made to Modell for loss of his tenant.
- Season starts with many holdouts, after Browns sign free agent Raymond Clayborn for big bucks.
- The year is the worst in franchise history, with a 3-13 record.

Every year but 1985 was full of setbacks and disappointments. The bright spots were snuffed out by all the glaring negatives. But 1985 produced Bernie Kosar, who in his first year brought Cleveland into the playoffs with an appearance in Miami against Don Shula's Dolphins. Ironically, the one decent year fell about midway during this infamous decade; maybe God thought we needed a reprieve so we could withstand what was yet to come.

While Art Modell was readying his announcement that Bill Belichick would spearhead the "hope" for resurrecting the team's fortunes, he was also telling fans about personnel changes in the 1990 team. "A lot of players you see on this team will not be back for the 1991 season. There are players on this team who are not carrying their load and not keeping in the Browns' tradition, and I don't think they belong here," Modell said.

Belichick took advantage of the situation and extensively cleaned house. He described his objective as transforming the Browns into an NFC-style team, going from the "finesse" team more prevalent in the AFC to the power-football team so dominant in the NFC. Since the NFC was dominating the Super Bowls, it seemed that following the NFC design must yield superior results. So the roster was cleared of many marginal players. (Bud Carson would say years later that he was vindicated by Belichick's house-cleaning. Carson said he told Modell and the front office prior to the 1990 season that the talent was mediocre or aging. His answer: the players had been had been good enough to make the playoffs for five straight years, that he should have no beef.)

In 1991 many players were brought into camp for a "look-see," and just as quickly sent packing. Belichick said, soon after arriving, "In order to get to championship level, we need a bigger, stronger, faster, and more physical team than was here in 1990." In the 1991 draft, Belichick's first, he selected safety Eric Turner as his first round pick. Turner was the big, strong, fast, and more physical player that would start rebuilding the Browns. When questioned about the pick, Belichick said, "Art told me it's my call, and I made it. I think it's important to have a big, physical safety who can control the middle of the field. Those guys can make plays that can turn games around."

In the front office we looked at each other with interest. This was a complete reversal from the script with Bud Carson at draft time and a return to the one with Marty Schottenheimer. But coming out of the draft room, all participants said there were no problems and they were in agreement with the selections and the process.

It is interesting to note the history of the Browns' head coaches and the swing in personalities. Paul Brown was the dominant, head-strong coach who would not last with Modell. He was replaced by soft-spoken Blanton Collier and Nick Skorich. Then Art Modell went back to the determined, regimented approach exemplified by Forrest Gregg, which after three years gave way to the more philosophical and understanding style of Sam Rutigliano. Sensing a need to go back the other way, Modell then selected the strong-willed Marty Schottenheimer, and when he had enough of that style, he returned to the soft-spoken, grandfatherly-type in Bud Carson.

After only two years with Carson, Modell decided a return to the youthful and energetic Bill Belichick was what was needed. (After the move to Baltimore took place, Modell would return once again to the paternalistic, kindly style exhibited by Ted Marchibroda.)

Belichick was given a lot of authority. He came to Cleveland with a game plan that made sense to the owner and the front office, and he was given the latitude to achieve his goals.

The Browns moved into their new facility in Berea just as the first season under Belichick was about to begin. The building was enormous, with wide corridors and spacious and elaborately furnished offices. The physical plant was beautiful, but something was missing. No one could quite put his finger on it then, but over time people began to agree: the place lacked the warmth and intimacy that the confined offices in Tower B at the Stadium had exuded. It seemed like miles from one end of the Berea complex to the other. The resulting isolation permitted coolness and eventually even coldness to develop among those who worked there. (Months after Belichick was fired, almost everyone still around pointed to him as the reason this attitude prevailed.)

Many former Browns' players were invited to come to Berea to join practice but didn't feel comfortable being escorted everywhere they went, nor did they relish certain restrictions placed on them. Security guards were ever-present: at the point of vehicular entry, at the front door, at the door leading to the practice fields, and so on. Visitors sensed a feeling of suspicion, maybe even paranoia, throughout the building. Former players would remark that it hadn't been that way in the past. While sponsors and guests of the marketing department were still invited to view practice sessions, it wasn't as comfortable for them as it had been. The media were "controlled" by placing them in a media room with a good view of the practice field. The new facility was surely state-of-the-art, but it lacked the warmth of the Browns' organization of yesteryear. Many would later say that it took on the personality of the head coach.

Bill Belichick worked his players hard. In training camp, they regularly had to climb "Mount Belichick," a huge mound of leftover clay piled off to the side of the four practice fields. The dirt was put to good use; players felt like they were running up a ski slope. Bill's objective seemed simple: if the Browns were better conditioned than their opponents, it might sometimes pay off in the late stages of a game.

Despite the conditioning, Belichick opened his first season with a defense decimated by injuries. Injuries continued to mount until the injured reserve totaled 17 players by December 1. Because of the many injuries, as well as the exodus of so many players from the 1990 squad, the Browns' roster in December listed an abnormally high 39 free agents.

Besides the injury factor, Belichick had differences with offensive players who resented the limited offensive schemes in which they felt their roles were restricted. Webster Slaughter and Reggie Langhorne were among the most vocal. Langhorne, who felt the wrath of the coach ostensibly because he was a holdout, resented being asked to run plays with the scout team when he came back. A confrontation resulted, and soon thereafter, Langhorne learned he would not be making the next road trip. Many writers sided with the players. They wrote that the offensive scheme had no identity, a problem that resulted from the constant turnover in offensive coordinators. In Bernie Kosar's seven seasons with the Browns, he was operating with his sixth offensive coordinator. Kosar had worked under Joe Pendry, Lindy Infante, Marty Schottenheimer, Marc Trestman, Jim Shofner, and now Gary Tranquill (or was it Bill Belichick?) Other writers were critical because they believed the coaches could better utilize Eric Metcalf's talents.

Every season seems to have at least one game that raises eyebrows. In Belichick's first season, that game might have been with Philadelphia. Despite the rash of injuries, the Browns were sitting with a respectable (considering the circumstances) 4-5 record, when they had to face the Randall Cunningham-led Eagles, who were coming off a big Monday night win over rival New York Giants. Going on the road after the big win should have left the Eagles ripe for a letdown. It looked like the script was playing out that way as the Browns shot out to a 23-0 lead, riddling Bud Carson's number-one ranked defense seemingly at will with 215 passing yards. During the game, Kosar broke Bart

Starr's record by throwing his 308th straight pass without an interception. But at halftime, Bud Carson made the necessary defensive adjustments to close down the Browns' effectiveness, holding his former team to just seven more points. Then, a banged-up Jim McMahon came on to captain the Eagles' charge back, as he threw for 341 yards in leading his team to 32 points. The game was still the Browns' to win until Webster Slaughter, fielding a punt on the two-yard line rather than letting it go for a touchback, started running laterally, only to fumble and lose the ball to the Eagles. The Eagles then punched it into the end zone for the winning points. This was a really tough game to lose as the Browns were embarrassed, 32-30, by blowing what was probably the biggest lead ever in team history.

Going into December, the Browns were at six wins and seven losses. When asked for an appraisal, owner Modell said, "Considering all the injuries, it's been a good year." Belichick did achieve his objective of transforming the sorry Browns' team of 1990 into a team that an opponent respected. While still struggling against the top third of the league, the Browns were playing even-steven against the rest. Much of this success was due to the excellent takeaway-giveaway ratio which at that point was listed as "plus 20."

The Browns then did an abrupt turnaround. They lost the last three games of the year, concluding the campaign with a disappointing 6-10 record. Obviously, Kosar's improved 87.8 quarterback rating and the exceptional takeaway-giveaway ratio helped keep it that close. But, more disturbing was the fact that seven of the ten losses that year were by a combined total of a mere 24 points.

During Belichick's first season, a serious problem began to emerge. A cold war between the head coach and the media was brewing. It seems to have started the first week of the season, and it festered with the passing weeks. Reporters at the weekly press conferences were displeased with the coach's lack of enthusiasm when answering their questions and with his lack of forthrightness when reporting the extent of players' injuries. The coach, on the other hand, felt that providing too much information could only help opposing coaches prepare for the upcoming game. Why help the enemy, he thought, and hand them that edge? But the media didn't accept that rationale. They preferred to believe he was being ornery and disdainful. "He'll be able to get away with that snippy attitude as long as he wins. But when he starts losing, he better watch out, because then he will get his," one media member told a group of us standing nearby.

The stated goal for 1992 was to take the team to the next level. That was not going to be an easy task. The team was showing the ill effects of the drafting mistakes of 1987 and 1988. One look at the existing roster showed only four first-round picks listed--Kosar, Matthews, Metcalf, and Turner--from the last 14 years. As Kosar said after the Browns lost the 1991 season finale to the mediocre Steelers, "I've known, and I think a lot of people have known, that there's still a way to go on this team."

The 1992 draft was one more step to that next level. To almost everyone's surprise, Bill Belichick selected Tommy Vardell, big running back out of Stanford as the number one pick. Vardell was a back who not only could run well but also block and catch passes; he was the "whole package." He also had a reputation for being mentally tough and not a fumbler. In his career at Stanford he carried the ball 418 times without a fumble. This statistic might well have been the most important consideration in selecting Vardell, for that would make him an important cog in the "ball-control" offense that Belichick was trying to design.

The media was surprised but generally in agreement with the pick. Even one of the Browns' most severe critics muttered, "That's a good pick," when Vardell was announced over the intercom. The surprise, of course, was that the team's strength was at running back (the roster already boasted Metcalf, Hoard, and Mack), and the team did not appear to be drafting in its area of need. But it was also apparent that when it was crunch time and ball control was needed late in the fourth quarter, it would be great to have a choice of big back to put into the game. Kevin Mack had a history of wearing down late in the year. As Modell commented later, "You can never have enough running backs."

Still, the glaring need on the offensive line went unresolved. In the first ten rounds, not one offensive lineman was selected. Critics might ask what good were running backs if there were no blockers out front. At his state of the team address after the 1991 season, even Art acknowledged, "We have to do something with the offensive line. That is an automatic." The 1991 season had ended with Tony Jones, Dan Fike, Mike Baab, Ed King, and John Rienstra as the starters. Not everyone found fault with those individuals. Leroy Hoard commented, "They need time to play together as a unit. They will get better."

Belichick explained his draft philosophy when asked about ignoring the needs at offensive line. He said he would only draft for need if the team was one or two players away from a championship. "Right now," Bill said, "we need a little more than that."

Another unusual phenomenon was occurring. Belichick was doing all the talking about the draft. Where was Ernie Accorsi? After all, when Bud Carson was hired, it was specified that the personnel department would direct the draft and that Accorsi and his staff were in full charge. Based on what was occurring, it came as no surprise when Ernie Accorsi resigned only days after the 1992 draft ended. Ernie apparently realized that Art was enamored with his new head coach and that the two of them felt they could operate without a "football-operations" man in between. Art said that Ernie had tried to resign earlier, after Belichick came on board, but Art would not hear of it. After the second attempt, Modell accepted the resignation.

As Ernie was packing up his belongings, he turned to me and said, "You know, Art does have some good, loyal people working for him. The trouble is, he doesn't always know who they are." I was beginning to agree with that assessment.

Accorsi was never replaced. David Modell began to work on player negotiations and player contracts. The head coach became the top man in player selection and pro-curement, and Jim Bailey, acting as Art's representative, oversaw the whole operation. This was the most meaning-ful position, since Modell was spending many days at home recuperating from his surgery. He wanted to redesign his modus operandi so as not to talk to the different department heads individually as he had for the previous 30 years. He wanted to work through Bailey alone. He asked me, for instance, to run everything on the Stadium Corp. through

Ernie Accorsi
Cleveland Stadium Corp. collection

Bailey, who in turn would run it by Art, "if necessary." The problem, as we were to find out later, was that Bailey didn't always attach the same importance to certain matters as we or Art might have. Years later, a Browns' official lamented:

> Things were never the same after Ernie left... there was no one left in a meaningful position who could, and would say "no" to Art Modell. Ernie was the last of the guys close to Art who would challenge the tide when it was turning against what Ernie felt was right. He didn't fear Art Modell, or what his reaction might be. He didn't fear that he was going against the majority. He fought for what he thought was best for Art Modell and the team, even though Art may not have been able to see it at the time.

With Art at home in Waite Hill most of the time, Ernie realized that Art was not able to see a lot of things. Art only knew what Jim Bailey chose to pass along to him. One of Accorsi's frustrations was allowing Bailey to decide what Art Modell should be made aware of. We were learning, sometimes the hard way, that Bailey was simply not passing certain matters along to Art, because "it would just upset him."

I challenged Bailey about not informing Art on one issue involving the Stadium Corp. Bailey's response to me? "Art couldn't handle the severity of the situation and wouldn't handle it right."

In Accorsi's last year on the payroll, he became aware through the club's security director of a situation involving some players on a road trip. Accorsi decided it was serious, and he wanted the club to take immediate action to contain further problems. Ernie dutifully went to Bailey and told him he was going directly to Art to tell him about the problem and what he wanted him to do about it. Bailey told Ernie that if it were he, he would not bother Art with the matter as it would "just upset him."

Jim Bailey
Cleveland Stadium
Corp. collection

That's how the team was starting to be managed: DON'T EVER GO TO ART WITH ANYTHING THAT MIGHT UPSET HIM. Well, that's just great, I thought. Why go to Art when things are going well? What would I tell him, "Things are good?" What's needed in managing a company is top-level caucusing and top-level direction, especially when things are not going well. Bailey's contention was that the timing had to be right, and he claimed he was able to decide that better than any of us since he was in hourly contact with Art. But we all knew Bailey's approach: If Art was in a good mood, Jim would choose not to change that mood with bad news; when he was in a "down" mood, why deepen it?

At the same time, Art announced that he would be more active in the administration of the club than before and would continue as general manager. Art's definition of general manager and the one most often held around the NFL were not the same. Typically in the league whoever was in charge of player matters--drafting, selecting, signing, negotiating--was viewed as the G.M. Art felt the general manager's function also extended to financial matters, including budgeting and treasury functions. In that context, Art felt only he was qualified. If not Art, then perhaps it was Bailey who was growing into the position as Art defined it. As to the definition generally held around the league, it might appear that Bill Belichick was assuming the G.M. role.

There was plenty of player movement leading up to the 1992 season. The opening day roster listed only 12 players Belichick inherited when he took over the team. Even though the team makeup was changing, the media were not yet impressed that it was vastly improved. No one picked the Browns to win the relatively weak Central Division. The main change in the offensive line involved the release of Mike Baab in late August and the signing of Jay Hilgenberg to replace him in time for the opener. (The last time the Browns changed centers, they did so just before the opener, and that season--1988--ended in disaster. The center being replaced at that time also happened to be Mike Baab). The only other new face on the line was free agent Bob Dahl, signed as a defensive lineman, but being converted to the offense.

The final pre-season home game may have been an omen of things to come. A loss to the Minnesota Vikings by a score of 56-3 hardly built hope a la Modell among the Browns' faithful. In 1992 another rash of injuries occurred. Michael Dean Perry started the year on DL, recovering from knee surgery; Kosar broke an ankle in the second week; Minnifield was playing hurt all year; Vardell opened the season out of action with a shoulder injury; and Patrick Rowe, the number two pick who was being counted on to fill the void at wide receiver, was lost with a season-ending knee injury prior to opening day. Complicating matters further, two of those departed in the off-season were long-time favorite wide receivers Reggie Langhorne and Brian Brennan. And Webster Slaughter was holding out. What a dilemma! Three of last year's front-line receivers were not back, and the top pick to replace one of them would miss the season. To make matters worse, Metcalf (along with Slaughter) was demanding to be traded, and Perry was openly feuding with the coach.

Modell must have been at the crossroads on this one. Many front-line players were hurt, and many popular players were at odds with his hand-picked coach. Callers into the radio talk shows were openly critical of Belichick. They missed their favorite players from former years and resented the coach's insensitive style of releasing players because they didn't fit into what he wanted done. They disagreed with Tommy Vardell as the number one pick, mostly because Vardell fit the coach's style of ball-control football, which in the fans' opinion was boring and ineffective. In face of this criticism, the front office cited the adage, "Wide open football scores points and sells tickets; ball-control football wins games."

Early in the season, the offensive line showed how much work was still needed. Kosar was sacked 11 times in the opener against the Indianapolis Colts, which the Browns lost 14-3. Four sacks came at the hands of Chip Banks, the Browns' former number one draft pick, and one of the touchdowns came courtesy of Reggie Langhorne. The offensive line, even with the addition of Jay Hilgenberg and Freddie Childress, looked pathetic and disoriented.

The Browns finished 1992 at 7-9, a one-win improvement over the prior year, but in so doing, lost the last three games of the year, just as they had in 1991. Four games had been lost by four points or less, and that was with backup quarterbacks Tomczak and Philcox playing 60% of the year. The game that Modell lamented over the most, however, was the home loss to Houston late in the year. Lorenzo White slipped through a tackle by Frank Minnifield and rambled 65 yards with less than two minutes left in the game, to allow the Browns to snatch defeat from the jaws of victory. Defensive lapses also cost the team a victory against San Diego when a mixup in the secondary resulted in a late come-from-behind touchdown pass to give the Chargers a 14-13 victory. All in all, with all the roster changes and the large number of injuries, Belichick's 13-19 record for the first two years was somewhat acceptable. His treatment of players who had been sports heroes in Cleveland, however, was leaving Cleveland fans with a bad taste. His attitude toward the media was giving writers an even worse one.

Modell held a press conference on December 30, 1992, in front of 50 reporters, six television cameras, and a live radio audience to give a "State of the Browns" address. He led off by saying, "I'll make this statement. I'm so positive of Bill Belichick's future here and that of the Cleveland Browns' organization that if we don't get the job done by the end of his contract (1995) I will get out of football and leave Cleveland. I'm so positive that he's going to do it, I'm not going to be looking for new excuses." Modell continued, "He's the last head coach I hired. I will not hire another coach." He refused to define what he meant by "getting the job done," but he said later it would have to be at least the playoffs with home field advantage. Modell gave Belichick total support for the job he was doing. He stopped short, though, in the area of Bill's role as offensive coordinator. He said, "Bill did not come in here to be in charge of the offense. He wasn't hired to be the offensive coordinator. We will be reviewing the offensive schemes for next year, and we will have a more organized approach to the offensive side of the ball in some form in 1993." With Accorsi gone, we all wondered who was going to advise Art on this point.

Translated, we knew it meant that Art wasn't happy with the sluggish offense, but we no longer had the receivers who had provided the big plays in the past. Instead, we had a young Michael Jackson, Metcalf out of the backfield, a part-time Lawyer Tillman, and Rico Smith. According to the experts, we had poor run-blockers on the offensive line, which accounted for the dismal total of seven rushing touchdowns the entire season. The first coaching change saw the departure of Hal Hunter, offensive line coach carryover from Bud Carson's tenure. Belichick sought a coach with more run-blocking expertise.

Modell recognized the difficulties the media was experiencing with Belichick. At the end of his address, he apologized to the media on behalf of the organization for anything which might have offended them during the season. He said he would see to it that Belichick became more sensitive to the media's job.

Modell was asked why he had issued his dramatic ultimatum. He answered, "I am putting pressure on myself to get the job done. I know the Browns' fans are angry, and you know what, they should be angry. This town deserves a winner, and I am reaffirming my choice of Bill Belichick to get it done. If I made a mistake, I'll move on." He then talked about the future:

We have a good future, and I am asking your listeners and readers to be patient because this team is going to rebound in a very dramatic way. Sports is made up of hope for tomorrow being better days. I'm optimistic, and again, I say, if I can't get the job done, using a famous saying, 'you won't have me to kick around anymore' in three years.

Art was sending an important message. He said we were going to be winners big-time in three years, and with Bill Belichick as the coach, or he wouldn't be in Cleveland, PERIOD. We all know what happened three years later.

In professional sports, it has never been unusual to have an abrupt turn for the worse in a team's fortunes. Even back in 1952, when the Indians were enjoying success as a baseball contender, Ellis Ryan, then team president, preached words of caution to his fellow investors. At the time he was concerned about the direction the general manager was taking the team. Attendance had fallen 300,000, down to 1,440,000 fans, and Ryan feared that if the Indians ever fell into the second division, as he told his stockholders, "You can lose your shirt in one season." The NFL owners, however, had a lucrative television contract to fall back on, and it seemed unlikely an NFL team could ever lose its shirt in one season. But over a couple of seasons? Quite possibly.

The two strike years in the 1980s wreaked havoc on the Browns' ten-year summary of earnings, and the consecutive profitable years in the 70s would be difficult to duplicate. While John Q. Public would understand that most companies lose money during a strike, he might think that everything is O.K. once it was business as usual again. Well, that wasn't the case with the Browns (or many NFL teams, for that matter).

To settle the strike, the owners made major concessions, and consequently players' salaries increased significantly, causing owners' profits to drop to levels where pre-strike 1982 results were difficult to achieve again. The loans made to finance the strikes also had to be repaid. Even folks who worked for the Browns (outside the finance area) did not completely grasp this unfortunate piece of reality.

The losses incurred during the 1982 and 1987 strikes exceeded whatever profits were earned for all the other years from 1980-1992. The strikes were not the only reasons for the losses. The sizeable legal costs incurred during the Gries litigation, paying off the contracts of numerous coaches upon their termination, and higher interest rates all compounded the severity of the situation. Team assessments from the NFL to cover league-wide litigation were running into the millions of dollars.

The company's financial condition was a well-kept secret among the Browns' finance department, the company's auditors, the banks, and the league until the Sunday morning *Plain Dealer* of July 12, 1992, appeared. Fans had to be shocked when they read the sports page headline, "BOOKS SHOW BROWNS DEEP IN DEBT DURING 80s." PD reporters somehow had ob-

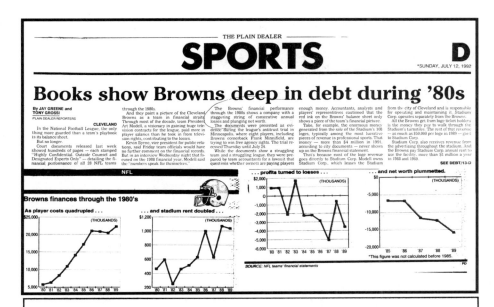

Reading about the Browns in the PD sport pages was like reading the financial pages with the related "Boardroom graphs." Focus turned toward the team's plunging net worth and consecutive operating losses, rather than wins and losses on the field.

tained confidential court documents presented in the league's anti-trust trial in Minnesota in which eight players, including Frank Minnifield, were trying to win free agency rights.

"In those documents," the PD reporter said, "was painted the picture of the Cleveland Browns as a team in financial straits. The Browns' financial performance through the decade of the 80s showed a string of staggering consecutive annual losses and plunging net worth." The report pointed out the differences in profits among various teams. For the same ten-year period in which the Browns showed accumulated losses of $12 million, the Cincinnati Bengals showed profits of $38 million, an alarming swing of $50 million between the two Central Division teams.

However, the players' lawyers argued the picture was incomplete, because lucrative loge and skybox revenues were not shown on the Browns' financial statements. The lawyers suggested revenues were "squirelled" away on another company's books, in our case, those of Cleveland Stadium Corp. They would not accept the rationale that those revenues did not belong to the Browns. The lawyers obviously did not understand that the loge revenues were committed to service the bank debt for the borrowings on capital improvements in the Stadium.

I recall this as the time when Modell and Bailey began to realize that like other professional sports franchises, only when the Browns could enjoy luxury suite revenues without being saddled by their construction costs could they ever hope to emerge from the spiraling debt situation in which they found themselves.

The *Plain Dealer* also listed the teams' bank debts. The PD reported that the Browns' line of credit (another term for maximum borrowing permitted) rose from $11 million in 1986, to $19 million, then to $21 million in 1988, and to $27 million in 1989. The Browns' debt limits were escalating, and of course the interest on that debt was also growing. In some years operating profits were no longer sufficient to cover even the interest load. The mortgage on the new training facility was soon going to take the debt well over $40 million.

The PD was able to obtain more confidential data, including all the NFL owners' salaries. The documents showed that Art Modell was the lowest paid president/CEO of any team in the AFC Central Division. The newspaper reported that in 1990 Paul Brown of the Bengals received $386,000, Pittsburgh's Dan Rooney earned $375,000, Houston's Bud Adams earned $409,000, while Art Modell was at the bottom, at $195,000. A few of us in the front office recalled when Art was sued by his fellow owner years earlier when he increased his compensation to that level from a base of $60,000. Art's pay remained in the bargain basement.

When asked to comment, Modell said, "I'm a little embarrassed by this whole thing. The numbers speak for themselves. I never came to Cleveland to make money. I came to win. I guess this shows that this carpetbagger from New York City is not milking the franchise, huh?" That was in reaction to a remark Art heard when he first came to Cleveland in 1961. Some 30 years later, it obviously still bothered him.

During 1992, Belichick was the only NFL head coach with a defensive background serving as his own offensive coordinator. Ironically, it was the Browns' front office which had objected loudly to this same situation with Marty Schottenheimer just four short years earlier.

Running back James Brooks, brought to Cleveland for a tryout in 1992 and then cut from the roster during the middle of the season, lambasted the Browns' organization upon leaving, saying the offense was rife with problems. "The offense is way too basic," he said. "Belichick was the one calling the plays. He's a hard worker, but he needs an offensive coordinator." Whenever reporters asked the question as to who on the staff was calling the plays, Belichick was evasive. Brooks provided that answer as he was walking out the door.

Fans booed the conservative play calls. When Modell was told the fans were angry with the boring offensive product on the field, he said, "I'd rather have angry fans than apathetic fans. When we start winning again, they'll be back."

By the end of the 1992 season, Belichick's popularity was nosediving. Tony Grossi of the *Plain Dealer* attributed this to the fans' perception that the coach "is a dunderhead when it comes to offensive strategy." Grossi wrote that "if Modell were to fire Belichick today, he would be applauded by about 75% of the Browns' season ticketholders." Grossi said Belichick and Mike Lombardi , the personnel director, were both to blame for the failure of the running game. This, he said, stemmed from their overestimating the ability of the offensive line. With the likes of Freddie Childress, Ben Jefferson, Kevin Robbins, Houston Hoover, Chris Thome, and Kevin Simons being paraded in and out of the starting lineup, one had to wonder how long Bailey and Modell would be buying the Lombardi line that these guys were players. If there was ever an example of why Modell needed a football-side general manager, this was prime. Bailey did not have that background or experience, and Modell did not have the in-depth knowledge of football talent to question Lombardi's trans-actions.

Ray Yannucci, editor and publisher of the BNI, evaluated the perfor-mance of the 1992 Browns, by saying this was a team in need of much repair. He said that in 1993, the team needed another quarterback, a wide receiver or two, and help at cornerback. He cited Kosar's broken ankle, the extensive surgery required, and the question mark it posed for the coming season. Nor did he ignore the extensive pounding that Bernie had taken in recent seasons. The most seasoned receiver on the roster was Michael Jackson, and he had played inconsistently. Next on the depth chart were Patrick Rowe and Rico Smith, which illustrated the reason for concern. At corner, almost everyone felt that Frank Minnifield would retire or exit as a free agent. Yannucci was hopeful the Browns would resolve most of these problems through free agency, since there was a plentiful supply around the NFL. It was a good way to get competitive quickly, but also a quick way to run up the payroll with lucrative contracts and hefty signing bonuses. Yannucci reported that Modell had prom-ised, "We will be very active in free agency this off-season. There will not be a fourth straight season without a playoff game."

One other problem was cited from the season just completed. Scoring 15 points a game was not going to win many games in the NFL. While fans were clamoring for an offensive coordinator, it was clear from Belichick's com-ments that he didn't believe this was a problem. Neither did wide receiver Michael Jackson, who seemed to lend credence to the coach's stance in saying, "It's not as much who is offensive coordinator, or even what plays are being called, but it comes down to the way the play is being executed." It always seemed to come back to the weakness in the offensive line.

As the 1993 season got underway, new concerns were developing. The offensive line had four new starters, including rookie Steve Everitt at center, replacing Jay Hilgenberg. The preseason games also found Bernie Kosar not playing up to the levels of his better years. Fortunately, the Browns were able to sign Vinny Testaverde on the free agent market to serve as Bernie's backup. It was certainly a luxury to have a former starting quarterback accept a backup role while commanding the salary of a frontline player. This costly adventure gave the front office reasonable assurance it could continue winning if the "franchise" quarterback went down. The team made other major acquisitions in the free agent marketplace: Mark Carrier, WR; Najee Mustafaa, DB; Jerry Ball, DT, to name a few. Modell was sparing no money in buying the talent the team had been unable to obtain at the draft table. With all the new faces, and a substantial increase in payroll, the objective of upgrading the overall talent level was achieved.

Then a new problem reared its ugly head. It was hidden in the comment from Ozzie Newsome, who said, "We have the talent, but the chemistry and getting this team to play together as a unit is just as important as acquiring the talent. Until we get the proper chemistry, we're still constructing." That statement about "chemistry" sounded more than a little foreboding. Only one offensive lineman had returned to the position he played in 1992, Tony Jones at left tackle. Rebuilding continued, as linemen were moved around in different combinations.

Despite experimenting on the line, behind Bernie Kosar the Browns jumped out to a 2-0 record, after a 23-13 Monday night victory over the San Francisco 49ers at Cleveland Stadium. Fans probably remember clearly the spectacular touchdown pass play from Kosar to a stretched-out, diving-at-full-speed, Michael Jackson (Dyson) as he fell to the turf in the end zone in front of the Dawg Pound. Few, however, noticed the exchange between Kosar and Belichick as the quarterback came off the field after the play which put the Browns ahead to stay. That may have been the first time ever that a coach looked downright angry after a picturesque TD catch. Something was obviously wrong!

When Modell had been talked out of the need for an offensive coordinator in 1993, Belichick agreed that Ozzie Newsome and Bernie Kosar would contribute to the game plan. This sounded to most of us like "offense by committee." Well, on that particular successful TD play, it looked as though there was disagreement within the committee. As we found out later, Bernie had changed the play sent in by Belichick, and doing so had put him in almost total disfavor with the coach.

In the following week against the Raiders, with the Browns down 13-0 in the third quarter and after Kosar's third interception, Belichick went to his bullpen and brought in "reliever" Vinny Testaverde. The backup quarterback responded and rallied the Browns to 19 fourth-quarter points when Eric Metcalf swept left end with one second left on the clock for the victory. An out-of-character, ecstatic Belichick ran down the sideline to hug his diminutive running back. What a great victory on the road for the team and its fans, especially a win on a West Coast trip and against a team everyone loved to beat! The Browns, at 3-0, felt very good about where they were. Testaverde looked like the acquisition the doctor had ordered. If one can accept that quarterbacks are like major league pitchers who can have off days, then it makes sense to have top-quality backup "pitchers." It also brought injury protection, and given Bernie's recent history, that could be more likely than anyone wanted to believe.

In weeks 4 and 5, with Cleveland trailing Indianapolis and Miami, Kosar got pulled after halftime in both games. Going back to the Raiders' game, Kosar had gone five quarters without putting a point on the board. Against Miami, it was fourth quarter when Kosar, having been sacked five times and with only 82 yards in passing, was relieved by Testaverde. In neither case, however, did the change create a miracle. The Browns slipped to a 3-2 record.

During the following week, Kosar spoke out, saying his benching might not solve the offensive woes of the team. Tony Grossi asked a rhetorical question in his next column: Was it poor play calling or poor quarterbacking that doomed the Browns and cost Kosar his starting job?

Many players said it was neither, that it was poor play execution by the rest of the offensive unit. Grossi continued, "From a distance, it appeared almost as if the quarterback and head coach took turns defying one another. Belichick calling plays that brought out the worst in Kosar, and Kosar executing them with the self-defeating attitude that they would not work." Whatever the case, it was a plan doomed to fail.

Grossi reached Mike Tomczak, then a backup quarterback in Pittsburgh, for some insights into Belichick's handling of the quarterback situation. Tomczak said he empathized with Bernie, particularly when he got chewed out for audibilizing. Mike went back several years to explain why an acrimonious situation was almost inevitable. "Kosar was already there and set in his ways when Belichick was hired. Bill then went about implementing his program and his own ideas." Tomczak won four of the eight games he started during Kosar's rehabilitation from a fractured ankle in 1992. He said he detected a certain amount of satisfaction in Belichick after these victories because they showed the Browns could win without Kosar.

"But there were a lot of communication problems as far as who was calling the plays," Tomczak continued. "There were three or four people talking before every play, and all the talk went through Bill. If he didn't think it was a good play, it didn't get called. Sometimes, I think that hindered us to some degree."

Fans did not take kindly to Bernie's benching. The controversy was the talk of the town. Over the radio airwaves and in every sports bar, the debate raged on. While some agreed with the coach about the selection of Testaverde as the new starter, the preponderance of callers favored Kosar in this battle. These Kosar fans cast the blame on the drab play calling.

It was clear to Art Modell that he had to show support for his head coach. The Browns, therefore, announced a two-year extension of Belichick's contract. Modell said publicly, "I think he has been treated unfairly by the media and the fans, and I want to show my unwavering support for him. The players and the media will have to get used to having him around." Modell then added that Belichick was "pleased and flattered" with the extension. (This seemed to be a reference to Marty Schottenheimer, who had difficulty accepting a contract extension on the spot.)

Modell was questioned whether he took exception that Belichick had no intention of hiring an offensive coordinator. Modell said he did not, that "we have offensive coordinators coming out of our eyeballs on this team." Modell was then asked about the rift between his one-time starting quarterback and his coach. "I can't accurately assess what's behind this reported rift. But I think it's up to Bernie to co-exist. I think every player has to co-exist with his coach. I've got to go along with Bill and what he decides."

The popularity of the head coach and the owner was at an all-time low. Therefore, the conflict that arose that week between sports bar owners and the NFL over televising blacked-out Browns' home games could not have come at a worse time. Kosar was relegated to the bench, and the Browns and NFL lawyers were in court getting injunctions against bar owners for "stealing" the rights to their games with satellite dishes. Although this was an NFL issue, the fans locally chose to perceive it as Modell forcing fans to buy the last 10,000 tickets before the games became televised, just to line his own pockets. Increasingly Art was becoming a target for fans to vent on.

Well, as fate would have it, Testaverde went down against the Steelers with a shoulder injury, and Kosar returned as the starter. Kosar told a reporter it was imperative that he be involved in both the game planning and the play calling, and that he would be talking to Belichick about that. Bernie was of the opinion the offense ought to be stretching the defenses more as the team went down the stretch. When asked about that topic, Belichick said game planning would continue "just as we have been doing it." While Bill Belichick said that his door was always open, players said that he really didn't listen.

The week passed, and more furor was set off--this time by the totally unexpected release of two popular players, David Brandon and Everson Walls. Brandon was outraged by his release and took off after Belichick. He said Belichick was a terrible person who "didn't handle players with respect and who couldn't communicate." Members of the defensive unit reacted with shock and anger. Rob Burnett said he felt like crying. Brandon's place on the roster was filled by Pepper Johnson, one time Giants' linebacker who had played on Belichick's Super Bowl defensive unit in New York.

For the first time in four years, the Browns were back in first place, and all Art had in his midst were hordes of angry fans. Creative signs featuring the television network initials kept focusing on the head coach. Some samples from the Dawg Pound included:

Cleveland wants
Belichick in
Shackles

Nobody wants
Belichick in
Cleveland

Modell was totally mystified by this reaction.

With Testaverde out of action, Kosar started the next game against Denver (which turned out to be his last game as a Cleveland Brown). At halftime the team went into the locker room with no points on the board--the third time that had happened in Kosar's six starts. While Kosar had good stats for that game (16 for 30, 226 yards, 2 TDs, 0 INTs), he was sacked six times. Some people were sensing that Bernie's lack of mobility was stifling the offensive flow, and his sidearm throws were getting batted down at the line more often. Opposing defensive coordinators seemed to be blitzing more, coming at Kosar with everything but the kitchen sink. And poor Bernie did not have Slaughter and Langhorne as he had in 1987 to counter those blitzes.

Early in his career, statistically, Bernie Kosar was average in the frequency of getting sacked. In 1989, one of his better years, he was sacked 34 times, or 1 in every 15 pass attempts. But then in 1991 it got worse; he was sacked 41 times or 1 in every 12 attempts. In 1993, Kosar was being sacked in 1 of every 7 pass attempts. By comparison, Testaverde was sacked 1 in every 14 pass attempts. (Dan Marino, one of the best in the league in getting rid of the ball quickly, averaged one sack every 55 pass attempts.) One might argue that the questionable talent on the offensive line bore some responsibility for the "getting sacked" statistic, but Testaverde's greater athletic ability allowed him to elude the pass rush more successfully than could Kosar. Some of the coaches felt that because of these combined factors, Testaverde was the choice for starting quarterback. But, unfortunately, Vinny was out with injuries.

The Denver game ended with the Browns losing at home, 29-14. Again, Elway had a superior day (17 for 23, 244 yards, 3 TDs, 0 INTs) against the Browns' defense. And again, though the Browns were tied for first place with a 5-3 record, the fans left the Stadium very unhappy.

As most of us in the front office do after a game, we congregated in the Stadium Corp. conference room and watched the post-game interviews on closed circuit TV. The press conference with the head coach, the star(s) of the game, and usually the quarterback, was held on camera. As one might expect, these sessions were always more trying after a tough loss, but we found them interesting. The questions and answers were published in the next day's papers. As usual, Belichick went on first, and he was typically unresponsive with his answers. The answers were short, no elaboration offered. On this particular day, Bill wanted a very short interview. This he accomplished. Kevin Byrne then said he would try to get Bernie Kosar next. Normally there was a short wait before the next speaker arrived, but that day the delay seemed endless. We waited, and we waited, and we waited, and still no Bernie. Something resembling a test pattern appeared on the screen, but the audio remained alive. We heard mumbling and grumbling from the media about the wait. The wait, I swear, was almost 20 minutes, and at this point I was ready to start fidgeting with the TV set. I thought we had lost the picture. Because of the delay, many of those in the conference room decided to leave for home, as the mood around the office was not the best. The rest started into their post-game duties.

Only two other people remained in the conference room with me when Bernie came on and fumbled with his microphone. I noticed his hands were trembling and his voice was shaky. I commented to the woman next to me, a regular at these post-game conferences, "Something is wrong here. Something serious just happened. Bernie would never make the media wait like this without good reason." He was quivering like someone who had been in a confrontation/scuffle and whose adrenalin was still pumping. As the Q & A started, Bernie seemed strong in his comments, stronger than usual, and deferred questions on the questionable play-calling back to Belichick and the coaches. Bernie remarked that the information available to them about Denver would have suggested a different offensive scheme than had been utilized. Bernie then begged off, and the post-game conference ended shortly thereafter.

Our corporate duties normally took us into various areas of the Stadium after the crowd left. The staff had to review first aid and police room reports, check in with the cleaning staff, and verify receipts from food and novelty sales, among other things. Then we normally went back to the office to compare notes.

Most of the Browns' front office had left for the day. Ordinarily, Art and Pat Modell would already have been gone, along with David Modell and Jim Bailey and their wives. I checked the parking lot to see who was still in the Tower B corporate offices, so I knew whether to set the security alarm. An unusual sight confronted me. Not only were Bailey's and Modell's vehicles still on hand, two limousines had pulled up, and both Mrs. Modells, minus their husbands, were being helped in. Normally Pat and her daughter-in-law did not leave the Stadium without their husbands.

It was past 6:00 p.m., and the two Modell men were still in Tower B, behind closed doors with Bailey, Belichick, and Lombardi. I was then positive something had happened during or after the game. The closed-door meeting and the loud voices coming from within told me clearly that there was no joy in Mudville.

The next day all the customers at the Stadium Restaurant were buzzing as the lunch hour approached. The radio talk shows announced that a noon press conference had been called, and speculation was rampant around the bar. "Belichick is getting fired; Modell is tired of losing to Denver," one long-time patron offered. "Kosar is getting benched," another shouted. "Oh yeah, then what, we're going to have Philcox at quarterback? Get serious!" his buddy countered.

The press conference made it clear: Sunday evening a decision had been made to release Bernie Kosar. The Browns did indeed say that Todd Philcox would be the starter against Seattle. The front office believed that Bernie should not suffer the indignity, nor would he be comfortable with the decision, to play behind Philcox. Modell had asked that the club first try to trade Kosar to get something of value for the former first-round pick. Modell was told that several casual inquiries had already been made, but there was no interest. We heard that Modell wanted assurances that Kosar would not get picked up right after the waiver transaction was announced so the club would not suffer further embarrassment. He was assured no other NFL club was interested in trading for Kosar. So, the press conference was held. Belichick and Modell, side by side, talked about Bernie's "diminishing skills," that those skills, once so plentiful that they led the team to five straight years in the play-offs, were no longer being demonstrated.

The folks around the bar and other fans, for weeks and months to come, bemoaned the insensitive way the departure was handled. Bernie, the guy whom the citizens of Cleveland had idolized since 1985, the guy who had resurrected Cleveland's love affair with the Browns after the team had gone into a downward spiral following Brian Sipe's departure, was shuffled off like a piece of luggage.

Bernie gets Beli-checked

The PD editorial page, normally reserved for more important national and international issues, began focusing on the Browns' turmoil.

The surprising thing, however, based on my limited survey, was that about half the fans agreed with the decision. They thought that Kosar's lack of mobility had slowly weakened the team's offensive momentum. His arm, which had carried the team for five or six very good years, was banged up, and he was getting more passes knocked down. Never blessed with great speed, his rehabilitated ankle seemed a further question mark on his future. His brilliant mind still made him a valuable asset, and some of his supporters were hoping he'd retire into the front office as offensive coordinator. But there was no way that would happen with Modell's unlimited long-term support of his head coach. Nevertheless, many people accepted that Testaverde had been playing better than Kosar and deserved the start. Those supporting the decision felt that the sacks the Browns were enduring with Kosar were holding back the team.

But Kosar and Testaverde backers alike wished the announcement could have been made in a more compassionate or sensitive way. All that had to be said was something like this: Bernie Kosar has brought many years of excitement to Cleveland Browns fans since being drafted out of the University of Miami in 1985. We remember the five straight years in the playoffs and the exciting come-from-behind win over the N.Y. Jets, and many other memorable contributions. These are memories we will carry with us for years. Unfortunately, the coaching staff has now come to the conclusion that Bernie has lost his former effectiveness as a front-line performer. So that the Browns can again move forward toward our playoff goal, we have decided to use Philcox and Testaverde, and we have offered Bernie Kosar a chance to go with another club. We, in the Browns' front office, and we are sure we are speaking for all the fans of Cleveland, wish Bernie all the best of luck in the future.

Where was the input from the public relations department at a critical time like this? If the organization was doing what it believed necessary, then announcing it with a tinge of sensitivity should assuage the fans' sense of violated loyalty. Well, from that day forward we saw substantial erosion in Cleveland Browns' fan support. The rest of the year was not the same. There was also bitterness among the players. Bernie had been a well-liked guy and a team leader.

The Browns won only two more games the rest of the year and finished at 7-9, the same as the prior year. The saddest part? The Browns had spent $12 million more in player payroll costs for free agents and contract buyouts (a big part of which was Kosar's) that year, almost 40% more than in 1992. Yet there was no improvement on the field to show for it.

After reflecting on the move, both Bernie Kosar and his father concluded that maybe the dark cloud had a silver lining. As it turned out, Kosar was able to sign with the Dallas Cowboys, an opportunity that made itself available when QB Troy Aikman went down with an injury. Bernie was able to come in and play immediately with the Cowboys. He then quietly accepted a backup role when Aikman was able to return to action. Kosar rode with the team all the way to the Super Bowl victory, earning himself a Super Bowl ring in the process. Being liberated by the Cleveland Browns gave Kosar his chance for the Super Bowl ring, a prize many critics said he would never earn if he stayed in Cleveland. Maybe that was the silver lining.

The Kosar release was the biggest sports story in recent Cleveland memory. Almost every fan had an opinion about the way the waiver was handled, and almost everyone had feelings to express about the transaction. Callers jammed the phone lines day after day, the majority critical of the decision.

A Cleveland area management training company used the waiver of the popular quarterback as a "case study" in employee relations. The president of the company published his analysis in a local business newspaper. He attributed the Browns' decision to a disturbing condition he called GROUPTHINK. He said that based on statements made before and after the decision, "plenty of light was shed on the process." According to his model, GROUPTHINK has three key elements, and these elements were visible within the Browns' organization:

1)   Overestimation of management's abilities;

2)   Close-mindedness; and

3)   Pressure to conform.

The public perceived the Browns' braintrust to be extremely (and maybe overly) confident of their abilities. Perhaps the front office had reason to be confident, stemming from the early 3-0 record, which included a win over the 49ers; being tied for first place in the AFC Central; and the success of starting quarterback Vinny Testaverde. There were also, however, the releases of Webster Slaughter, Reggie Langhorne, and Brian Brennan (leaving the team thin at wide receiver), and Mike Johnson, without getting much in return. Yet management did not seem to register any concern, since the team was in first place.

Researchers in the company said that members of GROUPTHINK soon developed shared stereotypes of outsiders, seeing anyone not part of the group, as the enemy. (This could even include members of the Cleveland Browns' and Stadium Corp. front offices.) WE and THEY relationships form, and the WE group soon becomes paranoid that the THEY group are out to get them. Those of us in the organization who were not included in the WE group could see that this analysis was apropos.

Jim Bailey had become the leader of a three-man "WE GROUP" management committee, which also included David Modell and Bill Belichick. When the committee was expanded for special-purpose meetings, Bailey decided who else might attend. Bailey had ways of isolating his GROUPTHINK members by demeaning the outsiders. Much of his style incorporated ridicule, and he cautioned his members that they seldom had reason to communicate with the outsiders. The WE group might on occasion be expanded to seven or eight people, but the main criterion for inclusion was that the add-ons be "yes men." As the management company's analysis stated, dissent is discouraged, and there is constant pressure, sometimes subtle, sometimes direct, on group members to agree.

The analyst talked about the Monday morning meeting in which Modell reportedly spoke to the coaches and told them that Belichick had decided that Philcox would start against Seattle. He then asked each person his views about Bernie Kosar's ability. By this time, the author said, the handwriting was on the wall; therefore, who could support Kosar?

Was the decision to release Kosar the result of GROUPTHINK? I cannot say for certain, but having been in and around meetings with the top man in the Executive Committee, I can state that GROUPTHINK had been evident under his direction for some time.

Art Modell had formed the management committee of three to establish Cleveland Browns' policies and to establish control over payroll costs, the most significant cost incurred by the team. The committee was responsible for managing the newly-instituted NFL salary cap. Inexplicably, the Browns' committee did not include the keen mind of the Browns' long-time CPA/treasurer, Mike Srsen. Mike had solid ideas on "cap" matters, and sometimes he also rendered insightful opinions relative to the talent level of some of the players vis-a-vis the contract and bonus paid for that talent. The player personnel department was not always appreciative of his views, even though Srsen tried to be as diplomatic as he could in registering them. Because of the thin skin of the personnel department (and others), the Browns passed up the opportunity to use a talented officer in an area that sorely needed a dose of business acumen. Anybody can spend money; it was wise spending that was critically needed. Srsen could have contributed some creative solutions. The way the Browns operated, after a player decision was made, directions were sent to Srsen along these lines, "We're bringing in Joe XXXX. He's going to cost $XXX,000. Find the money."

I had a meeting with Art Modell in 1994 to discuss Stadium events. Although my opinion on the subject of Browns' budgeting was unsolicited, I told Art that he owed it to himself to make sure that Mike Srsen had the opportunity to provide regular input on the salary cap and on team budgeting matters. I said Srsen had in-depth knowledge and experience that others did not have. Art said, "Don't worry. You can be sure he'll be included."

Srsen told me months later that nothing had changed with regards to him participating in the salary cap review.

After the Kosar termination, Art's moods became ever more changeable, and one had to be near him to get the proper reading before addressing him over a major problem. Because he was no longer easily accessible, one had to run the risk of "plain ol' bad timing" if he had to phone him with an issue. More often he was escaping to his home, keeping in contact with the office by phone.

Neither would Bill Belichick ever recover from the shock waves caused by the Kosar termination. As Steve Belichick (Bill's father) would say two years later, "If Bill won five Super Bowls in a row in Cleveland, they would still never accept him because he cut Bernie Kosar."

In retrospect, the event marked a major milestone in the erosion of respect by Cleveland fans for Art Modell. The style and manner in which Kosar was dismissed were so distinctly "un-Modell-like" that it was evident that Belichick had gained tremendous influence over the owner. I believe that from this time on real Browns' fans finally quit on Art Modell, and finding themselves in a kind of sports vacuum, they turned to the newest darlings in town, the Indians.

As the 1994 ticket renewal campaign rolled around in the spring, Modell checked the season ticket sales count, just as he had always done. He was trying to reconcile the fact that the sale was down 10% from 1993, bringing the count to just about 40,000 fans. He recalled the good old days when the tally was near 50,000, but he would have to go back to the Kosar/Schottenheimer days in the 1980's for those memories.

Modell was a realist, though. He knew that the Browns' last playoff season was 1989, and the organization's record for the last three years was 20-28, hardly awe-inspiring. But, over and above the losing record, though the front office did not accept it as a concern, was the loss of the fans' favorite players. The cold dismissal of popular players like Langhorne, Brennan, Slaughter, and Kosar had left a bad taste. Then, during the ticket renewal campaign of 1994, news came of a few more heroes leaving. Mike Johnson, Clay Matthews, and Kevin Mack were out, never to wear the orange helmet again. The Cleveland Browns' players the fans so fondly remembered were no longer here in spring 1994.

Art Modell was also troubled for other reasons. One recent incident still gnawed at him. A game or two after Kosar's abrupt dismissal, Art received a harsh message from the Browns' ticket buyers. In that game, Browns' cornerback Najee Mustafaa had come up from the secondary to help stop an opposing ball carrier. He got crunched in a pileup and lay motionless on the field. Apparently wanting to determine firsthand the extent of the injury, Belichick jogged onto the field. As soon as he crossed the hashmark, an ugly crescendo of boos erupted from throughout the Stadium. The fans had decided to let the unpopular coach have it with both barrels. They did not like the way Kosar had been treated, and they were sending a message to the author of the transaction.

Art said he was appalled to learn how the fans felt about his coach. While he knew the Kosar waiver was not popular, he thought the feelings would pass, just as reactions to trades of other popular players had passed. He told a close friend he never thought it would have created such a stir. In fact, at a press conference some 15 months later, Art was still defending the transaction. When asked about the public relations fiasco that surrounded the event, Modell took all the blame. He said, "I take responsibility because public relations is one part of the business that I think I know something about. I miscalculated."

Additional insights into the decision continued to come forward. Bill Davis, Browns' personnel director during the Rutigliano regime and a Youngstown, Ohio, resident, had a weekly television show in that city, and he reported that a Browns' insider told him that Belichick and personnel director Mike Lombardi, in order to convince Modell of how far Kosar had deteriorated, had compiled a video of Kosar lowlights to convince the owner that Kosar's better days were behind him.   An unusual use of football film!

Around the office Lombardi's role in the matter was becoming more prominent. When I asked why--the answer was: Don't forget that Kosar was drafted by Ernie Accorsi; this team will never have Lombardi's imprint as long as BK is quarterback. Lombardi told one player in a semi-threatening manner, "Look, I got rid of Bernie Kosar. I can sure as hell get rid of you." I guess that was just to set the record straight as to where the power rested.

The Browns had unfortunately replicated the ugly scene of the 1960s when Frank Lane made the ill-advised trade of Rocky Colavito, the fans' darling in that era of Indians' baseball. The *"Lane Haters"* club was formed and was heard from around town for many years. After the Kosar release, the Cleveland Browns found themselves dealing with its own version of that club, this time named the *"Belichick Bashers."*

Nothing but smiles in 1985 at the press conference announcing the signing of Bernie Kosar.
Browns News Illustrated

Bernie Kosar brought many years of effective on-the-field leadership to the team.
Browns News Illustrated

Over time, failing pass protection and Kosar's declining mobility led to the signing of Vinnie Testaverde. *Browns News Illustrated*

By the end of 1993, Bernie Kosar was gone, but the fans did not forget. *Browns News Illustrated*

CHAPTER 14
GATHERING CLOUDS

Linda Goodman's *Sun Signs* has been a popular book with people who like to analyze others. In it Goodman analyzes people through astrology, using the location of the sun during their month of birth to ascertain the traits and qualities likely to comprise their personality. Many folks construe this kind of personality study as hogwash. Rush Limbaugh referred to it one day on his radio talk show as "cuckoo-ry." While for most of my life, I have considered this kind of analysis, horoscopes and the like, to be absurd, I had to give it at least a second thought after a friend of mine suggested I read about my Aquarian sun sign. After reading through four or five pages, I thought Goodman had me down well. We Aquarians are a breed all unto ourselves.

Out of curiosity, I decided to see if Art Modell's personality fit under his so-called "sun" sign. With his June 23 birthday, Art was born just inside the sign of Cancer, making him a "Moonchild." According to Goodman, people born under this sign tend to become entrepreneurs and generally are quite successful at it. Other prominent entrepreneurs in professional sports born under this same sign include George Steinbrenner (Yankees), Al Davis (Raiders) and the late Joe Robbie (Dolphins).

Goodman's book tells us the Cancerian boss is really in his element when it comes to trading, as he is a master at figuring out what people want and then supplying it at a profit. Not surprisingly, the people under this sign are generally self-made men and women.

Cancerians are known to be people of rapidly changing moods, fluctuating constantly from high to low. At one moment, a Cancer could be laughing heartily at a joke and the next moment sink into solid depression. When in the life-of-the-party mood, a Cancer is the funniest person in the room. No one likes a joke better. Goodman believes the Moonchild doesn't seek the spotlight, but has an uncanny sense of publicity, and secretly enjoys attention.

Crabbiness is one of the negative Cancerian moods. While Art made sure outsiders did not see him in this mood, his employees were subjected to this side of him quite often. According to Goodman, a Cancer may snarl at another, but the cause seldom is the other person; it is more likely to be over some disappointment. Although people under this sun sign can be irritable, their hearts are so sentimental that they are quite vulnerable. Nor can one be sure what mood a Moonchild will be in. I wonder how many times Art Modell's secretary, at the outset of a phone call, heard the question, "Well, what kind of mood is he in today?"

Finances interest the Moonchild. Quality and thrift are synonymous with the Cancer person. Business sense and bottom-line return are the measurements of success in their lives.

True Cancerians also tend to maintain a sense of formality. They like well-tailored clothes, may still prefer French cuffs on expensive shirts, and make sure their shoes are polished. As a boss, the Cancer expects employees to be neat, punctual, and put in a full day's work. Most Cancerians have an opportunity to earn large sums of money, but they are not greedy people. They are truly sympathetic and charitable.

My own sense was that Art Modell fit the Cancer mold rather well.

While it was refreshing from time to time to try to look at the organization and its principals from a different perspective, the daily challenges of Stadium operations usually kept me more than busy.

Cleveland Stadium's loge rentals had been registering 100% of capacity ever since they were built, and steady price increases were tolerated by the corporate customers. That's not to say there were no cancellations. Every year we announced a price increase, eight to ten loge tenants might cancel their leases. Loges had lost their novelty, or corporate budgets were getting squeezed; one or both of these reasons were the most-often reasons used for cancellations. While notices of cancellation disturbed Modell, I never worried too much, because experience showed the empty suites would be refilled. For a long period, we had the luxury of a waiting list of up to 180 names. It was comforting to know that even if every one of the 102 loge tenants would cancel, we could refill the suites with a complete new roster.

For the period 1975 through 1993, while the Cleveland Stadium Corp. continued to enjoy 100% loge occupancy, the waiting list had dwindled to around 40 names. Many names on the prior list had become permanent tenants, and others had become "time-sharing" tenants with original box-holders who no longer wanted to attend all the events. Even though the dwindling list caused Modell concern, up until then it had not caused us any loss in revenues.

We had also enjoyed at least one major event a year for the previous three years. The evolution of the field protection material, ENKAMAT, and good summer-like weather, had allowed us to host a couple of concerts with no field damage whatsoever. Paul McCartney brought his tour to Cleveland in 1990 and played to a sellout crowd of 66,000. In 1992, Phil Collins and Genesis played at the Stadium on a very cool Memorial Day in front of about 50,000 chilled fans. In 1991, the Stadium Corp. was fortunate to land a college football game, after a 13-year hiatus. With the help of local Buckeye Booster Bobby DiGeronimo, who had the ear of Coach John Cooper and Athletic Director Jimmy Jones, Ohio State University finally acquiesced to a Northwestern home game being relocated here from Evanston, Illinois. All it took (I say this facetiously) was a $1 million guarantee by Art Modell, payable to Northwestern. The guarantee alone was more than Northwestern would normally gross at the gate for its best-attended home game. The contract provided for even more revenue (50% of the gate) once attendance passed the 65,000 level. Cooper and the Ohio State athletic staff saw this as a tremendous opportunity to showcase their team and aid recruiting efforts in the Cleveland area, a hotbed of high school football talent that had been passing over the state school for some time. Many fine local players were leaving Ohio to play elsewhere. One prize player that the Buckeyes did land was running back Robert Smith from Euclid, Ohio, who was developing into one of collegiate football's top runners (Smith now plays for the Minnesota Vikings). All of our publicity material featured "Robert Smith from Euclid and the Buckeyes to play here in October."

We had reasonably expected 70,000 fans, with outside hopes for a sellout. Although the tickets were priced in accordance with the Browns' pricing structure rather than the lower college rates, neither school objected to the higher prices. Both schools realized that higher prices were needed to cover the sizable guarantee. We realized, however, that higher prices might be a deterrent to filling the house, but we still felt confident of a substantial crowd.

Tickets were scheduled to go on sale to the public during August, after the Browns' and Ohio State season ticket holders had exercised their purchase rights. As luck would have it, the very Saturday morning the public sale was to start, a headline on the *Plain Dealer* sports page revealed that Robert Smith had left the Ohio State football team after a spat with the coaching staff. His decision stemmed from a directive by one of the assistant coaches that he pass up a class to attend practice, which Smith refused to do. Smith never did play football for Ohio State during 1991.

Modell one month earlier had proclaimed in the newspapers that this game would be a sellout, "most probably as early as Labor Day." His prediction might have come true had Robert Smith remained on the team, but instead Stadium Corp. had to settle for a paid crowd of 73,800, 90% of capacity. Certainly nothing to be ashamed of. The game was played in a steady downpour, so any hope for a sellout via game-day gate sale vanished at 9:00 a.m. After it was all over, Northwestern received a handsome check in the amount of $1,154,000, and Stadium Corp. made more on this event than on any other in the company's history. Not bad results for an event that from the beginning promised to be a lopsided victory for the Buckeyes. Even the City of Cleveland did well, garnering $114,000 from admission taxes and additional rent from the Stadium Corp., an amount in and of itself sufficient to pay the mayor's salary for the year. All this was possible because of Modell's $1 million guarantee. Inexplicably, Modell was upset that entire week, and especially on the day of the game. He never explained, but part of his displeasure was that the game did not sell out. Just before game time that day, I had to explain to him why I thought it didn't sell out. I cited as possible causes the obvious: the inclement weather, the Robert Smith decision, the higher ticket-pricing structure, and the lopsided matchup of teams. He shouted back, "Look, I don't want excuses. I want results." Art never did ask how much the company made that day. He just acted as though the event was a failure.

Modell needed an event such as this for revenue generation as he was planning for the day that he would lose the Indians as a tenant and he would have to make a "go" of the Stadium without baseball. Events like the college game would have to substitute for the lost Indians' attendance in 1994 and beyond. Art was hopeful the public would respond, since big-time college football was so infrequent a visitor to Greater Cleveland. Art exclaimed, "It will be a tremendous treat for local collegiate football fans, especially those who can't get tickets to see the Buckeyes play in Columbus."

Through this venture another need was satisfied. Like many colleges, Northwestern was having difficulty balancing its athletic department budget. Bruce Corrie, the university's athletic director, seized this opportunity as a way to bring the program into the black. He made a decision to move not one, but two home games off campus. Besides the game with OSU in Cleveland, the Wildcats moved a future Notre Dame game to Soldiers Field in Chicago. Corrie explained to his critics that by going to Cleveland, the school would make "six or seven times as much as they made the last time Northwestern played the Buckeyes at home." He said it came down to simple economics. "We are not making money following the standard format. We certainly would never entertain the thought of moving the game(s) if we had been selling out Dyche Stadium." (Northwestern averaged 28,000 fans per home game.)

After a very entertaining event that rainy Saturday afternoon, most of us were astonished when we picked up the *Plain Dealer* sports pages the next morning. Headlined "GREED TRIUMPHS IN 'MODELL' BOWL," the Bud Shaw article protested the marketing of college football by taking games off campus. The writer did not point out that the Gridiron Classic had been doing the same thing since 1986 in the Meadowlands Stadium, nor did he cite the president of Meadowlands as a villain who exploited college athletics. While he thought the trend offended college football tradition, Shaw chose not to acknowledge the financial requirements in running a big-time college athletic program. Nor did he mention that rivalries like Florida-Florida State, at the insistence of state officials, relocated games more than once to neutral Orlando. How about the Army-Navy game relocating to California, and Notre Dame-Navy many times leaving the home field of the U.S. Naval Academy?

This particular column drew the ire of readers. Many could not understand where the columnist was coming from, and why he was so cynical. Then the headline writer put the crowning touch to the thesis with the words "greed" and "Modell" in the same line. Was this one more example of the city's only newspaper grabbing an opportunity to zing Art Modell? A Cleveland alumna of Northwestern expressed how thrilled she was to be able to see her school play in her home town, and that there were 1,500 others who felt the same way and who enjoyed a pre-game party in a tent done up in the school's purple and white colors. Even readers from Columbus and Detroit wrote to thank Art for the opportunity to see the Buckeyes play. Art had not sought any plaudits, but he wondered why the media had chosen to target him, once again, for criticism. He was growing very tired of the treatment.

Besides events like the OSU game, the Whitney Land Development Co., the Stadium Corp. subsidiary that had been the subject of the 80s litigation, was starting to generate substantial cash. New home sales were running at a good pace, and by the end of 1992, almost all the cash invested in the development had been liquidated. As in any real estate venture, the money invested usually stays invested until the tail end of the project. Then it comes out in pretty rapid fashion. With this project in the final stages, the company had been realizing $1 million a year or more for three straight years, and the cash was being used immediately to pay down debt.

From the standpoint of operations, profits, and cash flow, Modell did not have much reason to hover over the day-to-day business of Cleveland Stadium Corp. But he remained concerned about the future of the Stadium lease with the City of Cleveland. In passing one day, Art asked me what I thought the city and county could do for the Browns.

Based on what I read of the city's economic state of affairs in the *Plain Dealer*, I gave Art my candid reaction. I said, "Well, if what I read in the paper is true, the city has no money left to help the Browns. They must have over-committed their resources to the Gateway project."

I explained what Steve Strnisha, Cleveland finance director, had reported. The City of Cleveland was going to experience a deficit in 1991. That came as a complete surprise to city officials, and as a defensive measure they were restricting purchases to absolute necessities until the end of the year. Strnisha elaborated by saying that as an example he would consider items like toilet paper an absolute necessity.

The city originally had been expecting a positive turnaround in tax collections in the third quarter, but it failed to materialize. After a recalculation by the finance department, the city was facing an $8 million deficit for 1991, and worse yet, was projecting an even larger $14.8 million deficit in 1992. With that kind of financial report, the city could do nothing but try to keep its basic services intact. Funding for professional sports surely wasn't in the cards.

Art then assigned me a project. Since the city had no responsibility for Stadium upkeep by virtue of the lease, we reasoned the city's financial deficit would have been even larger if it were subsidizing the sports teams. Modell asked me to calculate the benefits the city was deriving from the lease. When I completed the report, the figures showed the lease as worth $3 million in cash benefits to the city/county annually, calculated as follows:

1)   cash rent paid to city by Stadium Corp.—$704,000;
2)   real estate tax paid on main parking lot—$47,000;
3)   annual maintenance paid by Stadium Corp, rather than by city—$469,000;
4)   amortization of capital improvements ($18,000,000 over 25 years—$720,000; and
5)   Interest on borrowings for improvements (average loan balance of $10,000,000 @ 10%)—$1,000,000.

Art folded the report and put it into his coat pocket. I recall him carrying that summary around with him regularly, hoping to have occasion to explain how much the city was benefiting from the existence of his Stadium Corp. But because the lease was so complex, we found few people took the time to understand how good or bad the lease was. The popular tide was to go against the lease. It was easier to blast Modell.

While the Browns were setting out to improve themselves in the 1993 campaign, Cleveland Stadium Corp. was enjoying one of its busiest years. It was the Indians' last season in Cleveland Stadium. Every home weekend beginning in early August was marketed as the last games ever to be played in Cleveland Stadium against the Yankees, against the Tigers, against the Red Sox, etc., and the fans responded. Total attendance hit 2,177,000 in 1993, 700,000 higher than our previous best season (1986). Surprisingly this large number of fans came to see a team that ended up in sixth place, 19 games behind the leader. Many came to show their children, or to see for themselves one last time, the Indians' long-time home. The season culminated with a sold out home stand, as the Indians drew over 210,000 people to a three-game weekend set that featured Bob Hope, at one time an investor in the Indians, singing on the pitcher's mound after the last game. While Hope was entertaining the misty-eyed crowd, the ground crew was ceremoniously removing home plate with a pick and shovel to be transported by limousine to the new Gateway park. The very last baseball game ever played in Cleveland Stadium was on

Sunday, October 3, 1993, a bye week for the Browns. Few people were aware that Bill Belichick was in attendance that day with his son, sitting high up in Section 4 in the upper deck box seats. Modell watched the game at home, probably pondering his company's future in a Stadium without 81 baseball dates.

More and more frequently during the latter half of the 1993 baseball season, our maintenance staff were finding chunks of concrete lying in the aisles and on the concourses. Director of Building Services Bruce Gaines came to tell me his worst fears. He said a chunk of concrete had fallen from the underside of the upper deck, narrowly missing a fan below. Because of the growing crowds coming to Indians' games, Gaines worried that the odds of someone getting seriously hurt were growing. Gaines said there could be a number of reasons why this was happening. The frequency of fireworks after baseball games in 1993 could have been a factor, as the Indians scheduled many more "extravaganzas" in their last season. Another possible cause was the climate extremes. Many more very hot days and very cold days would give rise to more extreme freeze-thaw cycles, which could cause the spalling concrete conditions. The concrete on the underside of the upper deck had no place to go when it loosened but down onto the seats below.

We summarized these events in a memo, including various cost estimates for repair, and forwarded it to Berea, attention Art Modell and Jim Bailey. Our timing couldn't have been worse, since the Kosar termination played itself out during this dilemma. With the Indians already pulling out of their offices in Gate A, the last thing I am sure Art wanted to talk about was our Stadium situation, let alone invest major amounts of money in repairs. Nevertheless we pushed for a meeting as we felt it was critical to arrange the repairs in the winter months, now only two months away. Modell did not even want to talk to us about it; the answer was to deal with Bailey on the matter.

We hired an engineering firm to do an exhaustive examination of the upper-deck concrete, row by row, section by section. Their review told us that 18 of the 43 sections were in dire need of corrective work. A contractor did the work in the January-March 1994 time frame, so when the first event was held in May, the problem had been corrected. Once again, Art was wondering how much longer his company would have to keep spending large amounts of money to keep Municipal Stadium from falling apart while Jacobs and the Gunds were having the community design beautiful digs for them uptown.

I couldn't believe that the spalling concrete problem had only begun to surface in 1993. In questioning Bruce Gaines about this issue, he answered, "The problem did not originate this year. It's been a problem for some time now; it just hasn't been this bad." I asked him how he had been treating the problem in the past, since I had not seen any contractor invoices for dealing with it. He said the problem was taken care of on Saturday nights.

On Saturday nights in the summer when the Stadium was closed to the public, the maintenance staff came down with shotguns. When they located an area with a visible crack, they blasted away with shotguns until the loose pieces dropped harmlessly onto the lower deck seats. These chaps should have been lauded for such creativity. They were loyal guys too, for any time they were ever needed, they were there for the company. And they never charged the company for the cost of ammunition on their expense reports!

The maintenance staff had its share of unusual jobs in the stadium. A book could be written of their interesting exploits. As one example, our maintenance staff learned about the Indians' promising rookie Albert Belle much more quickly than the media or general public. These lessons usually came on the mornings after Belle had a bad night at the plate. Our staff would get requests from Indians' clubhouse manager Cy Buynak to start off the day repairing the furnishings. A couple of strikeouts might have meant a full morning's work for the staff. Maintenance man Bob Metzger came in one morning and after assessing the extent of the damage said, "Holy cow, how many times did he strike out last night? It looks like a tornado hit the place." Doors were battered to smithereens, stalls between the toilets were totally destroyed, lights bashed out. When Albert slumped, maintenance charges to the Indians accelerated. Albert was one of the worst current offenders, but players from the past like Early Wynn, and Billy Martin as a visiting manager, did their share of damage too. Nothing breakable escaped their raging bats. The water fountain in the dugout was usually the first target, then all the lightbulbs along the lengthy runway between the dugout and the clubhouse. Doors, plumbing fixtures, sinks, were all subject to demolition if the ballgame didn't go in the right direction. After a hard loss, Early Wynn more than once took out his frustration on the food spread laid out for the Wahoos after the game.

At about this time, totally unrelated to anything else going on, rumors began circulating that Modell was selling the Cleveland Browns to his friend Al Lerner. These stories were mentioned in national publications and on national cable sports talk shows. Art could hardly go anywhere without being asked about the "impending sale." To quell these stories, Modell called a press conference on December 9, 1993, to say that he was planning to meet with city officials to discuss the Browns' future at the Stadium. He said, "We're not talking lease here as much as their plans for the lakefront--what they have in mind. They want to know what my plans are. I want to know what their plans are for improving the Stadium."

Modell was getting tired of the media's negative treatment of his coach and toward the front office, especially since the Kosar transaction. At various times from 1992 to 1994, the *Plain Dealer* took the plight of the Browns beyond the sports page to the editorial page. Bumping more critical national and city-wide issues aside, the editorial cartoonist several times depicted Bill Belichick (and Art Modell) in an uncomplimentary mode. Fed up with the treatment, Modell told an Akron *Beacon-Journal* reporter, "I don't know if the Browns can continue to compete in an area where there is so much media hostility toward the team." He added, "I can't say if we'll move or we won't move....What does bother me is that I think some of that (criticism from the media) is influencing our fans."

This early hint of a Browns' move was addressed by the *Plain Dealer*. It chided the owner for blaming fan indifference on the media, rather than on the coach and front-office decision-making. "Textbook case of blaming the messenger," the editor said. "But if he (Modell) is serious about leaving the city, those Browns' fans who have made him millions over the years at the very least deserve the courtesy of an advance warning so they can react appropriately." (That turned out to be one of the severest complaints uttered by Browns' fans after the announcement of November 6, 1995. Why didn't Art Modell ever tell us?)

This *Plain Dealer* cartoon wounded Modell deeply, and may have prompted
him the next day to say that he would leave Cleveland
in three years if he didn't "get the job done."

Art understood the city felt they had him and Stadium Corp. "under contract" for five more years; therefore why do anything now? But he also realized he could be strung out until 1998 and then left high and dry by a City Hall which so far had not shown one iota of willingness to help financially. In order for everything to be in place by 1999, agreements were needed soon, with actual renovation commencing not much later. Any extensive project would require at least four years of time and a lot of money.

As 1993 was coming to an end, we were trying to imagine how much different 1994 was going to be: no more number 19, Bernie Kosar; no more Cleveland Indians; no more Major League Baseball in the 62-year-old building; no more baseball infield, foul poles, or backstop. What we would have was a new agenda of events and a newly-designed football field and perimeter. For almost a year Larry Staverman and I had been planning a special events agenda for 1994, trying to replace some of the lost revenue heading to Gateway, while Vince Patterozzi, the Browns' groundkeeper, was studying new configurations for the 3 1/2 acres of field to create a new look for football in 1994.

The newly configured field is ready for football...August, 1994. *Mike Poplar collection*

Several times during my 22-year career with him, Art asked me why I thought he was taking so much heat. For what it was worth, I offered my evaluation of this stormy relationship. I told him not to take the criticism personally, because I knew he often did. I asked him if he remembered as a kid playing "King of the Mountain." The game is simple: Whoever takes over the top of the hill tries to keep from getting knocked off by the other players. It didn't matter who was on top. It was simply fun to knock down whoever was perched up there. I told Art that he had been on top in Cleveland for some time, and so people enjoyed trying to knock him from his perch. Whoever succeeded him would eventually be subjected to this same treatment. It happened with his head coaches, his star quarterbacks, as well as with many politicians. I don't know whether Art agreed with my assessment. The truth is he did take the never-ending criticisms personally.

One day Modell called me in and asked that I prepare another financial projection. This time the question was: Can the Stadium Corp. survive without the Indians, given our debt requirements? Art knew the answer depended on our being able to generate enough special event income. One question was: how much would that be? The other part of the equation was: How much in expenses could be saved without baseball games? Would it be significant enough to make a difference? Would downsizing in the company be required?

I worked on the answer to the second question first. Since almost all the expenses in the company, as they are with most real estate ventures, are fixed costs, the savings that can be realized are minimal. About 90% of expenses remained, whether we had two events or 22 events scheduled. Admittedly, expenses that involve event labor disappear, but while this could involve a lot of people, it was insignificant relative to the total budget. Only about 10% of the budget could be saved when events were not held. Some of those expenses included cleaners' wages, liability insurance (premiums were paid on a per-fan basis), and to a lesser degree, utilities since, for example, concession stands were in operation less often. But 90% of expenses remained even with a less active building---rent paid to the city (though the override portion could vary with attendance), property taxes, base utilities, property insurance, staff salaries, maintenance, and repairs (since most occurred due to age, and not use, of the building). Since the base corps of stadium personnel needed to operate the building numbered only 10, there could be no cutback in this number without affecting client service.

So the conclusion I drew and presented to Art Modell, was this: *if the loges continued to be sold out, and at prices comparable to what the Chicago Bears charged for the NFL season at Soldiers field ($65,000, $55,000), and if at least one million dollars could be generated from special event income, enough profit would be generated to pay all the expenses and retire the company debt by 1998.*

On the Cleveland Stadium Corp. side, 1993 was the most profitable year in our 20-year history, and it was a relatively easy year to manage. The profits came primarily from volume we had been waiting 20 years to see: two million baseball fans coming through the turnstiles.

What Stadium Corp. management had done that summer, though, was gear for 1994, a year when we knew we would have to either "make or break" ourselves in the special events arena. We had begun pursuing some unique events. We realized that events other than concerts would probably have to be produced by our staff internally. These would be time-consuming and require additional in-house marketing.

The Billy Graham Crusade had not been held in Cleveland for some time, and it seemed like an event that would fit nicely into our cavernous Stadium. Since Graham was enjoying a successful crusade in Pittsburgh in 1993, our staff concurred that we should extend a proposal for the event in 1994.

For years, Art had been encouraging us to produce a fair on the Stadium grounds. He had in mind something like a combination of Steve Bencic's popular Oktoberfest in Cleveland and the Westchester County Fair held in Yonkers, New York. An old fashioned carnival and fair in downtown Cleveland—all on the Stadium field—sounded like fun. After we had made the initial inquiries into the Graham crusade, we decided to pursue whatever was necessary to produce the fair.

Modell had arranged for Larry Staverman, Bruce Gaines, and me to fly to Yonkers for an all-day meeting with the Rooney family. The Rooney family (of the Pittsburgh Steelers) owned and operated Yonkers Race Track. We attended the fair, learned about the planning that was required, and reviewed the associated budgets and profit (loss) projections. We had to learn things like: how many weekends should a fair run; what type and how many attractions and booths should a fair have; what were the "hidden" costs in producing the event; and how much could be lost from a "rain-out"? Art Modell asked a favor, and the Rooneys graciously provided us with all the information we needed.

We then learned that the Billy Graham Crusade did want to come to Cleveland in 1994 but had set sights on the new Jacobs Field. But since the grass field at Jacobs was still new, the Indians refused permission. The Indians' groundskeeper was concerned about permanent damage to a playing field which still had not matured. A Graham representative then called me to contract for a June 1994 rally at the old Stadium. This turned out to be a stroke of good fortune as the record crowds that ultimately attended the crusade could not have been accommodated by the much smaller Jacobs Field.

Given the cool spring weather in Cleveland when outdoor events would not be appealing and the time needed to put in a field before the fall football season started, we found that we were left with a ten-week period in which to earn our budgeted $1 million in special events. In 1994, our event season was set to begin May 15 and run through July 20. To stretch the season beyond July 20 would have put the start of the football season in jeopardy.

Over 250,000 attended the five-day 1994 Billy Graham Crusade. Attendees were forging their way onto the field to give witness. *Cleveland Stadium Corp. collection*

Larry Staverman and I then set out to tour Michigan and Indiana to locate a respectable amusement ride company to participate in our fair-to-be. After discussions with three different companies over the summer months, we reached an agreement to provide our fair with 24 amusement rides, all on the playing field. We decided to call our fair STADIUMFEST.

Most of us at the Stadium missed having Art Modell in the Stadium offices or at the restaurant for meetings on a regular basis. The feedback and the give-and-take around the roundtable with the owner was always productive and interesting. Art called every few weeks, hoping to hear the entire 10-week calendar had been filled with events. Other than concerts, which were usually brought to us by Belkin Productions, we found that we had to "hard sell" promoters to bring an event to Cleveland Stadium. While we could offer a huge capacity, few promoters needed anything near that size. They also feared the need (and costliness) to educate the public about their product in a new marketplace. New promoters did not know us or our management capabilities, and so many were reluctant initially to set up shop with us. Modell, in the meantime, was eager to show a full slate of activity for 1994 and kept asking when the concerts were going to be booked. We kept reminding our boss we were still six months away from even hearing what groups were to tour. Art was not a patient man.

In May 1994 the World Cup-bound Team USA held an exhibition soccer match against Bayern Munich on the Stadium field before 14,000 fans, the first event in the 1994 special events program. By the time the rest of summer 1994 had passed, the Stadium Corp. had hosted a two-night performance by Pink Floyd, presented on a seven-story stage built with a light-studded arch on a clamshell proscenium; a Monster Truck jam; and separate concerts featuring the Eagles and the Rolling Stones. All this, besides the week-long Graham crusade and the STADIUMFEST carnival.

Art was reticent about what he expected from the events. He didn't seem happy having to survive on the whims of musicians. If big-name groups didn't choose to tour, then it was just too bad for the stadium operators. Art felt that he had been promised that he would be reimbursed by the city for the loss of the Indians, but that had not happened. Had Stadium Corp. received some monetary relief in this regard to take pressure off the need for event profits, it would have been indicative of at least some consideration for his changed circumstances. The city's financial circumstances, however, indicated otherwise.

After the Truck Jam was held in June and the results were calculated, we learned that the promoter had taken a bath on the show. The Stadium Corp., however, with a little over 14,000 people in attendance, did manage to eke out a small profit. I recall Art calling early in the morning to get a report. He went ballistic when he heard the attendance. "What happened to the projections of 20,000-25,000 fans?" he demanded. He went on and on about being misled by attendance projections, about who knew and didn't know what they were do-ing, and finally how were we ever going to make our budget for the year?

I tried to get him to understand that this was a new event in a new market, and that we should feel lucky to have held the show without a loss. I said, "I know you think we should have made more, but how about the pro-moter? He suffered a financial bath, as he spent an arm and a leg on advertis-ing and promotion. How do you think he feels?" I surmised that Art just needed to blow off some steam. After a few minutes, I decided to call Jim Bailey in Berea just to see whether some new problem might have created this kind of an uproar. I told him of Art's unexpected outburst, wondering whether something else was on Art's mind.

Bailey responded, "Well, I know he just had a tough meeting with Belichick. You know, he just can't bring himself to yell at Bill, so he must have decided to yell at you instead. Don't worry about it. You know how Art is." Yeah, I thought, but maybe Bill should be yelled at. At any rate, I didn't have time to worry about it. The big ferris wheel was outside waiting to be be set up for STADIUMFEST

The 1994 summer events season at Cleveland Stadium ended after the Rolling Stones concert on August 28, 1994, the Stones' fourth Cleveland Sta-dium appearance. After the profits and losses for all events were tallied and the final results were in, the Stadium Corp. earned a tad over $900,000, about 10% short of our budgeted goal for special events. Without the STADIUMFEST fair and carnival, the profits stood at $1.2 million; unfortunately the loss from the unsuccessful carnival event had to be absorbed by the profits from other events.

Art and I met briefly in Berea in mid-fall to discuss the events season. When he heard the profit total, he expressed total disappointment. Surprised at his reaction, I extolled the efforts of our staff and then asked him what his expectations had been, given that we were only $100,000 short of what we had projected. I told him that earning a profit on all the shows but the carnival was commendable in our first year of the endeavor.

He remained unconvinced. "We should have made at least $2 million," was his only remark.

Stadiumfest: An artistic success, but a loser at the gate. *Cleveland Stadium Corp. collection*

I was a little taken aback by his answer and replied, "I wish you would have told me that last spring. I could have told you then that given a ten-week event season that number was an impossibility. Maybe we could have spared you this major disappointment." I left Art's office wondering where he ever got that $2 million profit number. On the drive back to the Stadium offices, I couldn't help but recall Art's wishful but unrealistic expectations some 15 years earlier about tripling the profits on the sale of our hotel investment. He might have decided only during our meeting itself that he had expected the $2 million in events profits.

Lawsuits are a part of life for a facility manager. Liability insurance premiums generally increased every year because of the volume of suits that arose from fans attending entertainment events in public facilities. One of the zaniest lawsuits grew out of an incident which occurred during the Eagles concert at Cleveland Stadium in 1994. As most concert-goers can attest, many of the men's bathrooms became "unisex" during the show. A couple would stand in the line to the men's room; when they finally got into the room, the man generally went to the trough while the woman went into one of the few stalls in the room. On this particular night, the lines to the washrooms were extraordinarily long, and when this particular couple finally got into the room, the young woman found all the stalls in use. Reportedly, her call from nature was too urgent to wait any longer. Searching for a quick answer, she dropped her pants and leaped up to sit on the hand sink (apparently to relieve herself). She was reported to be a rather large person. After she landed in the sink bowl, it broke loose from the wall and dropped to the ground with a thud, with her butt wedged in it. The sink shattered, the porcelain breaking into jagged pieces and the victim receiving cuts to her buttocks and forearm. She had to be transported by ambulance to a nearby hospital for treatment.

Nine months later, Cleveland Stadium Corp. was served notice that it was being sued in this matter for $50,000, charged with negligence! How were we negligent? The lawsuit stated that Stadium Corp. had "breached its duty of care to the plaintiff...to provide a reasonably safe environment by assuring that sinks in the bathroom were properly affixed to the walls...."

After hearing from our legal counsel in rather strong language, the plaintiff eventually filed for voluntary dismissal of the action. We can only guess that she might have found it embarrassing at trial to have been asked to demonstrate to a jury how these injuries were sustained.

In the meantime, problems were mounting with the Browns. The team had completed three losing seasons under Belichick, and they were losing money each year under self-appointed financial steward Jim Bailey. The Browns had just overspent on a new facility in Berea with final costs running substantially over the $12 million budget, possibly reaching $18 million for the entire project. Instead of inviting closer scrutiny from the Browns' treasurer Mike Srsen during these troubled times, the management team continued to exclude Srsen from the important decision-making meetings. Bailey rationalized that personality differences made any other situation untenable. So now Jim Bailey was making the Browns' financial decisions. We all wanted to ask Art: Whatever happened to the line "Don't ever let a lawyer run your business for you." But just then Bailey was THE man in charge. He was doing most of the thinking for the organization.

The Browns were spending a king's ransom at Berea to replace the fields (one indoors and four outdoors). Belichick had complained that the fields, which had been in place for only two years, were not what he wanted his team playing on. The coach had argued that the field's sand base was responsible for the many leg injuries suffered by the players.

Another negative impacting Art during 1994 was the large number of loge cancellations that occurred after the 1993 season ended. For the first time ever, Modell realized he was going to have vacancies at the Stadium. Of the full complement of 102 suites leased in 1993, over 40 customers chose not to renew for the 1994 season. Many said that they had already subscribed to the new loges at Jacobs Field and/or Gund Arena, both at much higher prices than they had been paying before. The causes cited sometimes were expressed sheepishly, such as: "we're now tapped out," or "we're maxed out on our corporate budgets," or "we got our arms twisted uptown" (referring to the new Jacobs and Gund venues). Responses directed toward Stadium Corporation included, "We expected a greater price reduction now that the baseball team is gone."

Loge pricing was adjusted downward only slightly after the baseball team left. Formerly $59,000, a ten-seat suite in 1994 sold for either $55,000 or $49,000, depending on location, and the $45,000 eight-seat loges were offered at $39,000.

I strongly suggested that our new pricing schedule not be established from the standpoint of "deducting" value but rather by following the guidelines of what the NFL was charging in football-only stadiums. To establish a value for baseball and then deduct it from the 1993 contract price was certainly a debatable exercise. For years, many loge holders had allocated little or no value to their baseball season tickets. The main reason (in some years, the only reason) some loge holders subscribed was for the Browns' season. So in 1994, marketing brochures were prepared to educate the customer about the prices of skyboxes and suites in other NFL stadiums. We knew that at least a handful of people were still going to cancel, no matter the price. Their stated reason? We were now hearing, "This football team is too boring to watch," or "My clients don't care to watch the Browns play anymore; last year I couldn't get guests to come to the games, and that had never happened on a Browns' game before."

One loge tenant who canceled was former Browns' player Gene Hickerson, owner of a manufacturing business. He was extremely vocal about not renewing. He directed his venom at the head coach for destroying the interest of the community in the team by utilizing a nondescript offense.

Despite these kinds of comments, Art refused to blame the team's performance or its philosophy. He would say that not every team in every city can possess a winning record. The Indians had not played .500 ball for years, yet Jacobs Field sold out almost all its suites. Instead he blamed the corporate community for "abandoning" Stadium Corp. so they could support the civic effort at Gateway. After years of supporting Modell's quasi-civic venture through their Stadium loge leases, 40% of the tenants decided that they could not, or would not, do it any longer. More disconcerting to Art was that many of those canceling were companies of substance. Three of the Big Six accounting firms, four of the larger law firms in town, and several other Fortune 500 companies were among those who canceled leases.

The loge marketing staff was able to re-lease about 10 of the vacant boxes, in part on the strength of the significant number of big-name rock concerts scheduled in the Stadium that summer (since 1991 all special event tickets had been included in the price of the annual lease). But in the end, Stadium Corp. had to adjust its profit projections for 1994 downward to reflect 72 loge leases, rather than the 102 we had been accustomed to.

Modell feared he was witnessing the start of a declining cycle of support by the business community for his Cleveland Browns. Yet he knew that support would be needed in an even more significant way if Cleveland Stadium was ever going to be renovated on a major scale.

The 1994 Browns' season ticket sale held at 40,000 as the preseason got under way. There was a lot of competition for the sports ticket dollar in Cleveland, as the opening of Jacobs Field had built excitement, and the Indians in their new ballpark were playing like a solid pennant contender. When Art was asked his feelings about fans possibly spending their entertainment dollars on baseball rather than on football, he said, "If we're in contention, we'll draw. If we're not, ushers may be hard to come by."

The Indians were enjoying sellout after sellout, and the only negative looming on the baseball front was the threat of a strike. The media were speculating as to how the Browns would fare if they went head-to-head against the Tribe in September, especially if the Indians were in pennant contention. That would be a novelty in town, in that there had not been a pennant race in Cleveland for over 35 years. The city had never witnessed a football team vying with a baseball team for fans at the same time. But it didn't happen in 1994 either, since Major League Baseball went on strike in early August and stayed out for the rest of the year.

On Browns' opening day, September 4, Brent Larkin, the *Plain Dealer*'s respected columnist, led off his article with the headline, "Future on the line for Browns in '94," and he opened:

The Browns better win today against the lowly Bengals, and they had better win eight or nine more times by the time the season wraps up. Because more than the future of the lovable head coach depends on it....the future of the team in this town will be on the line. The reason for this concern is the Browns, in effect, will be on the ballot next spring as part of a package billed as a Bicentennial and lakefront development package....So, why all the worry about the Browns? Consider the results of a hush-hush survey of Cuyahoga County voters taken recently by Cleveland pollster Bob Dykes. When asked whether they would support a tax (the type of which is still undecided) to fix up the Stadium, 63% said no. When asked which project on the drawing board was the most important, 12% said an aquarium, 18% said the science museum, 55% answered the port, and 8% said the stadium.

Larkin went on to say, and many people on the street heartily agreed, that some of the opposition against fixing up the Stadium stemmed from the Browns' recent on-field mediocrity, and even more important, from the team's public relations disasters and the unpopularity of the head coach. Larkin pointed out that there had never been a negative reading as great as 63% during the polling prior to the vote for Gateway in 1990. And that was when the Indians were regularly a sub-.500 team. Larkin concluded with suggestions to help get the tax passed. He said Stadium backers would have to sell the issue on its own merits, "doing everything possible to avoid having the vote become a referendum on the Browns in recent years, and on Art Modell." "If that happens," Larkin lamented, "the issue gets clobbered."

(It was not too difficult to imagine how Art felt after reading this article, particularly the last line.)

Larkin continued:

Even if everything gets done right, this remains one very tough sell, probably tougher than Gateway---which passed by the slimmest of margins. Anti-tax sentiment has grown in the past four years, political instability at City Hall works against any tax prospects and public officials are hardly unanimous on the wisdom of pouring $130,000,000 into a 60-year-old building.

Larkin then quoted County Commissioner Mary Boyle, "I've always believed we need to take the Stadium off the lakefront and that any further investment in the existing facility would be a waste of money."

We faced another discouraging thought. When Gateway was narrowly approved, it was with the benefit of a county-wide vote. The suburbs carried the vote to a winning margin while the tally within the city limits was overwhelmingly a loser. At this time the Stadium renovation vote was being structured as a city-only vote, given the then fractured state of the county's finances.

We didn't know how much weight to put on this next fact, but it didn't appear that it could help much. We learned that by 1994 less than 50% of regular Browns fans were residents of Cuyahoga County. More than half of our patrons were from the six adjoining counties, other parts of Ohio, and a handful from out of state. Less than 40,000 fans, which equated to about 3% of Cuyahoga County residents, were regular attendees at the Stadium. That did not seem much of a hard-core base of residents/patrons /ticketbuyers on which to swing this vote.

I am sure that Modell read Larkin's piece on the plane trip to Cincinnati that morning to watch his Browns open the season. I am also sure he was starting to feel that any meaningful funding for the project was hopeless if it depended only on the city and the county. If Modell still had any hopes, they were certainly dashed when he picked up the *Plain Dealer* a few days later on September 13 to read bold headlines that Cleveland would be facing another deficit in 1995. The article explained how City Finance Director Katherine Hyer had gloomily forecast an expected $26 million shortfall, stating that it was basically a matter of less income tax receipts than anticipated.

The Browns started the 1994 season in Cincinnati feeling pretty good about themselves. The head coach seemed more relaxed than he had been in his first three years. Some key players said practices had been easier and that he was letting his assistant coaches coach, rather than running the whole show himself. PR Director Kevin Byrne suggested that Bill was more relaxed because he no longer had to deal with Bernie Kosar or Mike Johnson, two former players who had tremendous influence over their teammates. Byrne said they had presented competition for the fourth-year coach, but now these threats had been removed. Bill Belichick also felt good about his first two draft picks, cornerback Antonio Langham and wide receiver Derrick Alexander. He knew he had drafted two blue-chip players and that both would play a lot and make a big impact.

In the first game, Cleveland emerged victorious over a struggling Bengal team, 28-20. The Bengals were much more tenacious than anyone had expected, and it took big special teams' plays to make the conquest. Randy Baldwin and Eric Metcalf responded with 85- and 92-yard returns, respectively, for touchdowns. While everyone felt good about the victory, we knew the Browns would need more than special teams' touchdowns to win many games. Most Browns' fans gratefully accepted the win, but they wanted to see more production out of the offense.

In game two, the boo-birds showed up. The Browns fought the Pittsburgh Steelers tough, only to lose 17-10 in Cleveland Stadium's home opener. Testaverde's four interceptions brought out the worst in the fans.

While the Cleveland radio talk show hosts had a field day with hostile callers lambasting Vinny for throwing into coverage, for throwing off his back foot, for not looking off receivers, etc., Steve Crosby tried to present a level-headed picture. Steve Crosby bore the title of offensive coordinator in

1994, the first person to hold that position since 1990. He told the fans not to worry, that the Browns were going to be all right. He said the offensive unit didn't have its timing down quite yet, but it would soon, and when that happened, the touchdowns would be flying. Crosby was an upbeat coach who liked what he saw in practice and who wasn't afraid to go out on the limb and talk about it.

Crosby looked like a prophet. The Browns rolled off a string of victories in getting their record to 7-2. A loss in Denver (where else?) was the only blemish after the Steelers' loss. The achievement was even greater when one considered that several key injuries had occurred during this run. One came in early October when Tommy Vardell was lost for the season in a freak injury catching a dump-off pass over the middle. Walter Reeves, a big tight end, joined him on IR at the same time. Both were big blocking ingredients in Belichick's offensive scheme for 1994, and this combined loss at the same point in the season was disconcerting, especially since there were no interchangeable parts among the backups to replace the entire package the injured players offered. (Analyst Doug Dieken, in a late-year review of the team's performance, gave high marks to the coaches for overcoming this loss mid-stream, and "scheming" their way through the rest of the year.) The wide receivers were also banged up, and Michael Jackson and Mark Carrier had little playing time going into week six. Mark Rypien, Cleveland's backup quarterback, was called on for relief appearances more than once as Testaverde twice suffered concussions. Despite these setbacks, Cleveland players proved flexible and responded when necessary, sending the team into the playoffs for the first time in five years with a record of 11-5. Consistent defensive play under coordinator Nick Saban and exciting special teams play were major contributors to the season's success.

The Browns showed they were finally capable of beating the NFC teams as Belichick had sought to do. The Browns shut out Arizona and Buddy Ryan, 32-0; whipped the Philadelphia Eagles in Philadelphia, 26-7; and Dallas in Dallas, 19-14, when Eric Turner fell on Jay Novacek at the six-inch line as time expired. So elated was he after the Eagles' game, Belichick ordered game balls awarded to every employee in the Browns' and Stadium Corp. offices. He wanted to acknowledge their contributions.

Another pleasing statistic surfaced at year end. This offensive line led the league in the lowest number of sacks allowed, 14 for the entire year. Vinny Testaverde averaged a phenomenally low total of one sack per every 31 passing attempts. The offensive line of Tony Jones, Steve Everitt, Bob Dahl, Orlando Brown, Gene Williams, Wally Williams, and Herman Arvie, along with new line coach Kirk Ferentz, all contributed to a new Browns' record for fewest sacks allowed, snapping the old one of 16 set in 1970.

Saban's defensive unit excelled in 1994, allowing the lowest number of points in the league. Cleveland outscored its opponents by a resounding margin, 340-204, limiting them to less than 10 points in six games.

There were also discouraging aspects to the year. First, Testaverde, despite the excellent protection, saw his quarterback rating slip to 70.7, from an 85.7 in 1993. His 18 interceptions exceeded his 16 touchdowns. A new phrase was coined on a radio talk show during the season, as at least once a day a caller would announce himself as "Vinny Intercep-taverde." The interception total was a large part of the Browns ending the year with a negative takeaway-giveaway ratio. Secondly, management grew concerned late in the year over the alarming number of penalties. In the team's final three losses, an apparent lack of discipline resulted in 15, 11, and 10 penalties, respectively.

The week after the win over Philadelphia, Modell took the occasion to mildly chide some fair-weather Browns' fans for not believing. Claiming after the game that he was proud of the team and that the "defense might be the best in football today," he sent those fans a message: "If they don't hop on (the bandwagon) now, they'd better take up hockey. I don't mean to be facetious, but if they don't take to us now and start having more belief in us, then there's something wrong with my organization."

I felt he was directing his remarks not only to the guy in the street but also to those in the corporate community who hadn't responded to his call to purchase the 30 unsold loge suites. But he primarily wanted to boost demand for single-game tickets. To his dismay, and to that of the rest of the organization, only 65,000 fans showed up for the next home game to see the 8-3 Browns demolish Houston 34-10. I was still hearing the lingering fan backlash over the handling (or in their words, the "bungling" of) the Bernie Kosar situation.

With the Browns in the playoff hunt, my meetings with Art Modell on Stadium Corp. matters became increasingly infrequent. While I wanted to believe that this reflected his satisfaction with the financial results of the Stadium operation, I found out that just the opposite was true.

Late in 1994, at what was my last full length meeting with Art, I was asked to defend the size of the Stadium staff and how they were spending their time. The implication was that it was time to cut some personnel. Since letting any one of the nine full-time employees go would have negatively impacted fan service, I argued that the payroll should remain as it was, and I tried to get Modell and Bailey (who was at the meeting) to understand why that should be the case.

I compared the Stadium staff with that of the Browns. I argued, "The Browns' front office payroll is ten times that of the Stadium's, and the Browns earn less in profits. In theory, labor should generate profits, and it seems as though there is some disproportion between the two companies. In fact, the

Stadium's total salaried payroll is less that what the Browns are paying just one tight end. It would be penny wise and pound foolish to cut staff and hurt service."

Clearly my defense irritated Modell. He said angrily, "If you're so smart, why are you working for me?" His remark stopped me in my tracks. I didn't have an answer for that one.

Art then said, "We're not going to discuss this any longer. Jim Bailey and David Modell will review the Stadium payroll and give you their decision."

I started packing up my files, as I knew the meeting was over. I also knew that my entire relationship with the owner had changed. Art no longer wanted to make decisions about Stadium operations, and he didn't want me to make them either. As it turned out, neither Jim nor David ever called back with a decision. The payroll stayed as it was until the severance arrangements were decided on February 28, 1996.

Money Magazine published a report, "Best Buys for Fans" in which the best money values in sports were ranked. The Cleveland Browns were listed as number 54 in the study, ranked behind the number 4 Cleveland Indians, the number 40 Cleveland Cavs, and the lowly Tampa Bay Bucs (number 48). When questioned by *Plain Dealer* columnist Bud Shaw about the Browns' low rating, Modell said he wasn't surprised that the Browns were now the number three franchise in Cleveland. He said, "I went to the Indians' Opening Day baseball game with owner Dick Jacobs, and I was in awe of the park. My front office staff visited the Gund Arena and they were in even greater awe of that building."

Shaw said that "these are the bleakest of times for the Browns and Art Modell. The ugly old stadium is only part of it. The rest is four years of uglier (won-loss) records, an unpopular head coach and no superstars (on the team)."

When Art Modell was told that Mayor White held a meeting with area sports writers on December 9 and warned them the Browns could leave town if Modell didn't get what he wanted, Art denied that he ever told the mayor that. He explained:

I have issued no threat and will not issue a threat. I don't play the game that way. I'm working within the business community to see what can be done and how it can be done to refurbish Cleveland Stadium, period. I am optimistic that somehow we can find a way featuring the state, the county, the city, the private sector...to get whatever is needed to fix up this ballpark. They found a way to do it for baseball and basketball.

The interviewer asked him what would happen if a deal could not be reached.

Art responded, "If it can't be done, if the public wishes that it not be done, then I have to revisit my options. I have to protect my franchise and my family. But we haven't got to that point yet." Modell, Mayor White, and the Greater Cleveland Growth Association were scheduled to meet behind closed doors on December 12, 1994, to discuss the future of Cleveland Stadium.

On the front page of the *Plain Dealer* on December 10, Mayor White said the Stadium issue was now a top priority, and pleaded with taxpayers to prepare to open their wallets to help yet another sports franchise. White warned that if the city did not obtain the estimated $130 million needed to renovate the Stadium, he was convinced that Art Modell would consider selling or moving the team. The PD went on to report that "City Council members appeared fatalistic at the prospect of having to pitch another major project to the public with the construction dust barely settled at the publicly funded Jacobs Field and Gund Arena."

Councilman Michael Polensek lamented, "In light of the county's financial disaster (referring to the SAFE debacle), and in light of the fact that taxpayers can't even pass school levies, where is the money going to come from?" SAFE was an ironic acronym for Secured Assets Fund Earnings, an investment which turned into a $115 million loss. The crisis created a loss to county taxpayers in an amount, coincidentally, almost equal to what it would have cost to fix up the Stadium.

Plain Dealer editorial cartoon hints that Stadium renovation talks were becoming increasingly urgent.

Around the same time, contractors began to tell me about financial difficulties at Gateway Corp. Many of these contractors, who also performed work for us at the Stadium, were saying their Gateway invoices were not getting paid. Some bills were almost a year old, and vendors were coming to realize that the project had run out of money, although no one had yet come up with a complete and accurate accounting for the public. One rumor cited a $12 million shortfall; another had it as large as $20 million. (In March 1996, when the former Gateway chairman left and Craig Miller was named his replacement, it became clear that $32 million in obligations remained to be paid and that all the funds were indeed gone.)

Financial reports surfacing on the operation of the two newly constructed parking garages that serviced Gateway also were not good. City Finance Director Hyer announced that the city would probably have to dig into its $3 million contingency fund to make the 1995 debt service payments on the $40 million loan. The balance would have to come from the city's parking meter revenues, revenues which normally went into the city's general fund. The City of Cleveland, already facing a continuous run of operating deficits, would now have to subsidize the parking operations for the Indians and the Cavs.

Tim McCormack, then Cuyahoga County auditor, told PD writer Steve Luttner that county taxpayers were quietly starting to assume liabilities from this Gateway complex, without even being made aware of it. McCormack said that county real estate and sales tax collections were being used to subsidize Gateway. Luttner pointed out that county taxpayers were ultimately responsible for up to $189 million in bonds, plus interest, if revenues produced by Gateway were insufficient. Luttner also wrote that in 1993 the county had already paid $7 million in bond interest, some of which was obtained from the general fund. McCormack said, "For the first time the county's general revenue fund was required to pay for the debts of Gateway....I don't think anyone who is writing checks for their property taxes understands that a portion of that tax is going to pay for Gateway...that necessity is going to be there for many years to come."

McCormack, a persistent critic of Gateway financing, would say later that "we are corroding the very fiscal well-being of this community. The future holds potential for further troubles."

When I read this, I recalled the pitch during the Gateway campaign: "This will not cost the taxpayers anything. This complex will be paid for by smokers, drinkers, private corporations and the teams."

I also recalled the Cleveland situation back in 1972. What we were now hearing sounded like a re-run of the old days when the old Cleveland

Stadium operation was continuously "in the red," and creating a drain on the city treasury. That situation eventually led to the creation of the Cleveland Stadium Corp. I wondered if history would eventually repeat itself with these two sports palaces? When Art learned the status of Gateway, he lost whatever optimism he still had left that the renovation could be funded with county help.

In ensuing weeks there was plenty of commentary on the subject from political figures, none of which was very encouraging to me. While Mayor White characterized his posture as only the beginning of a process to educate the public, he was adamant that the state must participate in Stadium funding. He alluded to using lottery proceeds, an idea which had surfaced recently in Cincinnati in conjunction with discussions over a new stadium for the Bengals. Less than two weeks later, however, Governor Voinovich responded, "Anybody who thinks that the state will be paying for their stadium or stadiums is not really thinking very clearly." Tim Hagan, County commissioner, said very simply, "There's no money for the Stadium renovation."

Stadium renovation plans included removal of the roof and moving lower deck seating closer to the field. *Cleveland Stadium Corp. collection*

Brent Larkin was writing regularly on the subject. One of his more prominent columns carried the headline, "Voters won't OK a tax to save Browns." He concluded, "...if the city fathers can't find $130 million without going to the ballot, the Browns will leave."

On the same day that Mayor White was warning the public about what must be done to assuage the Browns, the daily newspaper reported another bit of bad economic news--that the Gund Arena would need a subsidy of $7.7 million from the county for the coming year (1995). In response to a question as to whether this loss would have an impact on the Browns' request for renovation of the football stadium, Mayor White said he didn't think it would be a tougher sell than it already was.

County Commissioner Mary Boyle said in an almost resigned fashion, "There could not be any set of circumstances more ill-timed for a major construction project."

Nonetheless, the mayor proceeded to form a task force of civic and business leaders to study the Stadium issue. The leaders of the committee vowed to develop a plan by mid-January 1995 to keep the Browns in Cleveland. Included was to be both a study of renovating the present stadium and also of building a new one, the related costs of each plan, and ways to fund each plan.

Privately though, some members voiced their opposition to the philosophy of renovation. Jim Biggar, former chairman of the Gateway project, questioned the continuing use of a prime lakefront parcel of land for something used as infrequently as a football stadium. He thought the location might better be used to complement the tourist attractions then being developed on the lakefront. Others said it would be folly to spend millions to renovate a building already 60 years old. It looked to us in the Stadium and the Browns' front offices that there was a long way to go to build a consensus in six short weeks.

On the NFL front, franchises were getting restless. During January 1995 the Los Angeles Rams announced that they had accepted an offer from the city of St. Louis to move there for the 1995 season. The offer was touted as the richest Stadium deal ever given to an NFL owner. This deal certainly gained the attention of owners around the league, especially those with large bank debts on their balance sheets.

When Modell gave his annual end-of-the-year press conference on the team's 1994 performance and corresponding expectations for 1995, the Q & A session inevitably turned to Stadium issues. The questions and Art's answers appeared in the *Browns News Illustrated* as follows:

Q.   There have been rumors you will move the team if you don't get a new stadium, or a vastly-remodeled stadium. Please comment.

A.   I wouldn't consider moving the team. Newspapers have been making more out of that than they should. I do, however, believe Cleveland Browns' fans deserve equal treatment as the Indians' and the Cavs' fans. I am not asking for a new stadium. I'm just asking for help to refurbish, in a major way, the current stadium. If I don't get a new stadium or a refurbished stadium by the end of the contract, I'm not going to move the team. But I will sell the team to someone who might move it.

Q.   Haven't you been grooming your son, David, to take over the team some day?

A.   Whatever I do, David will stand behind me. I'm not planning to sell the team. I'm not planning to move the team. I just want some help from somebody--the state, the county, the city. But those people all have their own problems. I don't want to tax the people. What I do want is a lottery like they have in Maryland. If people want to pay a buck to buy a lottery ticket, they can. That's a discretionary purchase. That's what I've been pushing. Not casinos. I say take 15 days a year, have a lottery, and (devote those revenues to) cover the expenses for all the state's stadiums----Ohio State, the Toledo Mudhens, Bowling Green, two stadiums in Cincinnati, Fawcett Stadium in Canton, and here. And after I made the suggestions, the *Plain Dealer* ran a hundred letters that kicked the crap out of me.

Q.   Would you prefer to have a new stadium, or the old one refurbished?

A.   I would prefer to have a new one, but there's no land downtown [recalling the futile search to find land for the Browns' practice facility]. I'm a realist. If I can't get $130 million for someone to fix this place up, how can I get $300 million to build a new stadium? If we were to refurbish this one, it would take four years; that's why it is important to get started right away so the renovation is complete and in place by the end of 1998.

Q.   Do you think that had the Browns won even one Super Bowl, that things would be different?

A.   No, because I'll tell you what would have happened. The headlines in the PD would say, "Can the Browns repeat?" And Tony Grossi [PD sports writer] would write an article saying, "Odds are 100-1 against the Browns repeating."

Q.   How would you like to be remembered?

A.   As the nicest 102-year old man in Cleveland.

To be liked by everyone in Cleveland was clearly an impossible dream. Judging by the tone of his other answers, I thought he had made it clear that he was tired of the negative tone of *Plain Dealer* writers. By the end of 1994, he was not up to the tedium of prolonged lease negotiations. He simply said, "Just give me the same deal that Dick Jacobs got at Gateway. Let's make it nice and simple."

While the Browns had made the playoffs in 1994, there were deep concerns after the Browns got pummeled in the second playoff game in Three Rivers Stadium on January 7, 1995. The Browns suffered dropped passes and sluggish defensive efforts, as they lost a 29-9 decision. The game was basically over at halftime. In the final record of 12-6 (including playoffs), three losses came at the hands of the Steelers.

The Cleveland defense, in its last game for defensive coordinator Nick Saban (leaving to become the head coach of Michigan State University), had a miserable outing against the Steelers. Despite winning the first game against the Patriots, the team's defensive statistics over the two playoff games were disturbing. In those games, Cleveland had only one sack. Michael Dean Perry had four tackles and Rob Burnett had three, while the safeties (Turner, Riddick, and Moore) racked up 41 tackles. Obviously, when the safeties were making most of the tackles, the opposition was making big gains carrying the football. More discouraging, the Browns defense allowed the Steelers to convert 8 of 15 third-down attempts. The Steelers gained 238 yards on the ground, and a total of 424 yards. Saban acknowledged, "The Steelers controlled the line of scrimmage, and ran the ball almost at will."

On offense, Metcalf carried seven times for 14 yards. But the most difficult offensive stat to locate, and maybe the most ominous, is the dropped pass. The Browns had too many and at the wrong time (as if there is a right time) as many drops were to wide open receivers, and this plague stopped the momentum of some good drives early in the game.

A further discouraging note to those of us in the finance area was that the success on the field provided no help whatsoever for the desperate cash flow situation. Despite the playoff revenues, the Browns plunged deeper in debt after the 1994 campaign. Although the Browns registered $7 million in cash operating profits in 1994, this amount was insufficient to cover additional signing bonuses, interest on debt, and ongoing Berea field improvements. Consequently the Browns went deeper in debt by another $8 million.

A few weeks later word came out of Columbus that the governor had a new thought on financing public stadiums in Ohio. Voinovich was considering asking voters to resurrect the one-penny-per-can pop tax, which had been repealed by voters the previous November. This would re-generate about $67 million in revenues annually. While the *Plain Dealer* responded with a lead editorial endorsing the idea, the Ohio General Assembly did not act on the governor's suggestion.

Even the *Plain Dealer* editors began making references to the difficulties emanating from Columbus when they referred to the state's lawmakers as having "an anti-Cleveland and anti-tax sentiment" which appeared to be working against some of the suggestions being generated by the governor's office. I wonder if the bungling of the Gateway budget, which had still not been resolved, was a factor in the state's hesitancy to dig deeper into its pockets.

The public heard another financing wrinkle as local promoters of dog racing publicized their concepts of introducing greyhounds to race almost year-around at the renovated Stadium, strongly suggesting that this new source of gate receipts and admissions taxes would help finance the modernization. This concept never gained a foothold as the Humane Society and gambling opponents were vocal in their opposition.

In the meantime, the Browns' Stadium renovation committee, which was comprised of one employee, Jim Bailey, and two outside consultants, Ann Bailey and David Hopcraft, had been meeting regularly with the Mayor's Stadium Task Force. It was at one of the later meetings that a new problem was introduced. Engineers had concluded, after completing repairs to upper deck concrete in March 1994, that if the entire upper deck concrete platform was not replaced by 1999, the facility could become unsafe. (This cost element had not been factored into the 1990 study, as the condition was not then known.) In addition to apprising the city of this add-on to the renovation plans, the Browns also made the Task Force aware of the following financial stipulations:

1) As part of this proposal Cleveland Stadium Corp. would insist on financial relief for the loss of the Cleveland Indians;

2) Cleveland Stadium Corp. would take that amount of money when received and re-invest the full amount into the pre-construction planning; and

3) Stadium Corp. would guarantee that the budget would be met by agreeing to pay for any cost overruns, as long as Stadium Corp. could act as construction manager.

There was no response from the Mayor's Task Force or from the Cleveland Tomorrow group with respect to this proposal. When the February 15, 1995, deadline had come and gone without a meaningful response, the Browns' group drew the inevitable conclusion that the city was unable to assist the Browns economically in the renovation.

One more deadline of April 15 was set to finalize a financial plan. Jim Bailey was still being told that the Stadium Corp. and/or the Browns would be expected to fund as much as $20 million of the project. Bailey responded that the $19 million already invested in the Stadium under the existing lease, plus interest, should be viewed as the team's investment (even though it was technically made by Stadium Corp.). After all, that value was still present in structural improvements: scoreboard, loges, concession stands, and equipment, and represented money that would not have to be spent in the renovation. Bailey told me that the Task Force, however, would not accept this past investment as a replacement for new money. The Task Force position made no sense to the Browns. Had Modell's investment never been made, the Stadium renovation project would have to start from scratch (as was done at Gateway) and the project would cost at least $19 million more (probably much more than that when considering inflation).

While these negotiations were going on, the Browns announced a general ticket price hike. The *Plain Dealer* used the hike to take the Browns to task once again for, of all things, raising the price of the best seat in the house, in the the the upper box, from $37 to $55. While the editor conceded the price hike affected only 7,000 of the 79,000 seats in the building the newspaper wondered whether "Arthur B. Modell secretly desired to incense the community and fans to the point where he will have no choice but to move the Browns out of town." The editorial concluded, "Finding the funds to renovate the Stadium and keep the Browns is a challenge all of Greater Cleveland must try to meet. It surely would be nice if the Browns didn't keep making that goal more difficult."

What a ludicrous position, I thought. No one outside the organization had any idea of the Browns' dire debt levels, apparently not even the PD, even though it had reported on this very situation in 1992. The newspaper should have been aware that the 1992 bank debt didn't just go away, and that Art Modell did what any astute businessman would do, given these same circumstances. Instead, the paper saw this as an attempt by Art to undermine renovation funding. The writer also failed to mention the high prices of other premium sports seats in town. At Gund Arena premium seats were priced over $100, and the very best floor seats over $200.

As we at Stadium Corp. went about business during spring 1995, we noticed more kidding from Browns' personnel around the Stadium restaurant. "Where will the Browns be next year?" someone bantered. "San Antonio," or "LA," would come the answers. The rejoinder would be, "I hope it's not San Antonio; I hate domes." Not very funny, but it remained a steady topic among the select few with access to Jim Bailey.

After hearing enough of this kind of repartee, I realized that I needed to speak with Bailey, since we at Stadium Corp. needed to be aware of the Browns' intentions as part of our own future planning. To my question he replied, "We'll probably not be here down the road....No one wants us in Cleveland any longer, apparently." It was April 1995, and the Browns were coming to believe that the community, the politicians, the business community, and the taxpayers, were not going to do what was needed to keep the team in Cleveland.

There were rumors that another NFL team might be moving. This time it was the Cincinnati Bengals who were exploring a move to Baltimore. For a long time, many in the Queen City had felt the Bengals had second-class citizen status behind the Reds. The football team wanted a new stadium like many NFL teams were then getting. Baltimore reportedly had the money to lure an NFL team there. It looked like the Bengals had an ideal opportunity, but after several meetings the Bengals were not convinced a move to Baltimore would completely satisfy their needs.

Negative reaction toward any kind of taxation for Cleveland Stadium renovation continued to mount. In a May 5, 1995, editorial, the *Plain Dealer* stated that Mayor White was hopeful the renovation might succeed without county participation. The *Plain Dealer* feared that county support for the Stadium could hurt the chances of a health and human services levy planned for the November ballot. Everyone, including Art Modell, was sensitive to human services needs, and I am sure that Art did not want the Stadium renovated at the expense of the downtrodden.

In Columbus a task force was addressing ways to pay for stadiums across the state. A spokesman for Governor Voinovich said "the State ought to participate in paying for all the stadiums in the state at about the 15% level." To service this amount of debt would cost the state a little more than $2 million a year.

It was interesting to note that the Browns' players and employees alone paid $3 million in 1995 state income taxes. By merely using these taxes, the state could have covered its cost allocation, and the Browns' players could have been viewed as directly funding the state's participation in construction of the building. In fact, the state could have increased its participation and still broken even. While the state might argue that this perspective could set an undesirable precedent, the unavoidable conclusion was that if the Browns ever left the state, that $3 million paid in state taxes would be lost anyhow.

Just days later, long-time Cleveland City Councilman Michael Polensek was quoted in the PD as saying, "If the Browns leave, it is not the fault of Cleveland or council. The foundation for this debacle was laid when they put in the cornerstone for Gateway. The SAFE fiasco burned up the rest."

The councilman's words were ominous. It appeared he believed a franchise move was going to happen. It was apparently time to start assigning blame because fans would be looking for scapegoats. That's how I translated those words. Commissioner Tim Hagan had a similar outlook. He said, "Look, we have an alienated electorate here...They don't feel that the Browns being here makes any difference. It's their way of saying, 'Screw the big boys. Let Modell pay.'"

Jeff Schudel, LCNH reporter, urged Browns' fans to support the stadium vote. He reminded voters the city has not had to put one cent into the upkeep of its stadium since 1974, the year Modell took over the lease, and he indirectly chided the *Plain Dealer* for a vendetta against the Browns' owner in recent years. Schudel warned that the voters' attitudes didn't sound encouraging as he published the results of a survey taken by Cleveland Station WJW TV-8: What would it take to get you to pay for the stadium renovation? The responses:

> 13 % -----hire a new coach
> 24 %----- get a new owner
> 23 %----- only if the Browns win more games.

About 60% indicated that unless the status quo changed, the vote would not pass. Other unsolicited comments pointed to the strong feeling that Modell should fix the stadium out of his own bank account if he wanted the renovation badly enough.

Interviews with ordinary citizens showed opinions to be split. A few said they wouldn't mind the team leaving town. "We can watch them on TV no matter where they go," said one. Others said the Cleveland schools needed help more than the Stadium. Even west side Councilman Patrick O'Malley sounded indifferent when he declined to rush his decision; "I want to see the Browns stay and I want to see the Stadium renovated, but if they move to Florida someplace, God bless 'em." He added that he would vote against the proposal.

In contrast, even to its own previous reporting, some *Plain Dealer* writers were beginning to put a positive spin on the Stadium project. They told readers that "it's important to remember that the city had not invested one dime in the Stadium" and that the city had only made money as a benefit from the Cleveland Stadium Corp. lease.

Shortly thereafter, editorials implored the city, the mayor, council, and the Task Force to act quickly to put together the $154 million funding package, as Art Modell kept warning that time was running out. Engineering efforts had to begin in June 1995 so that the project could be finished by 1999. The writers warned that Modell was not bluffing. Modell had said the city waited too long to appoint a Task Force to resolve the problem. It should have been done in 1994, but wasn't.

One PD editorial chided City Council for its constant sniping at the mayor. It said that the mayor's plan might not be perfect, but it was a beginning. "Constant complaining about the Mayor won't keep the Browns in Cleveland. If Council has a better plan, then it should move quickly to enact it."

Mayor White and Council then proceeded to get a parking tax passed. Cleveland was one of the few major cities in the country without such a tax. The parking tax became an important piece in the funding puzzle. What still remained dubious, however, was finding a source for the county's share and determining the extent of the corporate community's contribution.

One proposal to raise money for the renovation was to extend the sin tax. The term of the original sin tax, passed to raise $117 million for Gateway, was for 15 years, 1990 to 2005. The new suggestion was to extend the tax beyond 2006 to raise whatever amount was needed. A serious question was raised, however: If the money wouldn't be received until 2006, how would the contractors be paid during their work period from 1997-1999. The answer? A loan from the State of Ohio.

A senior vice-president from McDonald & Co. said that financing this way would lead to a problem. The county could end up by paying so much interest that less than $30 million would be available to pay construction costs out of a $100 million bond issue. "Because of the delayed revenue stream, resulting in a diminished revenue stream, the sin tax extension is not an efficient way to raise the amount of dollars that is involved here," he advised the mayor's task force. The city, however, did not heed this advice but announced it would place the extension on the November 7, 1995, ballot.

On the football front, several significant player transactions were made. Michael Dean Perry and James Jones left Cleveland as free agents and headed for Denver as a tandem. Eric Metcalf was traded to Atlanta. Mark Carrier went to Carolina in the expansion draft, and Randy Baldwin opted to go to Carolina as a free agent. These departures, along with that of Coach Saban, left some big dents in the Browns' roster. The only bit of good news was that when Pro Bowl players of this caliber were lost, the club generated room under the NFL's recently-imposed salary cap rules. This provided leeway to sign some big-name players the Browns knew they needed on offense.

Trying to create excitement for the 1995 season, the Browns had incurred some very large obligations by signing Andre Rison, Lorenzo White, and Tim Goad. Large bonuses also went to other free agents. Therefore, it was disconcerting to Modell to learn that another eight loge tenants were canceling their leases. Those defections would reduce the 72 loges sold in 1994 to 64 in 1995, reducing occupancy to less than two-thirds capacity. The loge marketing department eventually was able to negotiate 14 new leases before the season started, so the final tally for 1995 was 78 loges leased--out of 102.

Modell and Bailey were faced with the task of evaluating the likelihood the city could raise the funds needed for the renovation. The chances did not seem favorable. The city would need the corporate community to buy out the loges, and at significantly higher loge prices than currently charged. Our first-hand experience, in view of the recent dropoff in loge leasing, was that local corporations were "tapped out" and wouldn't be able to do it.

The city continued to say it needed the Browns to contribute cash in order for the plan to work. The $19 million made via the cost of Stadium Corp. improvements was not recognized for what it was, a previous cash investment, "paid in advance" if you will. Furthermore, since the Browns were literally broke, after tapping themselves out on "free" agents in 1995, the team had no more money to contribute. While Bailey remained steadfast that the Browns would put in no new money, the $154 million refunding plan formulated in June 1995 continued to call for a $10 million contribution from the team, and another $10 million from the private sector from the sale of loges and club seating.

County Commissioner Tim Hagan then put the timing issue into perspective. In June 1995 he said the commissioners would not commit to the financing package until they were able to resolve the $28 million construction deficit at Gateway. From all indications, the county wasn't close to getting this done.

When minicamp 1995 finally arrived in June, Art Modell had the feeling that this was his and Cleveland's year. He expected big things from his team offensively with the acquisition of Andre Rison, and he expected Testaverde to have an improved year. The offensive line, which had a good year in 1994, was expected to have an even better one. The road to the Super Bowl had started.

As the team was heading off the field in Berea on the second day of minicamp, a reporter approached Vinny Testaverde and asked, "What are your feelings about the renovation at the Stadium, and what are your feelings if the city doesn't grant Art Modell his wish for the renovation project?" Testaverde, taken aback, told the reporter he had no feeling about it either way, that he hadn't given it much thought. The interviewer persisted. "Well, if the renovation doesn't happen, how would you feel if the Browns start looking around to leave Cleveland?" Testaverde was eager to end the interview; he didn't know why he was being asked these questions.

Word quickly got back to Modell, and he became very upset. "What does any of this have to do with any of my players? I don't want any of them becoming distracted with this renovation issue. I want total concentration on this season. Damn it anyhow!"

Art didn't want anyone to have any excuses if the Browns did not win. He wanted no more discussion by anyone in his organization about the Stadium renovation. He had kept Jim Bailey and his Task Force on this project since 1994, but no meaningful progress had been made with the city. Art was waiting to see how the corporate community was going to respond to the unsold loges at the Cleveland Stadium. In the meantime, he wanted to make sure the entire Browns' organization kept on the mission: a Super Bowl season. To avoid further distractions and to make sure players like Testaverde were not approached by the media, Modell ordered Bailey to cease work on the renovation and instead to devote full time to keeping the organization focused on the task at hand. Then Modell declared a moratorium on further renovation discussions.

Some time after Art Modell announced his moratorium, the governor became more vocal on the Browns' situation. Earlier in response to constant criticism directed his way for not exercising more leadership in the Stadium financing discussions, the governor had succinctly replied, "The Cleveland Stadium is Cleveland's problem." Voinovich later said that Cleveland's leaders were not looking to him for leadership. He said that had to come from Mayor White and Council President Jay Westbrook.

The Browns' front office looked at the events of the past several months and evaluated the scene as follows:

1)   The state seemed to be putting a toe into the water, but not much more, nowhere near what the State of Maryland, for example, was doing to return NFL football to Baltimore.

2)   The county found itself immersed in two major problems, the unexpected Gateway overruns, and the SAFE fiasco, with no money to solve either, let alone to dig in for a new project.

3)   The city would have to take money from important city services to put into a stadium "for Art Modell," as Art feared the project would be presented. Besides, the city's school system was in shambles. And every time the city's financial status was reported, the annual deficit seemed to get larger.

And then another reality was setting in. The entire renovation package was being estimated at $172 million instead of $154 million. Upgrading external utility lines and sewers, improving access roads, outdoor ramps, and other site improvements, as well as removing lead paint were cost factors that had not been previously considered.

To secure another piece in the financing puzzle, the city was proposing an increase in the admission tax, increasing the city's take from 6% to 8%. The task force did not construe this as a contribution from the Browns, but from the public. The Browns disagreed. Their position was that such a tax increase would replace the next ticket price increase. This led Modell to tell Mayor White that an admission tax hike "would drive me into bankruptcy."

No one was sure if Art was making an exaggerated off-the-cuff comment or what he was thinking when he said that. I had never before heard him

Text of Modell's Letter

Dear Mayor White,

Following up our telephone conversation of last Friday, I would like to thank you on behalf of the Cleveland Browns organization for your work on problems at Cleveland Stadium. We recognize your efforts to be determined and sincere.

Not withstanding these efforts, I write today to inform you that the Browns organization cannot condone, support or participate in a continuation of the divisive and disruptive dialogue concerning stadium renovation. Nor are we willing to endure a campaign associated with either an initiative or recall referendum on the November ballot. Our decision derives from the following considerations:

1) The experts employed by your task force established professional criteria for the vision of stadium renovation. Because that plan was untracked, the project has been further delayed.

2) With that time now lost, we in the Browns organization must turn our attention to more immediate challenges; specifically, the 1995 NFL season. We have built a very good team, which earned a 12-6 record last season, into a better team for which we have high expectations. To subject this team, our organization and our fans to the continued distraction of this volatile debate and the likelihood of an expensive and negative campaign for almost two thirds of our season is unacceptable.

3) We hope a moratorium until the end of the season will allow the political and economic environment to stabilize.

For many years we have been told by community leaders that "now" is not the right time for the community to address the responsibility of repairing its stadium. At this time then, I hope you will understand that "now" is not the right time for the Cleveland Browns and their fans to address this issue given the negative atmosphere being fostered by special interests and resulting in tense divisiveness within the community.

Thank you for your consideration on this matter. I have forwarded a copy of this letter to the editorial director of the Plain Dealer with hopes that its publication will make our position clear to our fans and other interested community members.

Sincerely,
Arthur B. Modell

Letter to Mayor Michael R. White asking for postponement
of the decision on how to pay for Stadium renovations.

make a public statement in reference to his balance sheet. I believe Art was crying out in desperation, begging for understanding and for help. After incurring player signing bonuses of $40 million over the previous three years, the Browns' borrowings had reached $60 million, an amount that was coming close to fiscal strangulation.

The Browns had to sit back and ask the following questions:

1)   Have we waited long enough for a practical, workable solution from the political leaders?
2)   Will waiting any longer provide new answers?
3)   Is there any meaningful progress being made?
4)   Is there a likelihood that we can ever strike a deal?

Yes. No. No. No. Those were the answers coming through. The request for help went back as far as 1989. Others prior to Mayor White had been unable to offer meaningful solutions, nor since January 1994 had White or his Task Force. With all these delays, it was impossible for the Stadium to be renovated by the end of the Browns' lease.

Apparently feeling squeezed for time, Council President Jay Westbrook asked the Browns to accept an extension of their lease by two more years to allow further study of the situation. On behalf of the Browns, David Hopcraft responded, "No, because all Art Modell has been getting is promises....meetings were broken off when there was no answer to anything."

Some were wondering who David Hopcraft was, and how he became involved in public pronouncements for the Cleveland Browns. Hopcraft, once the executive editor of the *Plain Dealer*, had become friendly with Jim Bailey through their membership at Shaker Heights Country Club. After many rounds of golf together, Bailey eventually recommended that Modell consider using Hopcraft's public relations firm in certain non-football areas for the Browns. Kevin Byrne, public relations director for the club over the last 15 years, had his responsibilites confined to the football team and league matters by Bailey. Bailey then used Hopcraft to spread the message that the team needed to disseminate on Stadium renovation and related funding matters.

Pride was also at stake in the deliberations. The success of the Cleveland Indians, who had become legitimate World Series contenders, gained them increasing fan support, to some extent at the expense of the Browns. Brent Larkin wrote in his column "the Indians in 1994 had surpassed the Browns as the town's favorite, and the team stands to remain in that lofty place for years to come."

Art Modell would not accept that premise as fact. He had said in an earlier interview:

The fans are emotionally involved with the Browns far, far more than the Cavaliers or the baseball team. The bulk of the calls that come into the radio talk shows are about the Browns. On draft day, the airwaves are flooded with information. When they see what they like, they walk around with their chests out. When they don't, they turn on us. I like that. That's a hell of a lot better than apathy and indifference, like I saw with the baseball team for 40 years.

When Jacobs Field opened in 1994, the Indians became the toast of their hometown, and apathy was a thing of the past. One of Modell's close friends said the Browns' owner grew jealous of the Indians' success. "His ego was nicked," said the friend. "For the last two years, all you heard around town was the Indians. Suddenly, Modell wasn't top cat anymore."

Modell did not like what he was reading in the media on how to get the financing package passed. The local business journal suggested the success of funding the renovation "will depend on how often the campaign backers avoid connecting the name Art Modell to the renovation." Almost like Art Modell was a poison. Art must have seen he was a long way from being voted the "nicest 102-year old man in Cleveland."

In a comparable remark, Commissioner Tim Hagan responded to a reporter's question by saying, "We all wish Mother Teresa owned the Browns. It'd (the sin tax extension) be an easier sell."

Perhaps the articles that stung Modell most were in the *Plain Dealer*. These were delivered by columnist Joe Dirck, who was constantly "chiding" Modell for seeking public support for "his" stadium. Not so much what the reporter said, but how he said it, became the issue with Modell. This columnist portrayed his episodes in a cutesy fashion, creating a fictitious stadium committee to be known by its initials, EXTORTS, for the EXecutive Task-force On Renovating The Stadium.

His May 7, 1995, column was another chapter in his EXTORTS series. Headlined "One last chance for EXTORTion," he fictionalized a meeting between the Task Force and Modell. Several times in this make-believe meeting, a Task Force representative makes the statement that the committee was reacting as quickly as they could in response to the threat being made by....., to which Art cuts the speaker off with "I am NOT threatening...."

Art was very angry with being characterized as an extortionist. He said later (more than likely in response to the way he was being portrayed in this column) that he would never go public with what he needed to stay in Cleveland. He would tell the mayor and leave it up to him. The mayor had found a way to build two brand new sports venues at Gateway. But Art would not, and he repeated WOULD NOT, ever tell the public what had to be done and further subject himself to being characterized in the *Plain Dealer* as an EXTORTionist.

As part of the ongoing renovation study, comparative cash flow projections from Stadium operations were continually updated, and Bailey presented these to Modell under many different scenarios. Because the Los Angeles Rams were moving to St. Louis, a new thought was included in the revised projections for Modell's review. This new wrinkle was significant.

Modell was given this summary:

Anticipated Annual Profits	
1) under present lease	$107,000
2) under an improved lease in a renovated stadium	$2,000,000
3) in a new stadium in a surrounding county	$7,000,000
4) for the Los Angeles Rams moving to St. Louis	$20,000,000

As Modell liked to say, "You don't have to be an MIT grad" to figure out that the present lease wouldn't help sign free agents. Professional football was being driven by stadium economics. Under the existing arrangement, the Browns could never generate sufficient funds to acquire the players needed to win in the NFL. Even with revenue opportunities offered by a renovated Stadium (assuming a renovated Stadium was even a possibility), the $2 million in profits would fall far short in providing funds for future free agents, based on Cleveland's experience in the 1995 marketplace.

The Browns were also concerned about where the profits were going to come from to get the team out of its spiraling debt situation. The analysis made it obvious there was only one way to accomplish the task of reducing the company's debt and still permitting Art to retain Browns' ownership...or whatever their new name would be in 1996.

Modell explained later, "You cannot make it in sports today without what Orioles' owner Pete Angelos has with Camden Yards." Sometime during 1995, Art had come to realize that the only way to restore the Browns to fiscal health was with the amenities found only in new stadiums---skyboxes and plush club-level seats for well-heeled fans.

The 1995 special events season at the Stadium was a big disappointment compared to the almost-capacity bookings of the prior year. No stadium-sized concerts tours were available. Besides the Motocross Races in

May, the gigantic Rock-n-Roll Hall of Fame concert in September was the only major event scheduled. At the request of the city fathers, Modell provided the Stadium rent-free for the evening concert, held in conjunction with the grand opening of the Rock Hall of Fame on September 2. Ticket proceeds for the evening went to complete the construction and outfitting of the new museum. Business leaders thanked Art Modell for understanding and being a good "team player."

In two more months, that viewpoint would change dramatically

Modell's request for renovation funds evoked a public outcry in some areas, as depicted by this billboard message on Cleveland's near west side. *Mike Poplar collection*

In May the Stadium hosted a Motocross event, one of only two special events scheduled for 1995. *Cleveland Stadium Corp. collection*

CHAPTER 15

THE MORATORIUM
IS UNDERWAY

By the time the moratorium was declared, Art Modell had probably come to believe that Stadium renovation alone would not solve the Browns' fiscal woes.

Other NFL teams were finding ways to get new stadiums built. The Carolina Panthers, as an expansion franchise, for example, was going to receive a new stadium in Charlotte, with all the positive economic benefits that would flow from the amenities within. In Modell's own city, and in his own league, new venues were sprouting up almost everywhere. But Art felt he was expected to keep pouring money into "that old barn," as he so often put it, and he was without a baseball team to generate revenues with which to help fund the needed repairs.

He was very disappointed when Bailey told him to expect no reimbursement from the city for the loss of his baseball tenant. On top of that, his own committee advised him that there was yet no substantive plan to generate the money to renovate the Stadium or to build a new one. Talk of corporate support couldn't be taken seriously, because some businesses, rather than purchasing Stadium loges, were contributing to the new Rock-n-Roll Hall of Fame museum, which also was facing a shortfall in its construction budget. One firm had just canceled its Stadium loge lease and made a publicized contribution to the Hall in the same amount as the annual lease fee.

The local media kept testing Modell on his support for the head coach, hoping to catch Modell off-guard. Finally there was a note of weakening support. One interviewer told Art he didn't understand how an owner with such a gregarious personality could continue to tolerate his head coach's personality. Modell answered, "If he wins, I don't care about his personality. I did not bring Bill Belichick in here to be the house comic. I brought him in to coach and win. If he doesn't do that, having not built a reservoir of goodwill, then he'll have some problems. Follow me? He knows the franchise is at stake here, and he's trying."

Excitement greeted the Andre Rison announcement, but there were miles between this announcement and actually signing the four-time Pro Bowler to a contract. The holdup was the amount of the signing bonus. Although officials thought they had reached agreement on $3 million, Mike Lombardi had to call Art and tell him that the agent had reversed himself and wanted $5 million to get his client to ink the contract. Modell was taken aback, but he felt he had to sign the player his "football people" told him was the one missing ingredient in getting the Browns to the Super Bowl.

Many people around the office questioned the wisdom of this move. Of course no one in the "in" group wanted to hear dissenting opinions because speaking against the consensus was viewed as disloyalty. Some people thought there were other equally important needs besides wide receiver, most notably, at linebacker. Could that $5 million have been used instead to purchase two, or maybe three, very good players? We felt somebody needed to express some opposite views just to provoke some critical thinking. But with Ernie Accorsi gone, the checks and balances that once existed on football decisions were missing. Most of us thought Jim Bailey didn't challenge Art or the football staff enough in the decision-making process. More than once (when Bailey and I used to compare notes) I suggested that Bailey take a stand in questioning a football decision from the player personnel department. Bailey would decide otherwise, saying, "Let him have his way. If he's wrong, he'll get fired."

The problem with that thinking, of course, is that the financial damage was being done while we waited for the inevitable...the fatal mistake to surface. But that's how things worked during these later years. "Let him do it his way, and he'll get chewed up when he fails." Head coaches got their way in the draft because they might not play the guy if someone else in the organization had drafted him. If a groundskeeper prepared a budget for an expensive approach to field replacement when a more economical one would do, we didn't correct him. We let him do it his way and awaited the results.

At a golf outing a former Browns' wide receiver told me that although Rison was a good player, he thought the Browns might be expecting too much of him. "I hope the Browns discount those receiving statistics that he racked up in Atlanta, knowing that he came out of the type of offense the Falcons are known for. I'm not sure he's worth that kind of money."

Nonetheless, the Browns were determined to acquire Rison, no matter the cost. If it didn't work out, somebody was doomed. Art was relying on only four people for most of his advice at this time---Bailey, David Modell, Bill Belichick, and Mike Lombardi. It was a fair assumption that no matter what happened, David Modell and Bailey were safe. The other two guys were safe only as long as the Browns kept winning.

I figured one other problem would have to be addressed. Those of us with long memories remembered the 1982 and 1990 seasons in which the team had won-loss records of 4-5 (strike season) and 3-13 respectively. Bailey should have reminded Art of the dire consequences in those years. The Browns had signed Tom Cousineau for a whopping multi-million dollar contract and signing bonus in 1982, and Raymond Clayborn for a substantial $900,000 in 1990. The real problem occurred after the players arrived, in the form of dissension among the base player corps. The reason was obvious: the front office chose to pay huge dollars to outsiders who had not yet contributed to the team, while the veterans, the core of the team, were snubbed in their pursuit of equal money. When Clayborn signed in 1990, a Browns' veteran said, "There's only two problems with signing Clayborn. The Browns have to pay him more than any other defensive back is earning, and secondly, he can't play football any longer."

In 1982 both Chip Banks and Clay Matthews stormed into the front office asking for adjustments to their contracts after Cousineau had received his plum. Both received them after holding out. I feared a similar reaction would occur in 1995.

After Rison inked his agreement, Art Modell was going to have to deal with two other problems that he may not have counted on. The Browns' financial people knew the Rison contract would almost guarantee the Browns would end the 1995 season with a cash deficit, no matter how high in the standings they finished. And because player moves were happening so fast, it was probable that no one assessed accurately the impact on the salary cap beyond 1995. Had Browns' treasurer Mike Srsen been measuring the turbulent moves, I am positive the cap would have been watched closely. But those duties were spread over several other people, so it is difficult to evaluate whose responsibility it was. It probably fell on Bailey, who was functioning as the team's vice president of finance, although he did not carry the title in the team's media guide. Srsen continued to be admonished to "stay out of the football side of the business, and don't register any opinions on the players being acquired. Let the 'football' guys do that. We'll sign the players; you find the money to pay 'em."

To Modell's delight, Bailey found a way to sign his key player "within" the NFL rules for 1995. But could Bailey find the money to pay the player, and could he find a way around the salary cap in years to come if Rison did not work out? If there was to be a problem, it didn't matter then. It was next year's problem.

The salary cap was intended as the NFL's way of maintaining balance in the league, by preventing one team with loads of money from buying up the expensive talent. But creative minds can find ways to circumvent the rules. The whopping signing bonus became the way of luring players from other teams, which was certainly not what the league had in mind when it adopted the cap. But as well-respected Giants' general manager George Young said, "Under salary cap accounting, you better be damned sure that the guy you are signing will be with you for the entire term of the contract, or you are going to have hell to pay."

He also lamented the future of the game. To get around the rules, owners were paying players big dollars merely to sign a new contract, rather than to produce championship football plays. Young said, "Free agency and guaranteed salaries (in the form of signing bonuses) are going to kill our game."

While the Browns tried to find ways to meet the payroll, the newly elected Governor of Maryland, Parris Glendening, thought it timely to meet with NFL Commisioner Paul Tagliabue. He wanted the league to know that the State of Maryland had a new administration and a new attitude. He reminded Tagliabue that Baltimore was the only city in the country where all the funding for a new stadium was in place. He said that Maryland wanted a team, preferably an expansion team, or the money "goes away." In response, the governor was told that expansion was a few years away, probably not before the turn of the century.

While Modell wanted total concentration on winning football in 1995, he didn't plan on having to address Eric Turner's contract. Turner, who had an All-Pro year in 1994, was disturbed by the size of Andre Rison's contract and indicated that he wanted a "Rison-type" contract or he would hold out. Modell responded angrily, "I hope it won't be a long holdout. That would make me unhappy because I want no distractions this year...That includes stadiums, holdouts, and agents." Turner, however, was sticking to his guns. He resented being designated the team's "franchise player," which he felt placed limitations on his ability to get top dollar. He became unhappy with his $2.145 million salary, and was looking for Rison's numbers ($3.4 million average over 5 years). According to published reports, Modell scoffed at Turner making that type of money. "You can't compare Rison and Turner," he said. "In Andre Rison we got the home run hitter we were looking for. He's a four-time Pro Bowler and a major acquisition. He was the one element that we felt was missing to take us to the promised land, and we paid dearly for him. In Eric's case, we value him highly, but we have rights to him under the collective bargaining agreement, and we're exercising those rights."

Eric Turner was finally signed to a new contract just prior to the opener on September 3. The Browns agreed to a sizable signing bonus and a very lucrative deal for their "franchise player."

In addition to Turner, other players were asked to restructure their contracts in order to fit everyone under the "cap." That was the issue: to fit everyone under the cap in 1995, because the Browns were going for bust, even though the front office was laying the groundwork for potential cap problems in the future. Modell had said earlier that he was pleased how the Browns were managing the salary cap. He complimented Bailey, "No one is better at managing the cap. We've done very well. The 49ers do not have a monopoly on 'cap brains.'" When the problem of the out-of-control "cap" situation surfaced a year later, however, Modell placed the blame on Lombardi and Belichick.

Sizable signing bonuses were used as the lure to induce players to let the club rewrite their contracts. So, while player salaries, as calculated under the NFL salary cap, and for accounting purposes, appeared to be relatively reasonable, the cash paid to the players was enormous, and these funds were secured through bank loans. In fact, Modell said later that the club had reached the point where the bankers refused to lend him any more money for bonuses. Essentially, the club had reached its borrowing peak; the Browns were tapped out. Consequently, I was instructed to minimize all expenditures by the Cleveland Stadium Corp., and from our operations to make any excess funds available to the Browns. While Art would later say that the Stadium actually cost him money, it was Stadium Corp. profits in 1994 and 1995 that were being loaned to the Browns to help fund their operations. In reality, Stadium Corp. profits may have prolonged the Browns' stay in Cleveland by one year. (A year later it was disclosed that the Browns had spent $55 million in 1995 player compensation, while the salary cap was approximately $38 million).

Later I learned that in 1995 over $20 million was paid in player bonuses alone, bringing the total spent in bonuses *alone* over the previous three years to about $40 million, an inordinately excessive amount by comparative NFL standards.

Those of us not in the select inner circle of advisors wondered how other teams found a way to win without spending the money the Browns were doling out. Teams with better won-loss records were spending less money. Lombardi had often said, "Art will have to spend really big money if he wants to play in the NFL with the big boys." Those of us in the financial arena were constantly warning Bailey that pursuing high-priced free agents would mean economic suicide. But we were bucking the party line, and instead of being viewed as people who cared, we instead fell into disfavor. But it was still painful watching Art's investment slowly dissipated.

The Browns' debt had become obscenely high, so high that it could never realistically be reduced through future operations. Without bank access to funds to pay the bonuses the team committed to, the Browns had to ask some players to wait until spring 1996 to receive payment. Mike Srsen kept warning Lombardi and Bailey that the money could no longer be procured, but rather than heed Srsen's warning, Bailey simply instructed Srsen to do his best to "find it." The one remaining hope was to get to the Super Bowl. Maybe the revenues from the playoffs, to and including the Super Bowl, would rescue the Browns.

Art Modell told people that "on paper, the 1995 team was the best Browns' team since the mid-'60s, particularly in terms of depth." Many experts agreed with him. There was a lot of talk around town, just like in 1988, that this was the Browns' year to go to the Super Bowl. Peter King of *Sports Illustrated* picked the Browns to be in it. Commentator Dan Dierdorf also made Cleveland his selection, and many local writers picked them to win the

AFC Central. Still, most local writers were not yet convinced that Vinny Testaverde was a Super Bowl quarterback.

Earlier in the spring, Modell had expressed total confidence in the Browns' defense. He said, "We're very, very comfortable with our defense." About the departure of Michael Dean Perry, Art said, "This is addition by subtraction. He's a good player, but would not play within our system." Modell said he expected the defense to improve on its record-setting performance of 1994. He said he and the coaches were "very, very certain that the threesome in the interior defensive line of Footman, Sagapolutele, and Goad was an upgrade over Michael Dean Perry, James Jones, and Bill Johnson in 1994."

From the start of the preseason, however, some ominous signs were developing on the field. First and foremost was the loss of the special teams runback personnel. Eric Metcalf, Randy Baldwin, and Mark Carrier, all effective runners, migrated onto other rosters in 1995. These men had been instrumental in getting the Browns excellent field position after punts and kickoffs throughout the 1994 season, but they were gone. Who was going to replace them? This question was posed to Bill Belichick, and not only did he agree that the losses would create a void, he pointed out one more problem. He said, "I think just as big a loss is the departure of James Jones, who was a key blocker on the return team. We need to find someone to fill that role. Then it becomes easier to spring a runback man, no matter who he is, when you fill the blocking spot with a key player." Tom Donahoe, director of football operations for the Pittsburgh Steelers, said the Steelers were relieved that Metcalf and Baldwin were no longer in the AFC Central Division. He said, "Metcalf and Baldwin were guys our special teams' coaches lost sleep over." After hearing both Belichick's and Donohoe's assessments, I became more concerned than ever. But this was not to be the only concern in the coming months.

Another potential problem was the loss of defensive coordinator Nick Saban. Some predicted that Saban wouldn't be missed, that Belichick's defense would simply be passed to the next guy, in this case second-year Browns' coach Rick Venturi. Others felt that Saban's skill at making key adjustments was going to be missed on game day.

Besides all of the above, Vinny Testaverde would have to come out of the gate quickly, because no one wanted to have to count on rookie quarterback Eric Zeier to take the Browns to the Super Bowl.

In mid-August I received a surprising call at the Stadium offices from Marilyn McGrath, long-time secretary to Art Modell. She said Modell would be leaving Berea to come down to his office at the Stadium. Since it had been a long time since Art had been on the lakefront, he and I took a drive around the building, focusing on all the construction just east of the Stadium. Finishing touches were being put on the Rock Museum, and the neighboring Science

Museum was well underway. What made the most impact on us, however, was how the Stadium parking lot had disappeared. At one time that lot had held almost 3000 cars, and it was totally gone. The lot west of the stadium, which held almost 1600 cars, was scheduled for new warehouse construction in 1996. I shuddered at the thought of 80,000 football fans fighting for the remaining 2000 spots, in a "part-time" lot owned by the Port Authority on the waterfront. At times there could be absolutely no place left for parking. How could we explain that to our fans?

At that time I did not know Art Modell's real state of mind relative to the renovation project. Nor did I want to ask because the official word was that "a moratorium was on." Still, I couldn't resist giving my thoughts. I said, "How ludicrous it would be for the city to renovate this building and have the Browns invite 80,000 fans to come to the rebuilt stadium, and not be able to provide them ample parking." Art didn't respond. He just didn't want to talk. (I still feel that a new stadium should not be built in the old location unless adequate parking spaces can be provided.)

The Rock-n-Roll Hall of Fame concert promised to be one BIG concert on Saturday night, September 2, 1995. The stage was the largest ever constructed on the Stadium field. In fact, there were so many acts invited to perform that promoter Jules Belkin had to design a double stage, to include a revolving stage built on top of a standard but extra-wide platform. The idea was to allow the next act to get ready while the one before it was still performing. Down time between acts would thus be eliminated, which was important since the program promised to be very long.

Construction on the stage began almost two weeks before the show. Including the event and the tear down time, it was close to three weeks between the start of work and the time the last worker left the Stadium. During that period, the grounds crew was unable to apply even a single drop of water to the playing field. August 1995 was a very dry and hot month, so the grass was denied the natural benefit of rainfall. With all the hectic activity going on, the automatic sprinklers could not be used. But the Browns' groundskeeper still had hope the grass could hold up until the Wednesday after the show.

Because this concert promised to be something special, cable television giant HBO entered into a pact with the Rock Museum to televise the extravaganza. This added to the pressure; to accommodate the network, the setting had to be nearly perfect for the viewing audience at home. More carts and more people were continuously roaming the field. The Stadium staff could only hope that the protection platform on the field was doing its job. But with the ambient temperatures so high, we knew the heat below the protective surface had to be over 100 degrees.

The stage constructed for the Rock and Roll Hall of Fame Concert was so large it obscured the entire scoreboard. *Cleveland Stadium Corp. collection*

The day of the show finally arrived. The Browns had already landed in Massachusetts to play the New England Patriots the next day in the season opener. Many of the players were able to watch the show from their cable-ready sets in the motel. The show ended at 2:10 a.m., after 6 hours and 40 minutes of music. Forty-one different combinations of artists, who performed 68 songs, entertained 60,000 fans live and millions of others at home. I'm not sure we will ever again see Bruce Springsteen and Chuck Berry team up to sing "Rock and Roll Music" as they did that evening in Cleveland Stadium.

Concert-goers had to pay $540 to sit in the best seats in the house, and the average ticket buyer expended $75 for a ticket. The gross gate for the evening was $5 million, and except for show costs, the balance went to the Museum. The entertainers played for free, and Art Modell, Stadium landlord, charged no rent. We thought it ironic that the City of Cleveland asked for and received its 6% admission tax, which was close to $300,000.

The Browns' completed an erratic preseason with a 2-2 record. In two games, the running game looked lousy. The offensive line didn't seem over-powering. They broke the huddle with little enthusiasm. Stories abounded about how Belichick's tough practices had burned the guys out. Maybe some players figured that if they lost this year, the coach might get fired. Some players simply did not like the coach. Reports of his demeaning treatment were well known, and if the negative feelings ran deep enough throughout the roster, he would find it difficult to get the team to play hard for him. Eric Metcalf, then with Atlanta, was asked just before the Falcons' preseason game, against whom would he like to spike the ball after his first touchdown catch against the Browns. He replied, "Maybe their head coach." Almost every player leaving the Browns had something less than flattering to say about Belichick.

In Berea stories were surfacing that Art Modell had begun to sour on his head coach. People close to Art said he was becoming disillusioned with the coach's apparent lack of effort in improving relations with the media. As the Browns were ready to start the season, a picture was evolving of a team not quite ready to win it all.

Mike Lombardi, Art Modell and Bill Belichick engaged in a question and answer session at a Berea facility press conference. *Browns News Illustrated*

By noon on Sunday, the Browns were on the field in Foxboro, Massachusetts, ready to open the 1995 season. Their owner, however, was absent, missing only his second regular season game in 35 years; he was nursing an ear infection at his home in Waite Hill. Twenty-five miles to the west, at the Stadium, the concert was over and the cleaning crews were finishing their work, the sound towers were coming down, and the field cover was being raised.

Vince Patterozzi, the Browns groundskeeper, was getting his first look at the field in three weeks. The sight that greeted him wasn't very pretty. The intense heat and lack of water had severely stressed the turf, and the big question was: Would it have to be replaced before the Browns' home opener next Sunday?

David Modell arrived at the Stadium to meet with Patterozzi on Tuesday morning after all the heavy equipment was removed from the field. They assessed the field damage and decided to replace the damaged sections of the field with new sod before the home opener against Tampa Bay. Patterozzi worked around the clock, employing sub-contractors as needed to get the job done within 48 hours. Plenty of water had to be added for the next two days to get some knitting of the root structure prior to the first home game. I am sure Art wasn't happy about the field conditions, but he realized the risks that went into a project this size.

When Art Modell had offered to donate the Stadium to the Rock and Roll Hall of Fame Museum for a rent-free concert, little did he expect the show would be held during the football season so it could coincide with the grand opening of the Museum.

The Browns were facing the Tampa Bay game with a 0-1 record, after losing the opener to New England, 17-14. Belichick lost to his former mentor, Bill Parcells, after the Browns had been guilty of several crucial physical and mental mistakes. Poor tackling, dropped passes (one on the second last play of the game), and the questionable use of a timeout late in the game all played a part in the three-point loss.

Eric Turner, just returning from his long holdout, was guilty of poor tackling on a third-and-ten situation late in the game. New England tight end Ben Coates got hit by Turner after catching a dump-off pass, but he bounced off and ran for 9 1/2 yards. The Patriots then went on to convert the fourth down play, and eventually scored the winning points on the same drive. After the game, Turner said, "I just bounced off him. That definitely was a first-game-back, six-months-off-kind-of-thing."

Simple as that. As a holdout, he couldn't be expected to be as sharp as if he had been in camp for six weeks. The Browns were 0-1, but holdouts could not be held accountable. Those things happen. Art Modell would sizzle over situations like this.

Sports columnist Dan Coughlin commented as to what a difference 30 years made. Then Art Modell took a hard line against Jim Brown. In 1995 Modell and his "football people" just caved in to player demands.

That kind of rationale also drove fans up the wall. Most fans felt that had Turner been in camp, the Browns might have been 1-0. Over a year later, some fans still surmise the holdout was a consequence of the Rison signing. I'm sure if Rison hadn't been pursued to the tune of a $5 million bonus, Turner wouldn't have reacted as he had. I wondered if Bailey, Lombardi, and Belichick would be held accountable for that decision.

But the real tell-tale sign in the Patriots' game focused on the defense. The defense that Art Modell had lauded in preseason, and from which he expected great things, allowed the Patriots to gain 427 yards. Was this a continuation of how the Steelers had run right through the team in the last game of the 1994 season? Could it be that Belichick had taken on double duty of defensive coordinator (defensive coordinator Rich Venturi had suddenly taken ill) and head coach, thus stretching himself too thin? Or was the team not nearly as good as the high player payroll indicated it should be?

Steve Crosby, when asked to elaborate on the offensive game plan, said the Browns "were surprised by something we weren't ready for, as the Patriots came out and tried to do some of the things that Pittsburgh did in the playoff game last year. They obviously studied the film."

About 63,000 fans were expected for the home opener against Tampa Bay. Modell was immensely disappointed with the figure. In a year many folks believed the Browns were Super Bowl bound, the team was to be greeted by its smallest opening day crowd in over 20 years. Was it in part due to the fact that the Indians were going up against the Baltimore Orioles at Jacobs Field that same day?

While Modell was questioning the reasons for the languishing support from Browns' fans, the *Plain Dealer* editorial cartoonist offered his opinion.

On Friday, September 8, two days before the Tampa Bay game, the lead editorial in the *Plain Dealer* dealt with the dilemma of Gateway's unpaid bills. With Jacobs Field hosting its second season of baseball, it was disconcerting for Clevelanders to hear continuing reports that contractors were still begging for their payments. In the previous week, 22 contractors had banded together and filed lawsuits to recover $11 million owed them for work at Gateway. The editorial chided Tom Chema and the Gateway board for failing to adequately monitor the construction budget. Ah, Browns' fans must have thought, so much remains to be done with Gateway before anyone can begin thinking about a football stadium project.

When I completed reading the *Plain Dealer* that morning, I meandered out to the field to find Vince Patterozzi and his subcontractor putting the finishing touches on the repairs. Both had worked around the clock for the better part of three days. To keep the project within a reasonable budget and because of time constraints, Patterozzi couldn't replace the entire field. The sections under the sound tower, under the huge stage, and those which had seen heavy traffic were replaced in their entirety. Other sections under the protective surface, though, also showed signs of stress from lack of oxygen and water, but these couldn't be replaced. Vince seemed confident that Mother Nature would help those areas recover in time. On Friday morning the repair job was complete, and heavy watering was applied to the new sod to help the rooting process.

While there was excitement in the Browns' front office over the Browns' home opener, Cleveland sports fans were excited over the Indians. They had clinched the American League Central Division title, their first title in 41 years. Front page headlines greeted the reader: "Wahoo! Indians clinch title." The Tribe had built up such a lead (22 games) that the magic number for clinching the division was hit before September 10.

On Sunday morning, the headline on the *Plain Dealer* sports page continued to deal with the excitement over the Indians' clinching the championship, while a U. S Open women's tennis story featuring a picture of Steffi Graf dominated the front page. Graf's picture was larger than the story featuring the Browns' home opener. I don't recall a Browns' home opener ever receiving so little media coverage.

The Browns defeated the Buccaneers quite handily, 22-6, and on Monday morning, the papers talked about how Cleveland accommodated 103,000 sports fans downtown at approximately the same time. The Browns attracted 61,000 fans, 17,000 shy of a sellout, while the Jake was once again sold out to 42,000 fans.

When the Browns went back to practice following the victory, euphoria gave way to gloom as the injury report grew. The first report had four key players out with leg injuries, with Michael Jackson's pulled calf muscle the most severe. Tony Jones, Rob Burnett, and Dana Hall also were nursing injuries. Jackson reported that he pulled his muscle in pre-game drills on the "soft part of the turf," which, the reporter added, might have been the result of the Rock and Roll Hall of Fame concert re-sodding. Keenan McCardell, another wide receiver, also limped off the field after hitting a soft spot, but he later returned to the game.

With Art Modell less accessible to reporters as a result of his moratorium, David Modell was sought out by reporters for his views on the disappointingly low turnout for the Browns' home opener. David responded, "I can understand if this occurred last year, because we did not have a good home record the year before. But we were 7-2 last year. I figured that would have an extremely positive impact. I was wrong."

Season ticket sales increased by 1,000 over 1994, taking the total to a shade over 40,000. David Modell said, "That is a modest increase for a team that has real Super Bowl aspirations," and he went on to identify two reasons for stagnant Browns' ticket sales, the success of the Indians and the decaying condition of the Stadium. "Clearly, the Indians have taken a lot of disposable income out of the marketplace," he said. "Also, consumers want a product. Part of the product is the venue. Now that the fans have been exposed to these gleaming temples (Jacobs Field and Gund Arena), and then they come down to our place, they ask themselves a question."

In the meantime, on the renovation front, city leaders were calling upon Art Modell to "guarantee that the team will stay in Cleveland if a renovation package was assembled." It seemed as though the city leaders sensed something amiss. Modell, through spokesman David Hopcraft, called the issue a "distraction" and said he would not discuss it until the season was over. Hopcraft added his criticism of a suggestion to use proceeds from the sin tax extension both for Stadium renovation and to pay the remaining debt at Gateway. He said the Browns did not want to be "piggy-backed" to take care of another stadium's funding problems. County Commissioner Mary Boyle, seemingly always eager to zing Art Modell, accused Art of "showing his disdain for the community" by refusing to offer the guarantee.

Boyle then offered her own "un-scientific" survey of comments on the "sin" tax received from her constituents, saying that of 75 letters received on the subject, only eight people favored an extension to renovate the Stadium. She said that while this sampling was rather limited, she was afraid it was an indicator of prevailing sentiment.

At midweek league statistics showed the Browns after two games to be second last in rushing. How could this be? The Browns boasted the one-two running back punch of Leroy Hoard and Lorenzo White, along with what they considered a premier offensive line. If anything, the Browns should have been second from the top, not second from the bottom. Steve Crosby stated that he was "absolutely concerned why this unit wasn't more productive." Bill Belichick added resignedly, "We're not getting production out of anybody." One of the lowlights in the Tampa Bay game took place in the second quarter when the Browns recovered the ball on the opponent's two-yard line. The running attack proceeded to gain only one yard in three attempts. The Browns settled for a field goal. Most fans wondered where the power (and dominating) football was that they had been promised.

Thursday morning's headline returned to the Browns' injury factor: "Unsound footing hurts Browns." In the article, Belichick said, "We're pretty banged up. There was some inconsistency in the firmness of the field. They had the concert there last weekend, and both teams were slipping and sliding around a little bit. You plant and the turf doesn't give when you think it will, and then it does when you think it won't. I think a number of these injuries are related to that." Several players chimed in with similar comments.

Art Modell wasn't happy with the team's early performance. Of course, he wasn't happy with a lot of things in his life right then, especially being shunned, as he perceived himself to be, by the corporate community, through their lack of loge-buying support. After reading the comments by his coach about the condition of the playing field, I felt he wanted to make sure the coach was not setting himself up with a round of excuses if the team didn't get to the Super Bowl. Word got back to us at the restaurant roundtable that Art was livid about the coach's comments. He called Vince Patterozzi and told him not to worry about the coach's comments. Modell didn't want Patterozzi to feel that Belichick was speaking for the front office. Art may also have felt that the coach was putting the blame at the owner's feet for scheduling the concert during the football season. Modell downplayed the field conditions to reporters, saying, "Maybe the players got hurt because of the inconsistencies in the field, and maybe they didn't. If the field was a problem ... I'm very sorry...We won't do that again. It was a special commitment I made for the Rock and Roll Hall of Fame several years back, and I wanted to live up to that commitment." Modell explained that he had petitioned the NFL to let the Browns also play the September 10 game on the road.

"We wanted to have a two-week spread to get the field back in shape, but they couldn't accommodate us," Modell said. "It wasn't as bad as I thought it would be. The field should be in 100% shape for the Kansas City game on September 24."

While the Browns' players were attributing their injuries to the new sodding, the Tampa Bay Buccaneers reported no injuries. Modell added, "That should tell you something right there." Before the article ended, Michael Jackson made one last statement, "It was definitely the field that caused it (my injury)."

People close to the scene said that the relationship between the head coach and the owner was permanently damaged over the field situation. Art showed his feelings by calling the groundskeeper directly, rather than going through his management committee. Modell called Patterozzi daily for updates on the field. He told him to do whatever it took to get the field in the best shape possible, "regardless of cost." Very emphatically, he said he wanted the field to be "perfect" for the next home game. With the Browns traveling to Houston for week three, the grounds crew had a week and a half to complete the task. Modell did not want any more comments from the players, coaches, or media.

Several coaches had been livid over the field conditions. One said that the club had to decide if it wanted to win football games or be in the rock concert business. That comment also found its way back to Modell. Art did not enjoy hearing an assistant coach tell him how to run his business.

The Browns went on to eke out a 14-7 win in Houston over the Oilers, taking their record to 2-1. But, surprisingly, acrimony erupted in the Browns' locker room after the win. One might have thought the Browns had lost the game. The offensive linemen took umbrage with the offensive coordinator's play calling. Steve Crosby responded angrily with an expletive-laced tirade at the complaining players.

Despite the talent the Browns had at wide receiver, opposing defenses were not in awe, and they were still stacking up against the run. There seemed to be a lack of respect for the Browns' ability to strike through the air. And the Browns' offensive linemen didn't feel that the play-calling schemes stayed with the run long enough. Abandoning the run to throw deep, some of the linemen felt, showed a lack of confidence in the offensive line.

The Browns were well prepared for Marty Schottenheimer and the Kansas City Chiefs for Game 4 in Cleveland on September 28, pummeling Schottenheimer's normally-tough defense to the tune of 35-17. Beating a former coach was more than just another victory for Art. After the game, I passed Modell and his family as they were exiting the Stadium in a happy, but subdued mood. He was cordial but distant, and we exchanged only a few passing comments. It was the last time that I would ever speak face-to-face with Art Modell.

Months later I learned from *Baltimore Magazine* why Art Modell was so low key at that impromptu passing. Six days before that Kansas City game

Modell had met in New York City with officials from the State of Maryland to learn more about their offer. Modell was accompanied by son David, Jim Bailey, and friend Al Lerner. After passing out boxes of cigars to the smokers, John Moag opened the serious part of the meeting by telling Art, "And for you, Art, I brought you a $200 million stadium."

According to the article, Art Modell responded, "I know you've been burned time and time again, but I'm here in good faith. I'm not going to use you. I don't think it's appropriate to use Baltimore to extort a stadium out of Cleveland." (It was interesting to note that Art used the word "extort," probably because he had seen it so often used against him in the PD) Modell's voice shook as he talked of leaving his city of 35 years. Then referring to his stadium situation, Art said, "I've waited long enough. It's clear to us that nothing is going to happen." The Baltimore group listened to what Modell needed, item-by-item. It appears a deal was agreed upon that day.

On July 28, 1995, even though the moratorium had been declared, the PD might have known the Browns were history in Cleveland.

John Moag said to the reporter that in the era of moving professional sports franchises, one simple economic truth became clear: Cities that choose to make professional sports teams an economic priority--by spending big money on state-of-the-art facilities--will get and keep teams; cities that don't will lose them. The City of Cleveland had showed the Indians that it was serious in getting them to stay in Cleveland, but it had not done the same thing for the Browns.

Art Modell had felt rejected for some time, not necessarily by the fans, but by the community at large. He had not been courted for a long time. If anything, he was disliked by many, and no one was sure exactly why. For all that time, Modell never thought he had any options, so he lived with the disdain, constantly in pursuit of his one obsession: the Super Bowl. Then finally an alternative did arise. A Prince Charming entered his life, and Prince Baltimore brought with him a golden stadium opportunity, shining with significant new revenue possibilities. Modell had to seriously consider a divorce, something he had not contemplated before. He knew he would have to act fast, or the gift-laden Prince would disappear forever.

Kevin Byrne, the Browns' vice-president of public relations knew Art's moods very well. Byrne said, "I could see it (the lack of affection from the community) wearing on him, that 'I'm not going to get it done here.' People in the office, his family, and his friends on the company boards, were telling him, 'Go live somewhere else and be happy.'"

Monday night football was always a *big* night in Cleveland Stadium. As far back as I can recall, Monday night games in Cleveland were always sellouts. The NFL schedule makers usually blessed Cleveland with a formidable opponent on a nice fall evening, the combination lending itself to an electricity-filled atmosphere in the building and a great background for the television commentators. The Browns always seemed to rise to the occasion and provide a great performance on national TV.

On Monday night, October 2, the Buffalo Bills were the scheduled opponents, and in the crowd were Indians Mike Hargrove, Kenny Lofton, and Orel Hershiser, among others, taking in the game before beginning playoff action later that week. By the time the clock struck 12:07 a.m. the Browns had succumbed to the Bills 22-19, dropping their record to 3-2. Frustrated Browns' fans anguished over the loss; this was the second by just three points.

Disconcerting factors were evident when the game was scrutinized in detail: A) The Browns' highly-touted defense again surrendered over 400 yards; B) The running attack faltered with 90 yards for the evening, premier runner Leroy Hoard gaining only 13 yards in 7 carries; C) Dropped touchdown passes by Michael Jackson and Derrick Alexander were the difference between victory and defeat; and D) First-and-goal opportunities at the nine-yard line and at the seven-yard line yielded only two field goals.

While the offense sputtered, the consensus was that the defense lost the game. Late in the game, the team appeared to run out of gas. Defensive lineman Anthony Pleasant acknowledged, "Playing against a no-huddle offense for 60 minutes just wore us down at the end."

The fans left the Stadium that evening, needless to say, quite dejected. Bill Belichick said, "I don't think we played well enough in any of the phases to win the game. We didn't make the plays offensively. Overall, they outplayed us tonight."

The injury list continued to grow. Affected were six starters on defense and Michael Jackson. Modell said later that week, "It's (the number of injuries) a testimony to how hard we played. In fact, maybe we played too hard."

In retrospect, the Browns were unable to recover from this loss. The coaches and players seemed to dwell on their bad fortune in the Bills' game, unable to get it out of their minds and prepare for the rest of the season.

Art found himself in headlines the Wednesday after the game. "Dropped passes irk Modell" was the headline. Art elaborated, "Vinny's passes were right on the money. We hang onto those and it's a blowout."

The headlines on Thursday signaled a second controversial matter. Acting a bit out of character, Bill Belichick blasted Bills' coach Marv Levy for accusing the Browns of faking injuries late in the game, to gain an injury timeout and thus counter the Bills' no-huddle, hurry-up game plan. Belichick lambasted Levy for making the charge, but Bill did not stop there. He attacked Levy's coaching ability. Maybe forgetting for the moment that Levy had guided the Bills to four straight Super Bowls, Belichick continued, "Levy's a guy offensively who came in and tried to run the Wing-T offense in Kansas City. That was brilliant. Marv Levy's perception of what's going on out there and what's actually happening are two different things."

Art Modell had a deep respect for Marv Levy and did not take kindly to the tirade from his young head coach toward one of the NFL's most revered figures. Modell said later, "Maybe Bill Belichick ought to worry a little more about the Browns' struggling offense instead of how well the Bills are doing." The encouraging part of the season to date, in my mind, was that although this team was coming up short on defense, had a sputtering running attack, and a passing attack that looked out of sync on many occasions, their record still could have been 5-0 by eliminating only two of the many mistakes made so far.

With the Browns at 3-3, and going into their bye week after a loss to Detroit, *Browns News Illustrated* took stock of the team. The publisher noted that:

1)   After six games, the Browns ranked 25th in offense and 26th in defense, numbers hardly indicative of a Super Bowl contender;

2)   After six games, the Browns had only one rushing touchdown; despite having reworked Leroy Hoard's million-dollar plus contract and having signed Lorenzo White to a million-dollar contract, not to mention the million-dollar linemen.

3)   Rison, the Browns' $17-million-man, had 15 catches and one touchdown; (I am sure that statistic did not escape Modell's business acumen either).

4)   The defense was allowing the opposition to score an alarming 75% of the time they penetrated the 20-yard line, the so-called "red zone." Modell had always felt that a Belichick team would have a formidable defensive unit; with the team slipping in this area, it was not hard to understand Modell beginning to lose his heretofore unshakable confidence in Bill Belichick.

Tony Grossi's analysis of the Browns was simple: not enough speed on defense. He said they were not very good, either. They were either too old, not in good shape, or both. Grossi said, "the rest of the NFL has figured out how to beat Belichick's defense." If Grossi was right, that surely would spell trouble for the Browns.

The 38-20 drubbing by the Lions confounded even Eric Turner. He said, "This game was a slap in the face for all of us to face reality. We have to stop reading all that stuff in *Sports Illustrated* and *Sporting News* that says we will be in the Super Bowl, and start playing like champions." Thirty-eight points was the second-largest number of points given up by the Browns in the Belichick era.

Fox network analyst Jimmy Johnson criticized the Browns' offensive philosophy for not allowing Vinny Testaverde to open things up. Johnson said the Browns' offense was much better and more creative when Bernie Kosar was the quarterback and calling his own plays.

Belichick himself admitted, "I am not happy with the whole running game--the runners, the blockers, the receivers blocking down field, the tight ends blocking." One Browns' official said the coaches were not happy with Leroy Hoard's running, that he was not hitting the right holes or not hitting them at the right time. The problem, however, ran deeper than statistics and offensive and defensive schemes. The team did not look like it wanted to play.

There had been no commentary in the newspapers from Modell since several days before the Lions' game. Almost ten days had passed, and Modell's name was absent from the sports pages. Tony Grossi reported that Modell had left for a somewhat secretive getaway to Beverly Hills, California. Tony wondered whether Art had been testing the Los Angeles waters as a possible relocation site.

Art Modell's prediction from several years back came to mind. "If Bill Belichick doesn't get the job done in five years, you won't have me to kick around anymore. I'll get out of town and out of football." What had he meant? Did those ominous words have some deeper meaning, or had Art just been venting frustration? The way the team was playing, and given some of the injuries, the so-called 'job' (which was never defined, but was assumed to mean a Super Bowl appearance) was not going to get done in 1995.

More closed-door meetings than usual were going on, and not with the "insiders." The people attending these meetings were the three-piece-suit types, men who looked like bankers and lawyers. In these meetings, Modell was not to be disturbed. Several young loge marketing people who worked at the Stadium and who had been called out to attend meetings with David Modell found themselves waiting for hours as David was called into these private meetings. Back in the Stadium office, I would be getting hurried calls from either Bailey or Pat Moriarty about Stadium Corp.'s bank loan balances. (Moriarty, a former banker had recently been hired and named Browns' director of business operations.) There was no time to kibitz; the caller "needed the answer quick and had to run."

Why would anyone need to know Stadium Corp. revolving credit balances in the middle of October? Why were they asking for a projection of the loan balance at year-end? After all, I had a scheduled meeting with Huntington Bank to furnish them updated profit projections, and Art received cash reports every Friday from the Stadium division, so everyone had an idea about where the loan balance stood. Yet it seemed imperative that they have the exact loan balance projected for December 31. Very unusual, I thought. Perhaps Art is preparing to sell the team and get out of football. He certainly had been reclusive for several months. Maybe he was wrestling with that difficult decision. I felt sure that's what it was, but I couldn't imagine what could have triggered him to decide to sell the team! It must have something to do with estate planning, I thought. That subject was getting much speculation in the papers. I couldn't help but conclude that Art was getting out of football, just as he had promised the fans three years before. If so, it meant Art had given up on the season. But then I thought, that can't be true; Art lives on hope. He has to believe the team can bounce back. Maybe his health has taken a turn for the worse. Maybe all the meetings are planned, just in case.....

I had been trying to contact Jim Bailey on some inter-company accounting matters, but he never seemed to be available. The previous week he was "just out of town." Usually his secretary would share where he was, when he would get back, and possibly the nature of his trip. But not this time. Just "out of town." We would learn in two months that Bailey had been in Washington, DC, on October 6, discussing the draft of the deal with State of Maryland officials to move the Browns to Baltimore. Although there was a snag in negotiations, according to *Baltimore Magazine,* by mid-October everything was back on track. The main snag centered on PSL (personal seat licenses) revenues to be shared between state and team. Using the very lucrative St. Louis Rams case as the criterion, both sides agreed on capping the amount of PSL revenue which the football team could earn at $80 million. Art Modell was finally going to receive payment for the loss of the Cleveland Indians as his tenant, but it wasn't going to be paid by the City of Cleveland. The State of Maryland seemed more than happy to do so if it meant the return of NFL football.

The Browns' head groundskeeper had been spending much time in the Stadium during October, tending to the re-sodding project, and he would often join the Stadium Corp. staff for lunch at the same Stadium Restaurant roundtable where Art used to preside. Vince Patterozzi kept plugging away at both his assignments (he also tended the four practice fields in Berea) without ever complaining. When I asked Vince at lunch what he was hearing in Berea about the renovation of the Stadium, and/or moving the franchise, he replied, "That's already been decided. There won't be any renovation." Very matter-of-factly, between sips of chicken broth, Vince added, "We're moving. We'll be in Baltimore next year."

I looked at him aghast. I was taken aback by the certainty with which he had made that statement. He said, "What's the problem? Why look so surprised? This has been decided for some time now. I have already been asked to go there."

I was stunned! I put my sandwich down as I had just lost my appetite. But I was still not sure if this might be Patterozzi's idea of a joke. So I followed up with another question. "And just why would you have been asked to relocate already, when others haven't been?"

"Well," he said, "I have to be in Baltimore by December 1 to begin plans for laying out a new field at Memorial Stadium so the Browns will be ready to play in August 1996."

I then asked, "Vince, in your opinion, does it make any difference how the team finishes this year? I mean, if by chance we can still get to the Super Bowl, the club would surely change its mind, wouldn't it?"

Vince shook his head "no." He kept his eyes locked on his soup bowl.

While the front office wheels were turning, Coach Belichick was trying to muster his defeated, demoralized, and injured troops for post-bye week action. "Let's view the Jacksonville game as the start of a new 10-game season," he said. "We are tied with Pittsburgh for first place in the AFC Central division."

Andre Rison went out on the limb by guaranteeing the public a win over Jacksonville. This "guarantee" found its way into the Jacksonville locker room and was plastered all over the lockers. Did the Jaguars need more incentive than that? The expansion team was already boasting wins over Houston and Pittsburgh in this young season; being 13-point underdogs to Cleveland probably didn't sit well with them.

Three minutes into the game the first chorus of boos emanated from the crowd. Testaverde overthrew a wide open Brian Kinchen, and the impatient crowd, expecting a full recovery by the team after the week off, sounded their disgust. The fans would boo at least 25 times during the game, intermixed with calls for Eric Zeier to replace Testaverde at quarterback.

By 4:11 pm that Sunday afternoon, the ultimate humiliation occurred. The Browns joined the ranks of the infamous by losing to an expansion team, and at home, no less. The Jacksonville Jaguars dominated the Browns' defense and prevailed, 23-15. By the end of the game, the Jaguars had left the Browns gasping. To the team's and the owner's dismay, the fans were chanting, "Let's go, Tribe" as the game was ending, They knew the Browns were going nowhere.

Besides having to view a game he would later call "an embarrassment to the entire organization," Modell also wanted to know why Lorenzo White had been declared inactive. He was unaware of that fact before game time, and later questioned why the Browns would acquire a million-dollar player and then not even dress him for a game. To Modell it appeared an unwise decision over one of the team's most valuable (or expensive, at least) assets. He said he wanted explanations, but I didn't think he would be happy with them. Modell also wanted to know why Andre Rison was not more productive. Over the first seven games, Rison had only 17 catches, one for a touchdown. The one touchdown had him tied with backup wide receiver Rico Smith. Modell said he was upset by what he saw as a lack of chemistry between Testaverde and Rison.

Earlier that week I had received an e-mail message from Berea asking for a summary of loge rental revenues generated during the year. What wasn't asked for, but which could easily be calculated, was the value of the loges not leased by the corporate community. This information was requested "ASAP, so it could be passed along to Arthur B. Modell."

Presumably the loge rental information was requested for a Browns' board of directors meeting on Friday, October 20, to demonstrate the loss of community and corporate support as part of the rationale for the need to move the franchise. Bob Gries, who represented 43% of the voting shares in the team, said that when he was presented this news for the first time, he went into virtual shock. He told the group he could not deal with the matter then and asked to have the meeting adjourned until the following Tuesday.

Then came the fiasco of the Jacksonville game. It may have been the final disappointment that Modell could handle; snippets of overheard conversation seem to indicate that he probably made his final decision about relocating the franchise before he left his loge to go home.

Before Tuesday arrived, Gries told Modell he wanted no part of the move and that he would resign from the board and sell his stock in the team. When the stock transaction was consummated, Modell became a 90% stockholder in the Cleveland Browns, up from the 51% previously owned.

Everyone knew it was going to happen eventually. On Tuesday morning Bill Belichick announced that Vinny Testaverde was being benched in favor of rookie Eric Zeier. The official explanation was that the Browns needed a spark, and Zeier had demonstrated in pre-season that he could light a fire under the team. Everyone in the front office had noted the team's lack of enthusiasm, and part of the reason given for the lethargy was that the quarterback was too laid back. Testaverde's agent angrily responded, "He's being used as a scapegoat for a team that's playing terribly. He has ten touchdowns and three interceptions, and had eight TD passes dropped. He feels that he is not to blame. They're pushing the panic button."

Art Modell announced that he was 100% behind the decision to make the change, but added that he was not blaming Vinny for the team's poor overall performance. He repeated, however, his concern about the lack of chemistry between the quarterback and Andre Rison, adding that the play between the two had been "woeful" the previous Sunday, when they misfired on at least six plays. "They're not hitting on all cylinders, and it's been extremely disappointing to me," Modell said.

Testaverde's agent responded, "Vinny hit their $17 million man in the hands in the end zone, and he dropped it."

Modell was asked about the risk of starting a rookie on a Super Bowl contending team. "Based on yesterday's performance, we're not going to any Super Bowl, except to sit up in Section 103. Let's put that in perspective. It was a terrible performance. We had two weeks to prepare for Jacksonville, and that game was an embarrassment to this organization." He finished by saying he was "extremely unhappy" with the team and promised other changes before the week was out. I had the distinct feeling that Belichick was history with the Browns, but I seriously doubted Art would make a mid-season change. He had done that in the past only if he was comfortable moving one of the assistants into the role. From the word around the office, he wasn't convinced anyone currently on board could move up. What I (and many others) didn't plan for was the change that Modell might have been referring to—a monumental one which would leave 2.5 million Greater Clevelanders despondent and angry.

The next morning's *Plain Dealer* made me even more certain that my observations on Belichick's future with the team were valid. Modell was asked whether Belichick's job was secure, and for the first time in five years, there was no unswerving vote of confidence. Modell's words were, "I am not going to get into that. I'll make my assessment at the end of the year." He then elaborated:

What's so distressing to me is that this is a better team than last year's, based on the acquisitions that we made. I've invested a lot of money in this ballclub, and I expected better results. I don't remember the last time I felt this low. I'm extremely upset. This was a bad one (Jacksonville game). I don't want to underestimate the impact it had on me and others in the organization.

He finished by directing his anger at the Lorenzo White decision, lamenting, "I can't explain that one. We're going to get some answers soon. We didn't bring him in here to make him inactive." Modell told the reporter that he didn't have the answer. Since he could already have gone to the coach for the answer but had not, it was a giveaway, at least to me, that Bill's time was coming to an end.

In the next day's *Plain Dealer,* Andre Rison gave his views on his poor production to date. He told the columnist that his "free-lance style just clashed with Testaverde's precision passing style." I guess that meant the combination would never work out. Browns' football fans had already figured that out. Art must have been wondering why, given that assessment, he committed $17 million on Rison. One thing was sure. After Modell read that comment, whoever had recommended Rison would be out of work by year's end.

Baltimore Magazine reported that on Friday, October 27 at Baltimore-Washington-International Airport, just before 8 a.m., Art Modell, accompanied by David Modell and Jim Bailey, met with Maryland representatives Governor Glendening and John Moag. Art looked at the governor and said somberly, "This is one of the most difficult things I've ever done." Then the two engaged in small talk for about half an hour. When the moment of truth finally arrived, Art Modell did not hesitate. He and Moag signed two copies of the new lease, one copy to return to Cleveland and the other to be kept locked in Moag's desk. Both sides agreed the deal would not be announced until the end of December, right after the end of the regular football season. The plane returned to Cleveland later that morning. No one in the Berea or Cleveland Stadium offices had any clue as to what had just occurred.

Two days later, on Sunday, October 29, the Browns and Eric Zeier needed to go eight minutes into overtime before the rookie quarterback led the Browns into field goal territory and a final 29-26 victory over the Bengals in Cincinnati. Zeier obviously went into the game with a plan to look for Andre Rison, and the goal was accomplished. Rison had his biggest day as a Brown, catching seven passes for 173 yards.

Modell made his way into the locker room after the game to congratulate both Zeier and Rison, giving both players big hugs as he had been known to do after big games. Few people, however, noticed the cool confrontation minutes earlier as the owner and the head coach crossed paths in the hallway leading from the dressing room. There was a simple, rather perfunctory handshake and a few words exchanged. The state of affairs had become evident, and with Tony Grossi and other media starting to write about it, I felt assured that Art had already decided Belichick's future.

Two days after the Cincinnati victory, with the Browns record 4-4, rumors started to fly about the Browns moving to Baltimore at the end of the season. Callers to the local sports talk shows had ways of finding out, and they relished coming onto the sound waves and telling the listening audience. In Baltimore, a caller phoned WBAL radio, telling all within listening distance that he heard it from one of Governor Glendening's bodyguards that the Browns were moving to Baltimore. In Cleveland, at least two callers professed knowledge of the same information. One was a courier who had been delivering confidential documents between the Browns' law firm and the State of Maryland; another claimed that over lunch he had heard the news from a friend of the son of Bob Gries.

Many people were hearing the words "sale" and "move" in connection with the story, and they concluded that Al Lerner must have purchased the team and was moving it to Baltimore. That theory made sense, since Art Modell had said recently that he would never move the team as long as he owned it, but he had added that "he could sell it to someone else who might move the team."

Reporters were pushing Modell hard for answers. On Thursday, November 2, in response to relentless questioning, Art declared that his team was not for sale and that he would not address unattributed reports emanating in Baltimore. David Hopcraft said Modell had not sold his interest in the team to Al Lerner nor was he even discussing doing so. Hopcraft was then asked if

Modell might move the team without selling it. Hopcraft answered, "We're not going to confirm or deny or comment on any part of it."

Local politicians reacted to the story a bit more lightly. County Commissioner Lee Weingart said this rumor was being floated by those in Baltimore in an attempt to anger Cleveland voters into defeating the upcoming sin-tax extension up for a vote on Tuesday, November 7, 1995. Mayor White said there was no evidence indicating a deal had been struck between the two parties. But he did warn that "there's no doubt in my mind that the Browns will leave if voters reject the upcoming county-wide tax referendum to raise money for the proposed Stadium renovation."

The rumors of the Browns' move did not go away, and by the end of that week, despite the disclaimers and statements of disbelief by public officials, it became impossible to avoid addressing the issue directly. For Greater Clevelanders the upcoming weeks would be filled with anger and anguish.

Although on friendly terms with at least three presidents, Gerald Ford (left), George Bush (top), and Ronald Reagan, Modell was unable to generate political clout on the local front. *Cleveland Stadium Corp. collection*

CHAPTER 16

NULL AND VOID

It was sometime around 5:30 am, November 4, 1995, when Mike Snyder, WWWE (now WTAM) radio newsman, called Art Modell and apparently awakened him from his sleep. Snyder was following up on a conversation between Modell and several reporters on Friday evening during which he had broken his moratorium and suggested that the Browns were in serious discussions with the city of Baltimore. The dialogue between Snyder and Modell went like this:

MS: Art, certainly, this morning is, I guess, in a sense, a sad day in the City of Cleveland. Can you tell us basically what is going on right now in your mind with the Cleveland Browns? Are you going to Baltimore?

AM: Nothing has been finalized yet. Everything should be clarified and determined within the next two or three days.

MS: Art, though, but you have conducted talks with Baltimore. You said a while back that you would not move the team as long as you owned the Cleveland Browns. What has happened to change your thoughts in that direction?

AM: There has been a tremendous change. There has been a dramatic deterioration of the financial condition of the Browns, which changed the situation completely.

MS: As this occurs, Art, you talked about the financial situation. What has happened with your talks with the city concerning keeping the team here? Where is that right now?

AM: It would take an hour of your time to get into that. I'm not going to. We've been talking on and off for six years.

MS: And it just has not happened to your satisfaction right now. I mean, what you see right now, you just don't see anything that is occurring or will occur to change that.

AM: That is correct.

MS: Art, what do you think has happened right now? I mean, I was looking, you've got the beautiful facility in Berea. It seemed like in the last three years now this has all turned around here for football and for the Cleveland Browns.

AM: It has, sadly.

MS: Why do you think that's happened?

AM: The market condition has changed dramatically and frankly the city and county don't have the wherewithal to meet the needs of the Cleveland Browns. They chose to put their resources into Gateway and the Rock-n-Roll Hall of Fame, the Science Museum, all worthwhile causes, and that was their choice.

MS: Art, I think that people are going to say here, though, that you've not been talking, you've had a moratorium....

AM: That is not so. We've been talking, we've exchanged information, we just haven't gone public under the moratorium. We've had conversations now for two years.

MS: But the perception is that people have not...so who has known exactly what it is that you would need to keep the football team here, who's known that?

AM: Volumes of material have been sent to the people of Cleveland, to the officials, over the last two years, describing what is going on in our industry, and what the needs are, and I never did quantify it because I didn't want to be, once again, accused of shaking down or extorting the situation that has been described in print and on the air. I don't want to go through that but they know exactly; they know the dimensions of the problem.

MS: Now you had left it open for still a chance of keeping the team here. Is the vote on Tuesday (the sin tax extension) at all a factor now in your mind?

AM: No.

MS: And why is that so?

AM: Because, it doesn't do the job. It's just not the answer. The "sin" tax extension is a minor, minor factor in this whole thing.

MS: Has it been the case of the city and the officials looking, Art, to build, as you mentioned, the Rock-n-Roll Hall of Fame, Jacobs Field, Gund Arena, has it been the case of just not including the Cleveland Browns in all those plans?

AM: That should be apparent to you and to everyone else.

MS: (in a resigned and exasperated tone) That is what has occurred. Right now, you've got a season yet to play here in this city. You know this is pretty unbelievable, in the middle of the season, this is all going down. Why now, Art?

AM: It is beyond my control.

MS: And that basically, why would that be the case?

AM: Because the pressures were building to do something and I had no choice. I would have preferred waiting until the season was over, that's why I asked for the moratorium. The city officials, the county officials kept pressuring here and the situation kept building and building until I had no choice but to make a determination.

MS: You know, Art, I've known you for a long time and I really feel that you have been a man of your word and for you to say that, you know, you would never move the team as long as you owned them, have you changed at all in your ownership? Have you sold, or are you doing that, or in the process of?

AM: No, on the contrary. I have acquired more equity in the Browns. I'm not selling. I have a significantly larger stake in the Browns than I had before.

MS: You have been symbolic of the National Football League. When the NFL looks at the city and how it has supported football and the Cleveland Browns, won't the league look and say, "My goodness, look at your television ratings last year." I believe they were through the wall. Doesn't that mean something, I guess from a fan's standpoint, in terms of keeping football in the City of Cleveland?

AM: The fans have been superb for 50 years. That does not answer the problem.

MS: So really there's nothing the fans can do. So really, Art, from what you're telling me then, we really come back to where there was literally a fumble among the political powers that be in the city.

AM: I'm not in the blame game. Mike, you've known me a long time. I'm not going to point a finger at anybody. I think Mayor White has worked tirelessly for years on this problem and deserves high marks. It just wasn't there to be.

MS: Art, I thank you for being with us on News Radio 1100, 3WE. I'm hopeful too, that maybe something can be done so you're not going to Baltimore. I thank you for being with us this morning.

That's the message early risers received on Saturday morning November 4, 1995. It was repeated throughout the day. The *Plain Dealer* graced its front page with the oversized morbid headline, BROWNS MOVE IN THE WORKS. Early in the article, the PD reported that Modell would receive from Baltimore about twice the revenues he was currently receiving from his stadium situation in Cleveland. Modell was asked by reporters why he had broken his vow to Clevelanders that he would never move the Browns as long as he owned the team. "As long as I owned the team, and as long as I was given any cooperation at all (that vow stood). As far as my proclamation that I would not move this team, that's gone, that's null and void because the game has changed considerably. We've suffered enormous losses in the last four years." He elaborated that because the franchise had "lost a bundle" it was in no shape to be sold. Furthermore, Modell said economic factors that once contributed to his demand that the Stadium be renovated could now drive him away.

Modell continued:

All I want to do is compete. I'm not in this thing to make money. I'm not in it to go bankrupt, either. I have to do whatever I have to do to protect my family and my franchise and employees. I cannot surrender 35 years of living in this town overnight and say I'm a happy guy--of course not. But I have to do what I have to do---if I do that. If I go.

Art said he was not envious of the Gateway complex and that he wished Dick Jacobs well. But on the one hand, while the Indians had received new parking garages to go with their new ballpark, the Browns had been squeezed out of parking by the new museums. Art closed his interview by telling the reporters "to take notice of the easterly parking lot, where the only people that can park near the bleacher wall are motorcyclists." If any sport should have received additional parking spaces, it would logically have been the football team which drew almost 80,000 to its home events. The baseball team needed to accommodate 42,000 and the basketball team about 20,000. So for the greatest sporting need in town, in 1995 the city provided the least number of parking spots.

In the midst of all the uproar, some people actually forgot the Browns were still in the throes of their 1995 football season. The Houston Oilers were due in town on Sunday. Some fans were convinced the Browns were moving, so why attend the game. Some 57,000 of the 61,000 ticket buyers did come to the Stadium, ostensibly to give Modell a piece of their mind. In the paper that morning Art said he would not be deterred from attending, but Kevin Byrne explained later that Modell did not attend on advice from his close friends. Those 57,000 who did attend witnessed the Browns' most lopsided loss during Belichick's five years as head coach, 37-10.

One fan said, "It was more like attending a funeral than a football game." How else could one feel, at least until they heard more from Art in Baltimore on Monday. Would their greatest fears be true?

On behalf of the Browns' players, linebacker Carl Banks told a reporter in a post-game interview in rather succinct terms, "We stink."

An Oilers' linebacker told reporters after the game, "It's about time that we played against a team whose owner is hated worse than ours."

Bud Adams, owner of the Houston Oilers, a team ready to bolt to Nashville for big-time money in the stadium game, sounded sympathetic towards Modell, "Cleveland has this new arena and new stadium. Poor Art's playing on that 85-year-old field. He was the third man out. Cleveland's been a great city for the Browns and for the NFL, but they haven't been getting Art Modell the support for a new stadium."

That began to sound like the NFL party line. If the city can do "new" for Major League Baseball and NBA basketball, then the NFL would accept nothing less.

I got to the office early on Monday morning. On my computer was a brief message from Jim Bailey. "Mike, please have all Stadium Corp. employees come out to Berea for a half-hour meeting to get a status report."

At the time, the Stadium Corp. employees could best be described as "basket cases." Questions like, "What does this mean?" and "Is this just a bluff?" and "Do you think we will be asked/expected to go to Baltimore?" were all being asked. The only answer I could give was "We'll know by noon today."

I closed down the Stadium Corp. offices and was the last one to arrive at the Berea facility. Waiting outside the auditorium was a teary-eyed Marilyn McGrath, Art Modell's secretary. Jim Bailey and Pat Moriarty, Jim's right-hand man, were there too. From the tears in Marilyn's eyes I knew the "tentative" decision was actually final. It was just a matter of how it would be conveyed. I entered the auditorium and sat in the first row. Then Bailey, McGrath, and Moriarty came in.

Some said they had hoped Art Modell would be there to talk to us, but the first words out of Bailey's mouth put that to rest. "Art surely wanted to be here in person to talk to all of you, but as you know he is scheduled to be in Baltimore today. He asked me to tell you that he'll try to get back to town in the near future, and he'd like to talk with each of you." There was some grumbling from the back of the room. One secretary muttered, "If he really wanted to be here, he would be here."

Bailey then went on to say what a great deal the Baltimore lease would be for the Browns. Everything the team had wanted to do but couldn't because of financial restrictions would pass, he said. He complimented the audience, telling them they had been a good staff, one that had carried the team through tough times. Bailey asked us to hang together for a while longer. He said that when the time to move to Baltimore came, he hoped to move the staff intact. To achieve this, the team would offer generous moving allowances. Those who could not make the move would receive a severance arrangement. It would be on a par with what other NFL teams had recently offered their employees.

Based on Bailey's speech, we didn't have to listen to the Art Modell-Parris Glendening noon press conference. We already knew the results: The deal had been made; at noon would come the announcement.

I doubted that many people were going to be asked to go to Baltimore. I recalled a meeting I had with Bailey a year and a half earlier, in which he was complaining of the high staff payroll in Berea. After having just recently expanded the staff, there could be no seemingly justifiable reason to begin cutting so soon, even though payroll costs needed to be brought under control. This move, however, would be the golden opportunity for Bailey to trim staff, as it would make economic sense to start lean in Baltimore. Knowing this, I sincerely doubted that Bailey had any intention to move the staff intact.

While we were hearing Bailey cheerfully tell us of "this great opportunity awaiting us in Baltimore," Pat Modell, her son David's family, and several house employees were hastily packing. They were scheduled to be Florida-bound by noon. Art had told Pat, "You can't be living here when I make this announcement." Pat would do whatever Art asked, and she knew as she was leaving that she might never see her home in Waite Hill again. Their private plane was flying over Virginia when Art's limousine pulled up to the dais in downtown Baltimore as the crowds chanted "Art! Art! Art!" He was given a hero's welcome by the local crowd. It had been years since he had heard anything in Cleveland that resembled those friendly overtures.

Modell sat on the dais, listening to Governor Parris Glendening announce that the Browns' franchise would be coming to Baltimore. The Cleveland football team would become the second professional BROWNS sports franchise to relocate to Baltimore (the St. Louis Browns baseball team made the move in 1953 to become the Orioles). The Cleveland Browns would also be the second modern NFL franchise to abandon Cleveland (the Cleveland Rams moved to Los Angeles in 1946).

In the days following the shocking announcement, *Plain Dealer* sports columnists annihilated Art Modell's character. Most Browns' fans heartily agreed with those judgments. In the paper we read, "Null and void .....do those words absolve a man who has always said his word is good?" and "Modell always had trouble with the truth .....how much double-talk will Modell use to convince you that at the time he said those words, he was absolutely sure he was speaking the truth."

I believe Modell needed one of his advisors to suggest how he might have restated his earlier position prior to moving the team. Not that it would change anything, mind you, because he would still be the guy who signed on the dotted line to execute the transaction. While he would still be considered a villain, people then couldn't accuse him of breaking his vow.   Art might have said something very simple, along the following lines:

I have said many times before that the Cleveland Browns would never leave Cleveland as long as I am the owner of the team. While that was my most sincere feeling at the time I made that statement, our club has experienced several substantial financial setbacks. Now that player free agency is a way of life in our industry, it gets very expensive to become, and stay, competitive. I still sincerely hope that a move will never come to pass, but in the era of cities bidding for NFL teams, a new option is being presented to owners. Please don't misinterpret this as a threat to leave the city, but I would be less than honest with you if I didn't inform you of these changing circumstances. I therefore can no longer say, as I have in the past, that I will never move this team. I am working with your political leaders to develop a mutually acceptable plan that can work for both of us, much like the region has already done for the Cleveland Indians and the Cleveland Cavaliers.

But Art never made a public statement like that. His position was simple: those realities would be passed along to the politicians, most notably the mayor, either directly or through an emissary, and it would be up to the mayor to pass the message along to the task force, the business community, and even the public. Art insisted that for him to make that statement to the public would leave him open again to be castigated as an "extortionist." Therefore, he would not do it.

The mayor's top legal advisor, Fred Nance, was told by reporters of the revenue estimates being offered to Modell by Baltimore, and he was asked to compare what the City of Cleveland had been offering. Nance said, "We're not going to come close to meeting the $29 million a year for them in Cleveland, even with our enhanced package. Our goal is not to get them in the top two, three, or four in the league. It's to get them in the top third."

With 30 teams in the NFL, that would mean city officials were hoping to get the Browns at least the tenth best lease. It was ironic, I thought, how close this conversation was to 1983 when Stadium Corp. was trying to satisfy the Indians in much the same manner. The Indians' lease was already eighth or ninth best in the league without any improvement. Although our proposal was structured to get them the fifth best lease, that was not satisfactory to the Indians. To get improvement beyond that required major financial assistance from Mayor George Voinovich and City Council on behalf of the city. The city turned down that invitation, and the rest of the story has already been told. Now the shoe was on the other foot. It was the city facing the difficult job of trying to satisfy an unhappy tenant.

Modell told the newspapers that he had been open with both the governor and the mayor in a letter to both on October 5, warning that the passage of the sin tax extension on November 7 would not be sufficient to meet the Browns' needs. In his letter, Modell said, "I am troubled that the public and the business community may be led to believe that the sin tax extension will solve the problem when, in fact, as we have explained... it will not. I urge you...to use your best efforts to make sure that they are not misled."

One of the most scathing editorials came on November 7, 1995, and was entitled, "The Art of deception." The *Plain Dealer* editorial director wrote, "...Art Modell, the Browns' majority owner, would have us believe that he was unable to compete financially with other teams in the league. Don't you believe it." The editorial continued:

Anyone who regularly fills more than 60,000 seats, and often upwards of 70,000, ought to be able to make a decent profit. After all, the Pittsburgh Steelers have done it with a stadium that holds barely more than 50,000. We might also note that they do it successfully, having won four Super Bowls while Modell and the Browns were watching on television. No, if Modell were the smart businessman and the smart football man he thinks he is, the Browns would be both a money-maker and a contender. But because he couldn't make the Browns a financial winner, he went searching for a Baltimore bailout that rewards even his mismanagement with windfall profits.

"Woulda, coulda, shoulda," I guess the saying goes. The Browns should have made money, but they didn't. Pure and simple. The Browns were broke, and they had to find the money they needed to survive. Sadly, it wasn't in Cleveland, Ohio.

Andy Frain security guard Bob Wahr worked the security gate on the north side of Cleveland Stadium from 6 a.m. to 6 p.m. every day. Through his gate entered almost every contractor and visitor who arrived during non-event hours. Wahr also had the additional duty of answering the company telephone in the off-hours when the office switchboard was closed.

On November 7, the day after Art Modell appeared on nationwide TV from Baltimore, the Stadium switchboard was unable to handle all the calls that came in. Every caller wanted a piece of Modell's hide. The vulgarity and profanity that pierced the ears of the telephone operator were appalling. Upset callers didn't stop to think they were yelling at an innocent party, who had no connection whatsoever with the decision-making process of the Browns' move. In fact, our telephone operators were themselves very upset with the decision. But not one caller was able to reach Modell, as he was presumably in his West Palm Beach home by this time. After a very trying day, the regular operator asked to be relieved at her normal quitting time of 5 p.m. rather than continue answering the same type of calls. When the switchboard closed, the calls were rerouted to the security gate for the next hour or so.

Bob was in his security cubicle, still in a state of semi-shock like the rest of us, when his phone rang. He was a little surprised that the board upstairs had already closed, but he answered the call anyhow. He was aware that bitter fans had been calling all day long, wishing all kind of evil on the Browns' owner and good riddance to the head coach. But this call was from a woman who was subdued but distraught and depressed by the news. She didn't wish harm to anyone but herself. She told Bob that she didn't see any way out of her dilemma but to kill herself, since she saw her life without the Browns as pointless and empty. The call got Bob's attention very quickly. He talked fast, empathized, sympathized, cajoled, babbled, and after a non-stop, one-sided gabfest, he summed it up by saying, "It's just not worth ending your valuable life over."

She said, "You know, you make me feel good about myself. You're right. I'm not going to let the Browns' moving to Baltimore get me down like that. By the way, what is your name? I want to send you $50. You do a better job than my analyst." They both laughed.

Bob hung up, and the phone almost immediately rang again. The next caller was mean and ornery. He warned Bob to get everyone out of the building, including himself, within a half hour. He said he had a machine gun and was coming down to "pepper the whole building with bullets." Bob reminded the caller that he would probably find himself in jail, and to consider whether it was worth punishing himself with incarceration over a "bad" football team like the Browns. Bob told the caller he understood why he felt he must do something to release this anger. He then suggested the caller buy a couple dozen of eggs, and then come down and egg the whole damn building. "But, leave the gun at home," the guard admonished.

Bob Wahr, a Stadium security guard who earned $6.00 per hour, may have saved one life and probably prevented another from going to jail and possibly injuring himself or someone else in the process. Little do we realize the talent people possess, talent that goes beyond the skill for which they were hired. Stadium Corp. and Andy Frain Security Services were fortunate to have an employee the caliber of Bob Wahr.

Wahr came to work the next morning, November 8, and chuckled when he found yellow stains splattered and dripping down the walls on the West Third Street side of the Stadium.

The Browns' players also came to work that Wednesday, as they always do, for a routine practice day, trying to avoid all the distractions and prepare for the upcoming Monday night game against Pittsburgh in Three Rivers Stadium. What the players did not expect that day, however, was the surprise appearance by Art Modell in the locker room after practice. Art had just held a press conference in Dallas that day following an owners' meeting. He used the occasion to call the team's performance against Houston "deplorable," and he blamed their performance on distractions over the move to Baltimore. Then he got on a plane and slipped into Cleveland to talk to his team firsthand. Realizing the Browns had lost four of their last five games and were in danger of going into a downward spiral, he implored the team to "play your rear ends off the last seven weeks." Also sensing the players were looking for some kind of indication about the status of the coach, Modell assured them that "in case there is any doubt, Bill Belichick will be your coach in Baltimore and hopefully for many more years after that." He then urged the players to salvage the season.

Modell continued, "We want to go to Baltimore as winners. From the bottom of my heart, I ask you to play for yourselves, to play with passion, to play to win."

As Modell was talking, many players hung their heads and listened. When the players heard that Belichick would continue to be the coach in Baltimore, muffled groans of "oh, no" emanated from the back of the room. That was the response to the owner's plea. After the brief meeting, Art left by private jet for West Palm Beach at 3:30 p.m. That was the last time Modell ever set foot in the Berea facility. When Modell held an interview with the Baltimore *Sun* a week or so later, he was less direct about Belichick's future. He told the columnist, "I made a statement to the players (about Belichick being the head coach next year), and I'm a man of my word. But I will review the entire picture with Bill from top to bottom. I'm not trying to leave myself an out, but I have some concerns that need to be addressed. We're in a tailspin, and we were in one before the announcement of the team's moving to Baltimore."

After the meeting the players warned about "a storm brewing on this team." As defensive end Rob Burnett said, "...and I am not talking about the move. This runs far deeper..." Running back Earnest Byner added, "There are a lot of things that contributed to the way we played last week. The move was only part of it. I could go into some heavy stuff right now, but I choose not to."

During the week, people in Berea were sought out for comments. Most employees were too distraught to make any. Bill Belichick said he had to prepare for the upcoming Pittsburgh game, and he was not going to worry about being asked to stay with the Browns, as it would not be his decision anyway. Player personnel chief Mike Lombardi said no one really knew what was going on, so he would just proceed with his job. But pro personnel director Ozzie Newsome said that he had already been contacted by Art about moving to Baltimore with the team and that he was planning to do so.

Looking at this sequence of statements, I thought it was pretty obvious that the people who fit into the 1996 Baltimore organization's plans had already been asked to go. If a person hadn't been contacted by then, she or he probably was not going to be included in future Modell family operations. Based on my conversations with the eight full-time members of the Cleveland Stadium Corp., I came to realize that only Bruce Gaines, director of building operations, had received any hint of an invitation. Only those in daily communication with Bailey were likely to be in the Browns' future plans. But foolishly many people were hanging their hopes on Bailey's exact words, "We will try to move this organization to Baltimore intact."

My parish priest sought me out after Sunday Mass. An ardent Browns' fan, Rev. Patrick O'Connor had hoped I could tell him that this whole thing was some kind of a Modell hoax, a threat to give the city one last chance to come up with the renovation funds. "But, Mike," he said to me, "this thing really won't happen, do you think? I know Modell is fed up, but he has to give the city one last chance, doesn't he?"

No sense in raising false hopes, I thought. "Father," I said, "it's not a matter of whether the Browns will move to Baltimore. The Browns have already moved. They already have established downtown Baltimore offices, had phone lines installed, and have executive offices in use. It's over. They have moved."

Poor Father Patrick looked like I had been feeling for the last several days. As Art Modell had always said of people, Father Patrick was living on hope, just like hundreds of thousands of Browns' fans everywhere. But true hope had evaporated a long time ago. The team's offices were picked out before Modell took to the dais in Baltimore on November 6. After all, Bailey and Pat Moriarty needed a place to work that week.

When Art Modell had addressed the owners in Dallas to justify his reasons for the Browns' planned move to Baltimore, he said, "The city is broke. It was broke in 1974 when I took over the Stadium, and it isn't any better off today. What we have here is far beyond the capacity of the City of Cleveland."

This statement would have generally been viewed as a fair assessment of the city's economic state, at least according to the perspective of John Q. Public. However there was one difference between 1974 and 1995. In 1974, while the city was broke, the Browns were a financially successful business; in 1995 both the Browns and the city were financially strapped. The average Browns' fan somehow was unable to conceive that the Browns were broke. "Ludicrous," they said, "Modell reeks of money." Seventy thousand fans and a fat network TV contract were factors that precluded Browns' followers believing that the team, as Modell had revealed in his November 4 radio interview, was "experiencing dramatic financial deterioration."

In his presentation to his fellow NFL owners, Modell revealed that the Browns had lost $21 million in the previous two years. While that number was a rounded-up estimate, it essentially was due to high player payroll costs, the result of chasing after (not-so) free agents. The guy on the street, even if he accepted Art's statement about the Browns losing money, still didn't understand why they had to move to resolve the problem. The perception was that the Browns had amassed millions of dollars in cash and investments from all those "prior years of successful 80,000 crowds at Cleveland Stadium," and the free agents were being paid from those "pots of gold" lying around in the money vaults. The fact is, if one looked at a ten-year summary of earnings from 1980 through 1990, the Browns would show red ink of between $5 million and $10 million in aggregate net results for the decade. Funding this ten-year loss was covered by bank loans. As even more significant losses continued in the 90s, the bank loans increased and increased and increased.

The bankers used Cleveland Browns' stock as collateral for these loans, and as long as the value of an NFL franchise kept appreciating, as it had, the banks really had no fear of losing their ability to recover the loan principal. While the banks would have preferred the company repay the principal in regular installments from operating profits, the fact is that after the players' strike in 1982, the Browns no longer could pay down any appreciable amounts of bank debt. Every year thereafter, the story might best be described as "one step forward, then two backward."

When Modell explained his rationale for the move, it came down to a very simple statement: "I had no choice." People found that hard to believe. Only the bankers, auditors, lawyers, and a handful of employees knew what the public would eventually find out in January 1996 through court discovery.

Of course Browns' fans were asking, "Why didn't you tell us how much was needed and give us the opportunity to match the offer?" No Browns' official ever attempted to answer that question, because an accurate answer could probably never be given. With the churning activity of signing and releasing players on a day-to-day basis, that number could, and would, change hourly. At any given time, though, Browns' officials could have accurately, if imprecisely, answered, "A lot."

Gib Shanley, former Browns' radio voice and then a sportscaster on local television, visited with John Minco and me for lunch the week following the announcement. He expressed dismay at what Modell had done. He said maybe Art would come to his senses and leave the team here. He still felt some hope that Modell and the city could work things out. I told him that I did not think that could ever happen:

The team's broke, Gib, simple as that. And going to Baltimore gives Art a chance to rid himself of his bank debt. Very simply, by moving to Baltimore, I think Art feels that he can have his cake and eat it too. If he stays in Cleveland, he must sell the team to get out of debt—if the team is even saleable at the price he would be looking for. If sold, the team is not in the family for David to operate. Furthermore, they don't have the luxury of waiting for the additional revenues that would come from a renovated Stadium several years from now. They need help right now.

In the meantime, almost everyone connected with NFL football had a comment on the move. "Everyone is chasing the buck," said Joe Gibbs, former Redskins' coach and analyst for NBC. "There is no more loyalty in the NFL."

Doug Dieken chastised the politicians when he said "they kind of let this one slip away. Maybe they didn't address some of the needs that should have been addressed. They haven't written a country and western song any sadder than this one." Always one to speak his mind when he had strong feelings, Doug cited the governor, local politicians, Modell, and the NFL as equally sharing the blame.

Tom Chema, former Gateway executive director who served on the mayor's task force for the Stadium renovation, said that in all his meetings with the Browns' organization through 1994, "they said repeatedly that if they had a renovated stadium, all of their revenue problems would be solved. Art personally told that two times to the task force."

If that was the case in 1994, then a lot had changed beginning in 1995. That change, we learned later, was primarily the cost of procuring players through free agency.

Ted Bonda, former president of the Cleveland Indians and a close friend of Art Modell, said that Modell left town for reasons that went beyond money. He said Art was very thin-skinned and sensitive. Bonda added that Art had told him he was offended by the treatment the town gave him, considering all that he had done for Cleveland over the years. According to Bonda, Modell said he had been taken for granted by not only government officials, but also by the business community. Bonda added, "Everyone else--the Jacobs, the Gunds---were treated so well, and everything came out so well for them. Why not for him?"

In his more than 30 years in Cleveland, Art Modell never had much to say about his Jewish heritage. But as his financial plight increased and as the business community was slow to hop on the Stadium renovation bandwagon and as their loge support wavered, he was heard on several occasions thinking aloud that his "rejection" by the town's movers and shakers had something to do with his ethnicity. (Once earlier, Jim Bailey had confided to me that he felt this might be the case.) Those emotional statements were clearly a sign of just how much Art was feeling the financial stranglehold.

While the daily newspapers were content to keep blasting Art Modell for his lack of loyalty, broken promises, lies, deception, and double-talking in connection with the move, *Crain's Cleveland Business* avoided the name-calling, and instead prepared a synopsis of three comparable deals to illustrate what Modell was facing when making his decision.

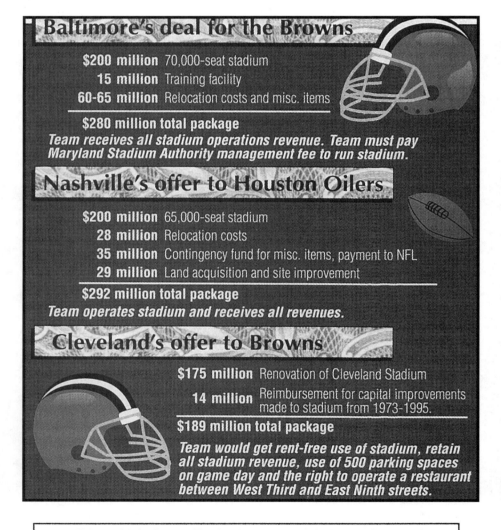

Baltimore's deal for the Browns

$200 million 70,000-seat stadium
15 million Training facility
60-65 million Relocation costs and misc. items

$280 million total package
Team receives all stadium operations revenue. Team must pay Maryland Stadium Authority management fee to run stadium.

Nashville's offer to Houston Oilers

$200 million 65,000-seat stadium
28 million Relocation costs
35 million Contingency fund for misc. items, payment to NFL
29 million Land acquisition and site improvement

$292 million total package
Team operates stadium and receives all revenues.

Cleveland's offer to Browns

$175 million Renovation of Cleveland Stadium
14 million Reimbursement for capital improvements made to stadium from 1973-1995.

$189 million total package
Team would get rent-free use of stadium, retain all stadium revenue, use of 500 parking spaces on game day and the right to operate a restaurant between West Third and East Ninth streets.

This graphic in *Crain's Cleveland Business* made it clear that Baltimore's deal was *$90 million* sweeter than Cleveland's.

The major difference between the deals was in the contribution by the states. Maryland was standing behind the entire cost of the Baltimore project with its special-purpose state lottery funds. Tennessee had provided about $80 million of the funds that Houston would be receiving from Nashville. In comparison, Cleveland would receive State of Ohio funds for Stadium renovation projected in the $20-million range. That disparity was the major disadvantage faced by the City of Cleveland and Cuyahoga County. In competing for NFL franchises, the City of Cleveland was contending with entire states!

County Commissioner Mary Boyle was vocal on this point. She lashed out, "If we are going to be major competitors, we have to be on an even playing field. When I think of losing out to the State of Maryland, it just galls me." Boyle also pointed out that adjoining counties were unwilling to participate in funding a city-owned stadium, and the City of Cleveland had refused to discuss any plan to make the stadium a regional facility. A neighboring county executive said that unless the city was willing to give up some ownership, maybe even consider a new location for the stadium, regionalization would be a tough sell.

And of course the reply from Governor Voinovich to Art Modell from several years earlier still rang in everyone's ears at Tower B. When Art pleaded for the governor to provide more financial assistance, Art reported that the governor told him, "Art, if something is done to help the Browns with their Stadium, then something will also have to be done for the Bengals." Modell, irritated with the apparent unwillingness to help, told us that he shot back, "Well, that's fine, but do something, and then help Ohio State, Akron, Bowling Green, and the Toledo Mudhens with their stadiums. But do it." (Incidentally, by 1996 the State of Ohio was boasting a $1 billion-plus "rainy day" fund, excess cash accumulated in the state treasury. Converting some of this "idle cash" into real estate would have been an economic boon to the state. It would have been inspiring to see strong leadership, as former Governor James Rhodes had shown in getting Riverfront Stadium built when the Cincinnati Bengals were awarded a franchise in 1968.)

Finger-pointing among the politicians continued. Democrat County Commissioner Tim Hagan charged Republican Governor Voinovich with staying on the sidelines. Voinovich responded by saying that finding money for the Stadium renovation was a "local issue." Hagan shot back, "If NFL football is an asset to the state...then the governor has to take a more active role in the future. This thing cannot be funded on a city or county-wide basis...George Voinovich has to accept the fact that the burden rests with the state first of all, and then on local communities, to contribute something." If Governor Parris Glendening and previous Governor William Donald Schaeffer had the same attitude toward the issue, Maryland would still be without professional football today. Governor Voinovich said he had done the best he could to provide state support for this project.

The football season was a little more than half over, and the fans felt betrayed, their high hopes smoldering in the ashes of an empty, fading season. The owner was no longer in Cleveland, and his son and lawyer-advisor were also gone. Modell's secretary, Marilyn McGrath, was spending time in both cities. Kevin Byrne, head of public relations, was the highest-ranking Browns official still around on a daily basis, but he was to speak only on football-related matters. All questions on Stadium issues and the move were referred to David Hopcraft, and he wasn't always reachable because he was frequently traveling between Baltimore and Cleveland.

The fans still remembered the last season of broken promises, 1990, when Bud Carson was to have led a strong Browns' team to the Super Bowl. Now the fans were watching this year's predicted Super Bowl contenders looking like "pretenders." "This team is lousy. Let them go to Baltimore. We're fed up. And Belichick better go with them," became the chant of the beleaguered Browns' fans.

Art Modell had never been "honored" by being placed on the cover of *Sports Illustrated*. Typically, that honor was reserved for athletes; that is until the December 4, 1995, issue hit the newsstands. The caricature of Art Modell that appeared on the cover might well have been the most unbecoming rendering of the Browns' owner ever seen in print. With a scowl painted on his face, he was shown sucker-punching a fan wearing a dog mask. SI presented the owner's proboscis in very exaggerated dimensions, something that Art was always sensitive about. Insiders reported that Modell was furious over how he had been depicted and that this stiffened his resolve to fight the matter through.

Clevelanders grabbed up every available copy on the newsstands. According to local distributors, normally 2,000 issues were sold weekly. That week, an extra 50,000 copies were requested, and all were sold in record time. Customers were buying two or more copies at a time.

When the readers got to SI's featured article, they were able to read Modell's first public explanation of what went into his decision to move the franchise. He basically said that the operation of the Stadium and escalating players' salaries were what unraveled the finances of his club and left him with no choice but to do what he had done.

The article concluded by pointing out that Modell profited handsomely by this move. Though Modell cited hard times at the moment, the writer pointed out that Modell's personal value in Browns' stock would increase approximately $100 million. Alluding to the stock buyout that was allegedly consummated with Bob Gries, the former 43% shareholder, SI pointed out that once the team moved, Modell's interest would be worth more than $180 million compared to $80 million when the team was in Cleveland. (Modell's value in Cleveland was based on 51% ownership of a franchise valued at about $160 million. His ownership share increased to more than 90% after he acquired Gries' share, this of a franchise the magazine estimated would become worth more than $200 million). Of course, the author failed to address the cost of purchasing Gries' interest, the details of which were never divulged. There were rumors of numbers as low as $50 million to buy the Gries group out. There was also a hint that the payout to Gries was structured over a long period of time. The real cost of buying the minority shareholder's interest was anyone's guess, but whatever the amount, it would still have to be subtracted from whatever increased paper value would accrue to Modell. But Modell's net value certainly did not increase $100 million by moving to Baltimore. (In May 1996, *Financial World* estimated the Baltimore Ravens were the third most valuable NFL franchise, at $201 million, trailing only Dallas and Miami.)

The publicity Art Modell received in the days after the announcement was not the type he enjoyed. The *Wall Street Journal* featured the Browns' owner on the front page during December, describing his recent woes in Cleveland. Referring to him as an "old-style" owner, the *Journal* made mention of him as one who had helped launch Cleveland's comeback in the late 1970's, first by staying downtown to continue playing in a run-down stadium rather than running to the suburbs as other NFL owners were doing. It was pointed out how he stood aside while other "sports palaces" were built, only to find out that no money was left to help save him. But the *Journal* still said that Modell had only himself to blame for some crucial mistakes. It said that he was "outmaneuvered" by Indians' owner Dick Jacobs (and Major League Baseball) and was "ill-suited" for the coming of free agency to NFL football in 1993.

Art didn't see this issue as a matter of being outmaneuvered at all, but he himself was quoted in the article as saying, "Keep in mind that the Gunds are worth $2 billion, and Jacobs is worth $400 million and little me, I say I'll step aside and let the Cavaliers and the Indians have what they want because my political and business friends had told me that my turn was next." Had the SAFE fiasco not caused a $115 million loss in county investments, Modell's turn might very well have been next.

Plain Dealer columnist Mary Ann Sharkey offered a different slant to the complexities of funding the Stadium renovation when she attributed the problem, at least partially, to political affiliation. "Modell's Republican activism hasn't exactly endeared him to the legions of Democratic officeholders in Cuyahoga County. It is these same officeholders who are being asked to risk their political necks by raising taxes for the Stadium renovation," she wrote. More than once I felt Art was too visible on the Republican front, especially since the majority of Cuyahoga County, and quite possibly the majority of Browns fans, voted Democrat at the ballot box.

In view of the tempestuous atmosphere in Cleveland, the Browns felt relieved to get on a plane for their next game. Leaving behind the controversy and bitterness in their home town, they arrived in San Diego on Wednesday night, two days ahead of the normal schedule. Having lost seven of their last eight games, they hoped getting to the other side of the country would help. At one point during this losing spell, the team had gone 25 straight possessions without scoring a touchdown.

In fact, the game in San Diego did turn out to be ugly, as the Browns lost, 31-13, and were embarrassed on national TV when the head coach called for a field goal try on the last play of the game. With the Browns losing 31-10 and one second left on the clock, the field goal unit was sent on the field. The announcers calling the game screamed in disbelief. They charged Bill Belichick with making a mockery of the game. "That," one reporter joked, "was the first time in the history of football that the losing team ran up the score."

The *Plain Dealer* was still striving for more insight into what had driven Art Modell to move his team to Baltimore. Since Modell had made himself unavailable for interviews, the reporter tried another angle by talking to Modell's fellow shareholder and friend Al Lerner. Lerner told the reporter that he had witnessed Modell's increasing discouragement over the Cleveland Stadium situation and explained, "You have to see the climate that was going on. He was not being viewed very favorably in the media. When he said what he wanted [to stay in Cleveland], he was being labeled an extortionist and a black-mailer; when he didn't say what he wanted, he was labeled as not being forth-coming, and he felt kind of trapped between those two lines." Lerner explained that Art was convinced no Cleveland proposal would be forthcoming, and know-ing the Baltimore opportunity would disappear at the end of 1995 and that his existing financial situation would not allow him to make it in 1996, he had to take the Baltimore deal. Lerner said, "Because the fact is, he was just getting deeper and deeper into hock. He was getting tapped out. And he is a proud man; it was very hard for him to say that."

The reporter pushed for specific debt numbers. Lerner replied, "My recollection is that there's $60-odd million worth of debt on the Browns...and $15 million plus or minus on the Stadium Corp. That's part of the problem: Stadium Corp. did with borrowed money what others did with public money."

A former *Plain Dealer* reporter, then a columnist for the suburban *Sun* Newspapers, Russ Schneider wrote how his former paper had handled Art Mod-ell. It shouldn't have been too difficult for the reporter interviewing Al Lerner to understand how Modell was becoming discouraged after reading Schneider's account. Schneider recalled that in January 1978 he was called into then-executive editor David Hopcraft's office (the same Hopcraft who later became Modell's spokesman) and told that he was being switched from covering the Indians to the Browns. Schneider asked why. Hopcraft said, "I want you to get Art Modell....I am tired of Art Modell getting a free ride in this town." Schneider claimed that he never set out to get anyone, but did cover matters "aggressively" and was "unreserved" in criticizing the teams. (Hopcraft, questioned about this later in 1996, said he was directed by higher-ups to go after Modell, that it was not his idea.) In reflecting over this time frame, I do think it was about this time that prevailing attitudes toward Modell began to turn negative. I had not known of a concerted effort to "get" Art, but by the early 80s it was hard to ignore the tenor of *Plain Dealer* reporting.

As in the previous home game, the Browns disdained the normal pre-game introductions for their final home game against Cincinnati on December 18, 1995. The team did not want to risk a player being singled out for boos. The team came onto the field as a unit, the only introduction, "Please welcome your Cleveland Browns." A crowd of 55,875 teary-eyed fans greeted the team with a long, standing ovation.

Former Browns' players were in attendance with varied agendas for memorializing the team and its legacy. Brian Sipe and Jerry Sherk had endured a week-long trip from California, visiting and filming Browns' Backers Associations along the way. Their trek culminated in Cleveland Stadium for a final filming of the highlights of the game.

Fans at the game displayed the gamut of emotions. No one wanted to believe he or she was attending the last Browns' game in Cleveland ever. Many fans in attendance were angry and bitter, and late in the game they vented their spleen by ripping out seats and throwing them onto the field. An even larger contingent wept in sadness and hurt, realizing a big part of their lives was over. The players came through and won the their last home game quite handily, 26-10. They then came out to the bleachers to thank and say goodbye to their staunchest fans, the residents of the Dawg Pound. They slapped hands and even hugged those who extended their hands. Earnest Byner took the time to go beyond the Pound; he trotted around the entire inside circumference of the Stadium bowl to say goodbye to the fans. No one cared about his fumble against Denver years earlier in the AFC championship game. And while some fans were bidding the players adieu, other were removing saw blades from their pant legs so they could take home their seat for a souvenir.

During halftime, Bob Costas, NBC's highly regarded commentator, let the Browns' owner have it with both barrels. He and Mike Ditka both blasted Modell, Costas saying, "If Modell is having financial problems, most of it is his fault. If Modell couldn't make a go of it, the only honorable way out was to sell the team to local owners." Mike Ditka didn't mince words either. He said the owner "destroyed" his reputation "in one greedy move." However Ditka then added his opinion of the condition of Cleveland Stadium which somewhat vindicated Modell. Ditka noted that the Stadium had "the worst locker rooms in the league." Irv Cross chipped in with "the Stadium was a dump in 1977, and it's a dump now."

The final Cleveland Browns' game was played on December 24, in Jacksonville, home of the expansion Jaguars. The Browns did not have much to play for, except to escape the ignominy of losing twice to an expansion team. I thought that alone should provide incentive to fire up the roster of millionaires. But the team was not inspired in Jacksonville and fell to the Jaguars for the second time.

An interesting occurrence, one that very few people noticed, was that Bill Belichick had his young son with him on the sidelines during the Jacksonville game. Was there any significance to that? Could it be that Bill knew this was his last game as head coach of the Browns and he wanted his son to share the experience with him? No one was making any predictions around the office. They were going by Art's statement to the team, "Bill Belichick will be your coach in Baltimore next year." But I also recalled what Art had said earlier, that he was in a five-year program to get to the Super Bowl, and enough money had been spent to get us there. I felt sure that Art would hold someone accountable, and I was equally sure that Art would not take kindly to the whispers that the players had "bagged" the season to get the coach fired.

The next day back to work, and with the "season from hell" over, employees found themselves wondering what the future held for them. The answer from Jim Bailey's computer terminal was, "You'll find out as soon as we know what is happening."

As 1995 was drawing to a close, the hullabaloo over the Browns' move was still dominating the newspapers. I was surprised then on December 28 to see Gateway back in the front-page headlines. The story announced that $21.5 million in construction bills remained unpaid, despite the lawsuits brought by the contractors earlier in the year. The real news was that Cuyahoga County agreed to loan Gateway $11.5 million to help clear up some of the bills. Aside from announcing this bit of news, recently-appointed Gateway board chairman Craig Miller grimly admitted that Gateway was "awash in red ink" and could run out of operating funds as early as March 1996. "It's an intolerable situation, and we can't go on living like this," Miller said.

Miller said that besides the shortfall in operating funds, Gateway still did not have enough money to pay the $330,000 due for county property taxes, even after cutting large chunks out of its operating budget. (Nine months later, September 12, 1996, Gateway was still on the front page of the *Plain Dealer*, which reported that unpaid property tax bills had reached $1.169 million. My own hunch was that this liability might never be paid, thereby converting this situation into a disguised form of tax abatement.

Something was clearly wrong with this picture, I thought. Gateway had the benefit of a playoff baseball team, a significant string of sellout baseball games, and euphoric fan sentiment supporting the team right into the World Series. Yet there was not enough money to pay property taxes, which were promised to the voters as a major selling point throughout the 1990 vote campaign. And now the voters learned that there was a money shortage not only for construction bills and taxes, but also to operate Gateway Corp. (the counterpart to Cleveland Stadium Corp.). Miller projected a $1 million operating deficit for each of the next five years.

And on the north end of downtown stood the old Stadium on the lakefront, operated under a so-called "rip-off lease" that Modell had with the city. Despite the foundering football record and dwindling fan support, the city would as always receive its full rent from Stadium Corp. (for 1995, it was $647,000, which included $354,000 for real estate taxes).

With this last payment on February 28, 1996, the Stadium Corp.'s financial performance under the lease showed that the city had received everything it was due, including a total of $5,634,000 in real estate taxes over 22 years.

The All-Pro balloting was completed before New Year's Day, and in pica-sized print buried near the back of the sports pages was a complete list of all players receiving votes. A detailed tally showed 151 NFL players receiving at least one vote, with the leading vote-getter at each position tallying anywhere from 40 to 86 votes. Since the Browns' salaries this past year ranked behind only the Cowboys, I wondered how many of the Orange and Brown showed up in the poll. Only three players got any votes, but given the team's performance, it should not have been a surprise, I suppose. Center Steve Everitt received two votes, placekicker Matt Stover tallied five, and safety Stevon Moore notched a lone vote. What disappointing results from a $50-million-plus investment in players!

The season from hell may have ended, but the city's lawyers were not giving up the Browns to Baltimore without a fight. Whether the fight was just for show, or whether the city really thought it had located the so-called "silver bullet," it appeared the city was going to court to force Modell and the Cleveland Browns to live up to their lease. There seemed to be one small problem: the city's lease was not with the Cleveland Browns but with Stadium Corp.

Stadium Corp. in turn had the lease with the Browns, and that lease was terminated between the two companies on October 27, 1995. Supposedly compensation was agreed upon between the two Art Modell-owned companies for the privilege of exiting the lease. If so, the Browns "bought their way out" of the Stadium Corp. lease. The sole issue remaining, therefore, was the lease between Cleveland Stadium Corp. and the city. Three years remained on that lease, and an early termination would certainly require some monetary consideration. Modell and his advisors felt certain this lease could be "bought out" also. The city, however, took the position that more than money was involved.

The Browns' lawyers contended that neither party could possibly benefit from a "lame duck" scenario. Fan support would drop drastically, and as Modell testified when called upon, "this would exacerbate an already precarious financial position." He pointed to the advertisers who in the two weeks after the announcement had canceled contracts in the game day program, in Browns' marketing sponsorships, and on Stadium Corp. signage.

The city basically did not subscribe to the Browns' pleas of financial woe. They demanded the Browns "open up their books" to demonstrate how they would lose money if forced to play in Cleveland through 1998. The Browns refused, saying that opening their books would put them at a competitive disadvantage by allowing other NFL teams to see how much they would have available to spend on free agents.

In the proceedings that followed, certain information was gleaned from public and private records filed with the courts, and on January 7, 1996, the *Plain Dealer* reported on the financial data it had extracted. It also sought out commentary from several managers and partners in major accounting firms. Noted Stanford economist Roger Noll was asked to add flavor to the numbers. Reporters focused on Modell's spending habits, indiscriminately lumping his personal spending and that for his company. It was pointed out how he permitted all the fields to be ripped out and replaced within a year or two of being installed, just because "Belichick wanted it done." This "re-do" easily exceeded $1 million. All this made many employees wonder. It had been a long time since most had been granted a raise, and they were regularly told that there was no money for pay raises. In reality, this was true: The Browns were earning no profits at this time. The projects were funded with further bank borrowings.

Modell avoided making extraneous commentary about the Browns' finances. He continually said that the 64-year-old Stadium was draining his resources. The PD gained access to Dun & Bradstreet files, which maintained a record of Stadium Corp. financial statements. Recent statements showed the track record of the Stadium Corp.'s profits, which the newspaper reporters reviewed and termed a "respectable $2.4 million." Yet Art hoped for more, since this amount fell far short of the $21 million he said the Browns had lost over the previous two years. Once the Indians left, however, there was never going to be more; in fact, there was going to be quite a bit less. Special event income could exceed the paltry baseball proceeds earned during the Gabe Paul era, but could seemingly never make up for a loss of two million baseball fans in 1993. That was why Modell wanted city officials to honor their earlier promises to make him "good" on the loss of the Indians.

Once the team's financial losses were out in the open, the public was unwilling to let Modell off the hook. The allegations were that Modell's lavish spending habits had severely aggravated the team's financial difficulties. People like me, who at one time had been close to Art, knew that Art did not have an insatiable need to spend money. However, some of his employees did. As Gib Shanley said later in commenting on Bill Belichick, "....he (Belichick) destroyed it all. He was a great part of why the team moved because of the money he spent."

In my opinion, Jim Bailey was just as, or even more, responsible. When he assumed the role of the team's so-called "financial director," he also assumed responsibility for fiscal control of the company's assets. Unfortunately, that control never quite materialized. The self-appointed "control-ler" was unable to get a grip on expenditures. In all the years that we worked together, I never thought Bailey had demonstrated the qualities that go with being "budget-conscious." He didn't seem to care how much money was spent. "Just get the job done," he would say. That was not the way, however, that the message worked its way back to Modell. This is the part that was puzzling. At one time Art wanted people around him who cared how the money was being spent, but the people who really cared and were frugal were gradually eliminated from the decision-making process in the last several years. We never learned if it was a conscious decision by Modell. It just gradually happened. Art put all his faith and trust into the hands of Jim Bailey.

At the same time, we all knew that Bailey authored the change. It was obvious he didn't want any opposition to his plans. Since Art was spending few days in the office, he could not see what was going on. His information came from his management committee. What Modell heard was whatever the committee, and only the committee, wanted him to hear.

During 1995 Art became aware of the dramatic increases in Cleveland Browns' debt. Reportedly, he was surprised at how large the debt had become, and he demanded an explanation. But rather than direct the question to Mike Srsen or myself, who kept such analyses in our files, he directed the question to Bailey. It was no revelation to either Srsen or me that when an organization excludes its top financial people from providing input on a daily basis, an inevitable financial debacle arises. Financial controllers are in place to do just that: control. Control budgets, control spending, and curb management's desire for free spending. Someone did not want this control to come from the companies' treasury departments any longer.

The *Plain Dealer* presented some balance in a later article by illustrating some of the shortcomings with the Cleveland Stadium situation from the team's perspective. It was pointed out that in places like Dallas the 280 suites commanded prices as high as $200,000. When loge prices were lowered to $55,000 after the Indians left, Modell was roundly criticized by some in the business community for not reducing them even further. It was conceded that one might conclude the team was losing corporate support when the first loge vacancies were announced in 1994.

The reporter appropriately noted the lack of parking spaces available to the team beginning in 1995 and the resultant loss of revenues. Most teams have 10,000 and more spots accessible for fan parking. The Browns had been squeezed down to where parking revenues on the Stadium Corp's books were so minuscule that this area was no longer even considered a "profit center."

Perhaps readers wondered why, with the continuing loss of revenues, Modell had actually accelerated the pace of his spending for players. David Hopcraft defended Art's recent spending binges, saying the Browns' owner was just trying to be competitive. "You have to put a good team on the field to get the fans' interest, and into the stadium. In order to get top players, you have to have (a lot of) signing bonus money."

In summing up the lengthy article, economist Roger Noll commented:

Modell's story about being under current financial pressure is, I think, not valid, but if it's the case that he's genuinely concerned about the near-term future, that's genuine. I think it's completely understandable that he did what he did, even though the reasons he gave publicly for doing it are not the real reasons.

To the contrary, I feel that if Roger Noll really knew the Browns' debt load, he would have realized that the financial pressures were indeed valid.

As I have thought about it, I've come to believe Art had a strong hunch early in 1995 that he was going to "have no choice" but to move the team from Cleveland. I also believe that Art deeply wanted to produce a Super Bowl appearance for Cleveland, as a "going away" gift, so to speak. I believe that when he was told Andre Rison was the key to getting the team to the big event, Art wanted so much to believe it that he went along with Rison's outrageous price tag. Finally, I think Art's deepest regret was not that he had to move the team, because I believe he had come to grips with that possibility earlier, but rather the team's dismal performance on the field. That inept performance would color the way his efforts would be remembered.

While the legal wrangling was going on, the Browns' and Stadium Corp. employees were kept out of the information loop. We didn't know what to expect. Most were living in a high-stress mode. Many weren't sure what their jobs encompassed any longer, nor how to carry out their responsibilities. Their supervisors were of little help, because they weren't being told anything either. The answer that kept filtering down was, "Don't worry; as soon as we know something, you will all be informed."

Few people, including me, knew who was represented in the pronoun "we" in that statement. Certainly it included anyone in the Modell family and probably Jim Bailey. Beyond that it was anyone's guess. With Jim almost permanently in Baltimore, a handful of people working in Berea carried out his orders. If I knew who was in daily contact with Bailey, I could figure out who would be moving to Maryland. He talked with no one in the Stadium Corp. offices. That seemed to make our future pretty clear.

As far as anyone could tell, Art Modell talked with no one outside football operations except for Marilyn McGrath and Bailey. Marilyn was still flying back and forth between Cleveland and Baltimore.

Marilyn called me at the Stadium on the last day of December and invited me to attend a Browns' supervisors' meeting at Berea at 7:30 a.m. on January 2, 1996. The discussion could be of interest to us at the Stadium, she suggested. No one was concerned with the Stadium folks, she hinted, so I might want to come, hear for myself, and draw my own conclusions. That clinched it. No one from Stadium Corp. was being invited to Baltimore, so we better begin making our own plans.

I found it surprising, and sad too, that Art Modell wouldn't call me about any business, but then I figured the advice he was receiving was: Go to Florida, rest up, and talk to no one!

At 7:30 on the morning after New Year's Day, there was little traffic, a bread truck, a newspaper truck, not much else. From all the anxiety surrounding the event, I found myself up early that day and the first one to arrive at the meeting. At the meeting there was no Art Modell, no David Modell, and no Jim Bailey.

Pat Moriarty, the team's director of business operations, greeted the group that morning. Pat was the last man to enter the board room at 7:30, and he began with business matters immediately. No small talk. The first thing Pat said was, "We are moving to Baltimore, no matter what develops from the court proceedings in process."

After a pause, he said, "Even if we should lose the case, and have to play in Cleveland Stadium through the end of the lease, our team will head-quarter in Baltimore, we will practice in Baltimore, and we will fly in for the eight so-called home games. So we must proceed with our plan to move from this facility to Baltimore."

Despite that opening, details about moving plans were not discussed. The discussion was about severance pay, relocation packages, early retirement considerations, and employment termination dates. I shuddered when I heard the word "termination," as it brought home the finality of the decision. Yet no hint was forthcoming of how many people were to move and how many to be terminated. Naturally letting this information out could be no advantage for the team.

Moriarty explained that whatever plan was finally developed would follow researching the relocation and severance pay packages presented to former employees of other NFL teams who had recently moved to other cities. One feature in the Browns' package was a "transition incentive" bonus. This was to encourage employees to make the transition as easy as possible. The implied threat was there, though. If management found out a person was doing anything to undermine the move, he or she would not receive the bonus.

Department heads were instructed to tell their employees that the Browns had retained a counselor to help them deal with any stress. The counselor would be available for both group and individual counseling, as requested. The first group session was scheduled for the coming Friday.

The meeting was adjourned, and the department heads then met with their respective employees. It seemed though that allowing the employees this sketchy amount of information only furthered their level of anxiety. They really wanted to know two things: if they were going to Baltimore, and if not, when they would be terminated.

City leaders were coordinating their efforts to bring added pressure on the NFL, as evidenced by a full-page ad in the January 16, 1996, *Plain Dealer* paid for by Cleveland Tomorrow. The ad, in the form of an open letter to NFL owners and Commissioner Paul Tagliabue, was signed by 43 corporations. It committed the signers to the purchase of loge suites and premium seats, and to support Stadium advertising packages. The ad was impressive, I thought at first glance. However, after a good look at the 43 signataries, I spotted some-thing odd. Twenty-four of the signing corporations were NOT Stadium loge customers in 1995. Here they were, pledging to support the NFL, but where were they during 1995 or 1994 or 1993? Those 24 corporations could have supported the Browns. Sadly, they didn't, but now they wanted the NFL to believe they would do so in the future.

During the court proceedings that followed, more reasons for confusion came to light, this time between the city and the county. It was about who was taking the leadership on funding Stadium renovation. The *Plain Dealer* reported that city lawyer Fred Nance referred to "a fact that this working group (the city task force) was putting together a plan that assumed (added emphasis) the county would be the primary source of money and that those plans went awry because of the SAFE failure and cost overruns at Gateway..." Court records indicated that the city assumed funding would be available by raising (the county) sales taxes.

County Commissioner Mary Boyle said the commissioners were never involved in any talks in this regard in 1994. County Administrator Danny Williams confirmed that after the county experienced its own financial dilemmas, it was in no mood even to discuss Stadium funding. He said, "There was an unspoken consensus among commissioners not to get in the same area code. We had our own problems to take care of."

Mayor White in an interview said that he kept the commissioners informed, but "I never at any time said they are absolutely on board."

After hearing all this, one could better understand why the Browns were dubious that the project was ever going to be funded. Furthermore, where did the financial turnaround come from which allowed for the new proposal given to the Browns on November 8, 1995? Of course, no longer did any of this make a difference, but a city operating under a deficit year after year, a county laden with its own financial problems, and an unwilling state government would equate to, in my crystal ball, a highly unlikely scenario for Stadium renovation.

The move to Baltimore and the ensuing fight with the City of Cleveland's lawyers were covered in the newspapers almost daily. Art Modell was judged the guilty party by almost everyone offering an opinion. National TV commentators blasted his lack of business acumen, and then his greed in running off to take Maryland's offer. *Newsweek* magazine headlined a column, "Modell Sacks Maryland," with a sub-title..."Average folks are building suites for rich fans so rich owners can pay rich players." The writer started out with "Art Modell made dumb business decisions and needed the money, or at least wanted it more than he wanted the affection of his community where he once was a leader and now is a pariah. .....this deal will make Modell the latest proof that there often is no penalty for failure in America." *USA Today* covered this endeavor almost daily until its final resolution. *Sports Illustrated* also covered the proceedings, and just prior to the hearings in February, reported that Cleveland's lawyers would present evidence that Modell had threatened to field a lame-duck team and unload his marketable players if forced to stay in Cleveland. What we understood later was that Bill Belichick, under contract for two more years, was designated the coach of this talent-less squad if the team were forced to play in Cleveland Stadium.

The question in everyone's mind was whether Belichick would still be coach if the courts ruled the team could play in Baltimore in 1996. Rumors were circulating that Art Modell had made inquiries of Jimmy Johnson and Don Shula as to their interest in taking over the reins in Baltimore. Most people felt that Belichick was indeed finished, but Art's words that "Belichick will be going to Baltimore as the coach of this team" were still fresh in people's mind, so they were not quite sure.

It was simple for the other NFL owners to realize that playing in Cleveland in 1996 would be a losing proposition. Carmen Policy, president of the San Francisco 49ers, said that the emotionalism has to be removed in order to deal with the situation. He added, "I think the time has come where we no longer try to ascribe blame... If you want to talk about a culprit, probably the most significant culprit of all...would be the aging facility. Because, ultimately, that would have to be dealt with."

Paul Tagliabue noted that while the Stadium-generated revenues were not as paltry as the club had indicated, they were insufficient to cover the cash drain being experienced by the Browns. "The real issue was," he said, " the condition of the Stadium, as it was far from being an adequate venue for NFL football."

With minimal gate receipts likely to be generated to watch a talent-less team, the visiting team's "cut" of the gate in Cleveland would be far less than the historical norm, and far below what could be earned in a new market like Baltimore. Likewise, the City of Cleveland would learn that its share of admissions taxes and rent from Stadium Corp. would also suffer. Probably with this in mind, on February 8, 1996, a deal was reached by the City of Cleveland, the Cleveland Browns, and the NFL. Final approvals were to be rendered during March.

As Art Modell returned to Baltimore the evening after the arduous ordeal was over and the deal was finally agreed to, television cameras zoomed in on him exiting the aircraft. When asked for a comment, he said, "I'm happy to be home again." That remark hurt and saddened thousands of loyal Cleveland Browns fans, not to mention his employees. For them, those words felt like *Sports Illustrated's* sucker punch in the stomach.

The agreement brought the City of Cleveland about $11.5 million, plus the name "Browns" and the team's colors of seal brown, orange, and white. The $11.5 million was chiefly intended to encompass: 1) $9.3 million for all the estimated rentals which Cleveland Stadium Corp. would have paid the city for 1996-1998, along with the estimated admissions taxes the Browns would have paid; and 2) $2.2 million for the city's legal fees, estimated at $1.75 million, along with $500,000 for other administrative costs. Modell had told writer Hal Lebovitz after the infamous announcement that he would get out of the lease by "buying my way out." That seems exactly the way it happened.

All of which again reminded me of Cyrus Eaton's words, "Anybody who goes through with a commitment when he is going to lose money, is a sucker." Art Modell may have been "suckered" at times, most notably and most recently by his own employees' recommendations on signing a wide receiver, but Art was no sucker. His business may have momentarily lost its liquidity, but he was not about to allow himself to go under with his most prized possession.

As far as leaving the team colors behind, Lebovitz reported that was a "given" back in November, and Lebovitz objected to Mayor White presenting this element as a victory for the city. Lebovitz said that Modell found out quickly that Baltimore fans did not want the "Browns" name. A vendor from Cleveland went to Baltimore loaded up with Baltimore Browns' tee shirts immediately after the announcement was made, but he could not sell them. Modell knew then that the name had little value, and so he would relinquish it. Modell's lawyers recommended, though, that he hold back any announcement until later so this could be used in future bargaining.

After the agreements were in place, Art Modell had this to say:
I don't fault the fans for feeling the way they did. I have a different thought about the media that fed the frenzy, and some thoughts, some private thoughts, about the politicians, who fed the passions of hate and vilification....I feel sorry for those fans, but I'm delighted to know that the Cleveland Browns will remain there and the team will play there in a stadium worthy of their attendance....I did not expect the national reaction over our move to be what it was. Maybe I'm kidding myself but I think it was a tribute to the national recognition of the Cleveland Browns organization and team over the years. It's a great legacy...started by Paul Brown. I'd like to think that I did something right in 35 years to make this somewhat of a popular franchise. I'm proud of that. But I did not expect this kind of outrage. The national outrage was disconcerting to me, but time will pass and that will heal.

The Washington *Post* reported soon after the deal had been made that Modell planned to have his conversation with Bill Belichick the week of February 11. It turned out to be Wednesday, February 14, when Art sent his Valentine to Belichick. What had been rumored for weeks finally came to fruition. Modell fired the head coach who he repeatedly stated would lead his Browns to a Super Bowl. Belichick was fired by telephone. He was "cut" in much the same cold fashion he had used when letting his ex-players go.

Bart Hubbuch, Akron *Beacon-Journal* writer, wrote, "A stormy tenure that included the release of Cleveland icon Bernie Kosar, the alienation of fans and eventually, the relocation of a 50-year-old franchise ended yesterday with a five-minute phone call."

Clevelanders must have wondered what Modell had meant when he said that Belichick was going to be his head coach when the team moved to Baltimore. When the team moved to its Baltimore headquarters in January, I suppose Belichick was still technically listed as the Browns' head coach on the organizational chart. So, with a little linguistic stretch, Modell could always say that he kept his word. I am sure that on this issue most fans would not press Modell; most were glad that Belichick got his due.

Modell had also mentioned to the Washington *Post* reporter that he wanted to return to Cleveland to see his employees, particularly his older employees. He was quoted:

The first thing I want to do is go to Cleveland. There are people I worked with, many of them for years and years, and I want to say goodbye. I am not going to bring the whole organization to Baltimore. All these people are waiting to hear from me. I want to treat them very, very generously as far as termination and severance pay, so they can land on their feet and not be hurt too badly.

After not having heard from Art for months, many of us had hopes that with the deal finalized, he would feel free to come back, say his goodbyes, and give us a chance to say whatever was appropriate. Some people even had hopes that they might receive a personal invitation to Baltimore. The employees waited, and waited. But Art's trip to the Cleveland and Berea offices to see his long-time employees never materialized. Nor were any telephone calls ever placed.

We did hear, though, that Jim Bailey would be in on February 28 to give the final decisions to the employees. At long last, the employees would know what lay ahead. No matter the news, bad or good, at least the wait would be over. Since November 4, 1995, almost four months, we had been left in the dark, and most employees no longer even cared what the decision was.

At about 4:00 p.m. on February 27, Bailey stopped in the Stadium offices, with one hour's prior notice. Knowing there were only nine Stadium Corp. employees to deal with, and that he personally had to deal with only two of us, he chose to do that first. He started with me. Very quickly, and without fanfare, I was told that I would not be going to Baltimore (no reason given), but because of my 21-year tenure, I would receive the maximum severance allowance. He asked me to stay as long as needed to wrap everything up. That was fine with me because I wanted to make sure no loose ends were left with the city on the lease, since I had been the liaison on behalf of Cleveland Stadium

Corp. for many years. Since I was 55 years old, I thought some mention would be made of early retirement, but none was offered that day. Bailey then detailed the severance package for the other employees and instructed me to convey that information the next day. He said the last day of work for most people would be March 31, 1996, unless they were needed beyond that date. He said I should make that determination for the Stadium folks. He then directed me to handle the termination announcement with each Stadium Corp. employee. That was the last time I saw Bailey and the last time we talked to each other.

Everyone was interested in knowing who was being invited to Baltimore. Aside from the football staff, about 16 administrative employees made the invitation list. This meant approximately 50 salaried people would be left behind and entitled to some measure of termination pay. Several folks had firmly believed that they would be invited and were shocked when they were not. One employee asked whether his wife could have access to the psychologist brought in to deal with employees in need, as she was having a difficult time with the turndown.

Specific media attention was focused on whether Mike Lombardi would survive the events of 1995. *Plain Dealer* columnist Bill Livingston likened Lombardi in some ways to the deposed coach. Livingston pointed out how Lombardi had cut Ernie Accorsi out of the picture with Modell, just as he had cut Bud Carson out of the picture with Accorsi. While Lombardi played a prominent role in running up the player payroll, many not worth the money paid them, Livingston said the full extent of Lombardi's role in the collapse of the Browns might never be fully known. When it came to light that some of the players had accused Lombardi of a potpourri of misdeeds and broken promises, it didn't seem that Mike had much of a chance of reaching Maryland. And in the end he didn't. He was left to begin collecting on the payout of his multi-year contract.

During this post-season timeframe in January and February, Cleveland Stadium's director of building services Bruce Gaines was quietly asked to meet in Baltimore with Bailey and several architects and engineers. Gaines was told that preliminary work was underway to design the new Baltimore stadium, and that his services were in demand.

When Gaines returned two days later, he reported that Ann and Jim Bailey were in attendance at the meetings, along with designers and architects. It was astounding to me that only a month or so after the 1995 season had ended, work had already begun on designing the new Baltimore stadium and its loge suites. Pat Modell had been in some of the early meetings deciding on the layout and selecting decor for the loge suites. Gaines mentioned that during one session a difference of opinion arose over four options for the club seat area. Gaines said each option had both advantages and drawbacks. When

Bailey asked his opinion, Gaines cast his vote for a certain option, which was contrary to what the rest of the group wanted. Bruce said with all the pros and cons involved, he felt Art Modell should make the final decision. Bailey told Gaines, "We'll decide what option we want, and we'll present it to Art as a given. Art will not be given a choice, so Art won't be making a decision."

Back at the Stadium restaurant, Gaines told me he was stunned by Bailey's statement. Bruce commented, "You know what, Art isn't included in the decision-making any more."

I said, "I don't think he has been for some time. When he is included, the facts presented to him are slanted, reshaped, or omitted, whatever it takes to let Art make the decision the group (or more specifically, Bailey as head of the management committee) wants made."

On a March afternoon in the Stadium Restaurant, Doug Dieken, former Browns' tackle and current sports commentator, stopped by for lunch. The conversation inevitably turned to "the Move." We were getting a refill on our coffees when a stately looking gentleman came toward our table and introduced himself as Allie Sherman, former coach of the New York Giants. He and his family were in town for a wedding, and he wanted to show them the inside of Cleveland Stadium before it was torn down. "I spent many years in your visiting team locker room, and I'd like my family to see it." He then asked, "Art Modell wouldn't be here by any chance, would he?"

I answered, "No, he hasn't been here since November, and hasn't been in this restaurant for two or three years." Sherman said, "I wouldn't think he'd be here." He continued:

You know, Art Modell was one of the few class owners in the league. I remember during his first year in the league, the Browns played in New York, and we were lucky enough to win. After the game, this new owner came into our locker room in his camel hair coat, and asked to see me. He shook my hand, introduced himself, and congratulated me and my team on beating his Cleveland Browns. I thought to myself, 'What a class act.' But what he did (moving the team to Baltimore) was just plain wrong. You just don't do that. You just don't take a team with all that tradition and move it. You just don't replace teams like the Los Angeles Rams and the Cleveland Browns with smaller markets like Indianapolis and Nashville. I don't know what everybody is thinking.

It was a sad day for Allie Sherman, and he never even lived in Cleveland. As we traipsed through the locker rooms with his family, noting how small these rooms were to accommodate today's over-sized athletes, I couldn't help but notice a small sign over the sinks, "Do NOT share your razor blades with others." It hadn't been necessary to post such signs when Allie was coaching, but it was important to players in the AIDS generation. A sad commentary, I thought.

March was when each employee had to begin deciding his or her own future. The Cleveland Browns provided counselors to assist employees with career changes, helping in the area of résumé preparation, interviewing techniques, and advice for starting up a business. The counselors also provided a shoulder to lean on for those who needed a boost in self-confidence or who just wanted to vent. The Browns also paid the fees for professional computer-training classes for any interested employee.

March flew by. Before we knew it, the farewell dinner on Friday March 31, 1996, in the Stadium Restaurant was upon us. Yes, that same restaurant where Art Modell spent almost 25 years of his life in business lunches and light-hearted joke-telling sessions and where in pre-management committee days he benefited from the counsel of all his department heads.. The former employees of the Cleveland Browns sat down one last time to break bread together. But not before they all went down on the field for a group picture standing under the Cleveland Stadium scoreboard.

The evening was wistful and filled with reminiscing. As dinner ended and people began saying good-bye, a final round of hugs and handshakes was exchanged. We all appreciated the support we had experienced during the trying past five-month period. We did not know if we would ever see some of our fellow employees again. What we did know was that beginning on Monday, we would be receiving our severance paychecks from Maryland.

An artist's rendering of Art Modell and Jim Bailey sitting in their loge while witnessing a Browns' loss. Bailey usually made sure no one got between him and Art.

CHAPTER 17

EMPTY PLACES

On the first work day of April 1996, the Berea offices of the Cleveland Browns and the downtown offices of Cleveland Stadium Corp. had less than a dozen people still on the job. The accounting departments of both companies were busy assisting auditors in wrapping up the 1995 audits and preparing tax returns. The city was planning a fall auction of Stadium equipment and memorabilia, and it needed the help of Stadium personnel to prepare the manifest.

While we were in the midst of closing down the operation, I still was trying to piece together what really had gone wrong here in Cleveland.

In the middle of April, I received a call from an insurance executive who at one time had handled the Stadium's coverage. He told me an interesting story of a friend of his, now residing in Baltimore, who years earlier had known Art Modell in Cleveland. He said this individual had attended that "infamous" announcement on the makeshift dais in downtown Baltimore on November 6. According to that friend, Art Modell was searching the crowd, looking for a friendly face, and found one. They chatted briefly and agreed to have dinner.

Following that dinner date, the Baltimore friend called the Cleveland insurance exec and reported, "You'll never guess what Art Modell told me over dinner. He said, 'Nobody would believe this, but I'm broke. I'm just about tapped out.' Can you believe that? With all the money he supposedly got for moving?"

The insurance man asked me incredulously, "Now, Mike, how can Art be saying he's tapped out with all the money he got for moving the team to Maryland?"

I said I thought Modell was telling the truth. From what I read, it was clear that the $70-75 million the team was to receive for moving was to come from the sales of PSLs, whenever that would occur in the future. For the present, though, the football team received none of that money. Modell was hoping to borrow from a Baltimore bank against that future stream of revenue.

Secondly, I told him I thought management got a big surprise, that I didn't think anyone with the team ever expected it would cost the Cleveland Browns over $55 million to exit the city. This $55 million, of course, arose from a combination of the following:

1)   the money which would be paid to the other 29 NFL owners who signed off to permit the move ($1 million per team);

2)   the $11-plus million due the city as a payoff to fulfill the Stadium lease commitment; and

3)   the payoff of the approximate $15 million in unpaid Stadium Corp. loans to Cleveland banks.

Then added to this total of $55 million were additional items, such as: the Browns' legal fees, the cost of paying off the Berea facility, severance pay to the employees, the cost of relocating staff to Baltimore, and the moving costs for the organization. A quick try at addition would show the total already exceeded the $70 million mark. This would leave next to nothing to retire any of the sizeable Browns' indebtedness, which was probably the reason the move was made in the first place. I wonder if Modell's advisors made these calculations before the move was decided upon. If they had, the decision to move might have changed, or at least been delayed. (Almost a year after the move, Vito Stellino, football columnist for the Baltimore *Sun* warned his readers to be prepared for lean years from their new football team. "Well-run teams don't move," he wrote. "If you don't get an expansion team, this is what you're stuck with.")

A few days later Hal Lebovitz reported that Modell's football team was over $100 million in debt. (That amount could very well be fact, if the liability to re-acquire Gries' stock was being reflected on the balance sheet.) Hal astutely pointed out that the team's interest expense, even at a favorable rate, would result in an annual tab of at least $7 million, a substantial amount for a business the size of an NFL team. Lebovitz cited his source as someone with access to the NFL office in New York.

Terry Pluto of the *Beacon-Journal* said in his column, "We are paying for Modell's army of debts. And while Modell was worried about looking like an extortionist to his fans, instead, he looks like a traitor."

Around this same time, the problems of the Cleveland public schools were also in the media spotlight. Plagued by politicized decision-making and insufficient funds for almost three decades, the schools' efforts were showing disappointing results. In April 1996, Richard DeColibus, president of the Cleveland Teachers Union, was threatening a strike. DeColibus got on the radio stations and challenged Governor Voinovich with this statement, "The Governor has $1.2 billion in this so-called "rainy-day" fund. We have our umbrellas out. It is, and has been, raining in Cleveland....The state sees us starving here, and they turn their backs on us."

I too had to wonder when the so-called "rainy day" would ever arrive. If building a Stadium to save a business and the stream of revenues it had generated for years, or saving a dying school system in the state's largest metropolitan area, did not qualify, what would? I agreed that it had been raining in Cleveland for some years. The governor just hadn't noticed.

While most would credit Voinovich's non-confrontational style during his mayoral years as a major factor in his being able to lead the city back from default, even then his approach had some critics. Back in 1983, *Plain Dealer* editorial writer Brent Larkin observed, after both the Indians and Browns turned to Council President George Forbes rather than to the mayor for help with their lease problems, "...that the Indians and Browns would originally turn to Forbes goes to the heart of Cleveland's ever-present leadership problem. It's worth repeating that it is the lack of heavy-handed leadership, the type that throws political caution to the wind, that goes to the heart of so many of the city's failures."

In September 1996 as the Cleveland City School District talked of strike, Voinovich, who labeled himself the "education" governor, took a week-long vacation. The *Plain Dealer* said, in reference to the hiatus, that he had continually ducked the problems of his hometown schools, but that his reluctance to get involved was consistent. When the paper had asked him in 1981 what he planned to do about the city's debt-ridden school system, then-mayor Voinovich replied, "I don't intend to do anything. I've got my hands full. There are already too many voices speaking out and my involvement would do more harm than good."

The *Plain Dealer* labeled Voinovich the "epitome of frugality, who constantly exhorted citizens to do more with less." Both as mayor and governor, Voinovich contended he had cut government's cost and size and that he was proud of his tax record. "I'm more proud of my fiscal conservatism and the ability to reduce costs. There's no government official in the United States who can compare their fiscal record with mine." With that philosophy in operation, it was folly for Cleveland Browns' fans to have hoped for the state to provide a major portion of the financing for a so-called "state-of-the-art" stadium for northeastern Ohioans.

County Commissioner Tim Hagan said about the governor, "It's fair to say that Voinovich shies away from any kind of controversy." The *Plain Dealer* said of Cleveland's loss of its football team, "While no Ohio politician had a better relationship with or greater access to Browns' owner Art Modell, Voinovich stayed on the sidelines while negotiations between Cleveland's leaders and Modell were foundering."

Former Cleveland Stadium Corp. executive Eddie Uhas told me that he had happened to meet Berea Mayor Stan Trupo in the church parking lot after services. Uhas had worked for the Cleveland Browns since 1968, and he was a long-time resident of Berea and knew Trupo well. The mayor was reminiscing with Uhas about the sad circumstances left by the Browns' departure. Trupo then said, "You know, Eddie, I know Art Modell is a good man. This never should have happened. He just got bad advice from his key advisors."

Trupo reiterated what Sam Rutigliano said more than once following his departure from the team in 1984. "Art listens to the wrong people," Sam said. "He doesn't want to hear bad news, so he surrounds himself with guys who won't kick the gorilla in the ankle. It's always been Larry, Curly, and Moe around him."

It has been my experience that strong, secure managers demand to hear about problems as soon as they crop up, so they can nip them in the bud. If, on the other hand, a leader does not solicit reports on impending problems from his top executives, then it is not surprising to find a myriad of problems lurking just inches below the surface. When these problems eventually break through, as they surely will, they are usually too overwhelming to correct.

During July word reached the media that David Hopcraft was scheduled to speak at a luncheon in Painesville. The subject, of course, was a discussion of the move from Modell's viewpoint. During the luncheon, Hopcraft made several points, one to the effect that no one in the Browns' organization really ever believed the city had the wherewithal to offer a reliable economic deal because the city was tapped out, as evidenced by its inability to resolve the Gateway debt crisis. The second point Hopcraft made was that when Modell finally realized the severity of the team's financial crisis in September 1995, his only choices then were to sell the team or to move it. By moving the team, Modell felt he could buy time and gain access to the funds necessary to continue operating. He also would still have the team to pass on to his heirs.

I had to wonder why Modell did not recognize the financial crisis until late September. Was it because, as Rutigliano had phrased it, "Larry, Curly, and Moe" had refused the previous winter to tell him that the Browns couldn't afford Andre Rison? Someone should have calculated that the cumulative effect of $40 million in signing bonuses was too much for the team to overcome.

Various newspaper accounts, however, do seem to bear out Hopcraft's statement about the lack of substance in the discussions with the city. For example, in March 1996 City Council members were complaining that they had not learned all the details of the deal the mayor had made with the NFL. Included in the deal was a $10 million loan from the Cleveland Tomorrow group. In November, however, Mayor White had said that as part of the city's last-minute offer, Cleveland Tomorrow was going to "contribute" $10 million. Sound confusing? In March 1996 City Finance Director Kathryn Hyer didn't seem certain when she said she was hopeful the city might not have to repay the funds. If it were a loan, and had to be repaid at 7.5% interest, the total repayment would amount to $46 million, which would have to come from parking tax and sin tax collections. The *Plain Dealer* reporter added that no independent financial analysis had determined whether those sources would be adequate to repay the debt.

Every few months during 1996, another account of the still-unpaid Gateway construction bills was reported in the *Plain Dealer*. The state was still unwilling to cover the costs of this overrun. A representative of the governor said that "a bailout by the state represented a bad policy." The state had already participated in the Gateway project to the extent of $46.6 million, or about 11% of the total cost, and apparently felt disinclined to increase that amount.

Craig Miller, acting board chairman of Gateway, the lone active management employee/volunteer remaining, faced the almost insurmountable task of rectifying a difficult situation created by others. While recently enacted austerity measures helped reduce the deficit, Miller knew those measures were insufficient to create a positive cash flow. He said he was dealing with a "ticking time bomb" and that help was needed from the Indians and Cavs. Miller then wrote a letter to both teams, almost pleading for their help. Miller also mentioned the possibility of Gateway selling some of its vacant parcels of nearby land to raise cash to cover the deficits, which seemed to me a move more of desperation than of sound future planning.

On July 24, 1996, the *Plain Dealer* reported that the county started making waves with regards to the loan it made to cover part of Gateway's unpaid bills. The county had loaned $11.5 million to keep the sports complex solvent and to pay some of the contractors. It wanted to arrange for repayment. It proposed receiving $5 million from the Convention and Visitors' Bureau, $4 million from Gateway, and $2.5 million from the city, all to be repaid over a ten-year period. The PD reported that none of the parties was eager to pony up. Further complicating this matter within City Council was a concern that the state was also pushing to get its $10 million loan repaid. Under the terms set by the legislature, the city and the county were obligated to repay $5 million each. A lot of money was still owed for Gateway and there wasn't any local money left to resolve the problem.

On this same date, two other pertinent and somewhat-related articles appeared in the papers. One was buried back in the PD sports pages. It reported that a groundbreaking was taking place in Baltimore next door to Oriole Park. Construction of the new $200 million home for the former Cleveland Browns football team was underway. Art Modell was getting himself a new stadium.

Then, flipping through the *Wall Street Journal* (WSJ), I noticed a report from the Cato Institute evaluating the fiscal performances of the budgets and tax records of each of the states. Fourteen different variables were examined as part of this review, and the states and their respective governors were graded, just as in a school report card. Most of the grades were "B's and C's";

only three "A's" were awarded: to the states and governors of New York, New Hampshire, and Arizona. There were also four "F's" meted out to the class. Besides Florida, West Virginia, and Delaware, Governor George Voinovich and Ohio were adjudged by the Cato Institute to earn a failing grade.

In its commentary on Voinovich's performance, the WSJ said:

(He) boasts that no one 'can match my fiscal record.' Thank goodness. The only GOP governor to rate an F, Mr. Voinovich flaunts his contempt for supply-side tax policy. In 1993, he passed a billion-dollar income tax rate hike. He grudgingly signed a tax cut last month, but only after reducing it by nearly one-half. From 1991 to 1994, state spending ballooned...more than 20%.

I sat back and reflected on all three newspaper reports of the day. I couldn't help wondering at the irony. Art Modell was getting a new stadium in Baltimore, and after three baseball seasons in the new Cleveland ballpark, our local political leaders were still squabbling as to how to pay for its overruns (although no one was demanding accountability for the apparent mismanagement), and the financial newspaper flunks the governor with a billion dollar-plus surplus.

Who are the winners in all this chaos? It is clear who did not come out ahead. The financial losers are the citizens of Greater Cleveland. They not only lost their Browns, but they also face the specter of continuing deficits from Gateway. The state was also a loser; it lost the taxes from the Browns' players' salaries and from wages paid to those who worked in peripheral occupations. According to the Cato Institute, the constituents in the State of Ohio were also losers. Browns' football fans will suffer through football-less years for a period of time, before finding eventually, I suspect, something to fill that chasm. Even Art Modell, who should have gained much more from the move, will probably have to wait years before he sees any substantial benefit. Eventually, the rent-free use of the building and other favorable lease terms will result in fiscal benefits the Browns could not have attained by staying in Cleveland.

I think the only substantive winners in the Cleveland sports scene are the Cleveland Indians and the Cleveland Cavaliers who with plush new venues and sweetheart leases have significantly improved their fortunes since moving to Gateway in 1994.

The plight of Gateway reached the national press by late summer. *Barron's* published an article "Foul Play? Team owners get sports palaces and fat concession deals. Taxpayers get stuck with the tab." It cited the financial troubles at Cleveland's famed sports complex. The article stated in part:

...the project's finances continue to deteriorate....[due to] the fact that [Gateway] isn't getting enough from its leases with the Indians and Cavs to pay debt service on some $120 million in bonds. As a result, Cuyahoga County has had to ante up some $23 million to cover Gateway's arrears, and will likely be forced to lay out at least $70 million more over the next 16 years. Meanwhile, the city is taking a bath on the $40 million in bonds it sold to build two parking garages for the Gateway complex. The county's director of accounting said, "We're paying a hell of a price for downtown economic redevelopment."

In July 1996 the city celebrated its bicentennial, marking 200 years since Moses Cleaveland had founded the city on the banks of the Cuyahoga River. A three-day weekend celebration was planned, and as part of the commemoration, a beautiful all-color souvenir program was being sold for $5. The highlights of the weekend revolved around the Flats, the area where Cleaveland's party had originally landed.

In the program were photographs of different Cleveland neighborhoods and ethnic groups. The program also highlighted the Cleveland Clinic, the Cleveland Orchestra, Jacobs Field, and other notable institutions. It talked of Cleveland being the "Comeback City," and of its bright future. But while the program touched on a lot of history, it contained not one mention of the Cleveland Browns or of Cleveland Stadium. I thought that was sad. For 50 years the Browns were a big part of Cleveland's history, and for a long time Cleveland was known for having the largest baseball-football stadium in the United States. The Stadium's day has passed, I recognize, but history should have guaranteed it a place in the Bicentennial program. A piece of Cleveland's history took place there, the Rolling Stones concerts, the high school Charity Championship football games, the Notre Dame-Navy games, and so much more. Obviously, the Bicentennial program chose not to cover all the highlights of Cleveland history, only those which might also be part of the future.

Before I left Stadium Corp. for good on July 31, 1996, I called Craig Miller, acting Gateway manager. We wished each other luck in our future endeavors. Then he added, "I guess (after reviewing the present Gateway leases) we now can all see that the city had a pretty good deal with that Modell lease after all."

I told Craig that over the years, several outside audit consultants had told various City Hall administrations that very same thing, but since officials had no other sports leases in town to compare it with, I assumed they never fully comprehended just how good the old Stadium lease actually was. Now that its economic value was finally being judged favorably, it was too late. I doubt the City of Cleveland will ever get from sports teams in the future what it gained when Mayor Ralph Perk entered into the lease with Cleveland Stadium Corp. That lease, in my opinion, was a "win-win-win" situation for everybody---the city, the Stadium Corp., and the fans.

"PAY UP" was the headline of the *Plain Dealer*'s unusually lengthy editorial on August 5, 1996, in which the city was taken to task for not coming up with its share of the Gateway overrun. Stating that this was supposed to be a joint city-county project from the very beginning, the PD said that the city was getting most of the financial benefits from taxes on the boost in downtown business related to Gateway events, and therefore was morally obligated to do its part. The PD went on, "(mayor) White reneged on the (his) lobbying pledge (to city council, to the Convention and Visitors Bureau, and to the state); in fact, he suggested the money go instead to the city's empowerment zone....Nor has White done anything to advance the legislation authorizing a direct city contribution. As a result, six months have passed without action."

The editorial also delved into city council's failures in this regard, the wrangling over the sharing of future excess sin taxes, if in fact there would be any, and a myriad of other disputes, before it concluded:

County commissioners have been widely and justly criticized for their part in permitting Gateway overruns to occur, but they have been commendably diligent in trying to clean up the mess they made. It is to their discredit that the same cannot be said of Michael White and city council.

In the meantime, in Baltimore, many former Browns' players were being lopped off the 1996 roster. Maybe it was just coincidence, but it seemed to be the highly (over?) paid players that were getting the boot. First came Andre Rison, followed by Pepper Johnson, Carl Banks, Tommy Vardell, Don Griffin, Lorenzo White, and Leroy Hoard. While their 1995 performances were below expectations, it would seem that more than anything else the salary cap led to the terminations. The former Browns' organization had to make room under the cap for the next crop of players, and this was the quickest way to do it. Unfortunately, it was also a costly and expensive way.

On the day that Rison was released, PD columnist Tony Grossi wrote that the Rison ordeal "symbolized the incompetence of the Modell organization." He said Modell was suckered by Mike Lombardi, the "fast-talking pitchman for the acquisition" who made the foolish judgment that the "undisciplined Rison and robotic Testaverde could be anything but the worst possible match of receiver and quarterback."

Later Rison signed with another NFL team, reportedly for three years, including a $1 million signing bonus, a much more reasonably priced acquisition than the Browns' braintrust had made a year earlier.

Leroy Hoard, the running back whose contract was restructured to the tune of $2 million in 1995, was later signed by the Minnesota Vikings for a reported $275,000, plus incentives. Someone on Modell's staff had again seemingly overestimated a player's worth. Maybe that would not have happened had Modell hired himself a football general manager who would have been able to work with a tough-minded CPA like Mike Srsen. The difference of just Leroy Hoard's contracts between the two years was equal to what used to be the amount of one entire year's profits ($1,700,000)!

Art Modell had entrusted the operation of his team to Jim Bailey. Thus the final decisions on many football matters, before being presented to Art, were made by a lawyer, without assistance from in-house CPAs. I guess, therefore, that it should come as no surprise that the end of the Browns in Cleveland was the result of economic chaos. Modell's creed from 20 years earlier kept returning to my thoughts. "Don't ever let a lawyer run your business for you, kid! They just don't have good business instincts."

What Art Modell was even more guilty of, in my opinion, was not retracting his vow that "I will never move the team as long as I am the owner." He should have done so when he first became aware in his heart that he could no longer be bound by his pledge. I believe one reason political and business leaders in Cleveland dragged their feet was because they believed that Art would never renege on his pledge.

Some have speculated that Modell made the move in order to facilitate his estate planning needs. I question how prominent a role, if any, estate tax planning played in the exodus of the franchise. It was my experience that estate planning was not a high priority with Art, because he was uncomfortable dealing with death and mortality, especially his own. Art felt that this would not concern him for years as he said he expected to live to be a well-loved 102-year-old. I don't think he felt any urgency to deal with wills and estates and their tax consequences. If the estate tax problem could be handled within the decision to move, then he would have considered that a plus, I suppose. But I would bet this was not the primary consideration for the move.

Many critics feel that had the Browns' business dealings been better managed, there would not have been the pressing need for fiscal help in 1995. In retrospect, I think the Browns' finances could have improved if three realities could have been achieved:

1)   A better drafting record between 1986 and 1993; this would have produced a more talented football team, and one with more depth. More successful April drafts would have alleviated the need to delve so deeply into the costly free agent market in 1993-1995, which rapidly increased the team's bank borrowings.

2)   A more personable head coach; a person like this could have produced better attitudes, better relationships, and better team chemistry. This might have resulted in a better won-loss record but if not that, then certainly in better relations with the media and business community. Those factors would have made it easier for the community to talk about providing funds for a new stadium.

3)   A strong football operations-oriented general manager who maintained checks-and-balances over the head coach and the team's personnel needs. I agree with Bob August, the veteran LCNH sports columnist, when he wrote that Modell's one flaw as an owner was his disinclination to hire a strong general manager. Knowing every head coach wants all the best players he can get, regardless of cost, this general manager would have kept Art from overpaying for some of these players, especially the vast number of marginal and mediocre players we watched play in recent years.

Realistically, how could Art Modell, as president of the Browns and Stadium Corp., who over the years had his hands full with:

1)   facing protracted litigation on various fronts,
2)   negotiating the NFL television contracts,
3)   working on Stadium lease extensions,
4)   serving as president of Cleveland Clinic,
5)   dealing with a serious team drug problem,
6)   deciding on a never-ending series of stadium repairs and improvements,
7)   undergoing three major surgical procedures, and

still have the time and energy left to function effectively as general manager of the team? As sports commentator Dan Coughlin so succinctly put it, "This was nothing less than incredible."

As Bill Levy, author of the book, *Sam, Sipe & Company,* wrote in reference to the team's demonstrated weaknesses during the football drafts of the 70s, "the Browns have been poor judges of talent in both the draft and in trading. If they hope to remain in the National Football League's elite, they must do a better job."

But in the 80s that was not the way it played out. The Browns went on a trading binge, exchanging high draft picks for aging former All-Pro players Lyle Alzado and Joe Delamielleure. It required a number 2, a number 3, and a number 5 pick to acquire Alzado from Denver, and then a number 2 and a number 3 to obtain Joe D. from Buffalo a year later. The Browns then kept the phone lines open with Buffalo and dealt with the Bills in two more major trades. Over the next several years, the Browns gave the Bills three number 1 draft picks, two number 3 selections, one number 5, and a number 6 to acquire Tom Cousineau and Bernie Kosar. To acquire the aforementioned four starters, the Browns surrendered draft picks that should have yielded 10 very good players for years to come. By succumbing to the urge to fill their immediate needs, the Browns' organization allowed these headline-grabbing transactions to suck the lifeblood from the vein of the team's future talent pool. One has to wonder how much these trades helped tip the balance of power to propel the Bills to the Super Bowl during the 90s, while relegating the Browns to sub-par years.

But regardless of how the team's business was being managed, the political leaders had placed their priorities on other matters, and failed to lead on the Stadium issue. After November 6 they found it easy to point the finger of blame at a businessman who responded to a better offer. Those politicians, however, were not going to raise money for the Cleveland Browns in spring 1996, when it came time to sign the new crop of rookies. No, in our capitalistic society the risks and rewards belong to ownership. When a business gets into trouble, the capitalist has to find a way out. Art Modell believed he found the way out. He found a governor in another state who had the money to buy the rights to his team. Ohioans did not have political leaders who felt that providing funds for professional football was a high enough priority.

As the *Plain Dealer* reporter aptly put it, "Somehow after all these years, Art Modell felt that Cleveland owed him. Cleveland fans felt Modell owed them."

Callers on radio sports talk shows could not drop the subject of the Browns' move, and well into 1996 they still seemed to want to exact a pound of flesh from Art Modell for this dastardly deed.

Former WKNR talk show host Bill Needle blamed the media for both the Art Modell and the Albert Belle situations. He said, "In our zeal to satisfy the insatiable appetite of the public to vent on somebody, we paint people like Art Modell and Albert Belle as natural targets."

Another former WKNR sports host, Mike Wolfe, answered one of the many callers who questioned whose fault it really was that the Browns were no longer Cleveland's team. Wolfe did take Modell to task for his failures as club president. He said Modell's style was to put guys in charge, and then blame them when there was failure, rather than participate as the leader of the organization. Wolfe, however, offered that, "I've come to the conclusion that no agreement would ever have been reached between Art Modell and Mayor Mike White on a new lease here in Cleveland. Both had king-sized egos, and their egos would not allow for any kind of agreement to be reached."

Perhaps Modell did have that kind of ego, but it was not his ego that drove Art Modell and the Cleveland Browns to Baltimore. The team needed a new source of funds with which to keep operating, and they were called "PSLs."

FINAL THOUGHTS

I left my office in Cleveland Stadium for the last time on August 1, 1996. After more than 21 years as part of Art Modell's Browns/Stadium Corp. operation, the end for me had finally come. It was not easy. Over the following weeks, I read and reread reports, clippings, and memos, and I talked with many people as I tried to piece together the complex web of inter-related events which brought 50 years of Cleveland Browns' history and 65 years of Cleveland Stadium history to so sad an end. This book was the result.

I wrote at the beginning that each person would have to decide where to lay most of the blame. And as is usually the case with blame, there is always plenty to pass around.

I imagine that in spite of the good works that Art Modell accomplished for the city in his 35 years in Cleveland, most Browns' fans will consider him an arch-villain. He took our team away. Just like the kid on the playground who took his bat and ball and ran home and left the rest of us standing bereft on the ballfield, so Modell's decision deprived us of our football heritage. Guilt for that tragic event, however, is not Modell's alone. It must be shared by others who by their mismanagement, disinterest, or unwillingness were indirect accomplices to the deed.

I don't think Modell's blame comes so much from what he chose to do but rather from what he failed to do. Somewhere after his first heart attack his previous dynamic hands-on leadership of the Browns and Cleveland Stadium Corp. gave way to a less involved role. He allowed himself to be isolated, and he too often acceded to the less-gifted insights of his so-called management team. In the end his own hand-picked committee members--Jim Bailey, David Modell and Bill Belichick--let him down by managing the Browns into a deep financial hole with their costly player acquisitions. But Art Modell selected these individuals and gave them free rein, and ultimately, therefore, their decisions were his responsibility.

Modell's other committee, the Browns' Stadium renovation group--consisting of Jim Bailey, Ann Bailey, and David Hopcraft--came up empty in trying to convince the city of the Browns' desperate needs. How close the city came to saving the Browns for Cleveland is really known only by these three people.

The absence of a true financial director on these committees still confounds me. How Art Modell could have continued to allow these committees to operate without one defies comprehension. Obviously Bailey convinced Modell that he had the requisite financial expertise and that other views were not needed. Unfortunately, Modell bought Bailey's advice.

A second factor in the loss of the team was the political leadership, or lack of it. City, county, and state leaders all gave priority to the needs of the baseball franchise, and while that in itself may not have been an error, in doing so they neglected to estimate just how much that priority would cost the coffers of the Browns and the Stadium Corp. Then when they finally perceived that the situation with the Browns was indeed growing critical, they were unable to speedily build the necessary consensus or to find the financial resources to solve the growing problem. In spite of a billion-dollar surplus, the state wouldn't stretch beyond its self-imposed limits; the county found itself in a double whammy due to the mismanagement of its investment portfolio and its failure to monitor the construction budget for the Gateway project; and the city continued to struggle against a string of annual operating deficits threatening even its critical city services.

This leads to the third source of the problem. Since the early 1980s and the time of the lawsuits, Art Modell was subjected to a hypercritical media. Some of this criticism came as a reaction to Modell's unfortunate penchant for grand overstatement, and while it would be easy to say that Modell should have developed a thicker skin, the fact is that the constant barrage of negativity eroded his own former ebullience and confidence. Even more damaging was the loss of support for him and his enterprises that the criticism evoked from the fans and from the business community. After 34 years, Modell was still heard to say that he never felt accepted in Cleveland.

Finally, perhaps too many good intentions were on the civic plate all at one time. Planning and funding for the Rock Hall of Fame and Museum, the Great Lakes Science Center, the city's Bicentennial celebrations, and most of all, Gateway, all demanded time and resources at much the same time--not to mention the crisis in the Cleveland public schools. These worthy concerns not only preoccupied the elected leaders, they also significantly absorbed the interest and tapped the checkbooks of the business community. Renovation of Cleveland Stadium simply had to wait its place in line.

So it very well may have been a combination of all the above factors that resulted in our Browns leaving the shores of Lake Erie for Chesapeake Bay. By 1995 the team's financial situation was precarious, and the team needed help faster than the political community was willing or able to give it. With the banks no longer willing to loan the over-extended club another dollar, the team was facing financial ruin. At this point Modell must have believed that he "had no other choice" but to sign on the dotted line and move the team that Clevelanders really thought of as their own.

My attempt at an autopsy is finished. I have laid out the facts as I remember them, and you may judge how important each was in contributing to this painful result. As I have indicated, accountability can be apportioned. You the reader are free to make your own decisions.

The Cleveland Browns as we knew them are gone, and parts of Cleveland Stadium have been consigned to the deep for a Lake Erie reef. The concrete floors of the second level of Tower B where my fellow workers and I paced for so many years are to be the spawning ground for Lake Erie perch. The upper deck ramps which carried passionate Browns' followers to their seats every Sunday will now contribute to the pleasure of the fisherman rather than the football fan. And I can't imagine how another team playing here in a new stadium in 1999 (or later) will be able to re-create the thrills that for so many years I experienced as a Cleveland Stadium Corp. employee and as a Browns' fan. I don't think that, at least for me, it will ever be the same.